Provence . 1977 .

SNAKES & LADDERS

SNAKES
& LADDERS

DIRK BOGARDE

HOLT, RINEHART AND WINSTON

NEW YORK

First published in the United States of America in 1979
by Holt, Rinehart and Winston, 383 Madison Avenue,
New York, New York 10017.

Library of Congress Cataloging in Publication Data
Bogarde, Dirk, 1921–
Snakes & ladders.
Sequel to a postillion struck by lightning.
Filmography: p.
Includes index.
1.   Bogarde, Dirk, 1921–   2.   Actors—Great Britain
—Biography.   I.   Title.
PN2598.B647A37   1979   791.43′028′0924 [B]   78-23877
ISBN: 0-03-047161-3
Printed in the United States of America
1 3 5 7 9 10 8 6 4 2

For
Elizabeth and George

A NOTE ON THE SOURCES

My principal sources have been my note-books, diaries and letters written to my parents, during the period 1941–1947. I have also drawn on a daily journal which I have kept from 1950 to the present day, as well as scrap-books, many personal letters, and in particular a collection of about 650 letters written between 1965 and 1973 to a friend in America, and which were returned to me in accordance with her will after her death. *The Films of Dirk Bogarde* by Margaret Hinxman and Susan d'Arcy (Literary Services and Production, 1974) has also been invaluable.

ACKNOWLEDGEMENTS

I am indebted, first and foremost, to George Courtney Ward who was my personal photographer at Rank for many years. Also to Mario Tursi, for allowing me to reproduce his stills from "Death in Venice", and to the owners of individual photographs, by whose courtesy I have reproduced many of the pictures. My gratitude to E. L. L. Forwood for taking on the Index with such care and patience, and also to Søren Fischer who traced and secured the scene written for Judy Garland. I am grateful to Miss Rosalind Toland who has waded through years of newspapers in search of information and headlines etcetera; and above all to Mrs Sally Betts, who once again, has managed to cope with my incomprehensible typescript, spelling and punctuation.

In order to save any embarrassment I have, very occasionally, used pseudonyms.

ILLUSTRATIONS

Following page 116

Catterick Camp, Yorkshire, May 1941.

St. Suplice, Normandy, July 1944.

My mother, Elizabeth, and my father, 1942.

As we are now: Elizabeth, George, Mark and Sarah. Christmas day at my house in Provence.

With Beatrice Varley in "Power Without Glory", Fortune Theatre, 1947.

Bendrose House, Amersham, 1950.

Kay Kendall and Olive Dodds, Bendrose, 1951.

The Sketch, 1947.

Elizabeth Taylor in the cherry orchard, Bendrose.

Jean Simmons and Anouk Aimée in a heat wave.

Kate dressed for a Sunday walk, 1952.

Beel House, Amersham, 1954.

The Green Study, Beel House, 1955.

Tea in the "Out-Patients", July 1956.

With Elizabeth and my brother Gareth.

Natasha Parry and Lusia Parry at Tamariu.

Following page 180

The 21st anniversary of Pinewood Studios.

The bar of the Hotel Terminus, Bourges, during "A Tale of Two Cities", 1957.

Christmas day, Westbury, Long Island, Self, Rex, Kate, Tony Forwood, and "June".

With Betty E. Box and Ralph Thomas.

Victor Aller, my loyal and devoted music coach, on "The Liszt Bio". Vienna, 1959.

Capucine and the dogs. Christmas day, 1960.

With Elizabeth in a mistral at Cannes, 1961.

My mother and father. Cagnes, 1965.
The Palace, near Beaconsfield, Buckinghamshire.

Hans and Agnes Zwickl: my cook and housekeeper.
A courtyard at The Palace, with Sinhue and Bogie.

Following page 244
Judy Garland with her children, 1962.
Welcoming Judy to a party at the Ad Lib Club, London, 1964 (photo untraceable).

A break during "Hot Enough for June".
The Elephant Gate. Red Fort, Delhi, 1957.

The last film in the Rank Programme: "The Singer Not the Song", 1960.

With Joseph Losey on location for "The Servant".
Self as Barrett, with Wendy Craig and James Fox in "The Servant".

Nore, Hascombe, Surrey.
Nore: the drawing room.

With Julie Christie, 1966.
Ingrid Bergman and Gareth Forwood at Nore.

Following page 316

Jack Clayton on "Our Mother's House", 1967.
With Gussie Henry. Croydon, 1967.

With George Cukor, working on "Justine".
Arriving at the Barberini Cinema, Rome, with Luchino Visconti for the premiere of "The Damned", 1969 (photo untraceable).

Self as Friedrich Bruckmann in Luchino Visconti's "The Damned". Rome, 1968.

Six-photo off-set sequence from "Death in Venice" (By courtesy of Mario Tursi).

SNAKES & LADDERS

I

WHEN I started to write the first book about the story of my life, which took me up to the age of eighteen, it was with motives which were, I suppose, rather muddled. One, certainly, was to try to discover whether or not I had any ability for writing as such, another was to occupy myself when the weather was too bad for me to work my few acres, and somewhere, buried in the midst of it, was the idea that I might be able to say something about the whole process of becoming an actor—the kind of natural instincts given one and the manner in which they were gradually developed both by myself and by the people I met along the way, so that they were ultimately fused by experience into something usable in a profession which I desperately wanted to follow. I imagined that what I had to say about myself *might* offer some clues to a new generation of would-be actors and actresses, or even to parents, who so often oppose the longing to enter a profession which is insecure, and by some people still denigrated.

One of the things which I have learned is that for a good ninety per cent of the people who want to become actors it is a mistake, and leads to poverty and unhappiness. For the other ten per cent it can be, as it has been in my case, in varying degrees, rewarding and enriching, and because I have had quite a few letters from young people as a result of the first book asking me how one does it, I have been encouraged to write most of the rest of what is inevitably something of an ego trip. Well, ego, for better or for worse, is very much involved in this business of being an actor, because we are creatures who are obliged to use our own beings as our instrument, and we tend to have to keep reassuring ourselves—and looking for reassurance—as to how good that instrument is. It tends to make us very boring as people unless we are on constant guard against a total self-preoccupation. And it has the more dangerous hazard of cutting us off from what I think to be the mainspring of all good acting, which is the minute observation of one's fellow creatures, who are really the fuel which feeds our attempts to create a living character.

So this book, the continuation of my ego trip, is also an endeavour to portray just a few of the people who have helped me to become whatever sort of an actor I may be. Living their own lives, they are also my life. In trying to compress thirty years of living into a book which may well be too long anyway, it is inevitable that many of them cannot appear, however important they may have been. Perhaps they may be only too pleased *not* to be mentioned . . . time will tell; but I, at least, am sorry. Anyway: to begin with, there was Gooley.

When we got to York the woman who had been sitting in the corner window-seat, knitting something fluffy, took a couple of brown paper parcels off the rack, slung her chintz knitting bag over her arm and threaded her way carefully past our disconsolate knees. We didn't try to help her. She wrenched at the door and clambered down on to the platform without a backward look, slamming the door hard behind her. We sat in dejected silence, as we had ever since we left King's Cross. None of us had spoken throughout the journey, except the woman, who had said that this was a Non Smoker and that if any one of us tried to smoke she'd vomit. So we had lumbered into the corridors and lolled against the windows, watching the rain start as the train trailed smoke across the grimy fields of the Home Counties shortly after Watford.

Now we had creaked and huffed into York. I stared at my own reflection in the dirty window; fist screwed into my face mottled with sooty raindrops down the glass. A tropical disease. Cholera. Something dreadful. Mazawattee Tea . . . Swan Pens . . . Careless Talk Costs Lives . . . Stephens Ink . . . Claudette Colbert in . . . but the title blurred away as we jolted into movement. Air Raid Shelter . . . Waiting Rooms . . . Gentlemen . . . we gathered speed for Darlington.

The compartment gradually relaxed with the woman's departure. We spread out a bit, and pulled crumpled cigarettes from pocket-squashed packets. The air was pleasant with the hazy blue of smoke, the sweet smell of tobacco. The youth sitting opposite me, short, thick, muscular, with greasy black hair spiky like a wet cat's, chucked his Gold Flake into my lap. I had run out ages ago, neurotically, in the corridor.

"Dere you are. Help yourself. Two packets in me case. Got a light?" I had, and we lit up. He pushed the crumpled packet back into the sagging pocket of his tired grey cardigan.

"De ould bitch! 'Dis is a non smoker . . . I'll vomit.' Dat's a *real* civilian now, a real bastard civilian for youse. I know de kind.

I know 'em." He slumped down into his corner and stared back at his reflection with hatred. The fact that we all were, at that moment, civilians seemed to have escaped him . . . we would only cease to be human at 23.59 hours when the barrack gates shut behind us and our own particular Hells began. But until then we were still free. Civilian and free. The Army waited.

Suddenly he leant across, prodding me into attention on the knee with a dirty thumb. "You know someting? As a matter of fact it's one of dem civilian women like her is de reason I'm sittin' on me arse in dis fucking train at all . . . an ould bitch, just like dat, t'in and scrawny like an ould hen. It was in dis little sweetie shop, you see, up Charlotte Street, she was ironing or doing some fuckin' ting in de back shop, and when she saw me picking up a few little bits and pieces like, she let out wid such a screaming and a hollering I had to hit her hard wid de little iron she had, to stop her, you see? And den she fell on de floor squawking like she had seen de Resurrection so I hit her again, not much of a whack, wasn't *dat* hard, just a couple of times to be sure. And would you believe it, dat evening de papers said an ould woman had been attacked by hooligans and was near to death." He stared away from me out at the darkening sky. Suddenly he snorted. "Hooligans!" He shook his wet-cat head in amazement. "Dere was only me!"

No one took any notice of him, or showed the least interest. We all had our own problems and worries, and I wasn't sure that he wasn't bluffing anyway out of boredom. But he had given me his cigarette. He might offer me another later.

"And why are you on the train then? They didn't get you?"

He looked at me with thin eyes and blew smoke down each nostril separately, which I thought quite effective.

"Not me. Paddy Gooley? Dey never caught me for nothing. Joined the King's bleeding army, didn't I? Took his shilling; a good boy from the Republic. Well . . ." he squashed his cigarette stub on to the floor, "dere was no point in hanging around just *waiting*, now was dere?"

"Won't they catch up with you in the army even so?"

"Once I'm in, I'm in and safe, and, me darlin' boy, the first ting Gooley does on his first leave, in twenty-t'ree weeks' time, is to slip back to me lovely Emerald Isle with me boots and battledress, never to return. You tink I'm soft?"

He was grinning cheerfully and gave me a long slow wink as

if we had both been conspirators in the little sweetie shop. His implied acceptance pleased me. Only I felt that I was the one who would be caught.

"You're a toff, aren't youse?" he asked suddenly.

"I don't think so, why?"

"Ach . . . you talk like one. I don't mind. What was you in Civvie Street den?"

"An actor."

"Sweet Christ! An actor! Would I know you den?"

"I don't think so."

"Was you ever at de Bedford, Camden Town? Or Chiswick? Dey had real good shows dere."

"No never. At the Q . . ."

Suspicion crept into his bashed face.

"Where's dat den?"

"Outside London really. Kew Bridge. I wasn't famous or anything."

"Oh." He dismissed me, and looked out at the sombre May sky. Across the fields a woman cycled, head bowed against the rain; it was almost dark. The man sitting beside me, older than the rest of us, leant confidentially towards me and said in a low voice: "I heard you say you were an actor which is very funny, you see, because I was with the Palmers Green Light Operatic Society for quite some time. It's funny you and I being of the same persuasion, so to speak, in the same compartment! Only amateur status, I'm afraid, me I mean, still we did some lovely shows there, you know, before this caper started. Last one we did was 'The White Horse Inn'. A very jolly show. Lots of very hummable tunes. A jolly show but most tasteful. *Rather* expensive." He smiled knowingly, as one professional to another. "We had a bit of trouble with the boat, you know. There's a paddle steamer type of thing, end of the Second Act, cost us a lot of headaches, as you can imagine. But Ileen Mirren and Mrs Croft did a remarkable job; it brought down the house. Funnel smoking, paddles turning, all that sort of thing, really marvellous. Of course the Chorus said it made them cough. They are for ever complaining choruses are, aren't they? Proper prima donnas the lot of them; but I don't think anyone really noticed very much. I must say it *was* a jolly show. I thought you'd be interested, you being an actor as you said. Birds of a feather, you might say! Quite a coincidence really."

He smiled at me encouragingly. I nodded and smiled back like an idiot. Across the compartment Gooley had taken out a rosary and was absentmindedly fiddling with it, the crucifix winking in the mean blue light from the electric light bulb in the roof. I didn't want to talk about the theatre or acting; that had been all put aside. Now I would only think of the future and how best to bend it to me, how to save myself in this new, daunting life which lay a very few hours ahead. But Palmers Green wasn't going to give in easily. After a while he asked me in a low, gruff voice, as if he was soliciting, whether I knew Richard Tauber or Binnie Hale, and when I said no, not personally, he smiled sadly and looked away into a past of smoking paddle steamers.

For my part, grateful for the respite, I stared out at the now dark countryside. The gleam of wet roofs here and there, a chimney stack hard against the scudding clouds, telegraph posts whipping past like sticks in a fence. I remembered my father's words of only last night, at our last family dinner. "It'll take a bit of getting used to, of course, but it will be a good experience for you; you may one day look back upon it all as among some of the happiest times of your life. I know that *I* did." And I knew that he was telling me an arrant lie. His had been an appalling war and he suffered from it for the rest of his life. All he was doing, I knew, was jollying me along at that particular moment. Like the dentist who says this won't hurt you. No point in frightening the wits out of the patient before the operation. The operation itself would see to that.

*   *   *

At Darlington we had to change trains for Richmond. It seemed to be the middle of the night. The cold dank of the North, smell of gas lamps and wet concrete, of soot and oily engines; draggled shadows bumping suitcases across the crowded station, in and out of the pools of light from the blackout shades, the hiss of steam and the clatter of tea trolleys; blindly we swam through the cross currents of hunched commuters like a shoal of fish, instinctively, mindlessly, until someone in uniform at the head of the shoal halted us into a colliding huddle and directed us raggedly towards another platform and yet another train. At Richmond in a wet moor-mist, on gleaming, slippery cobbles, in a biting wind and with only torches flashing about like distracted fireflies, we stood miserably about while other uniformed men barked orders and forced us shuffling into what were called "Alphabetical Groups" . . . all the A's and all the B's and so on. As V*, I found myself down at the far end of the long line of shuddering trucks, loaded up, tail boards slammed shut, bolts run home, tarpaulins roughly pulled down to protect us from the misty rain, and in darkness, and silence, we moved off through the night to Catterick Camp. All I knew was that we had to report to "Lecatto Lines", and that I was suddenly very hungry. I had had nothing to eat since the morning with Vida at Lyons Corner House, when misery had doused my appetite even for a lump of squashy gateau. The truck was full, some of us standing among the knees and suitcases of the luckier ones sitting on long wooden forms, hanging on with one arm to the steel supports of the roof, empty suitcases in the other. We rumbled and bumped along twisting roads and hills for an eternity. No one spoke.

Catterick Camp was a bleak, lightless huddle of hut roofs, jagged against the steel night sky. Torches flashing at the Main Gate, sentry boxes, wire, questions shouted and answered. I heard the phrase "New Intake" a couple of times and realised that that was what we were.

We crunched about on gleaming gravel for a time, bumping into each other, then were formed into squads and marched through the wet night to huts. Ours was up a muddy track. We slid and clambered along in the dark, snagged by bushes on either side. The hut was bleak, cold, two lamps whipping leaping shadows round the brick walls and tin roof in the draught. We were told to choose a bed site, from piles of grubby mattresses on the floor, shown where the Ablutions were, and where to put our personal possessions. Large metal two-door meat-safes evenly spaced all down each side of the cement-wet hut. "Three biscuits each for your beds," said a weary corporal indicating the pile of mattresses, "and if anyone wants extra, there's straw out in the yard. Help yourselves."

Later we were marched back down the track to the Mess Hall. A gaunt raftered shed, scrubbed tables and benches, three iron stoves smouldering sullenly down the middle, at one end a long counter with urns, mugs and bundles of knives and forks in cardboard boxes. Condensation sweated down the yellow walls.

Sitting, twenty to a table, we ate fried sausages, boiled potatoes,

* Van den Bogaerde, the family name.

6

carrots, two slices of thick margarined bread, with a pint mug of scalding tea. In the centre of each table, a bottle of Daddies Sauce. Next to me, Palmers Green, exhausted, eyes glazed, face soapstone. Opposite, a tall blond boy, cool, spruce, his mouth a coathanger of disdain.

"Won't quite do, will it? Should be organised by now . . . we'll lose the war this way. Name's Tilly, P. W., Chartered Accountant; you know Hendon Central? Thought you might." He looked coldly round the chewing mass. "Hope they put up the lists pretty soon, get our names down right away . . . want to avoid any mistakes, don't you think? I'm in your hut if you need any advice."

I thanked him and told him that I was perfectly happy, wanting only to live a quiet life, giving no trouble and receiving none. He cracked a couple of knuckles loudly.

"Stay a ranker for the duration? More responsibility as an officer surely?"

"I don't *want* responsibility!"

"You'd rather stay herded together with this crowd for the rest of the war? Not me. I say! I think your friend's going to be ill."

Back in the hut we scrabbled about laying out our mattresses, stacking suitcases on the meat-safes, sorting out washing kit and the sad relics of home in the shape of our colourful, personal, hand towels. We queued to wash hands and teeth and to urinate. The concrete floor awash with water, suds and spittle. The weary corporal shouted, "Lights out in ten minutes, you lot," and everyone struggled back to undress and some, not all, to drag on a sad variety of pyjamas. Then to bed. Two hairy blankets stiff as card, a round, striped, greasy bolster, clothes neatly piled beside one's head for the morning. I wound my watch and realised that it had been 14 hours since we had all said goodbye at home that morning in the bright, sharp, Sussex light. I wondered, as the lights switched off, if my mother had managed to put in her rows of wintergreens; when I'd be able to write to them; what Vida was doing at this moment? Was there a raid perhaps in London. Had my father got home from *The Times* or was he, like me, sleeping on the floor in his office, as he so often had to do? Was it warm down there, as it had been last night by the pond when we sat watching the dog snuffling about for a rat in the sedge? A great welling misery rose in my heart and swept swiftly to my throat. Tears, unwanted, salt and hot, swelled through tightly closed eyelids; I thrust my face into the greasy bolster and hoped it would smother them. My shaking only lasted a moment or two, and then I lay silent, staring into the blackness. I was more than relieved to hear, about me, that one or two other people were in the same condition. Someone coughed gently, and blew his nose. Gradually the hut became still. The cinders from the dying stove rustled into the grate. The man on the floor on my right started to snore. Someone farted. I thought it was probably Gooley.

* * *

After they had issued us with numbers, handed out sizeless new-smelling uniforms, boots made of forged iron, button sticks, gas masks and a heavy Lee Enfield rifle, plus tin helmet and camouflage net, I folded my green tweed suit from Gamages Fire Sale, the canary yellow polo necked shirt, my suede shoes a size too large, the colourful personal towel, shoved them all in the empty suitcase which had travelled with me from home, and bundled it all back. I was left with only my washing gear, a photograph of the family standing smiling by the pond, a copy of *The Oxford Book of Modern Verse* and a pile of blue notebooks ready for the Poetry which Vida felt sure, although I was much in doubt, would flood from me in the moments when, as she had put it cheerfully, "the others were cleaning their rifles or boots". Little did we know on those halcyon evenings at her flat during the blitz in Belsize Crescent, that when they were doing that so, indeed, should I be. Poetry waited for the quiet times in the NAAFI on Sunday afternoons after we had marched to Church, had lunch, and the rest of the day to ourselves.

I think that the very first thing which helped to break me into the life was the Haircut. For endless hours we queued in drizzling mist to be shorn like sheep. When my turn came the hefty bruiser with the clippers pronounced it as long as a girl's and asked what I'd been before. This eternal question. Unthinkingly I said that I'd been an actor. "Aha!" cried the bruiser with relish, and shaved me down to a prickly, almost naked dome. Everyone crowded round to see; gleeful that it was not they; goading him on in his surgical efforts to reduce my morale, my appearance, and my spirit.

I remembered a rat that some of the village boys had trapped on a brick in a water tank up at the farm. They were stoning it into the water with half-bricks, it kept falling off and swimming desperately round and round the brick-pile, blood running into the water, its hair sticking up like mine now, its nose split. They stoned it until it quietly gave in and floated, pink feet upwards in supplication, tail trailing, dead.

No rat I. I had to start proving, and show them what I could do. I joined in the laughter. My laughter stopped the others. I departed in a curious silence. I had learned my first psychological trick. Laugh with them at you. And then you win. As long as you can follow it up. I did by being the best boot-polisher in the squad. For one cigarette a time I offered to do it for all the others who found it difficult and, after a very short time, had enough to open a shop. I stitched on badges and "flashes" and buttons, thanking God all the time for my training in the theatre wardrobes of "Q" Theatre and Amersham. It was not, you understand, the most elegant of stitching, but it was able to pass muster at inspections and kept me busy in the long dull evenings while the others lay disconsolately on their beds reading *Health and Strength, Tit-Bits,* or just staring into space.

I never had any spare time. I excelled at Drill. Theatre training again. I enjoyed marching and about-turning, by the right and by the left. The precision of it interested me, the effort very nearly killed me; but I did it, and did it moderately well. I worked so hard in fact that every time I clambered down on to my hard bed I was almost immediately asleep. No haunting nightmares of misery assailed me. Self-preservation was strong, thanks to the theatre and a determined, sensible, family training before that.

Out on the range, scrubby heather, mist, a brick wall and rows of targets, I learned to shoot with my heavy Lee Enfield. I was determined to be best in the squad. Tilly, who was equally determined, but who could neither sew nor polish, was a comfortable second.

I was very good at everything except the one thing for which I had been sent to Catterick initially: to be a signaller in the Royal Corps of Signals. My father had been as much surprised as I myself at the arbitrary, seemingly idiotic, decision to draft me into the Signal Corps. I who had the co-ordination of a bursting dam and the technical intelligence of an eft. We had decided that it was probably due to the fact that I had had to state my school

9

background on my papers and that I had attended, for some time, a highly technical school in Glasgow which may have, erroneously, given them the idea that I was qualified. At school I had been so dense that I was finally removed from all the Technical Classes and allowed to follow my own pursuits in Bookbinding, Metalwork and Pottery. Which is why, to this day, I can sew on buttons, marble paper, open tins brilliantly, and glue the handle on to a cup. Everything else had been a total mystery to me, and remained so. And so it was with Morse Code and all the other bits and pieces which went with the Course. I was baffled, uncomprehending, lost. And although I tried to learn the handbooks as I would a play, like a parrot, the practice of the exercise left me floundering in a mess of wires, bells, batteries and code. I knew that in this instance I was utterly doomed. Polish boots I could, sew on badges, hit the inner, outer, magpie, and bull's-eye time after time with my little gun. I could throw a grenade, wash a floor, drill like a demon, pass Kit Inspection with top marks, write excellent, if mawkish, letters to a girl named Kitty who seemed to be the dominant factor in Gooley's life. But I could not perform any function, whatsoever, required by the Royal Corps of Signals. I couldn't even send the S.O.S.

So, when the time came, I volunteered for the cookhouse. And because no one knew quite what to do with me, I was left there, peeling potatoes by the barrel, scrubbing down tables and benches, bashing about in a lather of soap and swill in the tin-wash, opening tin upon tin of bully beef, liver, pilchards and plum and apple. I hoped that my diligence would not go unremarked, and that perhaps after a time they'd forget all about me and let me off the Morse Code thing and allow me to spend the rest of my war washing up. Fat chance. But for a time I was in a busy fool's paradise.

Sunday was a dreary day. After Church Parade and lunch, I wrote letters to Kitty for Gooley who was in my hut and to whom I had become very attached in spite of his violent past, and wrote reams and reams of frightful poetry in blue notebooks about Isolation, Loneliness, Shells, Death in the Mud, Barbed Wire, Larks and Cornfields. I wrote them all, without exception, like the mouse's tail poem in "Alice". Long wriggling columns without rhyme, or very much reason, usually ending in a single word like "dead" or "cigarette" or "stench". My war poetry, after about three weeks, was still completely second hand, and borrowed exclusively from my father's war, about which I thought I knew a great deal. It took me six years to realise I knew nothing. It was not, however, a total waste of time. Just putting words down on paper was something. Out of the welter of rubbish bits and pieces emerged, shyly, causing me great delight, and forcing my Venus pencil to even wilder efforts. It also passed the time in the grey, brown, greasy room with its scattered tables and sagging posters of the "Night Train to Holyhead".

Except for Tilly and Gooley, I didn't get to know anyone else very well. Because of my accent I was called, as indeed Gooley had done in the train coming up, Toff, but was excused for that in some dumb way by the fact that I was good at polishing and volunteered hysterically for practically anything. Usually a frightful error. I had, I thought, my own methods for survival. Blithely unaware that there were other factors working against my conceit.

Palmers Green, my light operatic companion from the train, was not very happy. I did his boots and sewed on his flashes free. Not out of any form of generosity, because he didn't smoke and never had cigarettes, but he was, as he had pointed out a number of times, a fellow actor, and loyalty came into it. He suggested one Sunday over slopped tea in the NAAFI that perhaps we should try and start a Concert Party. It would give us something to do, and he felt sure that the lads would enjoy a bit of a sing-song or some sketches which he suggested he would write. He himself, he pointed out, with his operatic background could oblige with some renderings of familiar and well loved numbers . . . and he had two sisters who could send him all the scores and song sheets collected from his past glories at The Society. I thought it quite a good idea myself, and began to rough out a few ideas. But first we had to get people together. And then where was the stage? Not, for sure, in the NAAFI. Tilly said there was a Garrison Theatre just outside the camp, and that if we did decide to form a concert party he'd be very pleased to supervise the lighting because apart from accounting his main hobby was electricity. I might have guessed. So now there were three people ready to start things off.

We pinned a notice up one Friday evening and settled down like anglers to wait. Palmers Green became almost cheerful. Writing off to his sisters in Hammersmith for the scores and libretti, daily scanning the notice board as if it was a rat-trap. We didn't appear to be attracting anything. One or two hesitant names; someone who could play a viola; someone who was a carpenter. And then it fizzled out. After a couple of weeks I gave in and forgot all about a concert party. And then one evening Palmers Green came into my hut with an ashen face, his thin hair straggling from under his cap, his fatigues drooping round him like ectoplasm. In his shaking hand, the notice, ripped hurriedly from the board. With a smothered cough he handed it to me. Someone had drawn an enormous, detailed, erect penis, plus optimistically splendid appendages, and under it, in block letters, had printed, WE WANT TO SCREW NOT SING! I tore it up and shoved it in the stove.

"They're animals," said Palmers Green hopelessly, "simply animals, there's nothing you can do with people like that. Beasts, that's all. What's the use of trying to help people in life, to bring a little cheer into their lives, what's the use, I ask you?" He was distressed and near to tears as he ambled miserably across the hut. I was forced to follow him for comfort.

"It's a joke, really . . . you see. We'll put up another tomorrow."

"They won't care. They are all obscene. It's hopeless. They'll take over the world one day, you see if I'm right."

I leant against the door-post. "We'll try again. Just give it time."

He wandered down the steps. "In my hut, you know, they all call me . . ." he screwed up his eyes and I thought he was going to cry, but they unscrewed and he said, "Hilda." We stood in helpless silence looking at a row of fire buckets. "I don't know why," he said, almost to himself, "I try to do what I can, but it is difficult. The Morse, the marching . . . I do my best. It's just not something I'm used to at my age. Difficult to look neat in this stuff too, isn't it? Do you know," he pulled out a handkerchief, and blew his nose hard, "do you know, I haven't even whistled since I got here, not a note, and I was always so full of melody, little snatches here and there, really very cheery, but I just haven't the heart these days." He shoved his handkerchief back and tried to cram the wispy hair under his cap. "You've been very kind, very kind," he tried a wan smile. "I did say 'birds of a feather', didn't I? Oh well, I'll be seeing you quite a bit this coming week. Cookhouse Fatigues. The Kit Inspections, you know. I don't seem to manage very well."

I watched him wander sadly down the track in the soft June

evening. It had rained all afternoon but now the sun was out, glistening in the puddles, the tin roofs of the huts shone like silver paper. Gooley and a skinny man we called Worms, because he was so thin and ate faster and more than anyone else, came down the hill. Gooley threw an affectionate arm round my shoulders.

"Come on, Toff. I'll treat you to a bromide tea. Me auntie sent a postal order yesterday."

We walked off together, avoiding the puddles because of our polished boots, and Worms made us laugh because he said that even if they did put bromide in the tea he still felt horny every morning and woke up with an erection like a tent pole. I wondered what Palmers Green would have thought of that.

*   *   *

The frozen Argentinian liver came in blocks eighteen inches long and five square. It had the texture of iced sand with veins running through it like string. This we cut into slices, tipped into boiling cauldrons, fished out after fifteen minutes, slapped into shallow tins, twenty to each, smothered in what was euphemistically called gravy, and bunged in the ovens. Then we had our breakfasts. Up since five-thirty, we ate fried eggs, leftover potatoes, bread and marge and a mug of tea in the peace of the empty Mess Hall. A moment of luxury. I only ate liver once, ever. At seven on the dot the Army arrived, clattering blearily into the Mess, faces pink from shaving, hair, or what remained of it, sleeked with water or Brylcreem, mugs and eating-irons clutched in their fists.

We shoved the liver tins on to each table, the Daddies Sauce, the margarine-bread, and filled the mugs with bromide tea as the noise of a cattle fair mounted. For all the disadvantages of working in the cookhouse, there were excellent advantages, I found. We fed better than the others most of the time, avoided the misery of Roll Call, kit inspections and the general daily chores of the barrack room life. We also missed out on Drill for a while, which, even though I liked it, was a bit of a relief.

But best of all, I was able to avoid the absolute terror of motor bikes. This was a hazard which I had not been expecting at all. Gas, bombs, bullets, mud and discomfort, all these. But never for one single split second did it ever occur to me that I should have to sit astride a giant motorcycle and learn, not only how to drive it, but how to care for its incomprehensible guts as well. My complete lack of co-ordination rendered the whole enterprise of riding a bike into something as dangerous and unreasonable as crossing Niagara Falls on a rope. I could seldom start it, and the only way I could stop it was by falling off as gracefully as possible. I developed the agility of a tumbler.

For all these reasons I was happy in the cookhouse even though the work was hard, dirty and often long. But it at least sped time along and kept our minds off the submerged wreck of fear which lay just below our fragile barque of courage. The Draft. Sometimes we dared to speak of it . . . but not often. A rumour would sometimes weave a thread of chill vapour into our overtly medical conversations. We were going to Madagascar, to Iceland, to Singapore; improbably far away places, never, alas, Europe. For that was long since sealed off from us. Once someone said that they had seen hundreds of sun helmets in the Q.M.'s store hidden under blankets. Which meant the Tropics for certain. Africa maybe . . . even, God help us all, India! Panic, always latent, surged within each breast, until someone mentioned tits or farts and then we relaxed back into laughter, instantly banishing Madagascar.

Washing up in the tin-wash was so unpleasant that it was ranked as a punishment for anyone slack enough to have a dirty bolt to his rifle, an unblacked-out window, or a messy kit inspection. Standing at the concrete sinks, arms deep in filthy, greasy water, hands red from corrosive soda, feet soaked from the spilled swill and muck on the floors beneath us, it ranked high as disagreeable. I saw poor Palmers Green clonking and scrubbing away there, his thin hair limp with sweat, his smile, when he saw me, tremulous, his elbows raw-boned, going up and down like a wooden monkey's. For me, there was a certain satisfaction to be gained by wiping clean a battered two-handled tin, once foul with grease and caught liver or frozen kidneys, and polishing it into a brilliant shining mirror. One always felt that it might be the one to come to one's own table the next day. It never was. But one hoped. Without hope there was not the slightest possibility of surviving those initial twenty-five weeks. Some did not.

One morning, while finishing off the last of the fried bread, a man crashed into the Mess looking as if he had been hit by a falling wall. Hair staring, shirt-tails flapping, trousers, clenched in two anguished fists, sagging round his knees, braces flying like hoops, he stood barefoot, shocked. We stood up in mute surprise. He was handed a mug of tea which he waved aside and slumped on to a bench. "There's a geezer hanging in the pisshouse."

In the already warming June sunlight an aimless huddle of men stood about outside the latrines waiting, presumably, for Authority to arrive and settle the business. Half dressed, some with toothbrushes or washing bags, they shifted from foot to foot in the embarrassed silence reserved for death. The door of No. 8 was wide open. In the vivid shaft of sunlight which illuminated the cubicle like a pin spot, hung a man. Dressed in striped pyjamas, head on his chest, one leg twisted cruelly in the pan, the other almost kneeling on the filthy floor, a stretched figure of supplication. The cord from the cistern was as tight as a bow-string, buried deep into his livid neck, forcing his fat tongue through blue lips in a final obscene gesture at the insult of life. His hands swung gently, a ring glittered. He had messed himself. I turned suddenly away and pushed through the silent herd with its toothbrushes and washbags. Hunched against a brick wall I fought a desperate, and successful, battle to retain my breakfast. Heaving and retching, fighting down the rising nausea, I pressed my face into the rough, warm bricks. After a while it started to subside. I gasped for breath, wiping my snotty nose and the cascading tears of effort from my cheeks. In a blurred instant I saw the worried, caring face of Gooley. Gently he put out a hand and patted my shoulder.

"Silly boy, you was. You shouldn't have looked, you know. You shouldn't have looked."

I shook my head hopelessly, brushing the muck from my face with a shaking hand. I knew damn well I shouldn't have looked. It was Palmers Green.

* * *

We prepared for the funeral with all the excitements and terrors of a First Night. Boots were honed to a brilliance never before seen, even on Colonel's Inspection, badges glittered, trousers were creased like knife blades. Soap rubbed down the inside of the crease, and then ironed hard, belts blancoed, brasses shining like a Whitbread's dray horse. We were determined to do our first official Show as well as possible and to give the deceased a far better send off than he had ever had welcome.

They had asked for volunteers. Palmers Green's family, shocked and dazed, one presumed, demanded his body to be returned to them in London. Pall bearers, six, were to cart the coffin from Richmond Station along the platform to the London train. I was first, this time because of Palmers Green and the odd, unwanted bond which he had forced upon me. Tilly and Gooley came in also when they knew I was on, and a small, neat, cherubic youth called Derek. His had been one of the few signatures on our ill fated notice for the concert party, and it had written beside his name, "Dancing, acrobatics, splits, etc." With his wide blue eyes, pink complexion, soft blond hair, delicate voice, and pleasantly defined figure, he had become a fairly frequent visitor to the Sergeants' Mess up the hill, and so no one dared to openly insult him. Behind his back was a different matter altogether. But it was felt that one false step or word with this angelic, helpless, little fellow would lead straight to a Madagascar posting or anywhere else east of Suez. Without any questions. So he was tolerated. Just about. He never got into the tin-wash or did Pack Drill at the double or anything disagreeable. We were still two short, and finally we were lucky to get Piper, who was a Christian Scientist and said that death was all in the mind so he didn't care much one way or the other, and Grimm who said that he had been sorry for the poor sod and he ought to have a fitting farewell. They were matched for height and we were off most duties for rehearsals.

For a couple of days we did our polishing and preparing, had a sort of frantic dummy run with an empty pine coffin round the Drill Yard, and one bright afternoon were loaded on to a 15 cwt truck, with Palmers Green lying boxed at our feet.

At the station, among a little group of curious citizens, there were two pale women in black, clutching handkerchiefs. The sisters from Hammersmith come to conduct him home. The coffin was hastily covered with an immense Union Jack, for which we were quite unprepared, having humped an unadorned coffin round on our shoulders during the rehearsals. On top of this, even more worrying, was placed a wreath of yellow flowers, presumably from the Royal Corps of Signals, although I couldn't see the writing on the flapping label. To add to our growing un-ease, sparkling away in brass and blanco in the hot sun, we became aware that there was a small flight of steps to be negotiated, and we hadn't actually rehearsed steps. However, out of sight of the mourning sisters, and without a great deal of elegance, Palmers Green was loaded on to our brave young shoulders. We immediately sagged and buckled at the knees. The shortest were in the front, Derek on the right, Grimm on the left, in the middle Gooley and Piper, behind, as we were marginally taller and therefore presumed, inaccurately, to be stronger, Tilly and myself supporting the head-part of the coffin. The heaviest we supposed, and envied Derek and Grimm having only the shins and feet, so to speak, to carry.

It was an uneven stagger which brought Palmers Green towards the steps and his black clad relations from Hammersmith; he seemed rather small for his coffin. Slid about a bit, up and down it seemed, as we angled him upwards. Gooley cursing under his breath, Tilly muttering "Steady, lads, steady," as if we were at sea, and the sweat beading under our caps, trickling into the serge of our uniforms. Mercifully we negotiated the steps, shoulders aching, legs slightly splayed, arms locked in desperate attachment to the ever increasing weight of our lost companion. "It's de wind," said Gooley under his breath, and trying to catch it, "dey say dey always blow up wid de wind after a few days. Sweet Mary! but he's a heavy bugger."

Exhausted, blinded with a mist of sweat, breathless, we reached the entrance to the platform and started down the endless vista to the Guard's Van. Right at the end of the train, practically as far away as York. The escort marched glitteringly ahead of us, the draggle of people, plus the two black women with their handkerchiefs, trailed along on either side and then a sudden gust of wind riffled the immense Union Jack causing it to whip about like the sail of a yacht in a force nine gale. Tilly and I, separated as we were by the apparently enormous bulk of the coffin, could only see to our immediate left or, in his case, right, but we did hear the smothered cry from Derek in the front as he stumbled suddenly, swirled about in the Union Jack. We felt, all too helplessly, the wild lurch of our possession, saw the yellow wreath slither out of sight, the flag cascade in a shimmer of red, white and blue about our feet, and in spite of desperate struggles on the part of all the rest of us, Palmers Green slid inexorably, and not ungracefully, to his feet, almost upright, on the wide platform. Derek lay wrapped in the colours, with Grimm beside him and the wreath between them. I don't know what happened to the mourners. The escort broke formation and rushed to our assistance, Derek was on his feet, the flag whipped out of sight, the coffin reverently placed back on our aching shoulders and with squint caps, sweat coursing, and a Lance Corporal carrying the wreath like a suitcase we made the Guard's Van and bundled our load into the more expert hands of the L.N.E.R. An ignominious attempt at chivalry.

Riding back to Camp in the 15 cwt, we smoked nervously, wondering if we would be put on a charge or what exactly would happen. Derek was on the point of collapse most of the way, and Grimm had to bawl at him to "belt up" at least three times before he subsided into hiccups.

"It was that bloody flag," he said in between trying to hold his breath and count to ten as Gooley had told him. "Whipped round my face, I couldn't see a thing, not a bloody thing, dears. Smothered I was, simply smothered. I wouldn't have done it on purpose, you all know that. I just buckled and went over. Oh the shame of it, and I've always been able to manage my skirts." But we were all too exhausted to care. What kind of punishment was there for dropping a full coffin, we wondered? All that actually happened was that we got a severe dressing down about being slack, weak, and a disgrace to the Royal Corps of Signals from the RSM, who finally admonished us into shame by saying that it was the last time we'd ever be entrusted to carry a coffin again in public. Which made us wonder just how many more he was envisaging during our stay.

2

BOREDOM, as my father had prophesied, began to leak into life, indeed into all our lives, after a few weeks. Sitting about in the grey NAAFI with a slab of sodden cake and diluted coffee, at ringed tables under a flat light made us all depressed and stale and it was during one of these deathly evenings, with someone bashing out Ivor Novello medleys at the upright piano in the corner, that Gooley had the bright thought of starting up the abandoned concert party idea. So the notice was, once again, put up on the board and this time, to our surprised delight, or mine at any rate, we got a much better haul and auditions were started round the Upright every free evening. It seemed that almost everyone in the camp had discovered a latent talent for singing endless versions of "I'll Walk Beside You", "Because" and "Ave Maria". In stultified misery we heard them all and realised that these splendid tenors, baritones and hog-callers would only compound the boredom, not relieve it. And after one or two extra talents like conjuring, impersonations, and when Derek of the cortège had given us some pretty fancy high kicks and a couple of agonized splits, which hurt him, because, as he pointed out, he was "not in practice", we settled for a Dramatic Society instead.

At the end of June I was promoted to Lance Corporal. And smirked with astonished pride. Someone seemed to think that I was at least showing signs of something, perhaps in leadership if not in Morse or the rest of the required activities. Slightly weighed down with the importance of my chevroned arms, I moved into the small cubicle at the end of the hut with a real bed, and assumed the responsibilities, unwittingly, for the entire Squad Hut. I lost no time in informing my father on a postcard of Richmond Castle, in heavy pencil, stiff with exclamation marks of false surprise. Overstating as usual.

The Dramatic Society flourished. We started off with a thriller, Patrick Hamilton's "Rope". Fairly easy since it had one set and only two parts for women, and a splendid part for me. The women's parts were willingly filled by ladies from the Officers' Quarters up the hill outside the camp who were just as bored with the Yorkshire moors as we were, and enjoyed their evenings, bringing all their friends, their knitting, thermos flasks of tea or coffee and sandwiches, imbuing the whole business with the atmosphere of a mixed Women's Institute.

We even managed a small orchestra for the intervals and the overture. Instruments were sent for from home, band parts scored, and before you could say "Curtain Up" we were off. The play was a whacking success, so much so that we had to play it for four nights instead of only one, and travelled it about the county to less fortunate companions in arms. Bundled into trucks, with our costumes in kitbags and the band parts of "Roses of Picardy" and "Me and My Girl: Selections", we covered Yorkshire. There was usually a party in an Officers' Mess afterwards, with sausage rolls and small gins and limes, and warming congratulations for boosting the morale, which pleased us since the main object had been to boost our own. However, ambition had been roused and was not about to be quenched easily. I decided on another play, and before the course was over we presented a more ambitious effort in Elmer Rice's "Judgement Day", which was an even greater success. It hardly felt like being in the army at all. If this was what it could be like, if I was crafty, I'd perhaps never have to go to Madagascar or Singapore, but might just manage to stay put and boost morale. After all, I reasoned happily, someone had to do it, why not me?

But that sort of idiocy came to an abrupt end when Tilly and I and a couple of others were sent for to be interviewed as officer material. Worriedly we cleaned and polished and blancoed days before the event, and one hot morning were summoned to our inquisition. Tilly, I noticed with regret, sparkled like a Jewish wedding. I felt sure that he would pass, he was so determined, and that I'd probably be set aside, for I looked anything but chic in my battledress, even though my brasses shone like bright deeds.

A large horseshoe table; about six or seven officers. One very tall and elegant, who made little paper darts most of the time; three or four with tabs and redder faces; and another who sat at the side of the table, crouched over his papers, wearing rimless glasses looking like Himmler's aunt. I was last to be called, on account of being "V". Tilly was second last and came out grim and soldierly; he gave such a smashing salute as he left the room that I feared he must have hurt himself. He about-turned and marched blindly past me, giving me no clues whatever. Sick with apprehension, I entered. There was a lot of tittle tattle over my papers; my schooling, family background, and all the rest. The thing which seemed to stick in their craws was the unacceptable fact that I had been an actor. This, I gathered, was a sign of an unstable temperament. The elegant officer who stopped making paper darts for a second asked me what I had done in London in the theatre and looked completely blank until I mentioned "Diversion" at Wyndhams. At this he seemed to recognise something far away across the room and, staring into the breeze-block wall, he said mildly that he didn't remember seeing me. I was not fool enough not to realise that this little pleasantry could be a trap: they did this kind of thing, I had been told, to try and throw you off kilter and see your reactions. Mine, I thought, were perfectly reasonable.

"Well . . . I was in it . . . but it wasn't much. I had a few lines in a couple of numbers and a bit of a song in a kilt."

He looked sadly at his collection of darts. "Doesn't ring a bell."

"Well, I don't suppose it would, Sir, I was a sort of chorus boy really."

A sudden hush. A red-tabbed one cleared his throat and echoed "chorus boy" as if I had said "child molester". I felt the earth slipping away very gradually. Chorus boys, even I could see that, were probably not officer material.

I tried to repair. "A glorified chorus boy; not really a dancer or anything like that, you know . . ." ending helplessly.

But no one did know. They leant together and muttered away. Eventually another one, with red tabs but a younger face, asked about "Rope" and "Judgement Day", to my astonishment. Until I realised that everything I had ever done in my life was set down in the papers before them. There was a murmuring about "jolly good show, boosting morale"—how that phrase cropped up with them all the time—and "organizing powers". My heart lifted a little and the languid officer folded another dart.

Suddenly a voice barked at me from Left Field.

"Nothing to it, of course; acting." He was older than the others, very red-tabbed, probably a General.

"No, Sir, not really."

"Acting's easy stuff. Girls do it."

"Yes, Sir." Agree with him. Clearly he's General Public.

"Done it meself . . . so I know. It's the organisation that counts."

"Yes, Sir, that's really very hard . . ."

"Did both, you know, so I know what I'm talking about. Heard of 'Aladdin'?"

"Yes, Sir."

"Bloody good show. Did that."

The languid officer was stilled with deference. "You did, Sir?"

He beamed round the table having caught their full attention. "Wrote it, played Widow Twankey, and produced it, what! Marvellous fun."

Everyone smiled politely and he turned his jealous eyes back to me. "Boosted morale no end, frightfully good show. Tickled 'em pink. Amritsar, 1926."

"It must have been marvellous, Sir."

"But acting's all twaddle, anyone can do it."

"Yes, Sir, of course."

For a moment he glowered at me and then barked: "Your father!" Father, for God's sake, what about him?

"Yes, Sir?" Eager and with a pleasant filial smile.

"Art editor of *The Times*, I believe. It says so on your papers."

"Yes, Sir."

"Well, what exactly does the art editor do? I mean, that is to say, what is the art editor?"

"He's responsible for the picture page, all the photographs, and the arts page generally . . ."

"Takes them himself, does he? Snaps, that sort of thing?"

"Yes of course, Sir, but naturally he has hundreds of photographers of his own."

"Naturally," the voice was ice.

Hasten in to correct.

"He selects the photographs for the News . . . landscapes . . . all those pictures of Sussex and Scotland . . . the half-page on Saturdays. Perhaps, Sir, you saw one he did of the Isle of Wight from Ashdown Forest. It was infra-red . . ."

The elegant officer folded, very carefully, another paper dart.

"Infra-red?"

"Yes, Sir; actually he managed to save a great deal of the South Coast from ribbon-development, from things like Peacehaven . . . you know . . ."

I was talking far too much, and perhaps he liked Peacehaven. Impatience eddied in the air like a bad odour. Time was running out . . . the elegant officer gave a little laugh and said: "All rather high quality stuff, General . . . not *Men Only*." There was polite laughter, and throats were cleared. I lied swiftly.

"Of course he knows all the other editors, you know; they er . . . work together really . . ."

The General looked up from my folder which he was in the act of closing gently. Like a curtain falling slowly on a play.

"Does he, indeed? Knows the editors? Of *Men Only* as well? *The Times*?"

"It's all journalism after all, Sir, they all know each other."

"I know that!"

I stood stiffly to attention, the elegant officer leant back in his wooden chair. The General stroked his nose.

"Perhaps *The Times* might care to send us a few snaps, shall we say? To cheer up the Mess, what? Something half-page size . . . that sort of thing?"

Don't be over eager. State a fact.

"Yes, Sir, I'm sure."

"But not landscapes of course . . . ha ha ha . . . something a little more, can we say, inspiring?"

"Of course, Sir." Lie as hard as you can and hope to God that your unsuspecting father will come to your assistance. This is the point of no return.

Shortly afterwards I was dismissed, threw a correct salute, about-turned under the stone eyes of the RSM, and left the room, just as a small paper dart skimmed through the air and plummeted against the windows.

That evening, from a call-box outside the NAAFI, reversing the charges, I telephoned my father.

"You do know the editor of *Men Only*, don't you?"

"No."

"Well, could you arrange to send me, oh, something like a dozen, quite big, photos of nude women? But quickly . . ."

"For your Mess?"

"No, for the Officers' Mess. I've just had my interview for an OCTU."

The line crackled for a few seconds. "I see."

"Quite large, you know. And coloured if you can."

"I'll do what I can. What is *Men Only*?"

Fourteen anxious days later Tilly and I and one other fellow saw our names on the board stating that from such and such a date we were now Officer Cadets and should put-up our white-tabs forthwith.

My father had been as good, as they say, as his word.

* * *

I had just finished Gooley's weekly letter to Kitty. It had become a firm routine over the weeks, and I sometimes felt that I knew Kitty almost as well as he did himself. It was a very intimate relationship, his and mine, for in charging me with the task of writing his passions to Cork and the girl he loved, he had placed himself confidently in my hands. In fact, after a time he simply indicated more or less what he wanted to tell her that week, and left me cheerfully to find the words (which I did, with the aid of the *Oxford Book of Modern Verse*), most of which he didn't know himself, and many of which I felt pretty sure Kitty wouldn't know either. However, he was always filled with self-pride when I read them back to him and sat in stiff amazed delight, shaking his cropped head, bemused, often moved to the point of tears.

This latest letter was the cruncher, for it was the Proposal Letter and we had spent some considerable time on its composition. He was determined that it should not sound daft, and that it should be more businesslike than poetical. "Her Dad owns a pub, he's no fool, you know . . . It's not de pub I'm after, Toff, it's de daughter . . . get that straight and clear." He insisted on the final lines himself, choosing, "Be assured of my strict intentions, my darling girl, Kitty, from your respectful, hoping-to-be-accepted-husband, Patrick Gooley." He scrawled a signature, the only thing he could actually write with any authority, and read it through slowly and carefully.

"Dat's beautiful!"

"I don't know why you don't write your own letters, for God's sake."

"I just haven't de touch, and anyway she enjoys your letters more dan mine, she says so every time. Dat's de only ting dat worries me . . . when I leave here she'll not be gettin' any letters and she'll likely be expecting me to talk like you write, and dat's going to be a bugger, I can tell you." He folded the letter carefully, put it into the envelope and, with his fat tongue sticking out, laboriously printed, in his own hand, the address.

I folded my arms behind my head and looked up at the ceiling: there was a dry moth in a cobweb.

"Gooley. When you hit that old woman on the head, that time, with the iron, what did you feel? Do you remember?"

He shook his head looking vaguely worried.

24

"Nothing?"

"Well . . . I was shit scared dey'd hear her screeching away . . . you know . . ."

"Did you think that you'd killed her? Or could have?"

"Naw! Wasn't more dan a little tap-like . . . couple of little taps . . . just to keep her quiet, you see. It was her or me, you know, and she was a ould bitch."

"No remorse?"

"What's dat den?" He looked blank.

"Well, it didn't worry you, afterwards, I mean?"

"Mary, no! You know? I never even mentioned it on me rosary . . . not one bead did she get from me . . . after all it's her as got me into dis bloody ould army, isn't it?" He slid Kitty's letter carefully into his breast pocket, and thumped my knee. "What's up wid you? Dere's someting worrying youse . . ."

"Well . . . the other day, you know when we were up on the exercise in the woods . . . with the dummy ammo that leaves a stain, and I got Ernie Basset in the chest . . ."

Gooley cuddled his knees happily. "Ah wid dat last little shot our side won, didn't it den?"

"Yes, we won. But, you know I really thought that I *had* shot Basset. I thought it was real suddenly." I could see by his eyes that he didn't know what the hell I was talking about, and I knew that I would not be able to make him understand.

"But it was just an ould exercise! It was like a game is all! What's dere to upset you about dat den?"

"It suddenly didn't seem to be a game, is what I mean. I felt sick, do you know that? When Basset just fell forward on his face out of that bush, I was sure he was dead and that I had killed him. I can't get it out of my mind, Gooley."

He sighed with kindness, impatience and incomprehension. "Youse daft, Toff." He got up and went to the door of the cubicle. "It was just de same as me and de ould woman, Toff. It's dem or you. Nothing to it," and patting his breast pocket with the letter inside, he winked his wink and was gone.

Somewhere, buried under layers of romantic nonsense, I knew that he was right; it *was* just an old exercise, I had been on many before, but none had had this effect on me. Sitting up there in the little wood that day I was calm, serene, detached, curiously watching an ants' nest which I had thoughtlessly disturbed with a stick. I heard someone suddenly crackle through bracken, the wispy whisper of fronds against a body; heard the heavy breathing, as if that person had been running a long way; heard the little groan of effort as it buried itself into some bushes not far in front of me; saw a branch tremble violently, and then become still. Through the fretted leaves a gleam of sunlight flickered through the slender trees, glanced off a steel helmet. He was one of the enemy side; our side wore forage caps. Quite suddenly, for no apparent reason, my mouth went dry and I was frightened. Perhaps it was his almost tangible fear coming across the little clearing, perhaps the silence suddenly of the wood; still, still. Away down on the road I could faintly hear the voices of the others who had dropped out and would be sprawled about smoking. Apparently we were the last two left unaccounted for. I glanced at the magazine of my rifle. Two bullets left. I hunched back silently into the bole of a tree, bracken screening me. I think I stopped breathing.

And then I saw him. Cautiously he raised his pale helmeted face from the bush, and blindly looked about him, straight at me but unseeing. He was sweating with effort, or fear, for fear emanated from him like mist. He moved very slowly, as someone in a dream. His helmet shone in the filtered sun. He gave a little grunt of satisfaction that he was safe, and I watched as he quietly, carefully, secured his position, in the springing branches of the elder bush, lowering his gun and slowly wiping his nose with the back of his hand. My heart thudding, my body tense, I raised my gun and got him securely in my sights. A bellow of distant laughter came from the road, he instantly pulled up his gun and stiffened. I saw the clean steel of the muzzle ring, the black hole from which his bullet would speed, the trickle of sweat running down his jaw beading under his chin. For seconds we faced each other, then he relaxed a little, the muzzle dipped, he looked up into the trees and I shot him.

The report of the rifle shattered the wood and smashed my shoulder into the tree behind me. A bird went off chittering through the branches. He opened his eyes with wide surprise, his mouth in a soundless cry, and pitched forward on to his face among the branches. For a second I sat hunched, frozen with horror. It was only when he started to move that I started to shake. I recognised him immediately, Ernie Basset with red hair from H Hut. In the middle of his chest a large crimson stain from my killing bullet. He looked down at it with some consternation, and then called out to the wood loudly: "You sod! You got me!

Morocco, and that since he was a Swede, very strong, and five years older than I was, it might be tactful to keep out of the way for a while. Which I found to my surprise I accepted with almost unseemly alacrity. She was rather expensive anyway. And heavy to move about.

And so, apart from friendly little waves across Class, and stolen, rather smothered kisses and fumbles in the lockers, we drifted apart comfortably and I went on with my interrupted journey towards the theatre. The April sprig, the late developer, was starting to put out leaves, of a sort.

But Ernie Basset, and all that he stood for, was something very different, and something which shocked me deeply. After all, sex was what everyone did, or had. But killing a man, even with a dummy bullet, and finding almost the same pleasure in release at his death, was both frightening and surely wrong?

Hunched on my blanketed bed, staring worriedly at the knot holes in the floor I began to realise, after a very long time, that this was really what war was about. Killing each other. Simple as that. Him or me, you or him, it had never remotely occurred to me before. Now that it did, I would have to come to terms with it pretty quickly and put aside the romantic notions I had so firmly cherished. Now I could perhaps really understand Sassoon, Owen and the rest, and one day, not so far distant it would appear, I would have to use a real bullet against a real man, and that would be the final test of growing up, which I had delayed so long. I would put the thought of that aside until it actually came to pass. But of one thing I was perfectly certain. That when it came, I would be able to do it. It terrified me far more than it gave me courage.

Every night before going to sleep, practically without fail, I mumbled silently my prayers. A firm relic of a swiftly fading childhood. It was a sort of charm thing, rather than a religious thing. Habit rather than faith. But it also comforted me greatly, and I still do it. No set prayer, a familiar pattern of words only, beginning with "God Bless Mother, Father, Elizabeth, Gareth ..." and so on down to the dog. Sometimes, over-tired, exhausted from route marching, or work in the cookhouse, or even just mildly pissed on NAAFI beer I slid, without awareness, into a much older prayer which bubbled from my subconscious like a meadow spring:

"Gentle Jesus, meek and mild,
Look upon a little child,
Pity my simplicity,
Suffer me to come to Thee."

It went on for a bit longer but I had usually, by that time, fallen asleep. Now, shuffling about my six foot by four foot cubicle, changing my boots for gym shoes in order to go over to the NAAFI for a beer, I knew that all that simplicity stuff was bunk. Innocence was melting around me like snow in the heat of the sun. I could no longer ever say that absurdly childish prayer again; all that had gone. Exit my simplicity more like. Not pity. Kiki, Palmers Green, now Ernie Basset, Innocence. Odd, I thought, growing up seems to be all exits.

*   *   *

Jammed at a corner table under the sagging "Night Train to Holyhead", with a beer, I opened my much abused blue notebook and, heading the first clean page with the title "Man in the Bush", I wrote my first poem for Vida. Straight off, in one ordered series of line and words, without corrections or additions or pencil lickings, it all fell into clean, simple shape. My muse had entered at last. I had thought that she would arrive with a crash of thunder, in a blaze of glittering light, a golden pen in one hand, my inspiration in the other. But that is not how it happens at all. As someone has said, when she comes, she comes stealing in, gently, softly, almost shyly, and taking your hand she says: "Come and look! I have got something I want you to see." And I had. I hoped that Vida would like the result.

Just before Lights Out, sloshing through soapy swill of the Ablutions, Gooley and his chum Worms, towels over their shoulders, washbags swinging, caught me up and we walked across the square to our hut. Gooley slung his arm round my shoulder.

"Are you better now, Toff? Was you writin' to your Ma about your problems den all dat time in de corner dere?"

"No. I wrote a poem."

He looked patient. "What for? A pome, for de love of God!"

"A girl I know in London."

"Ah. A girl. Like for Kitty . . . dat sort of stuff, fancy?"

"Not very fancy, it was about killing Ernie Basset."

"For de love of God! She'll love dat for sure. Have you told Ernie? He'd piss hisself wid laughing."

*   *   *

There was a leave somewhere during the course. I don't remember much about it beyond the fact that I clambered off the bus at the crossroads in the village hung about with respirators, tin hat, kit bags and haversacks, and, I seem to think, my fateful rifle. I can't be quite sure but I have a vivid picture of my happy mother proudly marching along beside me with it slung over her shoulder, and my sister Elizabeth and Elsie, the Rubens shepherdess, humping along cheerfully, proudly, with bits and pieces of army equipment between them, as if they were fishwives marching on Versailles. And that evening, with my father, who came back from his blitz-beleaguered office at *The Times* for the special occasion, we all went up to the King's Head where I was fêted and wined as if I had won the V.C. It was all quite moving and faintly absurd. The civilians, whose war was far more uncomfortable and dangerous than mine, were enjoying themselves. It seemed a pity to spoil the fun. But I felt not-quite-right-somehow; I didn't fit. I felt taller, everyone said that I was. The women put it down to the rations we got, and the men down to the broads, as they said, with which we appeared as far as they were concerned anyway, to be liberally supplied. Everyone was delighted that the war had made me into a man, implying that I had returned from ten months in the trenches and the Battle of the Somme. Everything, so I began to believe, was applied to their war of twenty-two years before. I was quite unable to tell them, nor did they wish to hear if I tried, that all I had seen of a war was the inside of Catterick Camp and a few acres of the Yorkshire moors. If I had grown taller it was only because I was growing up a bit, being exercised, and living a healthy life. If anything had started to make me a man it was merely a sort of rough school life. Cosseted, isolated, cared for, taught. Nothing to do with rations or broads.

But that's the way they wanted it to be, and so let it be. I felt strangely detached, distant, like Alice after she had swallowed one of the potions. Familiar things were smaller than I had remembered; my own room, my books, pictures, sketch books, even my clothes had shrunk. The old rowan tapping as it always had done against the window, the wardrobe door creaking open spitefully, slowly, as it always had done, all these things had the ring of familiarity but from a long distance. It was rather as if I was poking about in the room of someone I had known long ago, and then but slightly. The things, the possessions, evoked memories, but hazy ones; the person that I must once have been had gone and had left behind a not very interesting collection of inanimate objects. I handled them all with careful astonishment. The white Staffordshire pug, a paper-weight of the Eiffel Tower, the snow storm now long since gone dry, the tin lay-figure my Grandfather had given me, legs awry, one arm missing, head squint. I set them all back exactly where they had stood, fearful lest the owner might suddenly return and find my prying into his possessions. I could not reconcile myself to the fact that I was the owner and that this room had been, was indeed, mine. I was a stranger here; I knew, certainly, that some odd metamorphosis had taken place when, finding my old, unfamiliar bed too soft, I dragged the covers on to the floor. And slept there.

It was the same a few days later when, eager, anxious to the point of rudeness, I went up to London to meet Vida. I went in uniform because I felt strange, uncomfortable, in civilian clothes, which was another surprise. We met, as we always had in the past, outside the Warner Cinema in Leicester Square, and walked arm in arm, momentarily shy of each other, down to the Olde Vienna in Lyons Corner House, where, after all, we had said our farewells together only a few months before. But that was all changed too. The place was the same, red plush, little marble tables, papers still on sticks, gateaux and thin coffee, elderly Jews sitting silently staring unseeingly across the room to Warsaw, Berlin, Vienna. It had the crushed air of a waiting room at a Consulate.

We tried to start a conversation. I looked well, she had lost weight, what was she doing, where was I going, did I like the army, had I made friends, had she seen anyone from "Diversion", what did she really think of her poem?

"I loved it. I told you so. I mean I told you you would write something good, didn't I?" She smoothed down the cloth with a plump, generous hand.

"You always said that war made men very odd, and it was true really. It all came at once, you know. Just as I wrote it, I didn't even have to re-write or correct much, a word here and there . . . and it was for you . . . *because* of you really."

She bowed her head very gently and went on smoothing the table cloth slowly. "How did it get into the *Times Lit?* Was it your father?"

"No. I sent him a copy, after I sent you yours and his secretary found it and sent it over to them without telling him. I think he was a bit shocked."

"But pleased?" She looked worried.

"Oh yes. Especially when they sent me three guineas."

"I didn't tell you, did I, I've taken a cottage in Wiltshire for my father and mother. It was getting a bit too noisy up in Belsize Park—all the bombs. It's very small, but I go down at weekends, and when I'm not working . . ." She stopped suddenly and started to unfasten a brooch at her neck. Her eyes were full of tears. I reached across the table and offered her my hand. She went on struggling with the brooch, a tear welled and slid down her round red-lipped face. She got it off and started to examine it as if she had just found it.

"I don't know what's happened to us. You and me. I'm shy. It's idiotic, but I'm shy. I don't know what to say . . ."

I took her hand and squeezed it hard, the brooch spun across the table and lay winking its cheap light by the coffee pot. "I'm shy too. It's all different. Isn't it strange, nothing seems to be as it was before. It's all gone, I wonder why?"

She looked up at me with swimming eyes, and made a blind reach for the glittering paste brooch. She shrugged hopelessly. "The war, I suppose. We blame everything on the war . . . it seems to be going on and on . . . it just seems to bugger everything up. I don't know . . ."

"It can't go on for ever, honestly. I mean, after all, I haven't even gone in yet!"

A floppy joke, she smiled wanly and refastened the brooch carelessly. "I hope you don't have to, that's all. I hope it's over by then."

"So do I. I'm not very good at it."

"Really not?"

"Can't do the Morse and ride motorcycles and all that stuff."

"Well, I don't suppose the others can write poetry, can they?"

"I can't even send dit-dit-dit-da. For God's sake."

"What's that?" She was incurious, busy repairing the eye-black which had run.

"It's the letter V. You know, dit-dit-dit-da, Beethoven. The Victory Sign."

"Oh that!" She was weary suddenly and snapped shut her powder compact so that the dust flew up in a little cloud between us; she blew it gently across the table and started to button her coat. "That's a hell of a long way off," she said. "Come on, you'd better get the bill, the big picture starts in fifteen minutes."

*   *   *

There was no Gooley to welcome me when I got back to Le Cateau Lines. Tilly was there, smirking and strutting about, and old Worms who had had an exhausting time dipping his wick, as he called it, all over Wimbledon, Wandsworth and Battersea Park, but Gooley, my first real mate, had gone, as he had always promised he would from the first time we met in the train up from King's Cross. I felt a hard thrust of despair. Leave had been gloomy enough, and now with no one to laugh at the miseries of civilian life, and make comparisons in our attitudes and points of view, the future looked glum indeed. There was still a long time to go until February when the course ended. My cubicle was dank, and dusty. The *Times* calendar squint on the wall, the leave dates blocked in. I unblocked them, in so far as I blacked them out. It was over, that part, and now I settled down to the following months with something akin to despair.

I remembered our last night, Gooley and I, together in here, on the eve of our first leave. After the almost euphoric hysteria of packing kit-bags, polishing boots and brasses, and handing in the bits of equipment we would not be taking away, he came and joined me, sprawling, cigarette in mouth, across my bed.

"Who can tell, boyo, who can tell when we'll meet again? After de war, Toff, and you sitting across from me at me own bar, Kitty dere pullin' de handles and bloody great jars of Guinness slopping all over de counter! Ah de bliss of it all! Mind you, so long as I play me cards right, that is . . . de pub'll be mine, and de drinks is all on de house, I can see it now. Only, one ting, Toff," he leant up on his elbow and wagged his cigarette butt across at me seriously, "one ting, don't you go getting yourself killed and that. It'd be a waste, a terrible, terrible waste." I promised, in my cracked mirror, that I'd take care.

"Better chance of survivin', Toff, if you'd only stop volunteering for every damn little ting dat comes along. Hang back a little and give the Sweet Lord a little chance to see youse . . . he can't

keep his eye on us all at de same time . . . he'll lose you in de crowd
. . . all dat stuff about him havin' his eyes on de sparrows is all
blarney, you remember dat. And you tell dem I told you so, and
I'm a good Catholic boy!"

I was struggling with the cords on my kit bag and wasn't really
listening to him. He yawned heavily and eased himself off the bed
and shuffled towards the door. "Hey!" he called softly, "catch
this, you bugger!" and threw something through the air towards
me. I ducked and missed the catch and it slid and scattered,
glinting in the harsh light from the lamp. His rosary. "It's not
for keeps, mind; you'll give it back when you comes to Cork."
He went away whistling, his hands shoved into his pockets. I
never saw him again.

Now the little dusty room seemed emptier because of remembering, and I stared miserably at the calendar which still said
November. Time past. Nothing seemed good; I started unpacking
slowly, cigarettes, a fruit cake in a tin, Evelyn Waugh, John
Donne, a pound of winter apples from home. There was a sudden
commotion through the partition in the hut. People started
clapping, and cheering. I was putting everything neatly away in
my locker when Worms shoved open the door, his face scarlet.

"You heard, did you?"

"What?"

"The Japs."

"What about them?"

"They've gone and bombed some bloody harbour in Hawaii.
The Yanks are in!"

3

FIVE and a half years later I was out; my war was eventually over and after a long and uncomfortable trip from Singapore on the *Monarch of Bermuda,* filled with anticipation, relief, and a modest sense of a modest job well done, I reached my Regimental Headquarters on a dank October morning outside Guildford, where I was issued with a pork-pie hat, a cotton-tweed suit, a pair of new black shoes, a ration book and a travel warrant for Haywards Heath. Nothing could have been more prosaic, dull, or flat. Dragging a cardboard box of ill-fitting clothing to the gates on the way to the station I was accorded my last salute from a pale young Sergeant.

"Is that all there is to it?" I asked him. "I mean, I just go?"

He smiled a weak-tea smile. "That's all, Sir," and then flicking a wan eye at my thin line of ribbons he added, "thanks for the help, Sir." He wasn't even wearing the Defence Medal. I supposed he must have been fourteen when I joined up. Help be buggered: where, I wondered, wandering down to the station, had all those years gone? A Morris Minor stopped beside me and a man asked me if I wanted a lift. I hadn't thought about a taxi—and wasn't sure of the rate of exchange even, for I had not handled English money for a long time. We drove in silence for a while. He had assumed, correctly, that I would be going to the station.

"Been away long then?" His voice was kind, not curious.

"Not long. A couple of years."

A woman at a crossing suddenly slapped her child, shook it angrily, and then pushed her pram hurriedly over the road.

"You'll see some changes here then, after two years."

"I expect so."

"People are fed up really. Can't blame them, can you? A war's a war. They don't know what to do with the peace now they've got it. All at sixes and sevens."

So, I thought, am I. What lies ahead for me now? I don't think *I'm* all that used to a peace. Two weeks left to wear the uniform which, after five years, had given me a sense of identity, then into the cotton-tweed and then what? An interview with some head-master in December and, if I passed, a temporary job teaching at a

Prep School in, of all God-forsaken places, Windlesham. Did I want to go and sit among the pines and heather of Surrey and teach scrappy Art, History and, possibly, English to a lot of stinking little boys in grey flannel suits? And supervise their cricket, I who couldn't even buckle on my pads, or tell the bails from the ball? Was this all that I was any use for now? I was, indeed, most grateful to my brother officer who had made this temporary job even possible, for he taught, or had taught, at the same school before the war, and had put in a good word for me some months ago when I had written to him, in despair, saying that I would not, after all, make the Army my career, and would be demobilised in October without any chances of a future job, and could he suggest something for me to do. I was not, I added, ever returning to the theatre; I had been away too long, it would be impossible to try to start again; and in any case I reluctantly agreed with him that he was right when he had once said, years ago in Shrivenham where we had first met, that acting was a pansy job. So the theatre was out . . . what could I do? Windlesham and Cricket?

My silence in the car was impolite. I apologised.

"I know how you feel; at sixes and sevens yourself. Married, are you?"

"No . . . not married."

"Just as well really. So many of them didn't last the first bloody leave; all done in hysteria, really. Sad."

At the station he pushed a packet of five cigarettes into my hand. "Have these, not much, might cheer you up. I can get more, don't worry. Know a girl up at the Wheatsheaf." He drove off before I could thank him.

"I can see you been in the sun, mate," said a porter, shoving my box and bits and pieces on to the rack. "Where was you, Alamein then?"

"Calcutta . . . Java . . . Malaya."

"Aha! The Forgotten Army, eh?"

"No . . . no! Nothing as brave as that."

"Well, welcome home, though you won't get sunstroke where you're going, but I expect you'll be quite glad of that. Can't stand the heat myself, brings me out in a rash."

Friendly, kind, solicitous; traditionally English. Like the tidy little back gardens whipping past the window. Neat, dull, familiar. Here and there a row of houses rubbled by a bomb, washing fluttering, children playing in a school-yard, a red bus turning a corner. The flat October light grey; grey as the brick houses, the autumn gardens, the pearl sky above. Through the rumble of the wheels I heard, distinctly, the bull-frogs in the lily pool outside my house in Bandoeng, the clatter and clack of the evening wind in the bamboos, the soft rustle of the frangipani leaves, and the quarrelling of the parrots, swooping low over the eaves of the house, then spiralling upwards into the lavender sky, wheeling, diving, emerald turning to ebony, as they splintered and scattered hurriedly into the gleaming leaves of the great banyan tree to roost before the swift fall of night. And then the great hush which followed; the hills across the valley gently fading from deepest blue to blackest black, the sky vermillion and in that pure stillness the urgent, angry, reminding rat tat tat tat . . . tat tat . . . tat-a-ratter of a machine gun down on the perimeter wire.

It had been a goodish war, as far as wars go. I had survived, although I still wondered, slumped as I now was, looking out at Surrey, how the hell I had. Luck most probably. That and the very early training of my sensible parents and Lally, who had always insisted that one could do anything one wanted, if one worked for it; the working was the hardest part . . . the wanting came easier; but I had worked.

* * *

When the course had finished, eventually, in February, the Royal Corps of Signals, delighted with my theatrical ventures, distressed by my lack of any technical knowledge whatsoever, even after almost half a year under their very careful eyes, bundled me off, unexpected and unwanted, like a plastic netsuke in a packet of cornflakes, to the unaware Royal Artillery who, though quick to discover my talents as an actor (I started another Dramatic Society and flogged "Journey's End", playing Raleigh yet again), were equally quick to discover that I found guns just as incomprehensible as a field telephone, only more dangerous, so they in turn handed me on to the Infantry. Even though I had learned the handbook on the Bofors gun by heart, and was able to quote it in great chunks with the passion of a Lear, I was totally unable to do anything else with the thing, dropping dummy shells all over the place and most often on other people's feet, never, as far as I remember, on my own. I constantly jammed my fingers in the auto-loader, apologising with pain and dismay all the way to the M.O.

Defeated, therefore, once again by machines, which I came to dread and loathe for the rest of my life, I arrived at an Officer Cadets' Battle School in a wet cloud-sodden camp on the top of Wrotham Hill. There the only thing required of me was self-preservation. And since I had an extremely strong instinct for that I somehow managed to survive all the assault courses, bayonet drills, cliff-climbings up and down the quarries of Kent, and swimming, or boating, across every river and stream in the county. The fact that I couldn't swim a single stroke never daunted me. I just hung on to the nearest piece of floating matter, be it a log or a fellow cadet, and got through. My worst test of this came once at a public swimming baths in Maidstone where, in full regalia, steel helmet, boots, full kit and a clonking water-bottle on the hip, I sprang off the top board knowing that I would die. From the board the pool looked like a neat rectangle—a grave—and as I plummeted down, feet first thankfully, I knew that after this I would no longer have to try, no longer have to keep up with the best in the team, no longer have to make tremendous efforts to get myself into form as a leader of men. I no longer needed to prove anything. The angels, I had no doubt that there would be angels, could care for me from there on in; I took the sensible precaution of holding my nose. I seemed to go down a very long way, and bobbed up like an empty bottle, grabbed desperately at someone's threshing legs and was towed safely to the side. The angels receded for the time being.

I couldn't swim owing to the fact that I had once, at the age of ten, been encouraged by unknowing Lally to leap off a break-water into the sea at Seaford. She was sure that the water was shallow and that I would love it. The water was extremely deep, the tide was coming in rapidly, and I loathed it. Floating about in the pale green gloom, a large strand of seaweed drifting gently towards me, I knew that I was a gonner and was rather surprised to find myself on my stomach some miles, it seemed, along the beach, being thumped by a fat man in a red bathing suit. I brought up most of the English Channel, and stayed at the water's edge for the rest of my life. Shrimping was as far in as I ever went.

Then at school in Glasgow, dumped in a lavatory pan by mind-less classmates because I spoke with the accent of a Sassenach, I was once again immersed in roaring water and left half drowned in a sea of stale urine and floating effluvia. It was all I could do after that to take a bath. But, somehow, I got through five and a half years of war without once touching a field telephone, a Bofors gun, or swimming a single stroke. I wondered if that was simply luck or deception. No matter. Here I was in one piece, with all that, sadly, behind me. Sadly, strangely enough, because in spite of all the minor, and some very major, miseries, I thoroughly enjoyed all my war and had seriously contemplated making it my full-time career when the Americans dropped the atom bomb and war, as I knew it, came to a full stop. There was no point at all being a soldier without a war to fight: like a key without a lock, a meal without salt, or Androcles without his lion.

It was borne in on me very soon at Wrotham, among the blasted trees and bomb craters of the assault course that this was my third, and possibly last, chance to win through. No Morse Code here to trouble my idiot head, no auto-loaders in which to jam my hands, just me myself and my own deep sense of Self. The only way in which I could possibly succeed in this hell hole was by being, not The Best, I could never be that, but among the first five or six. In that way I might just manage to survive. I was always among the first handful up a cliff face, over a river, through the tunnels, across the mine-fields, over the palisades, along the greasy pole and in and out of booby-trapped buildings. I went like a ferret. Panic lent me winged feet and a lack of vertigo. Panic that I should have to stay behind with the slower members of the outfit who, struggling desperately over every obstacle, slipping in the mud, swirling in the swift currents of the River Medway, gasping and choking, were far more danger-ous than any stray bullet, coil of wire, or raging weir. A bayonet up the backside was something to dread, and most of them waved theirs around like parasols. So I let them all sink or swim as they chose and belted for dear life across acres of ravaged Kent as if the V.C. was my main objective.

In this rather shameful way I managed to clamber towards the heights of my Commission and become a fully fledged, even though unwilling, little leader of men. Which was all, in the end, that was required of me. I was given to understand that my life, in real action, would have the duration of about twenty-four hours. Which seemed to me rather a waste of effort; however, with all the supreme self-interest I could muster I felt quite sure that this unpleasing rule could only apply to the others. Never, at any time, to me.

On April 1st, 1943, a glorious, sunny, wind-whipped morning, I finally achieved greatness and marched solemnly off the parade ground at Sandhurst a fully commissioned Lieutenant. In my splendid uniform, fitted for weeks by a gentleman from Hawes and Curtis in a wooden shed near the barracks, wearing my father's Sam Browne, with the badges and buttons of the Queen's Royal Regiment flashing like the Koh-i-noor, my head held high, and before my somewhat astonished, but proud none the less, parents, I strode bravely up the stone steps preceded by a relation of the King's who rode a large white horse which defecated cheerfully when it got to the top. This was expected, and indeed hoped for, and to the strains of "Don't Fence Me In" rather oddly chosen for the march, and a wild roar of delighted applause and cheering, I set my right foot forward to what I sincerely hoped were better things.

They took a little while coming, but I was in no great hurry. First I was sent up to the Holding Battalion, or whatever it was called, in a deserted mill in Ramsbottom, Lancashire. It was a tedious time, spent mainly in a Lloyd loom chair in the Officers' Mess, reading old copies of *The Field* and *Everybody's*. No one seemed to know what to do with me. However, I was assigned to a batman, a sturdy fellow from Bolton who worked, before the war, in a brass-foundry, and it was he, more than anyone else, who told me what to do, where to go, and when I was on duty. I have always been deeply grateful to him, and never more so than the morning he came to call me with the news that I was posted to my first assignment. I was to join an Infantry Regiment as an L.O. the next morning.

"What is an L.O., Ben?"

"Liaison Officer, I think."

"What do they do?"

"God knows."

"Where is the regiment? Hope to God it's not near here."

Ben laid my gleaming Sam Browne carefully over a chair. "How the hell do I know, sonny? Go and read the Board, it'll be in yer Mess."

With this sensible advice, and no more, I discovered that my assignment was in a place near Redruth, which was, someone said idly over his greasy breakfast, in Cornwall. It was a long way to go to be an L.O. but one very quickly got used to that, and anywhere was better than the gloom and misery of the mill at Ramsbottom.

In an orchard, pleasantly set by a river, I was put into a tent, told we were all off to North Africa but that it was still hush-hush, and that being an L.O. meant that I should be used to send messages of a private and personal nature, rather like a pigeon, only that instead of using wings I would be required to ride a motor cycle.

Which was the silliest thing I'd ever heard in all my two years service. After a few miserable days' practice round the Cornish lanes, clutching a map and dressed as if I were about to be fired from a cannon, in breeches, boots and a too-tight crash helmet, it was deemed that I was ready for work and was given a small buff envelope marked *Secret*, a map reference which turned out to be a house in a large park which was a neighbouring Brigade Headquarters, and sent off with strict instructions that the Brigadier was to receive the envelope from my own gauntlet-gloved hands before luncheon. Or at the latest by thirteen-forty-five hours. Which was very confusing.

I didn't fall off once on my way to the HQ, but as I turned carefully into the rhododendrons lining the long drive up, thinking vaguely of "Rebecca" and North Africa at the same time, I stalled the machine, swerved into the bushes and fell off. Quite gracefully. Since I could already see the slate roof of the house and a large bay window, I decided that I would push the thing up the hill, and give it, and myself, a bit of a rest before the journey back. However, it appeared quite immovable. I pushed, tugged, dragged the bloody thing from the bushes and, helmet askew, sweat pouring down, strove to drag it up the hill. Someone came slowly down the drive, hands on hips, and stood for a moment watching my futile efforts.

"Having trouble?"

A pleasant voice, solicitous.

"I can't start this bloody thing."

"Apparently."

"I simply hate the buggers . . ."

He came a little closer, hatless and smiling calmly.

"I think you'll find it's in gear."

Shame flooded me, I cursed, slipped out of gear and started on up the hill puffing. He walked a little ahead, hands behind his back.

"Typical of the bloody army. I can't ride a motor bike and they make me an L.O. Have you ever heard of anything so idiotic . . ." We went on up, me pushing, sweat pouring, sunlight flicking through the trees, he scuffing along ahead with highly polished little boots. When we got to the front of the house, the land was flat, and I came to a halt in the gravel, thankfully. He turned at the steps to the house: "Have you a message or something?"

"Yes . . ." I fumbled in my battledress and found the rather, by now, crumpled envelope. "But it's for the Brigadier; I was told to deliver it personally."

"That's what you're doing," he said. "I am he."

*　　*　　*

I was told to stay to luncheon, since it was nearer thirteen-forty-five hours than it was mid-day, owing to my recalcitrant bike, and found the Mess a great deal more attractive than any of the others I had set foot in. This was a much jollier place; people laughed. Apparently my ill-delivered message, whatever it was, made everyone's spirits rise, and I was even offered a pink gin before the meal and a second helping of jam roly-poly. The Brigadier, a neat, compact little man, with reddish hair, brilliant blue eyes and a tongue like a whip when he wished to use it as such, fired questions across the table at me like balls at a coconut shy, and then disconcertingly announced that we would play a word game.

"Call it 'Derivations'; invented in this Mess. We'll do a dummy-run, you'll soon pick it up. Anyone care to start?" He peered round the table under sandy brows.

A scraping of knives and forks in the sudden hush; then the I.O. cleared his throat. "The Camberwell Beauty," he said.

The Brigadier looked thoughtful. "Camberwell. Not Gertie Millar, is it?"

"No, Sir."

"Well, some kind of Cabaret gel, a toe-dancer, eh?"

The I.O. shook his head.

A junior officer with a stammer took a risk.

"Some k-k-k-ind of r-r-r-r-ailway engine? Like 'The Flying Scot'?"

"No. Not mechanical. Animal."

"Ah ha!" cried the M.O. happily. "A horse, what? Derby winner, Fred Archer up?"

"Not a horse . . . six legs, I venture."

"Got it! An insect?"

"Hot! I say, damned good! Jolly hot!"

"A butterfly?"

"Scalding, old man!"

"Derivation!" snapped the Brigadier impatiently.

"No offers?"

"Not the foggiest," said the M.O. and helped himself to Malvern Water.

"Found there," the I.O. was beaming. "Cool Arbour Lane, Camberwell, 1740 something."

The Brigadier fixed me with blue lasers. "Got the hang of it? Stops the brain from getting soggy . . . on your toes, what? Have a think . . . but don't butt-in if someone else is playing; damned infuriating."

Since I was quite resigned, owing to my lamentable behaviour at our meeting, to being R.T.U. or court martialled for impertinence and ignorance, I ate well and joined in the absurd game with the greatest alacrity and good humour. The condemned man having his meal with the warders. I discovered, to my astonishment, that I was as full of irrelevant knowledge and jokes as a box of crackers; it might well have been the pink gin, but I really think it was hopelessness before the drop. They were amused with my derivation of the word posh (Portside Out, Starboard Home) and seemed intrigued when I explained that the nursery song "Ring A Ring O'Roses" was in fact a jingle about the plague. The Brigadier's blue eyes went into slits.

"Don't follow that at all . . . why?"

"Well, er . . . the ring of roses was the red blotches the disease made on their faces, Sir." I was nearly-overcareful about the Sir bit from now on.

"I see. What about the posies then?"

"Posies of cloves and flowers to keep the smell away, Sir."

"Smell, was there?"

"Yes, Sir, awful."

"And the rest? All the Atishoo Atishoo, that stuff?"

"The first symptoms of the plague, Sir."

"And All Fall Down?"

"Well . . . dead, Sir . . . you know . . ."

"Really. Well. I see. Would somebody ring for the coffee?"

I enjoyed my lunch immensely. Six days later, in some bewilderment I must confess, I strapped up my bed-roll, folded my collapsible canvas shaving-stand, packed my books and camp bed and moved into a very small attic in the roof of Brigade Headquarters to become the unofficial A.D.C. to the Brigadier. Unofficial since there was no such post; but as I didn't know that then, and as no one told me otherwise, or cared to, and since I had enormously disliked my sagging tent in the orchard by the river, I asked no questions and simply prayed to God that I would last out this extraordinary promotion. I felt almost fondly disposed towards the khaki motor bike which had delivered me at such an opportune moment. The old thing of "if I hadn't been there at the right moment . . ." For me, trundling up the drive that morning, pushing a stalled bike and catching, all unawares, the Brigadier on his way back from a quick pee in the bushes, was as decisive a change in my life as if the bike had heaved me over its handlebars in front of a tank.

For a week or ten days I sat proudly up front in the staff Humber, map reading us all over Cornwall and a good deal of Devon. I didn't get us lost often, and on a number of occasions got us there too early even, by taking side roads, at a frightening risk. I opened doors, stood to attention, carried the bumf without which no Staff Officer seemed complete, arranged thermos flasks of coffee with neat flasks of brandy alongside, had sandwiches ready for longer trips; I knew when to talk, and when to shut up, and how to arrange the seating at a dinner table if a visiting dignitary arrived with his A.D.C. from a neighbouring Brigade or Division. Added to which I memorised every single name that I felt would be needed in the job and a great many which only might be; a useful precaution. The training I had had as an actor, of all things, was coming in very handy, as Lally used to say. And I wasn't about to let anything slip from my joyful fingers. At last, at last, I was not a square peg. I was as round as a dowel-rod, and it seemed, I prayed deeply, that I fitted my equally round hole.

At the end of my trial session—for that's what it was naturally; no one was a complete fool; and just because I could read a map, and knew the derivation of a nursery rhyme, no one was going to risk me with anything more serious than a summer ride through the dog leg lanes of Cornwall—at the end of my trial a light remark at dinner that we were to go to London to the War Office, by road, for three days and would I please make all the arrangements, gave me hope that I had passed my test. I said, "Yes, Sir" with a quiet confidence which I did not in the least feel, and the Adjutant, who was sitting beside me vaguely stirring his coffee, thoughtfully picked his nose.

★ ★ ★

In the last days of July, I was made up to Full Lieutenant. My kite had caught the breeze. My Brigadier took me in hand and started my training in earnest. I really do not know why: possibly he had ideas that one day he would become a General and would have need of an A.D.C., or just possibly he wanted a dog's-body to run and fetch and carry for him. I have no idea. I only knew at the time that he had given me his implicit trust and that I must, indeed wished to, honour it to the very best of my abilities. After all, I had made a pretty poor showing in the Army for the last two years. Here was something that I could at least deal with. It was, when all was said and done, an actor's job. But there was a great deal to learn. I really had had no idea how to sit a table correctly: it was he himself who, at the very beginning, scribbled vague little sketches of his table and guests and told me who should sit beside whom and why. I soon caught on and, with the help of an old copy of *Mrs Beeton* which the Mess Cook slipped into my hands one afternoon on Kitchen Inspection, I was off. The tables got arranged, pretty well . . . with few mistakes; and Cabinet Pudding and Macaroni Bully Beef gave way to Chocolate Mousse and Truite aux Amandes. At first there were mild complaints but the Brigadier said everyone was getting too fat and that a little variation was essential. The Cook and I and *Mrs Beeton* did what we could to vary the monotony of the rations. It wasn't much, and sometimes was a disaster, but at least we were trying.

My absurdly boyish face was a very useful disguise. And a dangerous trap for many a Colonel or even, on a couple of occasions, a General or two. If the Brigadier wanted to find out a little bit of gossip which had so far not come his way, it was I who was set out to discover it. And after a meeting, wherever it might be, during a picnic on an exercise, a formal dinner in the Mess, or even a drink at the bar, it was my job to try and find out, in as casual a manner as possible, just what he wanted to know. I found other A.D.C.'s extremely useful for information. Usually given to bragging a little, and condescending, for they knew that my status as an A.D.C. was false, and that I had been an actor, they unwittingly fell into my traps without ever knowing they had. I didn't at all mind the patronage I often received at that time, for I knew full well what my job was, and that later in the evening I would be able to report to my Old Man and shake out a modest little packet of scraps—which only he could possibly manage to put together. It was a very successful relationship as far as that went, and I don't think that I was ever found out in my devious business. Added to which I thoroughly enjoyed it.

So intent was the Brigadier on bettering his unofficial A.D.C. that he sent me off on various courses all over the country, street fighting in Blackburn, a mortar course in Bury, a gas course at Frimley, most of which I managed to survive, if perhaps not excel in, except, unhappily as it turned out for him, one War Intelligence Course in Matlock Spa to which I reported in the October of '43 and left in the December as a fully fledged Brigade Intelligence Officer. He was pleased, I was staggered; but not very long after his pleasure gave way to white rage at breakfast when he chucked a signal across the table which said that I was to join 2nd Army Headquarters in London, directly, as an Air Photographic Interpreter. Although none of us knew it then, planning for the 2nd Front was beginning. There wasn't much he could do about it, since the order came from Montgomery himself, but he was unforgiving and when I asked permission to see him to say goodbye, and also to thank him, he refused. I left for my new, glorious job in misery. I didn't see him again until one misty October day just after the débâcle at Arnhem. There was no one I knew in the Mess in the shell-pocked red-brick château which his Brigade occupied. They were polite, if evasive, all looked rather young and new. Eventually he came into the room—we were having tea—glanced at me, sat down, crossed his shining little booted feet, milked his tea and asked me if I had enjoyed, what he called, "your cushy job". There was no forgiveness. He had lost too many since the Normandy landings, and made it clear. "Won't find anyone you used to know here now; all gone.

We lost more than half the Brigade. Bloody lucky for you that you got out when you did."

There was nothing to say. Useless to try and explain that he had been my catalyst, and that even though I was still alive and in his Mess, there had been times . . . useless. I left very shortly afterwards; he was reading and didn't look up.

* * *

But there wasn't really very much point in remembering all this sort of trivia rattling through the back streets of Clapham and Wandsworth, seeing, very clearly, the present and the future through the dirty carriage window. Gooley, Catterick, the first train journey up there to that starting point. Wrotham and Shrivenham, the Brigadier and the motor bikes, assault courses, promotions, D Day and Arnhem, Berlin and the stink of dead, the hysteria of Peace on the Heath at Luneberg, Himmler lying sprawled in the bay window of a villa, a blanket over his skinny body, British Army Issue boots sticking out at five-to-nine at the end of bony ankled legs; pith helmets bobbing on the water outside Bombay, like jelly fish, a trooper sailing majestically out past us, the singing voices thin across the sea in the fading tropic light, but strong with relief for all that, the voices, a swelling chorus to jeer us in . . .

> *"for we're saying goodbye to them all,*
> *the long and the short and the tall,*
> *you'll get no promotion*
> *this side of the ocean . . ."*

and five nights on another train across the stranger-continent to Calcutta. Monkeys as well as parrots in the banyan trees, Tagore's palace and the sudden monsoon, the rain falling like steel rods, iced lime juice in the sticky heat of Green's Hotel, the gentleness of the Indian, the startling, shameful, arrogance of the Memsahibs, mid-wives at the abortion of an Empire; Truman's gesture to mankind and the pulverisation of two Japanese cities, branding forever man as the descendant of the killer ape. And in the vacuum which followed, the slow trip across tropical seas in an L.S.T. to an island bent on its own self-mutilation in the name of Freedom. "Merdeka!" the word to ring with fear through one's head for months to come. A world turned upside down, the values back to front, the oppressed rising against the oppressor, all over again, and with what results? New oppressors, new oppressed.

But now it was all over for me at any rate, the brave new world lay all about me outside the windows, the world to which I now must belong. The past was the past and all I had to worry about was now. Childhood had been easy, beautiful, a glory . . . unforgettable. Adolescence had only just started to offer the most tentative of budding shoots when the burgeoning plant was culled, bound, and trundled off in a 15-cwt truck from Richmond station into what were now quite obviously, the best years of your life. No good carrying any of this stuff about with me like a bundle of crinkled love letters. Chuck it. The hardest part was yet to come, the growing up; I was going to find it harder than anything I had ever been called upon to do.

How do you, at twenty-six, green as a frog, join the team with all the years since nineteen missing? Who would care, or have the time? Where would I go, and what would I do now? A sort of panic mounted, Windlesham, if I was lucky. Little boys in grey flannels running up and down a cricket pitch. Or I could work in a pub . . . wait at table . . . perhaps get a job in a prison even? Something with men, something with the same sort of background which I was now being forced to leave . . . could I get a job with the War Graves Commission even? Hopelessness rose in me like a fever, I wasn't ready . . . don't get into Waterloo . . . don't start my new life too quickly . . . I'm not ready, I don't know how to do it.

The man opposite, hit by my unconscious kick, woke up and blinked. I apologised and he smiled through half sleep. "Nodded off," he yawned and stretched his arms wide across the near empty compartment, contentedly licked round his stale mouth, belched gently and asked me where I'd been.

"The Far East."

"I could see you had a bit of a tan . . . Burma, were you?"

"Partly . . . Malaya, you know . . ." lamely, leave it, don't ask me. Tears aren't far.

"Ah! The Forgotten Army, eh? Well, you're safely home now, sonny. Mind you, we've had our problems, oh yes! Not been easy. Dunkirk, the Blitz, and those V2s . . . shit, don't suppose you know about them, eh? And the V1s . . . very nasty . . . nearly did for us that lot did. But we won, didn't we? We muddled through

49

... can't say we didn't win in the end." He smiled again, "Course we had Churchill, but he had to go; a bully ... don't need a bully in peacetime." He pulled his mackintosh and a carrier bag off the rack, and stood at the door as we rumbled into a platform. "And," he said with a wink, "Waterloo's still here! But we had a bloody awful war, mark my words, we was under siege, you know ... under siege."

"But you weren't occupied, were you?"

He lowered the window and thrust his hand out for the handle. "Don't follow?"

"Occupied. You weren't occupied, were you?"

He swung open the door. "Occupied? This is Britain, mate. Good luck!" He jumped off and ran along the platform before we had finally stopped.

I collected my kit together, and the cardboard box with the black shoes and the cotton-tweed suit. I left the pork-pie hat, alone, on the rack.

★   ★   ★

If Waterloo was still there, home was not. Well, not the home that I had left five and a half years before. It was no longer the red-tiled, gargoyled, ugly, much loved house by the big pond. No more the bamboo thicket in the orchard, my tin studio called "Trees", the magnolias, the lawns, the Granny Smiths from whose scaly arms I had often stared, hopelessly loving, concealed in leaves, at Elsie Brooks in her attic bedroom changing into something pretty for the day off with her mechanic from Lindfield; no more spreading common ablaze with summer gorse, no lizards, no gentian patch, no pond, no rotting punt. That had all since gone, sold to people who ripped down the studio, hacked down the bamboo and the magnolias, cleaned up and cemented the pond with hideous crazy paving paths, and generally opened up the place to the light, leaving the unhappy house standing baldly four square and ugly to the winds.

Home now was a small cottage, badly placed under the Downs, on a narrow lane facing south and north. That is to say the back faced south into the hill and practically never got the sun, and the front faced north across rolling plough to the station at Hassocks. It was not unlovely, just uncomfortable. But with me half across the world, Elizabeth my sister, a WREN at

Portsmouth, and Gareth, now twelve, a boarder at Hurstpierpoint, the dog dead and Elsie married to her mechanic and a mother herself, it was the right size for what remained of the family.

"It is rather small, darling . . ." My mother wistful, apologetic. "But I think you can make do in Gareth's room . . . he comes home at weekends only, you see, and then he can sleep in the telephone room on a camp bed. But you can't use the bathroom while Ulric's shaving . . . he goes up to town on the 8.25 so we have to keep everything clear for him, you see; he doesn't get back until very late. I do wish he'd retire."

Gareth's room was very small, eight by six. A minute window looking out over the fields to Hassocks and Ditchling, a not-big-enough bed and some rather ugly bits of furniture I didn't remember. I sat on the bed and looked around the stranger's room, feeling very much as I had done in my own room on leaves long past, only in this private place there was nothing to remind me of myself. A German helmet, a jam jar full of used stamps, part of a wireless-set, coils and valves bloomed with dust, *Treasure Island, The Boy's Book of Hobbies 1912,* and handfuls of dried acorns, Sherwood Forest dormant in a Dolcis shoe-box. I didn't know the person who lived in this room any more than I knew the person sitting presently on his bed. I had been. Who was I now? Nervously, curiously, I looked for signs of myself . . . surely he must have something of mine from the days past? The Eiffel Tower was there! And the lay-figure my Grandfather had given me, legs and arms akimbo still, head pressed into its aluminium chest. In the meagre bookcase some old sketch books from Chelsea Polytechnic. I felt the pages for familiarity, riffling through them with affection. My old notebooks, filled with projects never accomplished, designs never designed, ideas long abandoned. All the help that I had been offered by Moore and Sutherland and my other teachers was intact. Sutherland's splendid Stonehenge, eight rectangles on a half sphere with a radiant sun, some of Moore's wrapped ladies helping to define form for me, they all were there still, half obliterated by crayon drawings of Spitfires, monsters, a sinking battleship, someone called "My Pal" wearing a hat and cross-eyes, and riotous squiggles of red, yellow and green wax. The sad ruining product of an idle day and a box of crayons by my little brother.

I had no present here. I had no past here. The October day was dying in wan splendour, a flock of lapwings eddied down into the plough opposite and scuttled about busily for the last feed before night, crests rising and falling in cautious alarm. Somewhere down below I heard spoons in saucers and my mother singing. It came softly up the little staircase through the door with a Japanese flag pinned across it, which I had sent Gareth from Sourabaya, long ago. The voice was sweet, warm, gentle, a remembrance of time gone by, of rooms gone by, of places lost and other evenings. But equally a reminder, a reassurance of now; of love, of belonging, of coming home again. I went over to the little desk and started to unpack the presents I had brought back; her singing filled the house.

> "I'll be loving you, always . . .
> With a love that's true . . .
> Always . . . ."

★   ★   ★

"What-did-you-do-in-the-war-Elizabeth, then?"

She laughed and brushed a silk-stockinged knee with a dismissing hand. "Nothing much, just a boring old WREN. Made a lake of cocoa, I should think."

"Nothing brave? Firing torpedoes or something?"

"No. Nothing. The only time I ever got really upset was when I got very muddled about all that twenty-three-fifty-nine business. You know, the time thing. I never learned that ten o'clock was twenty-two hundred hours. Did you?"

"Never."

"And I was late back from leave so I had hysterics on the platform at Haywards Heath."

"Real hysterics?"

"Screams and sobs, it was ghastly. People thought I was having a fit. I was."

"What happened?"

"Oh, Daddy telephoned the Head Nun, or whatever she was, and sorted it out. But it gave me a terrible turn."

"As Lally would say." We laughed together.

"She's married now, you know... terribly nice man, a footman to Lady Hedgerly. She's very happy. Are you?"

I shrugged. "It's all so different somehow, I don't know. I miss it all. Isn't it strange?"

"I hated it all, my bit. Yours was different. What are you, a Captain or something?"

"War Substantive Captain . . . but a Major, it's difficult to explain . . ."

She lit a cigarette busily. "Don't try, I'd never understand. But it's quite good, isn't it? Can you be a Captain in peace time?"

"They say I can."

"But you wouldn't, would you? You'd sound like something in a Club House. What are you going to do, though?"

"That's the whole problem. I don't know."

"Go back to the theatre thing?"

"No. Not now. Too late. I'm too old anyway. And it's a bit frivolous, isn't it? Shallow somehow. I'd feel . . ." I dried up, I didn't know what I'd feel. "Anyway, there is this school job at Windlesham . . . I'll try that. Got to do something, I haven't a penny."

"I'm going to get married, I think."

I was struck dumb with shock.

She nervously pulled down her navy skirt and shook her hair round her shoulders. "Mummy and Daddy don't know yet. Don't tell. It's not certain really."

"It's not The Prawn, is it?" An awful drip in a Guards Regiment she had known years ago on one of my last leaves.

She snorted with scorn. "God no!" she laughed. "He made a pass at Mummy one night in the pub, and that was the end of that, thank you . . . ghastly creature. Do you remember his whiskers!"

"Who is this one, will I like him?"

"George, in the RAF, and you'd better. I do."

It was a strange feeling, the two of us sitting in our uniforms, smoking with a couple of beers, in the little sitting room of the cottage. It was as if some great duster had wiped away a large chunk of our lives together, like a half-erased problem on a blackboard. The last time we had really been together she was still in her blue tweed school coat, I in my awful, but loved, green suit from a Gamages Fire Sale. And now I was talking of becoming a schoolmaster and she was talking of getting married.

I laughed aloud and she looked at me incuriously.

"George is a very nice name, you needn't laugh."

"I'm not . . . about George. About us really."

"What's wrong with us?"

"Nothing! Nothing's wrong. It's just so funny. You and I playing in those plays I wrote, do you remember. 'The Titanic', and pushing you off the wall into all the straw . . . Do you remember when we used Gareth as a baby and you dropped him on his head in the barn, on what you called the soft part, and we thought he'd go mad or something? Perhaps he still will; he has masses of time."

"I remember lots of things then, Lally most of all of course, Twickenham and Mrs Jane and those lovely chocolate cakes she used to make for us . . ."

"Madeira cake."

"I remember chocolate . . . it doesn't matter. You know I don't feel the least bit different inside, do you? I feel just the same as I always did. Isn't it awful."

"I feel just the same too. I suppose we are supposed to be different, but I don't feel it. I feel just as silly now as I was then. Sillier."

She sighed and went over to the window and peered out, her arms folded over her chest, she hunched her shoulders up high as if she was cold. "Isn't Mummy wonderful really? She's kept the garden going all the war, you know, vegetables, fruit, garlic even . . . always something; she used to eat huge garlic sandwiches all through the winters to keep well. Daddy nearly choked to death. But she never got a cold once. I wonder what happened to the time, all that time? I expect we grew up." She sounded sad, wistful, almost as if she hoped that I would say that she was wrong. I did.

"No, I don't think we did. I haven't, I know; what worries me so much is that I have got to start doing it now, right away, and I don't know how to begin."

She came slowly across and sat beside me, her arms still holding her body. "But in the war, in France . . . or even, you know, in Burma or India or wherever it was. I mean that all made a difference, didn't it? There were things which happened; things which make you grow up. They say so anyway, killing people, you know. Were you frightened?"

"Yes. Very. But I don't think fright makes much difference to it."

She leant towards me very secretly, as she had done so often in childhood, a very private matter between us both. "What was the most frightening thing?"

"Climbing a mill chimney in Blackburn."

"Whatever for?" Her eyes were wide with astonishment.

"It was part of a Street Fighting Course . . . we had been doing Hand to Hand Fighting in some ruined houses, with real bullets and stuff, tiles flying, and dust . . . and at the end there was this damned chimney, about eighty or ninety feet high, with little steel spikes driven into the brickwork all the way up . . . and we had ropes, and when I looked upwards it sort of reeled against the sky and I felt sick. I think you could have refused. Some people did."

"Why didn't you then?"

"I was too frightened not to. I didn't want to be a coward."

"I think you must be mad, really."

"Anyhow, when I got to the top it was about a yard wide all round and the Sergeant was covered in soot and very hearty. He made me look at the view. 'Grand view from here,' he kept saying."

I remember that I stood clutching his arms with my shaking hands, my legs weak, as if my knees had been removed. I forced myself not to look at the great black hole to my right, but to look up where he indicated out across the filthy city cupped in its rolling endless moors and dales, far below the pale faces of those who had not come up, or those who had already reached the bottom, stared up at us like a scatter of mushrooms. When I got down I was sick. Hopelessly. But the Sergeant gave me a pat, and stuck up a thumb. I had been frightened then. But I had been far more frightened of showing that I was.

She got up suddenly and, shoving her tie into her jacket, buttoned up her little buttons. "I'll go and give Mummy a hand with the table. She's made a meat-loaf or something with two sausage rolls she got this morning and some sage and onions. I do think she's clever; all I know is that I'm terribly frightened of growing up. I just wish I knew how to do it." She went off into the little hall and a few minutes later I heard my mother laughing in the kitchen and the door closed.

She had only asked me about being frightened, not about terror. I thought that terror, like responsibility, and killing people which I had done, might make a difference, but it hadn't, so it seemed. And there had been terror, but I didn't want to tell her that. I didn't even, when it really came down to it, want to remind myself yet either. It was an emotion which you could, after a time, obliterate more or less for a little. Only during really bad thunderstorms would I remember Belsen, and the girl, shorn head covered in scabs, face cracked with running sores from which she carelessly waved away the April flies, who grabbed my hand and stumbled with me along the sandy tracks amongst the filth, talking, crying, singing all at the same time, pointing me out proudly as we went, her filthy striped skirt flapping, breasts swinging like empty pockets against her rib-lined chest. A Corporal, red faced and gentle, took her from me and pulled us apart, thrusting her away. She stood appalled for a moment, and then with cascading tears pressed both hands to her lips and threw me kisses until I had gone from her sight.

"Sorry, Sir," apologetic, careful. "Typhoid. The place is full of it . . . I reckon they'll all go."

Outside the camp, in the pale April sun, the larches shadowy with spring, larks high above the rolling, sandy heath. Help had come, trucks and jeeps and cars still bumped slowly across the tracks through the huge wire gates into hell. I drove away.

And the wood outside Soltau . . . the dark pines and the earth below squashy, so that tent-pegs driven in slid into slime. The stench then, and the massed grave . . . legs and arms and swollen heads, the bloated, the rotten, liquefying, death beneath the pine-needles and moss. They had forced the people from the village to march past. Old men and women mostly, dragging, or carrying children. Some, the oldest, sobbed into handkerchiefs, the younger ones, white faced, spat, pointing out putrescence to unaware babies slung around their hips. Laughing, spitting into the grave, proud still, Germans.

That was terror. Because it was so completely incomprehensible. Being dive-bombed on the airfield, shot at crossing a July field of buttercups, chased by tracer-bullets at night among the dykes and ditches of Holland, getting lost in a minefield, staggering up the beach at Arromanches, seeing my very first battle casualty, a man in a kilt lying indecently sprawled among the cow-parsley, the *Daily Mirror* plastered, considerately, across his blown-away face, holding the shaking shoulders of a woman stretched out under a shattered roof, while three older women delivered a child induced by shell-blast and terror . . . they were not Terror for me, because those things, however bizarre and strange, however unexpected, were, in fact, to *be* expected in a war. Those things, because I could understand them, terrified me less than the terrors which began to emerge from a new kind of war. These things had not been in a textbook, and no one had been able to tell us that we should find them strewn along our victors' path, no one had ever said that perhaps this was what growing up entailed. If they had, I doubt very much that I would have believed them, for I tend to disbelieve anything remotely beyond my comprehension.

A limiting fault.

* * *

The light had died, the room was still. From the kitchen I could hear them clonking about, a tap running, the door opening and my mother coming into the little dining room next door; she rattled plates on to the table singing still.

"Are you hungry?" she called. "We'll eat early tonight, won't wait for Ulric, Elizabeth has to get the eight-thirty bus back. Darling! Do put on the lights, it's so gloomy in there."

The door shut. I put on the lamps and poured another beer. My father's portrait over the fireplace looked sternly across me to another time.

"I'm home," I said aloud. "You said at the beginning that I might enjoy it, and some of it I did. But I don't know what I had to go for, really, do you, now that it's over? But I'm back, and I have lost nothing much. Nothing I really regret. Nothing that I won't have a try at replacing, even adolescence. I must have gained something after all these years, but I suppose it'll take a bit of time to come through, won't it?"

Elizabeth came quietly into the room, pulling off an apron. "Talking to yourself, my dear . . . that won't do, you haven't gone do-lally-tap, have you, like Gooze at Twickenham?" She rummaged in a large leather hand-grip and found some cigarettes. "I suppose you'd got all lonely on your first night home . . ."

I offered her a beer, but she shook her head, and lit her cigarette blowing the smoke in a long stream towards me.

"As a matter of fact," I said, "I was having a bit of a chat to our father up there over the fireplace."

She was unsurprised. "And what were you telling him, if it's not private?"

"No. I was just telling him that it had all been a bloody waste of time, that's all."

"God! What a dreadful thing to say."

"And He's out too."

"Who is?"

"God. He's all balls really."

"But you used to be mad about God and Jesus and Mary and all that . . ."

"How does it go, do you remember? 'When I was a child, I thought as a child. But now that I have reached man's estate . . .' "

"I know." She was bored by my banality. " 'I have put away childish things'."

"Growing up," I said.

Later, when everyone had gone to bed, I sat in Gareth's little room among his dusty bits of wireless set, acorns and used stamps and sorted ruefully through my own collection of possessions and papers which I had kept with me through the years. There wasn't much; and what there was fitted into a worn crocodile briefcase which I had taken from a Japanese General later hanged for War Crimes in Java. My parents' letters in a thumbed bundle, a packet of assorted snapshots, my Identity Card and dog-tabs, polished with old sweat, a pressed daisy from the grass at Dover Castle, a Tiger's Eye ring which Harri had given me and which I had never worn, the blue notebooks in which I had written my poems for Vida, page after page filled with pencilled non-rhyming misery, and the small buff-cotton covered book, *Newnes Handy Touring Atlas of the British Isles*. This had constituted my diary and started on the first night at Catterick Camp.

It had belonged to my father, and when I ran out of pages I just inserted more so that it bulged lumpily. Every page was scattered with a wedding-confetti of figures and letters minutely inscribed with a mapping-pen and coloured inks. Every place I had ever visited, even for a night, was ringed in black on the maps, or else neatly squared if written on the extra pages when I had gone overseas. Every course I had attended, every promotion attained, every date was methodically inserted in the margins, over hill-contours, the green plains, or the blue spaces of the Irish, English and any other neighbouring sea or channel, even on the inside covers and across the Index. It was a flurry of indecipherable hieroglyphics which overlapped each other like chain mail and were as difficult to penetrate.

And in any case, what did any of these laborious entries mean now? It was all over for me, as I had been comfortingly reminded at dinner, and the past must be considered the past. I had survived after all; my war was officially done and something much worse, because I had forgotten how to manage it, was ahead. Peace.

I stuffed the little book back with the rest of the debris of time and stuck it in the bottom of the yellow-oak wardrobe. It was late anyway, and far too difficult to work out; leave it all for another time.

* * *

Which is now, thirty years or more later, up here in my work-room. The buff cover is stained, mosaicked with rings of long forgotten Bovril, tea, or beer, the spine shredding threads of cotton, cardboard corners split. Inside, however, all is pristine, hills and rivers, seas and lakes, woods and commons as bright as the day in 1906 when they were first printed, now densely annotated with the crimson, blue and green pen marks of my secret messages.

For secret is what some of them certainly appear to be. What on earth do they all mean now? For although I obviously set everything down minutely so that in some distant future I might be able to warm myself with the recollections so meticulously gathered there, I seem to have left very few clues to aid myself, and the code (why on earth did I try to use a code? Was I frightened that I, or it, might fall into enemy hands perhaps? Or was I just being unusually secretive, even for me?) seems arbitrary and to have no key that I can now remember. Some things are written in the clear; most in fact. And the dates present no problem, nor the places ringed or squared in black. "Blackburn", for example, is easy. An arrow to the margin says "Street Fighting Course. 30.4.43–3.5.43. Bloody. Sick after Chimney". But then there are scatters of jumbled letters and figures. For example, "T.T.H.PG.M.P.C." poses a bit of a problem. This set beside "Matlock Bath. Hydro Hotel. 26.10.43 APIS". More under-standable when you know that APIS stands for Air Photographic Interpretation Section. The other letters are the problem. The PG is isolated, without punctuation, which is presumably the start of the message. And I now remember that from the "start" I would place the first initial of each successive word left and then right of the unpunctuated two. Arriving thus at P.G.H.M.T.P.T.C. which I decipher as pathetically, Please God Help Me To Pass This Course. Which He did. With extremely high marks, which is why I finally became a fully qualified Air Photographic

Interpreter and was ordered to leave my furious Brigadier to report urgently to London. Air Photographic Interpretation (the reading of aerial photographs taken from a height of anything between 1,000 to 30,000 feet) is very much a question, in simple terms, of observation, an eye for detail, and memory. I was happily possessed, to a modest degree, of all three, due in the main, I feel sure, to an apparently witless game which my father made us play as children. In a shop window how many pots and pans, how many with lids, how many without? How many tea pots, plates with blue rims, jugs with pink roses? Make a mental list, look away for a moment or two, look back and check. In the Underground, look at the people opposite. Memorise the faces. Look at the feet. Look away. Who had the bunion, the toe-caps, the brogues, spats, lace-ups or buttons? Even the breakfast table was not spared. After a good look one closed one's eyes while he very slightly disarranged the setting. Look again. Was the label on the marmalade facing you before? Was there a lump of sugar in the tea spoon? Had the milk jug turned its back? Two or three pieces of toast in the rack?

I had no idea that this childhood game would one day prove to be the key to a life in a war; without it I would very likely have had my twenty-four hours (or whatever it was) life expectation as an Infantry Officer and that would have been that. As it was I became a moderately accomplished specialist in an extremely complicated branch of Army Intelligence for the remainder of my service. And no one was more surprised than I, or more delighted. I loved the detail, the intense concentration, the working out of problems, the searching for clues and above all the memorising. It was, after all, a very theatrical business. How many haystacks had there been in that field three weeks ago? Look back and check. Six. Now there were sixteen . . . did the tracks lead *to* them and not *away* from them? Were they made by tracked vehicles or wheeled ones? Guns, tanks or radar maybe? Or were they, after all, only haystacks, it was June . . . but the tracks led inwards. A hay cart would have been parallel and left turning-loops . . . these ended in the little stacks. Too short for tanks, too round for trucks . . . probably 88 mm guns . . . a long, silent, painstaking job.

In the high-ceilinged sitting room in a requisitioned mansion flat in Ashley Gardens, Victoria, sitting on folding chairs at rough wooden tables we were first shown a big relief map of a part of some coast-line. It stood squint on the dusty marble mantelshelf. Did any of us know where it might be? Some made guesses, no one was right. It was actually upside down we were told, could anyone say now? We twisted heads and necks and with a cheerless laugh the Briefing Officer swung his map into its correct position and before us stood the Cherbourg peninsula and all the Normandy coast. The planning of D Day had commenced.

It was not, as my Brigadier had thought, just a cushy job. To be sure at the beginning of planning I spent all my time in Ashley Gardens or hunched over maps and photographs in a servant's bedroom high in the roof of a hideous house once owned by a sauce and pickle manufacturer at Medmenham on the river. But as the time drew near for the actual assault I was moved down to Odiham RAF Station and seconded, for the duration of hostilities, to 39 Wing of the Royal Canadian Air Force. Where they went I also went, and since they operated from little landing-strips ripped out of the corn fields and orchards as near to the fighting as they could be got, life was not without interest. Preserving it being the main one.

I was a bit late for the landings as it happened. Packed and ready to leave, bad weather suddenly forced a postponement of the actual day, and worrying reports reached us from ground sources of a German Panzer Division moving, by a disastrous coincidence, into the Bayeux area which we had not expected nor discovered on our photographs, since this was a completely unexpected move. With twenty-four hours therefore in hand, and flying almost impossible because of cloud over the dropping zones, we none the less searched the new photographs which came in hourly, desperately trying to ascertain the whereabouts of this new Division. It took a good deal of time and when I was finally shoved on to a Dakota, minus my cap which I had left behind in the rush, and clutching a vast bundle of uninterpreted photographs and a small canvas kit-bag, everyone, or everyone who had survived, had landed, and after an extremely bumpy trip across the grey heaving sea, with bursts of German flak drifting below like dandelion clocks, I was set down among the trampled corn and told to dig myself a hole in a nearby hedgerow. The Flight Lieutenant who gave me this excellent advice, together with a small shovel, said that he really couldn't like the whole business *less*, but that there was some tea brewing and that as long as some idiot didn't drop a shell right into the middle of things it would be ready in a jiffy. It was a very confusing afternoon at St Suplice.

It was a pretty confusing kind of a war altogether. Fluid, sometimes dangerous, exciting, often uncomfortable but never, at any time, boring. There wasn't time for that. We never sat about, as my father's generation had had to do, trapped in waterlogged trenches staring bleakly across a hundred yards of mud to the German line for months on end. We were constantly on the move and the very nature of the work kept me fully occupied day and night, either working at the photographs which streamed into the truck hourly in fine weather, or down in the line briefing brigades, companies, platoons, sections and even individuals on the terrain and hazards they could expect to find before them during their attacks; the depth of ditches, width of streams, minefields and lines of fire. We worked shifts day and night . . . fourteen to sixteen on, ten or eight off. If we were lucky.

During what was brightly called the Rest Period I used to take my paints and brushes and go off recording what I could of that devastated summer landscape in company with my RAF counterpart, F/Lt. Christopher Greaves, an artist before the war, and together we sought some kind of relaxation from the stress in painting. Our perhaps eccentric behaviour did not go unrecognised. Owing to the fluidity of the line we were as often in front of it as in it, or behind it: generally unwittingly. Eventually the Air Ministry made us Unofficial War Artists and allowed us to continue, retaining the product of our free time as their property until the end of hostilities when it was all returned to us and we had an exhibition at the Batsford Gallery in London, only a few weeks after the events and sights we had recorded had passed into history. But the buff *Touring Atlas* doesn't say much about this; just the long lists of names and the jumbled letters too confusing now to decipher.

The names, however, remind, as well as the forgotten ones like Ste Honorine de Ducy . . . or Caulille . . . Paris is there, Brussels, Louvain and the drenching rain and mud . . . the race towards Eindhoven and Nijmegen Bridge, hearts high that a breakthrough was in sight and that we'd all be home for Christmas. Then the catastrophe at Arnhem and the dreadful days of fury, frustration, despair and defeat which followed. The brimming dykes at Driel; helplessly staring across the wide flowing river to the burning city, the chatter and crump of machine guns and mortars, crimson tracer-bullets ripping through the night, the little huddle of Dutch civilians weeping, not for themselves, but for the few returning guests departing from what someone on the Staff had chosen to call "a party"; scattered, ashen, straggling back desperately across the strong current hanging on to rubber dingies or anything which would float; the mouth sour with the bitter knowledge that we had lost. Ninety per cent successful they had said at Headquarters; what could a ninety per cent failure conceivably look like? The only decipherable mark I have made against Arnhem is a neat black cross. It seems fitting.

On my twenty-fourth birthday I crossed the Rhine and the curtain went up on the terrors. The first slave labourers, shaven heads, striped shirts, too weak to cheer; the ruined desolation of my ancestral town, Kleve (paradoxically a target which I had helped to select myself), the April sun in Belsen, the woods at Soltau, the empty eyed façades of thousands upon thousands of streets, and the sweet stench of rubble-buried-dead in Berlin. In Hamburg crumbling spires, twisted rusted girders silent as the mass grave it was, save for the lapping of water and the sparrows. All these are marked, and finally there is Luneberg and the capitulation on the heath. That evening, in a state of mindless euphoria, we set fire to the Mess tent and watched from a sandy hillock as it blazed into the night until all that was left were the glowing spiral-springs of six looted armchairs glowing like neon in the drifting embers. Behind us in the fire-reflection two German women stood holding silent children.

"Kaput," said the older woman, "Alles Kaput." They turned and moved away through the springy heather into the dark, leaving Christopher and I alone with the cooling symbols of our own finish.

But it was not, after all, the end for me; three weeks later I was on a troop ship bound for Bombay and Calcutta to join the planning for the next invasion. Malaya . . . and, after Hiroshima, off to another war in Java . . . a civil war this time in which we were to play no part save that of Police . . . and since there were no photographs and no sorties, for we had no planes there, I was jobless until I replaced the G.O.C.'s A.D.C. who was due for demobilisation, and thus came full circle in my military career. There had been nothing brave, no gallantry, no wounds, no grievous personal losses; what you might call a comfortable war . . . but quite enough to last me a lifetime. The final entry in the buff *Atlas* is written in the clear.

"Sail Batavia. Home seven weeks. The End."

4

IT was a tired, shabby, bomb-blasted London to which I made my nostalgic pilgrimage. However pleasant it was to be among my family once again, and it was, the changes had been too great for an immediate settling-down. I was restless, unhappy somewhere, bored truthfully. And running rapidly out of money. Hillside Cottage, cosy as it might be, was not the home in which we had all once been so young and happy, and in which our early years had been formed. I missed space, white paint, high ceilings, solid doors, the geography of hall and stairs and landings, of my father's office, the cool drawing room massed with philadelphus in June, my bedroom, private, rowan at the window, the little twisty staircase to the attics . . . above all the space and light. Now, familiar furniture in the cramped, low ceilinged rooms, was suddenly unfamiliar, and there was nothing to do at all beyond long solitary walks over the Downs to the windmills, or up to the Matsfield Arms for too many beers before lunch. And with Elizabeth, and even Gareth, away, there was no one to talk to apart from my mother, and she, busy about her small domain, admitted cheerfully that I got under her feet, so I moved listlessly from one room to another ahead of her Hoover.

Sometimes on my solitary walks up the lane to the Downs I used to meet a pleasant, pale woman pushing a pram looking almost as bored as I felt. We smiled at each other and one morning even greeted each other with something illuminating like, "It's cold, isn't it?" or "Might rain later", and on another occasion we actually stopped hesitantly and she said I had been away, hadn't I?, and I'd told her that I had, and she said wasn't it good that it was all over. Only I wasn't at all sure that I agreed. She pushed her baby on up the hill and I went on towards the windmills. I didn't speak to anyone else for almost a week . . . except my father when he came back, late from *The Times*. Apart from one or two passing commercial travellers in the pub, and the pleasant blonde woman in the lane, life was fairly silent for most of the day.

"That's Mrs Lewis," said my mother, over our heavily rationed lunch (another thing I was finding it difficult to adjust to). "She's terribly sweet, they bought that great big house at the end of the lane when the Blitz got really bad. Her real name is Vera Lynn, but you know her, surely?"

*   *   *

The bull frogs were croaking by the lily-pool. Below in the valley, the rice-fields lay glittering in the sun like scattered hand-bag mirrors among the plantations, blinding the eyes. Sitting on the little terrace of my house under the heavy speckled shade of the bougainvillaea, Harri and I sat listlessly in the Sunday heat drinking American beer from cans and listening to Vera Lynn singing, for the hundredth time of playing, "Room Five Hundred and Four", which made her, Harri, excessively sentimental and me beerily romantic. We usually followed it with Judy Garland and "I'm Always Chasing Rainbows" which she equally loved, a sentiment which Chopin might not have fully endorsed.

Every Sunday, when my duties permitted, and if there was no attack warning from the perimeter wire, she and I would sit together on the terrace and have our little concert in exactly the same way that Lally, my sister and I, in the distant days of the Cottage in Sussex, would have ours while we polished the lamps, trimmed the wicks, or just shelled the peas or top and tailed the gooseberries. Time lost. Time remembered. My collection of records was almost as small as Lally's had been . . . about eight or nine, looted from the already-looted bungalows and villas of the Dutch who had either been murdered in the name of Freedom or else despatched back to Holland by us, the unwilling Police Force in this sad, ravaged, island, Java. But Vera Lynn's record was the most precious since it was almost new and borrowed from an accommodating officer in "A" Mess who had recently come out, and who swapped it for my recording of "Great Themes From Opera" which was very much older, badly scratched by rubble and dust, since I had found it among a pile of debris and scattered papers, in the once-trim flowerbeds of a burning villa, and which we had played until we knew every note and every instrument—it took a great many years for me even to be able to bear Rossini whistled in a street.

"Room Five Hundred and Four" usually started the same old conversation off again, although I knew it would be hopeless.

"If you married me now, you'd have a British passport. We could go together."

65

"No. It wouldn't do, really . . ."

"But Pearl, Helga, Nellie . . . they're all going. They'll be on the same ship with their husbands. We could be too."

"Don't, please . . ."

"If I asked the General, now, today, he'd be able to fix things, you know he would, he's very fond of you."

"I know . . . but don't . . ."

"It is because you are half Indonesian, isn't it?"

"The British call it half-caste."

"But you aren't! You're only a third or whatever it is."

"Immediately even you start to explain . . ."

"I'm not explaining! Only to you, you are so silly."

"I'm not silly, I know what it's like, you don't. The Dutch didn't mind. We were encouraged to intermarry, it made the colony stronger. But the British do mind. I remember the British women who came here before the war, from Malaya and from India . . . polite, sometimes kind, patronising always. And they minded. I know, I was here. I was called a chee-chee." She laughed gently and repeated it, "a chee-chee."

"And it's because of that only . . ."

"Not only. No."

"Well, what else?"

"I don't think you really know what you ask. You are so romantic. You'll be bored with me in three months in England and then what would I do?"

"I love you."

But she wasn't really listening, her eyes closed in the Sunday morning heat, her long slender fingers scrabbling gently in the pebbles of the terrace, her lovely golden skin beaded with little mists of heat-sweat.

"Pearl says that Harold and she will go to live in Lewisham. Near London. Is it pretty?"

"Lewisham? Not very, not really."

"Will she like it?"

"I don't know."

"And Nellie goes to Chesterfield. Is that nice too?"

"It's prettier than Lewisham, it's got a church with a twisted spire."

She stroked her arm gently, and slid the bracelet I had given her slowly up and down. Her eyes were still closed, but she smiled. "We have many churches with twisted spires, I don't think

Nellie has ever seen them in her life. When she was fifteen she went straight to Madame Hue's . . . do you think they'll like Nellie in Chesterfield? The spires she remembers best were not on churches."

I remember being so angry that I left her and leant over the terrace wall looking down across the uncut lawns to the banana trees and beyond.

"It's not fair of you . . . you and Nellie are not the same . . ." I was lame with anger.

"Who can tell the difference in Chesterfield? You thought we were all alike just because we offered to work for you and the Dutch girls wouldn't because you are the Enemy."

"We aren't the Enemy!"

"The Dutch think you are. You're here as policemen . . ."

"We're here to repatriate the Dutch civilians . . ."

"They don't want to be repatriated . . ."

"I can't help that . . ."

"You let the Indonesians take over the country."

"They want Independence."

"And you do nothing to prevent it."

"But how can we? It's not our business . . . we can't even fire at them until they fire on us first."

She threw a scatter of pebbles at a long green lizard. "So you can't blame the Dutch; you're the Enemy. But whether we worked in a Massage Parlour or were rich and had servants of our own before, as I did, we were still the same to you. Easy women."

"Shut up! For God's sake, stop, it always ends like this . . . I can't talk to you."

"You started it again. Is there some more beer?"

We sat for a little longer, looking out on to the shining mirrors below, the pale blind volcanoes ridging the sky far ahead, bull frogs croaking, Vera Lynn long since silenced. We were silenced too, until Kim, my Gurka batman with golden teeth, came out to say that lunch was ready, he collected the beer cans and the dish of shrimp heads, and went away.

"Put her on again, please Pip. I like so much when she says 'We never thought to ask the price, but who can bargain over Paradise . . .' It's quite good, isn't it? Awful but quite good." She laughed and pulled her long dark hair up into a bunch on the top of her head. "I tell you what; at your farewell party next week, after they have all gone, I'll read the tarot cards again . . . just for you. Not for me, for you. Will you let me?"

I had always refused this strange gift of hers. Everyone else I knew had let her do it, but I was too afraid always for I instinctively believed in it, as she did, and I have never wanted to know what the future had in store for me, finding the present either pleasant enough, or difficult enough without having to be alerted to the tribulations or terrors ahead. However, miserable, irritated and angry as I was that morning, I said "yes", and we went into lunch and I forgot about it all, immersed in self-pity, rage at not getting my own way, and six cans of thin American beer.

* * *

"I'm afraid it's one of my messes, darling," said my mother with no apology since no apology was needed for, as I have said, she could conjure up a meal from three biscuits, a kidney, a piece of bacon rind and whatever vegetable she had been able to find in her garden, or from some generous neighbour's, or the village grocers.

"It's lovely," I said, "I hope there are seconds, I mean second helpings . . ."

She was gratified. "You just dice the bacon rind, the kidney, sauté them and mix them all up with a lot of carrots. Thank God for carrots. We'd have starved to death without them."

* * *

Vera Lynn. In my tent in the apple orchard at St Suplice, the night alive with sound; two idiots in Messerschmitts strafing us up and down, tracer bullets ripping through the leafy branches, the horizon beyond Caen white with fire, the earth shaking like a jelly with the thudding of the big guns; the Fall of Paris in that splendid, hysterical, final August week. The enormous tricolour floating gently from the Arc de Triomphe, tanks nudging about outside the Hotel Crillon like sullen carp, bullets chipping the stonework of the Cathedral, and roses, roses all the way. German faces, pale, gaunt, taut, watching as we crossed the Rhine, a toytown countryside with all the farms ablaze; slave labourers freed into the streets near Rheine, a band of shaven-headed women heaving a grand piano out of a second floor window so that it fell, with a wild jangle of wires, into a heavy white magnolia, the whole hanging for a moment in suspended motion, until everything crashed down amidst a torrent of leaves, blossom and splintered keys, the ashen-faced owners, with two small children, standing stupefied, silent beside me as slowly, their house began to burn; air raid shelters and the smell of dust, cordite and ashes. The slow swell of the Red Sea, flying fishes racing across the bows of the ship; lying naked on the decks in the sweating nights, a lifebelt for a pillow, still, save for a portable gramophone softly playing somewhere among the thousand black forms, "The White Cliffs of Dover", from which we were slowly steaming East and to which many of us would not be returning. And through it all, always, her voice.

★　★　★

"Your Ration Book has been a vast help already, I got two eggs from Bannisters yesterday . . . a Welcome Home present, I imagine, but the extra butter will be such a help, and the sugar. Sylvia gave me a quarter pound she didn't need, she's awfully generous, you know."

"When I come back from town, next week some time, do you think we might ask Mrs Lewis in for tea or something."

"Of course. She often drops in. There isn't much to do down here, as you gather; whenever you like."

"I'd just like to thank her really, that's all. Or do you think she'd think I was daft or something?"

My mother neatly placed her knife and fork together on her plate. "Not that kind of woman, darling."

★　★　★

Later, at the gate, she said, "You realise that this is the first time in years that you have gone to a train and it hasn't been a farewell?"

"We never did that, did we?"

"After you had gone I did. When I was alone. I cried; but alone. It's such a messy business, and you had enough to worry you anyway."

"You were very good and very brave . . ."

"I was, but you don't really know, you've never had a son."

Silly, bloody, Harri. My farewell party that evening had been quite good. Nellie and her future husband Roger, Pearl and Harold, Helga and Peter, two Yanks from Shell Petrol starting up the business again, some of the Dutch staff from Radio Batavia where, for a while, I was the British announcer, playing requests and sending messages between the many prison camps all over the island.

Harri was looking tall and cool in a steel-coloured satin dress which she had had made up to a design I had done for her, by a Chinese friend in the quarter in which she lived. Her hair long and shining, the wide pewter bracelets, like cuffs, on each arm, new sandals we had bought for her from an Indian in the city.

The party started off at sundown; drinks on the terrace, Japanese White Horse whisky, looted French wine, Bols Geneva, bowls of curried chicken, prawns, rice, mangoes and a big slab of oily cheese which the Yanks had brought from their Mess. We finished, and when they had all gone, leaving only Harold from "A" Mess and Pearl, who were to give Harri a lift home in their jeep, and me as high as a kite on Japanese White Horse, we did the tarot as I had agreed.

She was always very serious about the cards, and never drank anyway, which irritated me when I had had too much. She laid them all out as solemnly as a Mass, which, as far as she was concerned, we were attending. Pearl was a believer naturally, Harold was as high as I was and didn't really care much one way or the other. There seemed to be nothing very dreadful in store for me, or if there was she was not about to let on; she murmured something about "Lights . . . all lights, everything is light," and, after a long thinking pause, poking among her medieval pack, she suddenly shuffled them all together with a brisk laugh and thanked me for being so brave. Harold, I suppose out of relief, nearly broke my neck with an affectionate punch, and told Pearl to get her bits and pieces together. It was half an hour to curfew.

At the front door, waiting for the jeep, she suddenly thrust her hand over mine and crushed it hard. "You see; it wasn't so awful, was it . . . the cards . . .?"

"No. Not awful. Unless you saw something that you won't tell me . . ."

She laughed and shook her wild hair. "Nothing, Pip . . .

nothing bad, only light I saw, and that's good I think, don't you?"
She leant up and kissed me suddenly on the neck just as the head-
lights of the jeep swung into the forecourt.

She and Pearl climbed into the back, struggling and laughing
with their long, tight skirts, Harri clutching her box of tarot
cards and the little steel mesh bag we had found together in the
market. Harold revved up, and she pulled my head towards her
with her one free arm. "Thank you, Pip. Next time I see you you
will be in uniform."

"I know! Tomorrow."

"No, no, not this uniform. A different colour, different badges,
a bird I think, and there will be light everywhere. You see."

Harold said, soberly, "The big war's over now, for Christ's
sake."

"Not for Pip," she said. "The next time, you will see!"

The jeep lurched, swept round the lily-pond and raced off down
the drive scattering gravel into the canna lilies. I stood until I
heard them reach the main road, turn right, double de-clutch,
and roar off towards the city. All was still. Somewhere in the
house Kim was busy stacking glasses and plates; the sky shimmered with a billion winking, silent stars, up the hill in the
General's house there were three lighted windows. I went to get
my cap and papers, for the Nightly Report. The frogs began to
agree among themselves.

I never saw her again. She didn't come to the office in the
morning, or any morning following, and although I went again
and again to the little Chinese kampong where she lived, no one
knew where she had gone. The veranda was empty. Just the
two bamboo rocking chairs, the rain-warped table, vivid sun-
flowers thrusting through the palings, doors and shutters locked.
The Chinese smiled all the time, hands clasped, heads bobbing,
shaking sadly with gold and silver smiles; no one knew where
she was, or where she had gone. I left notes, but perhaps they
blew away.

*　*　*

Trailing up to Victoria through the misty decay of an English
October, my past seemed vividly clear; it was after all, only a few
weeks old. My present seemed, and was, indefinite, obscure, a
clutter of emotions. My future was imponderable, a long dark

corridor with all the doors apparently closed, and without even the very smallest candle to light the way. Had I been thinking these thoughts aloud it would have been extremely unpleasing, since all that would have emerged would have been a high pitched wail of whining self-pity. And I was not a whit different from thousands of others who were all in the same boat; the thought, when it came, gave me no comfort. They were just The Others, and I'd never had much time for them anyway. Muffled as I was in my tattered rags of self-esteem and selfishness, my total fear of the corridor ahead, my nagging worry of my own inadequacy, I simply hadn't got the guts, slumped in my 1st Class corner of the 2.45 from Hassocks to Victoria, to hazard a guess as to what lay before me.

*   *   *

With my rapidly dwindling Gratuity I took a small bedroom on the Strand side of the Savoy and, thumbing eagerly through my tattered address book, began to try and make contact with the friends from before the war. It was a dreary chore. Voices, when they answered, were pleasant, surprised, glad to know I was safe and well and otherwise occupied, or on Tour, or starting a Tour, or trying, themselves, to settle down to the exhaustion of Peace. But no one actually threw their metaphorical hats in the air and invited me to endless parties. The fact was that I really had no friends from before the war; and most of them had been older than myself anyway. The Blitz had forced people to move about a good deal, and the telephone numbers either didn't reply or, if they did, were no longer the ones where my acquaintances lived.

London was as suddenly empty as Sussex—and behind the pleased voices of the few I contacted there lurked a thread of fear that I might just perhaps ask for help in getting a job. Everyone was trying to get a job; the theatre was jammed, it was always explained, with returned actors trying to get a job. The message, though infinitely tactful, was infinitely clear.

In desperation one day, for I had to find some sort of work before Windlesham's term began in January, and the theatre was, much as I disliked the idea, the only thing I knew from the past to do, I went down to Kew Bridge once again to see Beattie de Leon in her little theatre hoping that perhaps she could find me a temporary fill-in job until I went off to be a Prep School teacher.

Apart from asking me, with mild surprise, if I had been away for the last six years, she said that after so long out of things I must be a bit rusty and that I should try somewhere else first, because the standard, as I must remember, was very high at "Q". But where else to try, I wondered?

I ate a miserable lunch in a pub near Leicester Square, bread and cheese and a half of bitter, and saw a poster announcing "Crime and Punishment" at the New Theatre starring my friend from long before, Peter Ustinov. Since we had joined the Army together, and since he was the first actor, all those years ago at the Barn Theatre, Shere, in Surrey, to explain to me about Dedication and the Theatre and had so fired my imagination that I had gone into the profession with all the passion, faith and determination of a nun taking Holy Orders, surely he must be the one to whom I could now turn for advice. And he was presently only round the corner.

It was a rehearsal, and he had not as yet arrived at the theatre. Thinking to surprise him in my tattered, but well-pressed, uniform, I stood among the huddle of pallid fans gathered round the Stage Door. Presently a low, smart, blue sports car drove up, and parked imperiously. There was Peter himself, a little plumper, beaming genially, clutching papers and books, his hair as wild as I had remembered it from '39 . . . but successful clearly. People moved in with books and he happily signed, saw me, smiled above the scarfed heads of his fans and said cheerfully: "Hello! If you have come to try and get a job, forget it! I can't get one for myself." He smiled at us all, made a little joke, and strode into his theatre.

It is fortunate for me that hopelessness has usually made me extravagant and seldom suicidal. By that I mean that rather than jump off a bridge, resort to pills or an oven, I nearly always go and spend whatever I have left in my pocket on something idiotic, joyful, useless, and pleasurable, and so it was that after three or four fruitless and down-casting days in the questionable splendour of my one-bedded room on the Strand side of the Savoy, I decided to spend the last of my slender means in a final burst of epicurian delight in the Grill; and return to Sussex the next morning broke, humbled, and not too proud to borrow from my parents and just live at home.

Someone waved across the room to my single table, and blew kisses. It was Lusia Perry. I have known Lusia for so long that I don't even remember now how or where we first met. Russian, or as near Russian as makes no difference, she was dark, cheerful, loving, vivid and as comforting as the samovar which she always had steaming away in her tumbled mews flat in South Kensington where she lived with her small daughters, Natasha and Nina. There was a Mr Perry but I don't remember that I ever met him. There was tea, or baked potatoes with heaps of rock salt, or bowls of borscht, and always love, encouragement, and laughter and, above all, conversation. With her aliveness, her interest, her tremendous vitality and Russianism, if that is a word, she attracted people in all walks of life to her untidy, noisy, delightful mews off the Brompton Road.

And there she sat, across the Grill, waving and laughing, the eternal cigarette between her lips, beckoning me across.

"Of course you are out of work, darlink . . . everyone is." She lit another cigarette from the butt of the last, and coughed cheerfully, "Haven't you got an agent or something?"

"I had . . . Tony Forwood, but apparently he has given it up, now he's an actor himself."

She laughed, and coughed again. "Of course he has. After seven years in the Army he couldn't possibly stay in an office. He spent so much time getting jobs for total idiots at twice his salary that he decided to go back. He got married, you know, to Glynis Johns."

"Yes, I knew; he wrote to me years ago."

"But they've broken up. It's sad because there is a baby, a boy, did you know?"

"No. Lost touch in 1942."

"Well, he's in London in a play . . . but he's wretched and ill, I hear . . . you should go and see him, he'd be pleased. He doesn't see anyone much now. It was a big blow, the marriage breaking up. Go and see him, and give him my love."

*   *   *

Chesham Mews was just like any other fashionable mews: narrow, cobbled, faintly incestuous. Window boxes, yellow, white, pale blue, the summer's geraniums and lobelia dying into November. Spring is fashionable in a mews. Not autumn. Louvered shutters, wrought iron numerals, carriage-lamps at every primrose door.

I rang the bell three times, waited patiently, rang again. A window above opened and he looked out blearily. Hadn't shaved, pale faced, hair ruffled.

"Yes, what is it?" He had been sleeping.

"It's me."

"Ah. Yes."

"Came to see if you were in."

"I've got 'flu. In bed."

"I knew . . ."

"The key is on a string, put your hand in the letter box."

A long, steep, flight of stairs. One smallish room. A large divan bed, some chairs, a cream painted table with a crackle-finish. Over the fireplace a Medici print of a scarlet amaryllis, a couple of Chinese tea-caddies, clothes scattered here and there, motor magazines; incongruously, a tapestried chair worked by his grandmother, claw and ball legs, squatting beside the gas-meter. He was in the bed swamped in crumpled sheets, blankets helter skelter, a pink rubber hot water bottle, cold, on the floor. He blew his nose hard on a bit of Kleenex.

"Well then."

"Well then."

"I have to play in the evenings, so I stay in bed all day . . . I've got 'flu."

"Yes, I know . . . Lusia told me. You've stopped the agent business, I gather?"

He scrabbled for another Kleenex and blew his nose again.

"Yes . . . so many idiots, thought I'd do it myself. More money, less work. You just demobbed?"

"Last week . . . I'm looking for a job."

"Everyone is. It's not easy . . . I don't know what I can do . . ." A helpless look into the middle distance.

"Marriage broken up, I gather?"

He plumped up a sagging pillow. "Yes . . . Lusia again?"

"She knows everything."

"So it seems. I've moved in here for a while. Give us time to sort it out; we were very happy together, but . . . well, Peace takes a bit of adjusting to, you'll see. I'm a parent too."

"Yes . . . what time do you have to go to the theatre?"

"About six. Do you want to see it?"

"Not much. Where are you?"

"The St James. A Boy Wonder Impresario. Daubeny. Quite pleasant. Bright. Might be useful for you to meet him one day."

"I'm leaving the theatre, I just want a job to carry me on until January. I owe the Army two hundred quid or something, they over-paid me, so they say. I'm broke. Can't go to my father after all this time and expect to be kept."

He scratched his head and yawned.

"Have you tried Actors' Reunion yet?"

"What are they; or is it?"

"A group of ex-service people; all actors. You do an audition and if you're lucky and get a part, the Agents and Management promise to come and see what you can do and you might get something from that. If you get a part, that is. It's very hard, you must realise; the ones who didn't go in are hanging on like grim death; and suddenly thousands of people who weren't actors before discovered they had a talent in army concert parties. They're in too. A chap who has done a couple of impersonations in a troop concert, or played Elvira in 'Blithe Spirit' in a prisoner of war camp, suddenly knows that he is ready for 'Troilus and Cressida', or his name in lights at the Windmill. Very optimistic and totally lacking in style. You'll find it all a bit changed."

On the crackle-topped table there was a dirty breakfast tray. I suggested that I might make a cup of tea, which I did on a sort of hot-plate in a corner kitchen, washing the cups, and chucking the sloshy tea dregs down the lavatory. It was quite like old times. I found some damp biscuits in a cupboard, a half empty packet of tea, and no milk.

He grumbled quietly. "Biscuits are all soggy."

"Well, they were on a plate beside an old cauliflower, that's why."

He looked surprised. "A cauliflower? Thought I'd had that ages ago."

"So you're not an agent any longer then?"

"No. Too much of a sweat, filthy job, idiot people impossible to handle."

"Where is this Reunion Theatre thing?"

"Not terribly sure. There's something about it on the desk there, among the papers and things . . . I should have a try if I were you, half London is anyway so you'll be in good company at least. And you were an actor before, it might help; most of them don't know Stage Right from Stage Left and they can't time an egg, let alone a laugh . . . try. Anyway you'll need a new agent, I'm afraid; it really is not my line."

The audition for the Actors' Reunion Theatre, which I had the good fortune to attend a week later, was held in the Duke of York's Theatre, on the set of "Is Your Honeymoon Really Necessary". Although it was barely ten-thirty in the morning the theatre was full from pit to gallery and I thought that a performance must have started and that this was the Show. The fact that it was merely one solitary, monthly audition daunted me very much indeed. Forwood's depressed words of the week before became facts. Here they all were, the out of work ex-actors, clambering for a chance, looking for the break, and here I was among them. I could now no longer wear my uniform, my two weeks grace was up, and the last of my money jingled sadly in my pocket.

I decided to sit where I was in the warmth of the auditorium, and then walk back to Victoria and get a train home. Realising that it might go on for some time—how could anyone in their right senses audition an audience of nearly five hundred for a one act play for children which had a cast of barely fifteen, excluding crowds?—I took a seat on the centre aisle towards the back so that I would be able to leave for the train without disturbing whatever was going on at the time. The more ambitious had all arrived early and were packing the Stalls nearest to the stage where, at a small trestle table, amidst the stag-heads and painted beams of Ralph Lynn's farce, a small, worried, body of adjudicators sat in a self-conscious line. Someone got up and called for silence, Ladies and Gentleman, and explained that the play they were about to cast this month was a one act-er called "The Man in the Street" and that the Director, present on the stage, would be Allan Davis, ex-The Buffs, and that he would now come among us to cast his play. It seemed to me a very dotty way of going about the business, and God knows what happened to the people who had jammed themselves into the Circle, for Mr Davis, ex-The Buffs, wasn't going to have the time to trot up there, which he very sensibly didn't.

Instead, with a spirited leap into the Orchestra Stalls, he hurried up the aisle, cast list in hand, looking for his actors. I remember that he was very spick and span and crack-regiment-looking; bright eyed, confident, a head as neat and smooth as a nine-pin, a voice, light, clear, authoritative and crisp. No wasting time . . .

Up and down the Stalls he hurried, peering along every row, pencil in hand. Like a ratcatcher.

"I'm looking for Jesus now!" he cried. "A young Jesus . . . no beards . . . smooth faced Jesus . . . anyone feel like a Jesus?" It was a rhetorical question, and no one answered. "I've got Mary Magdalene and Joseph!" He ticked off the names as if he was checking the company stores. "But what I need now is Jesus." He had reached my area by this time, tripped over my feet sticking into the aisle, and when I withdrew them hastily, apologising, he grabbed my arm, pulled me to my feet and cried, "Got him! I've got my Jesus . . . trot down there and give them your name," and as I bewilderedly walked down to the glaring stage I heard him hurrying up into the Pit calling out for Pontius Pilate.

We rehearsed in the Dress Circle Bar for a week or so, very seriously and with intense concentration, while charladies battered about with buckets and a long thin man hoovered the carpet round our feet. Mr Davis was very particular and gave the whole horrid little playlet the importance of "Tosca". I can't for the life of me remember what it was all about, save that it was a play for children and had a religious flavour if not much religious fervour.

We opened one morning, at the deathly hour of eleven, in modern clothes (there were no costumes or make-up naturally) on the stag-hung, chintz-settee'd set of the current farce before a sparse audience of Agents, Managers' Assistants, Casting Directors and what were called, in those days, Talent Scouts. Sparse they might have been, but at least they had showed patriotism in coming to give the "ex-actors" a chance. I remember that I wore my one pair of grey flannels from Whiteway and Laidlaws in Chowringhee, Calcutta, and a blue and white striped shirt which I had bought in the market in Batavia. There were hardly any lights, because there were power cuts at the time, and we were all frozen to death, and to my intense surprise I was a great success as Jesus; and after the play was over found myself jammed into a corner of the Stage Box surrounded by excited, complimentary, quacking people handing me telephone numbers and begging that I call them, all, it appeared, immediately.

In a slightly dazed state we, the cast and Mr Davis, withdrew to a pub in St Martin's Lane and had a stiff drink where he told us all how good we had been, and, leading me aside, told me that he thought I had great quality but to be careful and not let "anything go to your head". He needn't have worried. Though the exercise had been amusing, even in a way, stimulating, it had still not re-awakened the almost completely dormant desire for the theatre which I had allowed to slip away in the cornfields of Normandy. All I wanted was an immediate job to help me out until term time. It was uncomfortable borrowing a quid every time I wanted a drink or a packet of rationed cigarettes, from my patient, understanding, but hard up, father.

Forwood, adding up some bills, was amused and tried to give advice.

"It seems stupid not to go and see someone, if they were all so keen about your work . . . wasn't there anyone there you could deal with?"

"The lot of them sounded mad. All yelling and shoving telephone numbers at me . . . I frankly wouldn't trust one of them. I told them I really wasn't interested at all . . . there was one fellow though. Quite small, just gave me his card and said he'd be glad to advise me if I needed any help. I quite liked him. Very cool and collected . . . he just faded away, very sensible and sure."

"He sounds your best bet then: what's his name?"

I fished about in the pocket of my Calcutta flannels. The card was crumpled. "Fredrick Joachim, an address in Regent Street."

Forwood slid the bills into an envelope. "I'd give him a call. He sounds all right, never heard of him, but he sounds sensible."

Fredrick Joachim's office, three floors up in a shabby building over a coffee shop at the top end of Regent Street, was the exact size of his desk. That is to say, it was about six feet by four, and contained himself, crouching in a small chair, his pleasant secretary who crouched beside him, a chair for "The Client" and a slit of a window which faced a dark well. I asked him what he would do if there was ever a fire in the coffee shop below, and he said, very sharply, that he was an optimist.

He also said that he thought, but was not at all sure on just one performance, that I might have something but was unable to specify what exactly, and that if I cared he would try and get me a few bits and pieces and then we could all make up our minds together. He promised nothing at all, said that he was just starting out as an agent after six years as a War Reserve Policeman, and showed me his lace-up boots from the Force which, he said, were just the thing in this frightful weather. We exchanged telephone numbers and shook hands, a difficult effort, since I had to lean across the pleasant secretary and he had to hunch himself out of his chair, trapped behind his littered desk.

At first he sent me off on a round of all the Studios to meet the Casting People. Everyone was polite and kind but each asked the same question, "What have you done recently?" and when one said nothing since 1940, except be in the Army, they all looked sadly wise and suggested, as Beattie had done, that I must be a little rusty and perhaps I should call again later after I had done a little work. Sweet Heaven! What work?

"I think," said Freddy sipping a cup of filthy coffee in the coffee shop below his office, "I think this thing called Television could be useful, they say it'll be very important as soon as they can get sets and things . . . but people do watch it, quite a big public, about 9,000 sets, I gather, mostly in shop windows and so on, quite large crowds. We might try that. Since they are just starting up they'll not be too choosy. I think they'd take anyone—even you . . ."

We started on Television. And he was proved right. I got my first job, to my relief (funds were absolutely rock bottom by now, and the train fare from Haywards Heath was a killer at seven shillings return), in a television production of "Rope" . . . the play I had started out with in Catterick all those years ago. The auditions were held in a cold room in Marylebone and I got the part of "Granillo"—the neurotic killer, not the lead, to be sure, but I was more conscious of the salary than the billing.

"What are you going to call yourself?" Forwood asked, picking through a vegetarian salad, the cheapest meal on the menu, in the restaurant at Peter Jones, on the roof next to the Pet Department.

"I haven't thought really; I was D. v.d. Bogaerde at 'Q', sometimes."

"Sounds awful, and they'll never get the diphthong right."

"Well . . . I quite like the name Simon. How about Simon and Garde. The second part after the whatever you called it."

"Wet name, Simon. There has never been a star called Simon anything, it's weak."

"What about de Montfort? Or Bolivar for instance? I think Simon Garde would be jolly good. Neat and simple."

"Simple Simon. And dull."

"Well, Dirk, then, and the rest of the name without the diphthong, it is my name in Dutch after all. Dirk Bogarde. That sounds all right, doesn't it?"

"And drop the van and the den . . . and the diphthong? It's awfully foreign to me."

"Well . . . my grandfather's name was Forrest Niven. What about that? He was an actor too."

"I know that. But there is a Niven already. Leads to confusion."

I grew desperate over the salad. "Well, it really doesn't matter. It's not for long, it won't last."

He was reasonable. "It might. And you can't suddenly change it in mid-stream. Make sure before you start."

The chattering tide of Second Generation Harrods' voices threatened to engulf me; a grumpy waitress spilled a bowl of beetroot on the table beside us and little shrieks of "Oh! how *too* awful . . . how *maddening*!" shattered my head.

I pushed my half-eaten vegetarian salad aside and started on the caramel cream.

"I'm going to be Dirk Bogarde and that's it; that's my new name, no one else is called that, for God's sake."

Forwood finished the last of his shredded carrot. "There's always Humphrey, of course . . ." he said mildly.

"He's in America and anyway he's the same family and it ends in 't' . . . and the hell with it all. These bloody women are driving me mad."

I told Freddy that afternoon, and he pursed his lips and shook his head thoughtfully. "Doesn't feel right . . . too harsh, you want a nice easy name that people will remember instantly. What about Paul, or Robert, or James?"

"You tell them I'm that, and not to spell it like Dick . . ."

"Ah!" said Freddy happily. "Dick! That's the ticket! Dick is much easier than the other one: friendly."

A few weeks later at Victoria on my way home, I bought the evening papers. And there it was for the first time . . . splendidly new, correctly spelled, under the modest Television heading, squashed between Carrol Gibbons and The News (sound only), "David Markham and Dirk Bogarde in 'Rope'. A thriller." It was a beginning again.

Freddy soon had me whizzing round London like a cotton shuttle. I went to all the Casting Directors and Studios and met Theatre Producers who showed a singular lack of interest. Forwood, one evening, arranged an interview for me backstage at the St James Theatre with the Boy Wonder called Peter Daubeny in whose play "But for the Grace of God" he was playing; that was a total failure. Mr Daubeny, with tight crinkled fair hair and minus an arm which he had lost in some extremely brave encounter with the Germans in North Africa, smiled almost, and turned an implacable back, his empty sleeve neatly tucked into a pocket.

At the Rank Organisation, a flourishing empire founded on flour-milling, in a palatial house in South Street which had once belonged to the Aberconways, I was interviewed for half an hour by one of the Chief Executives in her Ladyship's ex-bedroom, a vast room filled with busy typists all clustered round a giant Partners' Desk like pilot fish about a whale, at which the Executive sat in a grey suit, carnation and cigar. Helpless, I was asked to stand on a pale blue dais before him—it had obviously once supported a sumptuous bed—and told to remove my coat, jacket, waistcoat and finally my tie. Bewildered but complying, I stood before the assembled typing pool of Mighty Rank and was asked to turn around slowly, like beef on a hook. Which I did unsteadily.

"Head's too small, kid," said Earl St John from behind his cigar. He threw a scatter of glossy photographs across the partners' desk. "We're looking for people like that!" he said proudly indicating Stewart Granger, James Mason, Dennis Price and a sundry collection of retouched, lipsticked, hair-creamed gods.

"Nice of you to come . . . but your head's too small for the camera, you are too thin, and the neck isn't right. I don't know what it is, exactly, about the neck . . ." he squinted through money-box eyes, "but it's not right."

Crestfallen, with a neck-complex, not to mention a too-small head, I went back to Freddy's flat, comfort and a coffee.

"I think it's time I really packed it all in . . . it's so bloody humiliating."

He was warmly sympathetic. "Well . . . they know what they want, you understand. It won't be easy. Your head *is* a bit small for your body, you know, and I think your legs are too long really . . . but they want you for another Television. At Alexandra Palace, something called . . ." he riffled about in his briefcase . . . "'The Case of Helvig Delbo'. It's a war story and you would have to be a spy I think, as I said, they are just starting up again, so they'll take anyone, they aren't the least bit fussy. Perhaps your small head doesn't show up on Television. I don't know, I haven't seen anything, not having a set myself. Anyway, quite good money. You start on Monday week." Which was just as well since Christmas was looming and term at Windlesham was not far behind.

I remember nothing whatever about "Helvig Delbo" except that I seemed to spend a great deal of time tearing about Alexandra Palace changing my costumes and leaping up in bits of set all over the place. It was over and done with in a matter of days, it seemed, and not a ripple did it, or I, cause.

No sooner was it over than Freddy had me out on the beat again—he never let the grass grow under his War Reserve Police boots.

"You are doing very well, you know," he said reasonably. "You have only been demobbed a few weeks when you think of it . . . and you have already done two television shows. I know that's not very important but it is a start, and now there's another one. They want to audition you this time, it's a very serious play, I believe. I don't think it is because of your head or your neck, but they said they wanted to see you before they committed. It's really not like them, they seem quite pleased to take anyone these days. Anyway," he brightened up a little, "anyway, it is good money and the Male Lead . . . perhaps they want to match you for height with the female star, although I can't for the life of me see why it matters on the television since everything is just big close-ups or whatever they call them. Four-thirty, Thursday, Aeolian Hall, Bond Street . . . oh!" Suddenly he had a thought and rustled through the papers scattered all over the cramped desk. "Tell you what, while you're there, go up and see Freddie Piffard; he runs a little theatre in the suburbs. Not much chance, but you can't tell. The play they are doing is cast already anyway, but there is no harm in your just meeting him, so that they can look you over. He's in the Aeolian Hall too . . . I'll telephone and say that you'll be coming in after the television thing. Studio 4a. Don't forget. And this is the script."

I went down the stairs into the bitter winter sun, filled with Freddy's negatives. I wondered, vaguely crossing Regent Street, what he would sound like positive. It was an improbable vision, so I put it aside and went on down to the Tube.

★   ★   ★

It was snowing heavily when I got to the Aeolian Hall the

following Thursday. However, the hall-way, guarded by a large uniformed, bemedalled, porter was warm, and having given him my name and the number of the studio where I was apparently expected, I settled down to wait on a hard bench with the floppy script from the BBC.

I noticed, as I arrived, that he did not write my name down in the ledger on his table, and that he was changing over duties with another bemedalled fellow. Shortly afterwards he came out of a doorway, changed into civilian clothes, and with a nod to his replacement, he tramped down the hall into the snow. I sat there for an hour and a half, and nothing happened at all. No one rang the telephone on the porter's table, or if they did it was not about me; people drifted in and out all the time, but I paid no attention to anyone, immersed, as I was, in the difficulties of reading a television script which contained more camera angles, it appeared, than dialogue. Eventually I plucked up courage, gave my name and studio number yet again and waited patiently while he thumbed through the ledger.

"You ain't down here," he said in a surly manner. "No one of that name here."

I was patient. "I gave it to the porter you relieved about an hour and a half ago . . . Studio 4a . . . perhaps he forgot to write it down."

He turned back some more pages and then closed the book. "Nothing 'ere," he said. "BBC was it?" He picked up the telephone and dialled something. There was a long time of unanswered ringing. He replaced it thoughtfully and looked up at the clock. "If it was BBC Studio 4a, they've all left. Closed. They don't work after five o'clock that lot. Been a mistake, I shouldn't wonder, try again tomorrer."

I went back to the hard bench and sat down miserably. My train from Victoria didn't go until 6.45, and it was at least warm in the liver-coloured marble hall-way. I'd wait, then walk down to Piccadilly, call Freddy about the muck-up and go home. It was just my luck to arrive at the bloody place the very moment that the damned porters were changing over. For the tenth time I opened my *Evening News* and started to read the Situations Vacant column. You never knew . . .

"You're late! You're late! You're late!" A shrill, angry, impatient female voice jerked me from the paper. She was hurrying down the staircase, coat over her shoulders flying like a banner, her reddish hair had unpinned and flew about her face like rope, she had a long, sharp nose and a cigarette stuck to the corner of her lips. "Come along, come along! Some people have no sense of time or discipline, it seems to me . . ." Grumbling furiously, and breathless, but with the cigarette still sticking amazingly to her lip, she hurried my bewildered body up the stairs and along a corridor into a small, smoke-sour little room.

A blaze of light, a table and two chairs, people standing or lolling around the walls. "People are so bloody casual these days." Her voice was exasperated. "I'm Chloe Gibson. Sit down there." She indicated the table and one empty chair. The other chair was occupied by a slim, dark-haired girl, who smiled, offered her hand and said her name was Maureen Pook. I hadn't even taken off my coat by this time. The angry woman with the rope hair shoved a couple of sheets of typed paper before me and said crossly: "Now; this is the end of the second act. You read 'Cliff'. You've done a murder, and you are confessing it to 'Anna', Miss Pook here. You can have a couple of seconds to read it through, don't hurry, then we'll go. It really is bloody tiresome of people being late all the time," she complained to the silent smoke-hazed room, lighting another cigarette from the smouldering butt glued to her lower lip. Taking a deep pull she sat down, crossed her legs, put one elbow on her knee, shoved her chin into her cupped hand and squinted at me through the smoke and her rope-straggle of hair. Her foot began to swing impatiently. "When you're ready bang off," she said.

For the next ten minutes or so Miss Pook and I read the scene together. It came quite easily, and since I had to do most of the talking I just ploughed on. I was flustered, irritated, cold, angry at having missed the BBC interview and frightened of missing the six-forty-five. No one interrupted us, and when it was done, I placed the loose sheets of the script neatly together on the table, and started to pull on my gloves for the walk down to the Tube.

The rope-haired woman was still sitting hunched intently, as if she was watching a cock-fight with a bet placed. Her cigarette, I noticed, had grown a long length of grey ash which spilled all over her red woollen skirt when she suddenly sprang to her feet and said briskly: "What's your name then, after all this?" I told her and she looked angrily at a sheet of paper in her hand.

"You aren't here!" she cried accusingly. "Your name isn't on my list!" She turned despairingly, arms thrown wide, to the room in general. "What am I to do . . . he's not on the *list* . . . where do you come from? Who are you?"

I told her about Studio 4a and told her the agent's name and that it had all been a mistake and that I was sorry for wasting her time. She threw her list on to the table, and spun round on one leg so fast that her coat fell to the floor.

"Dear God!" she cried. "These bloody agents . . . you're in the wrong place! We are casting a play . . . we aren't the bloody BBC . . . you are here under false pretences!" It was useless to explain to this hysterical virago about the mistake, so I just thanked Miss Pook, still patiently sitting at the table, and headed for the door. "Anyway that part was cast weeks ago!" the angry voice zipped across the room like a ricochetting bullet. "Weeks ago! I don't know what happens in this business. You aren't on the *list*!"

I walked slowly through driving snow down to Piccadilly underground. My feet sodden, the demob shoes as waterproof as a fishing net, my hands, in spite of the woollen gloves, wet and frozen. What I badly needed after such a wasted day was a good stiff drink, or even a cup of bottled coffee. However, all I had was the half of my return ticket to Haywards Heath, and a few coppers which I inserted into the telephone at a call box to tell Freddy of my failure.

"Afraid I screwed that all up. Missed the BBC, they forgot me or something, never saw the Piffard man you told me to, and went to the wrong room to read a play they have already cast. Terribly sorry. It's the first thing I have made a bosh of; I don't really know what went wrong."

Freddy's voice was calm and reassuring and quite unworried. "Never mind," he said, "these things happen. Fortunately . . . you've got the part."

I was stunned in my wet shoes. The khaki woollen gloves were steaming gently. "What part?"

"The thing you just read; they have just this minute telephoned to say they want to change their minds about the other actor and have you instead. Rehearsals start Monday morning at nine-thirty, New Lindsey Theatre, Notting Hill. Not much money, five quid. Still since you missed the BBC, you'd better accept. I think they are mad—but you never know . . . it may work out."

Someone tapped with a coin on the glass door and made impatient signs for me to hurry up. "Freddy . . . I've got to go

. . . I'll miss my train. I don't know what to do. It's cast; and the woman was bloody rude as well; I can't make up my mind." Freddy's voice was flat, clear and positive for the very first time. "You take it, that's what you do. I'll call them now and say it's set. Have a nice weekend." He rang off.

Crossing the wide underground circus, bashing into the milling throngs of commuters to Tulse Hill, Golders Green and Upminster, I found a wastepaper basket and shoved the *Evening News* and the floppy BBC script deep into its tin throat, then, unburdened, I joined the seething faceless mass and clattered down the escalator for Victoria. Entirely unaware that I was making my exit from privacy and anonymity for the rest of my life.

5

CAN a sky be the colour of opals? This one seemed to be; white, translucent with heat, little specks of green, blue and orange flicking across my tired eyes. It was not yet eight in the morning. What would it be like by noon? There was no breeze, everything still, silent, waiting, shimmering out of focus in little waves. I lay, half propped, half sprawled, against the trunk of a cusuarina tree, in the fretwork shade, where Johnny, George and a little Indian Corporal with brown teeth and a squint cap-badge had carefully set me down: my right foot hurt like fury, even though both boot and gaiter were removed, and the whole swollen lump had been carefully bandaged and eased, for some reason, into a thick, green woollen sock. An hour before Doctor Hubialla, with gentle hands, had given me a pain killing injection with a far from clean syringe.

"Is it broken?" My voice had a forced indifference.

"Oh . . . hard to tell, you know . . . could be . . . could be . . . angry swelling, I must say, but it's not broken off, is it?" He laughed cheerfully. "Oh no, goodness me no, whatever next I say, not broken off. You still have it, don't you? But hard to say without an X-ray." He shoved the needle into the livid ankle. "This is not really big enough, you know." He was apologetic. "Came in such a hurry . . . but if you keep still, like a good fellow, we'll unscrew the plunger, fill it all up again, re-screw it in, and then Bob's your uncle, to be sure."

He did; refilling the syringe carefully, the needle and the base still sticking awkwardly out of the swollen foot. I was beyond caring anyway, and the pain was easing. Or I thought it was. When he had finished he carefully removed his cap, placed the syringe neatly inside the cap band, and shook my hand warmly.

"How did you do it? Not playing dominoes, I'll be bound."

"I jumped out of a jeep."

"A jeep? Ah . . ."

"It was moving quite fast."

"Foolishness."

"Necessary."

"I follow. Heedless youth . . ." He left in a flurry of little bows and laughter.

Across the burned scrubby valley, the hills were opal too . . . white to grey . . . scabby thorn bushes, cactus, buff-ragged rocks as high as a house, and, running like a strip of dirty bandage trailed through the scrub, the zigzag white road through the gorge along which, very soon, the first of the refugees, some thousand of them, would appear dragging along in the heat. And then, broken foot or no broken foot, I would have to scrabble down somehow and join them, and lead them painfully and slowly to the plains below—men, women, many children, goats, some sheep. Above me, slightly to my right, a baboon with matted hair the colour of dirty cornflakes defecated into the dust at my side. It spattered across my leg, and the green woollen sock. Sweat ran down my face, my neck, stinging under my chin. Flies came, humming with pleasure. The baboon threw the last of his half-eaten fruit at me and, scolding angrily, scampered into the branches which sagged and swayed with his weight. To my left the burned-out hulk of a Ford V8, tilted on its side against a boulder, smouldered acridly, thin oily smoke weaving out into the still, breathless air, like a veil. Vultures dragged, and squabbled at something fleshy crushed into the backseat.

I heaved myself up to a more or less sitting position, and tried carefully to move my foot. The stabbing pain swamped me, and left me breathless: the injection was wearing off. I grabbed for the large piece of branch someone had given me for a crutch, and tried to haul myself to my good foot. The movement irritated the vultures who, with bloody beaks and beady eyes, battered and scrambled out of the wrecked car and lumbered, gorged, into the air, to float gracefully away across the shimmering valley.

On the little slope below me, seeking what shade they could from a thicket of baked bamboo, the Indian troops sprawled motionless. The hard morning light winking on the brass and metal of their equipment. One of them, fanning his face with a bunch of leaves against the flies, murmured something and a ripple of laughter rose and faded into the heat. They were still, save for the rustling bunch of leaves. Standing a little apart, incongruous in boots and breeches, Captain "Sonny" Herkashin tapped his glittering shins thoughtfully with a swagger cane, his eyes fixed tiredly on the road across the valley. He was handsome, twenty-five, and worried. Seeing me, he called up the slope and asked me how I felt.

"Not so bad, as long as I don't put my foot to the ground."

He looked sad. "You resemble a stork standing there."

"I feel like one."

"What a business, I must say. Rotten luck."

I hobbled down the slope towards him, sweat coursing down my throat, the green woollen foot swinging out before me like a gourd.

"It's almost nine o'clock, they should be due at any minute." I started past him, and he offered me his arm which, in a hum of flies, I brushed aside. He was stiff with hurt.

"Stubborn chap, you really are. I was offering you help . . ."

I was immediately contrite, took his wrist and rested on my crutch. "Sorry. Really . . . wasn't thinking."

His brown eyes, with the faint pink whites, of all Indians, were mournful.

"I must try and do it on my own, Sonny, don't you see? I have to. Discipline, all that shit . . ." I hopped on slowly.

"Ah! Sandhurst and all that, what?"

I went on down, stubbornly, and tripped over part of a rather large ant-hill.

"Sandhurst and all that: you've got it."

I stopped and looked back up at him standing on the little ridge. Impassive. Uncomprehending. His Sam Browne shining like conkers: suddenly he turned and walked away. I noticed he was wearing spurs and wondered if he'd trip in the sere, scraggy brush. At the bamboos he called out sharp, irritated, little orders and his Company started resentfully to straggle to their feet.

The vultures were wheeling, gliding, in the high draught from the plain. As soon as we were out of their sight they'd be down again, tugging obscenely at the muck stuffed into the back of the Ford. The valley lay before me, beige, still, and suddenly from the mouth of the gorge a low, open white roadster shot into view like a gleaming bullet. It whipped along the dusty winding bandage-road trailing a column of dust which rose into the motionless air like enormous plumes, higher and higher. Dimly through the fog, I could see a darker car following. Up on a rock behind me an English voice cursed splendidly, and someone came clattering down shouting orders beyond the reeking Ford. Captain Herkashin screamed at his Company, wagging his cane, straightening his jacket, wiping his forehead. The white car took a left turn, suddenly, and ripped across the valley floor like a toy gone wild— for a moment or two it was lost among the scrubby thorns and bushes—and then came on up towards my ridge. I stood stork-like; the dust was now so thick and so high that the sun was a crimson ball. English curses drifted back across the rocks as the white sports car slammed to a stop yards from my sagging body. She jumped out with the agility of a track-runner, trim white slacks, spotless white shirt, her initials in black on the pocket, long dark hair streaming, a ring glittering, bracelets, the buckles on her Gucci slippers flashing. She was dazzling, beautiful. Brushing hair from her forehead she came towards me smiling. The bracelets slid down to her elbow.

"Not late, am I? I told you I was a punctual woman . . . good training." She stood hands on hips, and looked out over the dust-filled valley. "Where are they? I mean, haven't you started yet? I haven't missed anything, I'd be furious." She smiled a wide un-caring smile. Up on the rocks the English voices were still complaining and grumbling.

"No. We haven't started yet. I think, as a matter of fact, that Your Highness has rather mucked things up for the moment."

She looked vaguely surprised.

"What have *I* done?"

"The dust . . ." It was thinning slowly.

"What of it?"

"Well, we can't shoot through dust; they'll have to wait until it settles."

She shrugged impatiently. "Oh, the cinema. I never will understand you people. But it's real, you know. There *is* dust here."

"I know. But you can't see through it."

A rather plump, saried lady with Bata sandals and an Instamatic camera round her neck joined us from the white car and I was presented, and bowed my head. She smiled and said that they had passed hundreds and hundreds of people and goats down the road, were they the refugees? I said they were and she looked impressed. "So many, maybe a thousand. And so tired and hot and the children crying . . . oh dear . . ."

"Well, they are supposed to be hot and tired and everything. They are supposed to be the last refugees out of Burma."

The saried Princess giggled and put her hand politely over her mouth. "How will they know when to start walking, I wonder?"

"We will fire a Verey Light into the sky. That's the signal."

"But first," said Her Highness, "we'll wait for my dust to settle, is that it?"

She wandered up the slope in her gleaming slippers effortlessly. Captain Herkashin screamed something into the morning air and his entire Company thudded to the ground like dead grouse. He threw a salute, his eyes wild as a mad horse's, belt and buttons gleaming. Her Highness walked past the grouse pulling a long strand of hair behind her ear. She murmured something to the Captain, who by the grace of her favour, and God, relaxed his anguished posture and screamed another order, and when the Company was standing once again in a row like a triple picket-fence, they were inspected and the fat Princess in the sari started snapping away with her Instamatic. Other Princesses, and a Prince and a scatter of people had clambered out of the dark Bentley which had followed, and a faint feeling of a picnic was in the air. The dust was clearing, members of the English camera crew were presented, and then everyone took up positions for the first shot of the day. A worried-looking boy called Eric, in a thick blue serge suit from Burtons, stood ready with the Verey Pistol.

"We won't stay long . . . just see the first march of the refugees. I suppose you'll do it again and again as they always do in the films?" She was cool and matter of fact. Bored really. "I have to get back anyway pretty soon; your party tonight. I think we have about five hundred coming, all in their traditional costumes; especially for you. They weren't frightfully pleased, but I insisted. The City Palace is only opened occasionally now, for honoured guests . . ." A bleak smile. "So we might as well make a splash, mightn't we? It will be almost like old times again. Not quite, of course." She smiled a vivid, accusing smile. "Not quite, but as near as we can make it. And, anyway, it'll be the last time too . . . this time next year it will be an hotel, full of Americans all over my tennis courts." She turned away with distaste. The Princess was photographing Eric in his blue serge suit. Up on the rocks someone yelled down: "We can go! Dust is settled. Eric?" He nodded blindly, pistol in hand.

"I'll give you a count down. On 'one' you fire, right?"

Her Highness moved a little nearer to me, on my slope, and shaded her eyes with a slender, ivory, hand. "It'll be very beautiful tonight. I hope you'll be pleased with it all. They are working on the water pumps so that all the fountains will play, and the little canals will flow, scattered with rose petals and jasmin and marigolds. What happened to your foot, is it for the film?"

"No. I broke it yesterday jumping out of a jeep."

Her laugh, at once derisive and unbelieving, frightened Eric, who, forgetting his position, cried out, "Shush! . . . please!"

"Oh we're used to broken feet and every other sort of broken thing here! Polo, you remember? We have lots of wheel-chairs . . . you'll come in one of them. I'll have someone very beautiful to push you about."

"It hurts like hell at the moment. I don't honestly think I could make the evening really. I'm terribly sorry. Can we just see how I get through today? I have to walk all the way down the valley with the damned refugees . . . I'm just terrified I'll pass out."

She was flat. "They have goats and sheep with them, the people in the gorge, we saw them on our way here. So no one will be walking faster than the cattle. You'll manage. And you'll manage tonight, I'm sure. A wheel-chair and Heaven knows how many nobles. All 'Our Court' . . . and all in honour of you, Sir." Her sarcasm was pointed if faint.

Eric fidgeted; from the rocks a voice yelled down and asked me if I was ready to start moving; I was to start my descent of the hill to the valley as the head of the refugee column reached a certain tree a million miles, it seemed to me, below. There was a moment of tense silence; even the Princess with her Instamatic was still. On the morning air we heard the count down start. A thick Cockney accent began the numbers: "Eight, seven, six . . ."

Her Highness turned slightly towards me, smiling, her eyes were very bright. "Broken foot indeed . . . goodness me! You're British, aren't you? Well, you must show us what you can do."

* * *

"You really must, dear. You must show us what you can do." Chloe Gibson's voice was dull with defeat and cigarettes. Her hair, which had once hung down around her face like old rope, was scragged back into an untidy bun. She dropped her cigarette stub into the thick coffee cup where it hissed sullenly for a second before extinguishing itself in the weak dregs. Hunching her shoulders, she leaned towards me: "I know you can do it. I knew that first evening when you came up late and read the part. I knew it . . . I *know* it. But it's the Company: they don't know. They can't judge what you are going to do. Or even if you can. It's nearly three weeks and you haven't given much of a sign, dear. Nothing. You can't go on just walking through it, the others are trying desperately hard to give performances, but it is completely and utterly impossible for them if you don't play back. You must see that?"

She was being more than reasonable, and I knew, with terror, that she was right. I was still walking through it; I hadn't even tried to give a performance. Yet. We still had another five days before opening and I was trying to save performance until we had the costumes and the props, the real chairs, tables and the chenille curtains at the windows. Walking about on the top floor of the dingy red brick building across the street, with chalk marks on the scratched parquet floor, two or three bentwood chairs and a Watneys beer crate, didn't, for me at any rate, hold magic. I was, I thought, storing up my work until the time was ripe. All the others were hard at it making characters; Maureen even managed tears, so did Beatrice as my mother: they were able, in their actors' minds, to transform the chalk marks into the walls and the door of the back-shop parlour as if it had the fireplace and the whole staircase down. They mimed brilliantly, teapots, beer glasses, door handles; they believed. And they obviously didn't like me much, nor, as it turned out now, did they get any help from me.

I was shattered by my selfishness, terrified by my innate shyness—this shyness which has inhibited me all my life. The wrong profession for such a malady; for malady it was which crippled me before I walked into a crowded room, theatre, restaurant or bar. But I knew, sitting at the tacky table in the Linden Cafe in Notting Hill Gate that day, that my time for timidity and selfish shyness was about up. Someone was calling my bluff. And she wasn't going to let me get away with it: her production, and her blinding faith in my capabilities, were at stake. I was at stake too. Windlesham still waited; I had not, as yet, cancelled my appointment with the patient Headmaster in the pines and heather.

She hunched and shrugged herself into her tweed coat, avoiding my assistance. "Of course," she fumbled about in her large, beaten, handbag, "of course, we could always postpone things for a week . . ." She pulled a stubby bit of lipstick across her thin, cracked lips, and smacked them together as if savouring a sauce. "Just for a week. It would give us time to re-cast you."

My heart stopped beating altogether. I looked out through the steamy windows into the dirty snow-packed street. The red shape of a bus slowly ambled past. Re-cast. In my first theatre job in years. The utter shame overwhelmed me. I was stiff with silence. She snapped the clasp of the bag, and studied the slip of paper which was the bill for our coffees and sandwiches. "If you would like that? The boy who was cast and went up to Newcastle with that Tour is free . . . they closed in Leeds last week. It would break my heart but I must think of the Company, and my play. I know you'll understand." She laid some money on the slip of paper, left three pennies under her cup for a tip and started for the greasy door.

I caught her up, pulling on gloves against the bitter afternoon. I couldn't speak. Crossing Notting Hill Gate, slithering among the lumps of packed, oily, snow, I kept behind her a little, watching the red tweed coat flapping, the battered bag swinging, re-membering that night in the Aeolian Hall when she had hustled me up the stairs and into the little smoky room to read the play and finally to give me the part. I couldn't betray her. At the door of the grimy red brick building I took her arm. She stopped. "What shall I do?" she asked. "Send them home and re-cast . . . or what?"

There were icicles hanging from a burst pipe just above us. "No . . . don't do that. Not yet. Could you, I mean would you, just let's run the play right through; from start to finish, no notes, pauses . . . all three acts . . . so I can get a run at it. Perhaps then . . ." I knew that then I'd be on trial, that I'd have to bash through, that shyness and timidity and all the rest of it would be put aside in the sheer exhilarating excitement of becoming another person. In becoming the man I was trying to play: "Cliff".

While they all sat about, the Company, on chairs round the wall of the beastly little room, I was sure that all they were think-ing was how bad I was; inept, thin, useless: irritation and dismissal floated from their slouched bodies like a gas. Of course this was arrant nonsense; they had their own worries and problems, their own fears and doubts, as I did. But, naturally, I only considered myself. And how I felt. Not how they did. I wanted it all my way. And got it. Chloe sighed, shoved a sliding pin back into her pot-scrap-bun, and nodded doubtfully. "I meant to do a polishing job on the Second Act. Still . . . if you think it'll help . . ." We started up the stone steps to the Rehearsal Room, slowly, her beaten-up handbag slapping the iron handrail.

The Company were assembled. Sitting round the small gas fire which blinked and popped (it was the coldest winter for fifty-three years) they looked up with no surprise. I almost expected it, because we have a cruel, and true, saying in our profession, should you be taken to lunch by your Producer, that you "won't be with us after lunch, dear"—a sure sign of re-casting. But perhaps she hadn't told them before . . . they might not even have known anything. Perhaps I wasn't so awful. I warmed. Kenneth More, sitting in his ex-Naval overcoat, badges of rank long since ripped off, a string bag beside him with a packet of cornflakes and a pint of milk (he'd collected his rations in the break); Dandy Nichols reading the noon edition of *The Standard* to find her horoscope; Maureen Pook just sitting and smoking and warming her frozen legs; Beatrice Varley knitting with the placidity of a country nanny. How could I have doubted them? How could I have behaved so badly? Self-pity started and was smothered swiftly by Chloe chucking her coat into a corner and announcing that we would forget the polishing of the Second Act, and instead we'd run through the entire play from start to finish, no pauses, no notes, no timing. "Just bash away at it," she cried, as if we were all novice jockeys. "Bash away and see what we get."

A slightly bewildered Company got to its feet, stuffed news-papers into handbags, knitting into chintz-holdalls, and Kenny slowly removed his heavy navy blue overcoat. We started on the First Act.

At the finish, two hours later, Chloe with swimming eyes embraced us all, said nothing, and struggled into her red coat. "There's a hell of a lot to do . . . but we still have time, thank God. Maureen, when you say 'Do you see?' go below the table, not above it, so that Beatrice can play downstage . . . must see her eyes. Kenneth dear; I think you could stay a titch bit longer at the door, only a titch mind you, in the Second Act with Cliff and Anna, take the shock, see what I mean?" She rattled off orders, suggestions, pulling on gloves, tucking a tartan scarf about the scraggy hair, cigarette dangling. Eyes bright. "Tomorrow, same time. We'll start with Act Two . . . and I'll give you notes then. What the bloody hell have I done with my lighter?"

It was dark when we reached the street. Lamps flickered . . . there was a power cut again. She shivered, pulling the red coat round her, the bag slapping. "Oh by the by . . ." she grabbed my arm, "pause a bit longer at the top of the stairs on your first entrance; don't milk it, just a beat longer, it'll hold." She suddenly leaned up and gave me a rough, completely unexpected kiss. "I knew. I knew!" she said, and hurried off down to Holland Park.

★   ★   ★

In 1947 India at last gained her Independence, and exploded bloodily; Princess Elizabeth married a Mountbatten and tied all that up; Henry Ford and Gordon Selfridge both died; Albert Camus wrote *La Peste*, and Michael Clayton-Hutton wrote, and had produced, on February 25th, at the New Lindsey Theatre, his first play, "Power Without Glory". A good many other events took place as well in that year, but nothing was so impacted on my mind as that solitary event off Notting Hill Gate.

At the fall of the curtain nothing much happened. We shuffled on to the stage in a complete silence, feeling drained, unhappy, worried. Kenny murmured under his breath at the line up, "They've all pissed off . . ." and then the place erupted. The applause and the cheering continued, after that first almost stunned silence, for so long that eventually we were all forced to take hands, on the stage, and stood grinning and laughing inanely at each other, as the curtain rose and fell. Chloe was standing in the wings in a long woollen dress. Smoking.

Up in the dressing room which Kenny and I shared on the roof, a long wooden shelf on one side, some hooks banged into the wall on the other, a washbowl crammed into a corner, we quietly removed our make-up and stared into the long, scratched mirror before us.

"I think we're a hit," he said presently.

"They don't often do that, do they? Audiences, I mean?"

"Christ! No. Usually the other way round with a try out."

"It's a very nice feeling is all I can say, isn't it?"

Kenny grinned into the mirror.

"Enjoy it. You may never see its like again."

A scuffling on the stairs; the door flew open. A bright-eyed man. "Van Thal. Pinewood Studios. Remember I saw you first!"

A woman behind him pushed under his arm. "And I saw you second!" They slammed the door and clattered away.

Kenny winked. "Must be agents!"

We laughed together and I started to dress hurriedly. There was a reception in the Club Bar; my Father and Mother had come all the way up from Sussex, and Elizabeth from somewhere else. Kenny was being maddeningly slow. He was still wiping muck off his face, still in his underpants, calm, as ever, unhurried.

"Oh come on, for God's sake! You'll miss the party."

He got up slowly from his wooden chair, greasy face, a lump of cotton wool in one hand, his pants slipping round his hips. He hugged me suddenly to him. "Off you go, mate, it's your night, I'll catch you up later."

In the excitement of the night I didn't really take in much of what he said. But somehow I did remember it. That evening I saw no further than the Club Bar of the New Lindsey, which was full to bursting with red-faced, jolly looking people. As I pushed through they clapped as if I was a dog at a Show, and some patted me on the back in the same manner. Freddy was in a corner with some people; he smiled cheerfully and raised his glass to me in a silent salute. I found my mother, and we embraced; people drew back for this moving moment of mother and son. "Marvellous, darling!" she cried. "Look, my mascara has all run, does it show? It hurts like hell." My father, quiet, smiling, amused at some secret amusement (one never knew what with him), took my hand and kissed me too. "Very good. Curious play. I've been talking to your Author. Seems very young . . ." His voice tailed away. My Author was hunched in a group by the small bar; a slight man, with blazing eyes like a lizard, a red carnation, fresh at lunchtime, a large gin and tonic. He was smiling his odd little twisted smile, which was attractive, and, tonight, kind. He winked only. I winked back, and he turned and talked to a fat hovering woman with a note pad and pencil. Elizabeth was there, in the middle of some people, splendid in a monstrous Chinchilla cape. Somebody gave me a whisky which slopped over her skirt. I apologised and started patting at it.

"Don't bother. It doesn't matter. It's old anyway." She was happy and smiling.

"Chinchilla?"

"Sylvia loaned it to me, belonged to her mother. Stored all the war in a tin trunk in the garage but they forgot the mothballs; don't *touch* me, it comes out in handfuls."

I hugged her to me laughing, whisky slopping unheeded, Chinchilla hairs wafting into the packed room. "You see! I'm moulting! They'll all get hay fever or something dreadful . . . some allergy . . . I wonder what there will be left to hand back to Sylvia tomorrow?" A tall, blue-suited oaf carrying three drinks in his podgy hands pushed between us. "How does it feel," he roared, "to be a Star Overnight?" He weaved his way through the pack.

Elizabeth looked quite put out. "How frightfully rude," she said.

★   ★   ★

Later, much later, in my small sub-let flat in Hasker Street (two rooms and a hot-plate on the landing; share of bathroom, for a quid a week), we sat together in the sitting room where I was to sleep on the divan, she to have my bed in the back room. The Chinchilla drifted hairs gently into the stuffy air. She had made some cocoa (habits die hard) in two mugs, we were both half asleep.

"What do you think it'll mean, then, all this?" She was curious, amused, not very serious.

"I don't know. Depends on tomorrow's papers and what they say really."

"But they were awfully nice, the criticky people, weren't they? That funny woman with the hat, she was someone frightfully important. She said you were spell-binding!" She laughed, knowing much better herself. Remembering my moods and torturing, and sulks and one thing and another; sister junk. They remember everything you ever do. If they love you. "But if it does work out, I mean, what then?"

"Well . . . we might transfer to a bigger theatre. Make more money. They might make a film out of it."

"With you?" Her attack was sharp, pointed.

"I don't know . . . probably with Stewart Granger or someone, I don't think with me, they never use the original actor, always film stars. It's a sort of rule."

"Oh dear! It's all ups and downs, isn't it. Like snakes and ladders." She looked downcast, and sipped away thoughtfully.

"I'm dreadfully tired, are you? You must be, all that acting and so on. I think Daddy quite liked it, don't you? Seemed really quite impressed; for him; he had a very long talk with the Author boy. Funny creature, isn't he? So young. Sort of desperate. I think they are all a very funny lot in your profession. Do you think you could become famous? Like Charles Laughton or Michael Wilding or someone?"

I started putting a pillow case on the grubby floral cushions for my bed. "I don't honestly know. Probably not. The people at Rank said my head was too small and my neck was all wrong."

She looked startled, and peered up at my neck curiously. "Your neck? Whatever is the matter with your neck? Herbert Marshall had a wooden leg, but you couldn't tell."

I was tired now. I didn't know what would happen, all I did know was that something had happened, and that it was warm and pleasant and rewarding. So far. "I don't know, honestly I don't. But if all went really well I suppose I might be a bit famous or something, if it lasted, and I could make a lot of money. If I was clever and all that."

She put the cocoa mugs on to the tin tray and took them to the door. "How much money, I mean sort-of how much?" She stood looking at me with interest. I pulled down the floral divan cover and revealed a grey-looking blanket. There were no sheets. "A hundred pounds a week even. I don't know."

She went out on to the landing and stacked the mugs, not clinking them so as not to wake the elderly interior decorators who lived on the ground floor. Coming back in, and closing the door gently, I saw that she was smiling contentedly to herself. "A hundred pounds a week! Goodness! I consider that very nice indeed," and seeing my worried face she laughed and added, "well, I mean, just for acting it's not bad, is it? I mean it's better than a wallop . . ."

I finished it off for her, "a wallop in the belly with a wet fish!" We laughed, tired, warmed by the childhood joke, Lally had said it was plain vulgar when we once dared to use it, and given us a cuffing.

"Much better than that!" I said.

*　　*　　*

The Press the next morning was all a Rave. That is to say we were a hit and I was "an actor to watch" and indeed, as the podgy oaf of the night before had said, and perhaps he even wrote it, A Star Overnight. My father telephoned from *The Times* with carefully concealed pleasure and read one or two bits over the line; my mother came up with Aunt Freda and had coffee—we laughed at the caricatures of myself; and Forwood called up in the middle of it all.

"Maddening having one's friends becoming stars overnight. Are you free for some lunch?"

I wasn't. "I have to take my mother and an aunt to lunch. I wish I were free."

I heard him stifle a yawn. "Never mind. But it is a very nice beginning, just don't let it go to your head." He hung up and we all went off to Kettners. At the door there, a thin, scraggy black cat suddenly sprang across the street and, arching its back, tail like a pole, it rubbed itself hard against my legs, and then shot back into the shadow of a bombed building opposite. It was a very nice start indeed.

In the late afternoon I walked from Sloane Square down to Notting Hill with all the evening papers, which were as good as the dailies had been, and sliding over the packed snow I knew, really for the first time in my life, just how splendid it felt to have wings on your heels, and in the theatre the Company were gathered together for Second Night Notes, and in a solemn ceremonial, presented me with an inverted china pudding bowl. To put on my head to see if it still fitted. We were all extremely relieved to find that it did.

And the day after I wrote a polite, and regretful, letter to Windlesham.

*　　*　　*

Although I had more or less scooped the pool with the play, we were all of us singled out for our individual praises. My part was extremely flashy, noisy, and centre-stage for most of the time. I also had a splendid scream in the Third Act, and that is usually irresistible to both audiences and critics alike, who tend to confuse the part with the player. You really can't miss with a good yell. However, the other member of the Company who was especially singled out was a quiet, pale, sensitive girl called Mary Horn whose work was, quite simply, staggering. She got a great deal of praise but eventually, after a year or so, she withdrew from the theatre and went off to be a House-Mistress in a boys' school in Scotland. A grievous loss to the theatre.

But none of this worried me at the time naturally. I kept my money safely in a large Oxo tin in my suitcase under the bed, and knew just where I stood in the world financially. I gave my ration book to a pleasant lady called Millie in the Express Dairies at the end of the road and lived on a diet of Weetabix, Kraft cheese, H.P. sauce and an occasional apple. I washed my clothes in the washbowl in the shared bathroom and took things like sheets and pillow cases down to Hillside Cottage once a fortnight to my unfortunate mother. I brought a few bits and pieces from the cottage to stick about the anonymous furniture of my two-roomer, got a cracked lustre jug from a junk shop in Walton Street, filled it with catkins, and settled into London life, if not exactly its society.

My demob suit was wearing out, worn as it was, daily. And the shirts and slacks which I had brought from Calcutta and Singapore looked faintly dated once they were unpacked and worn in the King's Road. My father sent me off to his tailor and I got a fine grey flannel suit made, bought a neat green hat from Henry Heath, some chamois gloves from Gieves, and succeeded in looking more like a trainer of horses than a moderately success-ful out-of-the-West-End actor.

The play was packed nightly and we became fashionable. Everyone came to see us. Film companies, agents, talent scouts and on one memorable night, Noël Coward. Nervously we were all told to assemble on stage after the Show since The Master wished to address us individually. We stood in a short neat line of seven. I was beside Maureen and at the end of the line. I didn't hear what he said to the others, saw him kiss Beatrice, wag his finger often, and when he got to Maureen I just heard him say: "The name Pook is disaster, change it immediately." Maureen, shattered with nerves, said, "It must be to something beginning with a P!" and Noël murmured gently, "We aren't playing word games, dear." And moved on to me. I got the finger wagged. "Never, ever, ever take a pill, not even an aspirin before a show, and never, ever drink until after curtain-fall." He said, in general, that we were all lovely, talented, moving and clever and thanked us.

As we wandered off to our dressing room, he shot out a very

firm hand and took my elbow: "And never, ever, go near the cinema!" and was gone into the night.

I obeyed his first commands implicitly.

Letters started to arrive from elderly Gentlemen Novelists, and odd-sounding ladies with double-barrelled names with addresses in Hampstead and South Kensington. Forwood got me a job in a Crime Film. It was hardly what you might call a part; just a policeman sitting in an office. And I was never noticed unfortunately. The uniform they gave me didn't fit and so was pinned up the front and the camera was behind me; however, I did have one line to say, "Calling Car 2345. Calling Car 2345" into a sort of microphone, and although it starred the Attenboroughs I never met them. But it was a start, and for that one day's work I earned double my week's salary in the theatre; and coming back to Town on the bus from Islington Studios I vaguely thought how simple it was, and how much better paid, and how I could, in a very short time indeed, fill the Oxo tin and move to a larger flat than the one with the hot-plate on the landing in Hasker Street. But equally I knew that it was a flashy sort of job, and that it didn't take, or need, much talent. The theatre was at least honourable. I had a lot to learn.

Eventually the snow melted, in this extraordinary winter, and the vague signs of spring arrived and with them came Peter Daubeny, the Golden Boy Wonder I had so briefly met back stage with Forwood, and who had been singularly, or so it seemed, unimpressed with me. Mr Daubeny bought the play, which impressed him enormously, and transferred us to the West End in April. We were giddy with delight, sure of a long, long run, rich with our new West End salaries (I got ten pounds a week now), and completely overlooked the fact, or chose to ignore it if we knew it, that our theatre was miscalled the Fortune, stood opposite the Stage Door of Drury Lane, had a public right of way running through the auditorium and across the stage dating from God knew when, and was extremely difficult to get to unless you were hell bent on being there. Which, in spite of magical critics again, no one was. No one even used the public right of way, and "Oklahoma" opened shortly after us, and filled the narrow street with steak-eating, jean-clad, healthy, Americans who all seemed to sing, dance *and* act. Confidently nursing our wounds we prophesied that we would get the overflow of those who could not obtain seats for this fantastic musical (we heard many curious stories from our dressers of people actually fainting in the Stalls and Circle from the sheer energy set before them), but there again we were miserably wrong. If you go out to see a new American musical, the first since the war, it is very unlikely that, being unable to get in you would turn your eyes across the street to our modest canopy and come in to see a tense play about the working class in South London. Forget it. And everybody did. After a very short time we slid into the eternal obscurity of the Fatal Fortune and our happy time was over. But not before Queen Mary expressed a surprising wish to see us perform, which threw us into complete panic and faint hope. Perhaps, if she liked it, we could solicit publicity from the Palace to help us fight the lusty Yanks across the street. But it didn't make a mite of difference. "Oh What a Beautiful Morning!" became, alas, our requiem.

Apart from Royalty, someone else came before the electric lights went out for ever on our humble, modest, moving play. Ian Dalrymple, quiet, soft spoken, thoughtful, articulate, who smoked his cigarettes through paper holders and looked more like a Cambridge don than a film producer, signed me up for his next film, "Esther Waters", showing either great courage or arrant stupidity. But he was so gentle, so persuasive, so unlike the kind of film producer I had ever expected to meet, that I was lost. Mr Coward's ultimate warning was drowned by Mr Dalrymple's charm and detailed explanations of my role of "William Latch".

"But what about my neck?"

He pushed his glasses up his nose and looked hard at me. "What's the matter with your neck?"

"The Rank people say it's too thin. My head's too small. I don't look like David Farrar or James Mason."

"I don't see anything wrong with it, your neck. Your head will soon swell anyway; and until it does we'll have your hats made by Lock and you'll be wearing stocks most of the time. I shouldn't worry. This is new Cinema." He seemed quite confident. So I decided that I should too; after all, he knew much better than I did. And wore glasses. So that when Mr Coward came to tell us all, just before we closed, that he had written marvellous parts for us all in his new play, "Peace in our Time", mine was the only heart which sank. I knew I would have to confess.

"You remember what I told you. Never, ever, the cinema."

"Yes."

"You ignored my advice?"

"I didn't know that you'd written me a part."

"You'll dine with me tonight. This is madness . . ."

It was not mentioned at the Savoy Grill—so many people came to the table that it resembled Gold Cup Day at Ascot. So we went back to his house in Gerald Road. It was not, as he pointed out, much more than spitting distance from Hasker Street.

I was miserably shy, and walked stiffly beside him down the street and into the yard of his house. Impatiently he stood at the gate. "Go straight ahead, that's the front door, I put on the light here." He pressed a switch in the wall. "I shan't jump on you. I'm not the type, and Gerald Row Police Station is immediately opposite you. Would you care for a whistle or will you merely shout?"

We talked for an age. His advice was considered, wise, careful. The cinema would ruin me, I had a great deal to offer the theatre, a whole new world was starting there now the war was over; I must be patient, loyal, devoted and learn from my new craft which had, so far, welcomed me with such warmth. Magic lay before me and he had, incidentally, written me a "walloping great part" in "Peace". But it was to no avail. I confessed that I had given my word to Mr Dalrymple, that I wanted to try the cinema and do the theatre as well, that my contract would allow me to do one play for six months every second year, that I had not abandoned the Proscenium Arch, merely postponed my moment. He was not at all best pleased. "I think," he said, "you are being a cunt. And I am very, very, angry indeed."

With thirty pounds a week from the Rank Organisation as a sort of holding-salary until the film started, and ten a week from the tottering play, I was richer than I imagined I'd ever be. And one day walked with great courage and my Oxo tin into an Estate Agents in Sloane Square and rented number 44 Chester Row for ten guineas a week. Furnished; with garden, three floors, and basement.

In the kitchen in the basement, with a quart of ale and a smoked haddock and mashed potatoes, and under the unbelieving, but pleased eyes, of Freddy Joachim, I signed my contract with the Rank Organisation for, at that time, seven years. In the morning I had gone along to Kettners Restaurant, found the black cat crouched in a wooden box in his bomb-site, and brought him back to S.W.1. I called him "Cliff" after the role in the play. As Freddy and I toasted ourselves in pale ale, I chucked Cliff the haddock skin, and then started on the washing up, with Freddy drying and stacking up the plates and things on the wooden dresser. We made a comfortable, domestic scene.

"Seven years seems an eternity," I said, wrapping up the remainder of the fish-skin and bones in newspaper.

Freddy wiped out the saucepan carefully, "Oh! They'll probably drop you long before that, you know, the contract is renewable every year. I very much doubt if you'll last all that time. It's a fickle business, and you aren't really the right type for the cinema, you know. Of course," he added brightly, "this role in 'Esther Waters' is what you might call a Character Part . . . probably why they picked you. You could be a very good character actor, I feel sure; but I can't remember a real cinema star who was just a character actor. They need a bit more glamour; anyway we must cross our fingers, work hard, stay modest, and hope for the best. Things change all the time, we really can't tell at the moment. Grasp the nettle, I always say." He slid the saucepan, cleaned and shining, on to the shelf and took off the towel which he had tied round his waist as an apron. And then all the lights went out. Another power cut.

"Don't move!" I cried. "I know where the matches are." By the flickering light of two candles Freddy took up the contract, and placed it carefully in his briefcase. "We don't want to lose this, do we. I must admit I really didn't expect it all to happen so soon, or even at all. You must feel very elated."

"I don't know really. Elated or not. It's all a bit frightening, signing your life away for seven years, and all those clauses . . . I wonder if I'll even last seven years."

He smiled his kindly smile, wrapped himself into his black coat, folded a scarf round his throat. "These spring evenings are very chilly . . . most treacherous," and patted my arm with an unexpected avuncularity. "Cheer up, do! You mustn't dwell on the gloomy side tonight, it's all gone so wonderfully well so far. It's been quite a big adventure, yes, I really think that we can say that. A big adventure in a very few months, now all you have to do is work very hard, and show us all what you can do."

*   *   *

Ten years later, on a scrub-covered hillside, in the centre of India, I was standing "like a stork" on one leg, with a broken foot, a clutch of Indian Royalty behind me, an uncertain future ahead, more than thirty films in the past and a thousand refugees starting their unhappy trek along the white twisting gorge road, vultures drifting in the opal light: it was a long haul from the shabby kitchen and the crisp new contract and Freddy wrapping himself up like a parcel for the walk to Sloane Square and the Tube.

And I was still trying to "prove", to show them what I could do. Would it ever end, this proving, this statement of determination? Wasn't it enough that I had done what I had done in spite of skinny neck, small head and a pair of too long legs? I had long since closed, with wry regret, my Oxo tin and opened an account in a high marbled hall opposite the Law Courts. I had played bookies and thugs, soldiers and sailors and pilots. Bombed Berlin. Braved a bursting dam; been various doctors, in the house, at sea, at large and in distress; suffered from amnesia, and shot a policeman. I'd even played Sydney Carton. God knows what I had not done. But my determination to prove was still insatiable, the need to show what I could do was still my driving force. Today, I realised as I started to hobble down the slope to join my thousand refugees I was heavy with despair. One had to go on doing it simply to survive, but, I wondered as I came abreast of the hot, sweating, dusty mass dragging along the road, was it really all worth it? Swinging into line with them, hopping with my crutch, with what I hoped was a noble lift of the head (to favour the main camera up above me), I could not rid myself of the thought that it was all a dreadful waste of time, effort and life. Surely there were better things to do with the years I had, so far, been given than forcing myself to prove continually?

Up on the ridge the first whisper of a breeze riffled the pink and silver sari of the fat Princess, billows of white dust swirled and eddied about our sweaty ranks. I could see the sunlight glinting on the three great cameras on their separate rocks, smoke drifting still from the wrecked car, the shimmering plain ahead. I looked, briefly behind me, and our trail seemed endless, a thousand people is a great many . . . sheep, goats, women in torn cotton prints, children dragging along, men taut-faced, sweating, some bandaged . . . an old woman with a white parasol being jostled along on a creaking cart surrounded with bundles and kettles and a clock. This had all once happened, not so long ago . . .

a few years before I had signed my virgin Contract . . . this had all been real. Today we were merely re-enacting what had gone before, and what unhappily would come again one day. An exodus. And I was at the head of the column of marching souls. I was the leader, broken foot or not; I had to prove only that I could do it; and in doing that I would be showing them, even as a cinema actor with a limp, what they could do as well. Setting a good example. An absolute essential, which brooked no despairing argument.

Of course one had to go on proving: that was what one was there for. I felt a great deal better, and threw my arm round the cotton print shoulders of a hot, dusty woman. She looked up at me with flat, tired eyes and smiled; she shook her head and straightened up, and calling across the straggle to a small boy of seven or eight, she told him that it wouldn't be so far, not to dawdle, and to give Felicity a hand because she probably had a blister on her heel. We marched on, and someone not far behind, started to whistle in the blazing sun. It spread gently through the column, raggedly but clearly on the morning air, the marching became less of a straggle, more of a determined walk. Felicity's mother said, "Do you know the words?"

The rocky walls of the gorge swelled with the sound of our voices, it drifted up to the fading cluster of Royals on the ridge; almost triumphant, pride regained, courage retrieved; a joining had taken place.

> "*I've got sixpence,*
> *Jolly jolly sixpence,*
> *I've got sixpence,*
> *To last me all my life . . .*"

Proving. Showing what one could do. That's all.

6

NUMBER 44 sagged dejectedly two or three houses along from a wide and deep bombsite where some pleasant artisans' cottages once had stood in neat Georgian modesty, until a land mine had hit them and scattered their yellow bricks and fragile timbers into rubble and my back garden. No. 44 had suffered from this cruel thrust of German might; cracks ran about it like inverted varicose veins, the top floor bulged heavily over the area railings, a brick pot-belly, the black and white tiled steps were badly chipped by falling debris, and the front door only closed after two good bangs. But it had a roof, and it had the garden. From the top windows you looked down on to the E. Box luxuriance of bramble, buddleia and bracken in the bombsite, and then the garden, scraggly, unkempt, cluttered with slate-shards and half bricks, a laburnum on one side, a red May on the other, and at the end, where the brick wall fended off the gardens of Cliveden Place, two giant limes which shed flowers, pollen, leaves and a thick sticky muck all through the summer. But to left and right, as well as below, one saw green; and above the green a couple of spires and the roof of the Royal Court Theatre. Not bad.

Inside, not so good; margarine yellow paint, faded cretonnes, scuffed once-elegant, neo-Georgian furniture. Curtains staccato with parrots rioting in writhing yards of peony trees. No paintings. A small engraving of Salisbury Cathedral, a black silhouette of two ladies in lacy caps taking tea. The kitchen, in the dark basement had a table covered in stained American cloth, a stove, electric wires trailing along every wall, a sink, a geyser, and a door to the area on one side and the coal cellar which ran right under Chester Row itself. There were four knives, four forks, four spoons, three saucepans and a frying-pan petrified in years of egg and bacon grease. The beds, all five in the house, had horse hair mattresses. And the lavatory was cracked and creamy with rime. But it was the first real home of my own, even though I rattled about in it like the pea in a whistle.

Millie at the Express Dairies had a sister called Rose who would "take on another gentleman" for two hours a day starting Monday. Rose came. Small, nervous, glasses, with a floral pinny and a voice which rang through the empty house with all the melody of a gull at a fishing-port. But she washed and scrubbed, wiped-down and told me what to buy from Vim to soda, lavatory paper to extra plates, and a mat for in front of the sink. When I got back from the theatre in those long spring evenings which seem so particular to London, I took my Weetabix and cheese and a glass of beer into the ragged garden, and under the May tree, with Cliff for company and a cod's head for him, bought from Macfisheries on the way, I sat and ate and felt well content with my lot. As indeed I should have been. But what, I wondered with a twist of alarm, would happen when the cinema part of my life began in the middle of the summer? It was easy while I was in the play—a few hours per day away from my new house, patching cracks, washing walls, heaving furniture about to suit my scheme. If scheme I had. But what then? Who to look after me, run the house, tend the garden, buy the cods' heads. Sort the laundry, go to Millie for the rations?

Who but Nan?

Calcutta. She was older than I by about six years, tall, grey eyes, good hands, a generous figure. "Ample", she used to call it, or, in a kinder manner, "my Edwardian body". Which it was. She wore her hair in a plait bound round her head, and had an ever ready capacity for tremendous laughter and a surge for living. She was like a crested wave, always about to tumble, full of excitement, cool, grey-green, poised, crest tilted towards whatever shore. Never quite breaking.

I first saw her in the Mess the evening I arrived after five days of travel on wooden seats from Bombay. Tagore's Palace, a low, crumbling elegant house with pillared veranda, standing in a cool wilderness of zinnias and pale lawns watered daily by unseen gardeners. In the centre of the lawns a long shallow pool skimmed by kingfishers, thrusting with the lilac lances of water hyacinth. The Mess was a high, white room; a long table in the centre, small bamboo bar in one corner, two or three rattan chairs, old copies of the air-mail edition of *The Times*, *Lilliput*, and battered *Country Life*, fans clickety-clacking slowly in the ceiling, blades wobbling, gentle air riffling the papers as they lay. She arrived suddenly through the doors flowing in long white chiffon, her hair tonight tumbling about her shoulders, in one hand a slim cigarette holder, in the other a book; the only completely unfeminine thing about her was the big Service watch on her wrist.

She came straight to the bar and slid on to the stool beside me and ordered a Gin Sling.

"Are you van den Thingummy . . . or are you Wallace?" Eyes grave, mouth smiling.

"Van den Thingummy."

"There were two of you on the Posting Order. I didn't know." She took her glass and prodded the ice cubes with a straw.

"What is Thingummy?"

"Bogaerde."

"Goodness! All of it? How grand. What are you called for short?"

"Pip."

"Better. For Philip?"

"No. For 'you give me the pip' . . . my first Commanding Officer's groan every time he saw my face."

She laughed, and bent her head, placing the book beside her on the bar. "Were you so awful then?"

"Pretty."

"I'm Nanette Baildon. Squadron Officer."

"Goodness! All of it? How grand. What are you called for short?"

She snorted a laugh, choked on smoke. "Touché! Nan."

"Is it all right, to call you that?"

"Nan is perfect."

I liked her very much. A large gecko ran up the wall and slid behind a picture of Their Majesties.

"I don't really know what I'm doing here actually."

"You are Photographic? An interpreter, I mean?"

"Yes . . . ex Second Army."

"I saw the little ribbons. Jolly. Come at the wrong time, haven't you?"

"The monsoon started as the train pulled out of Bombay Central."

"Always the way. They want you in a hurry and then nothing. No sorties now, no flying possible for weeks in this." She indicated the rain thudding down into the sodden Elephant Ears at the door.

"Still, the planning goes on, doesn't it? From the sorties flown?"

Her eyes widened slightly, she took the butt from her holder and squashed it out in a puddle on the bar. It hissed.

"What planning do you mean?"

"Singapore, the fall of, all that . . . I'm supposed to be working on the defences."

"Defences! We are up to our eyes in defences, been at them for months and months; you really are late! I don't know what we'll do now. You know it's unconditional surrender for the Japs, or else, don't you? A matter of time I'd say, really. Otherwise God only knows." She sipped her Gin Sling, clinking ice.

"It's so marvellous to see a woman in evening dress again."

"We always wear it for dinner. Evelyn and I are the only two girls in the Mess so it rather falls on us to keep up standards, don't you think? And it's nicer."

"Much; and you are wearing a scent?"

She looked at me steadily, grey eyes smiling.

"Clever old you. The last dregs of 'Je Reviens' . . . almost squeezed the bottle dry. Do you want another drink? On me . . ."

People started to wander into the room, gruff exchanges, hand shakes, drinks all round; then hands in pockets, rocking gently on heels, laughter too loud, conversation bored and falsely jolly, straight from the showers, all of them, talcumed, scrubbed; crisp uniforms already starting to sweat slowly down the backs, under the arms; foreheads beaded. Evelyn (apparently) came in, a flutter of green silk, a white flower in her hair. Scattered applause, she bobbed a curtsey, someone handed her a drink and she waved to Nan.

"What's the book?" I turned it up on the bar, covered in coarse brown paper, the word "Poetry" in big ink letters.

She shrugged, and her shoulder strap slid down; pulling it up gently she took the book and opened it. "An anthology . . . poetry, prose . . . this was a poet's house so it seems appropriate . . . do you know Tagore?"

My blank face betrayed me. She hurried on, amused, confused, finding a place marked by a dead leaf.

"Do you like this?

'The yellow bird sings in their tree and makes my heart dance with gladness.

We both live in the same village, and that is our one piece of joy . . .' "

She stopped and looked up. "Perhaps not. It's from the Bengali, of course; perhaps not your cup of tea."

"No! No . . . No . . . I did like it. It was just suddenly so odd.

Poetry, evening dress, scent . . . civilised; I didn't expect it. I've had six weeks on a troop ship and five days and nights on a train . . . I rather expected the Japs to be hissing from every bush and tree, and that I'd have taken my cyanide pill by now."

She closed the book gently, replacing the dried leaf to mark her place with Tagore.

"We are an awfully long way from Kohima or Rangoon here . . . Calcutta is hardly front line stuff." There was gentle reproof in the voice: "I think you can breathe freely, at least for the moment. And if you like, I'll start teaching you how to enjoy Poetry. We'll try simple things, Belloc and so on . . . then Yeats, Pound . . . unless of course you have other things to do during the monsoon?"

At dinner, she at one end, Evelyn at the other, she placed me on her left in someone's place who had gone to the Hills on leave. She rang little silver bells and Bearers flitted about with tinned tomato soup and a mild curry . . .

"What did you do before?"

The usual question.

"Don't, for God's sake, ask me at dinner."

"Why ever not? Was it something dreadful?"

"No, not dreadful. Embarrassing, that's all."

"How curious. You must have been about ten. Can I guess?" She handed me grated coconut. "You sold yo-yo's in Oxford Street? Trained performing fleas?"

"You're getting hot."

"Really? In a circus? No? Something on a trapeze . . . a trainee clown?"

"You are an idiot! I was an actor."

She laughed. "Well, that's not so awful, is it? Owen Nares, Godfrey Tearle, Ralph Richardson, all rather respectable, I should think. Were you any good?"

"Hard to tell, they got me for this job before I could do much. Out of the cradle."

"Well, you have plenty of time now; you can start on your Shaw and Shakespeare. And the poetry would be invaluable, stretching the mind, the Learning Mind, don't you think? Do you want cucumber? Marvellously refreshing with that . . ."

We read to each other on the cool of her veranda, and I learned blocks of Poetry and we discussed and argued while Evelyn, our chaperone, did lazy daisy stitches on cushion covers for her bottom drawer. Later I wrote a play, which had been struggling about in my mind on the journey out, miles and miles of it, which she bravely typed during the long, steamy days of rain. Sometimes there was a gentle flutter of work, but very little; and our lives started along a gentle, pleasant road together. We drove to the city and explored every market, bazaar, street and alley; joined the Saturday Club, an impossibly snobbish club, one hot morning by saying that I was Baron van den Bogaerde and that she was the Comptesse de la Vache. Improbably, but with sickening ease, we jumped a two-year waiting list and lunched in cool splendour. The Club became our Place, even though we detested most of the white clientele . . . Indians were not admitted. Apart from my Literary Education, Nan was determined that I should try to understand India and the Indian mind, and I was dragged from temple to temple, shrine to shrine and festival to festival, and in the evenings, when we rested up from MacNeice, Dorothy Wellesley, Spender and Wilde we talked about Gandhi and Congress and the Raj. It was a crammer's course. Her unashamed passion for this vast country was infectious, and I began to look about me now with clearer eyes and compassion, trying to understand as much as I could, before they threw us out.

One day, returning from the city alone (she had stayed behind to wash her hair, a tedious process because of its length), I came bearing gifts. A small bottle of "Je Reviens" which I had discovered by chance on Chowringhee, and a pair of lovebirds in a bamboo cage.

She was not on her veranda; no one was. The mosquito nets were down, the lights on; wild dogs barked across the compound. I went over to the Mess. It was full. Silent. Only the fans clickety-clacking and a faint voice through heavy static from the bakelite radio behind the bar. I saw her standing motionless, hair in a towel, hand to her face. Evelyn in a chair, head bowed. The faces round the bar taut. There were no cheers in our Mess at the news of the atomic bomb on Hiroshima.

It was still raining on V.J. Night. We drove into the Club and dined and danced to celebrate the end, for ever we all thought, of our war. There was great euphoria in the dining room, people cheered and sang as if it was New Year's Eve. At the next table to ours a party of six wore funny hats, and a mem-sahib in a crepe paper wimple hit a silver salver, offered by a bearer, high into the air. "I said mashed potatoes! Not boiled!" she shouted. The little white balls scattered about our feet. "Christ!" she said. "But you do grow to *loathe* Them, don't you!"

We drove home in torrential rain and struck a group of soldiers somewhere along the Barrackpore road. We turned over twice I seem to recall: Nan had a cut head, I was unhurt. There were two or three men sprawled in the muddy, roaring waters of the street. People came and took Nan back to barracks. I knew that two must be dead; but remembered, and remember now, very little. They were members of a gang of American GI deserters, known in the area, who high-jacked cars at nights. We spent weeks of misery in Court, and finally were exonerated, because witnesses had seen them link arms across the road and form a line to halt us. I had not seen them in the dark and the rain. I have never driven since.

It was decided that we should both go away on leave. To clear our minds. Whatever that meant. We took the train to Darjeeling and then up into Sikkim on stubborn mules, across the high plateau towards Tibet, which reminded us both forcibly of the Yorkshire moors and which was just as cold and uninviting. We saw dawn rise on Everest . . . the sun set slowly on the shimmering height of Kanchenjunga. In Tindzhe Dzong women hid behind the pillars in the market place horrified because Nan was wearing trousers; and somewhere else, which I have forgotten, she traded a tin of American bacon for two black agate rings, from an old man with a fluttering prayer wheel. We were hopelessly unprepared for such a trip but, like most idiots, Fortune cared for us, and we arrived back in Calcutta a month later, calm, brown, rather pompous, happy, to be welcomed in the Mess with cheers and tall John Collins's—and the news of my immediate posting to another war, in Java.

She came down to the docks with me. My exceedingly small L.S.T. was almost ready to put out for the long journey. It was the same farewell as always: the bright, uneasy chatter, the beating heart, the false bravado.

"Just remember . . ." she fiddled with the buckle of her sandal which had come undone, " . . . just remember. I'll be going home in about a month, I think . . . you have my address . . . my sister's house? Well, it's just that when you get back, if you need anything, or if there is anything I can ever do, just . . . well just . . ." the buckle came off in her hand. "Hell! Now I'll have to hop about looking for a taxi. But I mean . . . if you want me, just give me a call . . ."

*　　*　　*

So who, but Nan?

She came right away with three suitcases and her old tin trunk, a pile of books, and a cardboard box with a collection of doubtful Meissen, Augustus Rex, plates and saucers, and moved into the first-floor two rooms. Sitting room on the street, small bedroom over the garden, sharing the bathroom and the dark kitchen below. She had kept on her nine-to-five job because all I could offer was the accommodation and six pounds a week for house-keeping and Cliff, who took up his place in the house on the end of her bed. And we managed very well.

No more Weetabix and cheese. No more lonely suppers under the May tree. On two ration books we fared far better, and she knew a shop in Lancaster Gate where she got black-puddings and haggis and split peas and lentils and God knows what other delights. I began to eat properly, and was happy to do the washing-up in return. Walls got repainted, window boxes planted, the neo-Georgian furniture was arranged and rearranged and arranged again. I spent a lot of my time, and more money than I could afford from the Oxo tin, in junk shops up and down the King's Road; it was still, then, almost a long village street, with an ironmongers who sold hooks and bolts and pounds of nails, a haberdashers which sold woollen combinations in winter and muslin blouses in the summer, and a greengrocers spilling with cabbages, lettuce, green peppers, mud, and garlic. But the junk shops were my best place, and for a very few pounds, and often shillings, I carted back suspect Old Masters in heavy gilded frames, domes of stuffed birds shimmering with dusty feathers, cracked coffee pots and sets of odd glasses, jugs and bits of Staffordshire which, all washed and mended, suddenly gave a feeling of false richness to the sagging, margarine yellow house.

Then, just before the play finally closed, we attacked the garden, cleared all the rubble, whitewashed walls, pruned and cut and heaved the sour earth out in sacks. With the assistance of an old man with a cart and donkey whom Nan met in Elizabeth Street, we filled the place with geraniums and tobacco plants, laid out a lawn in strips of emerald turf which cost a fortune per sod,

Catterick Camp, Yorkshire, May 1941.

St. Suplice, Normandy,
July 1944.

My mother, Elizabeth and my father at the cottage. Clayton, Sussex, 1942.

As we are now: my sister Elizabeth, her husband George and their children, Mark and Sarah. Christmas day at my house in Provence, 1977.

With Beatrice Varley in "Power Without Glory", Fortune Theatre, 1947.

James Swarbrick

Bendrose House, Amersham, 1950.

Kay Kendall and Olive Dodds, Bendrose, July 1951. This was the day of Kate's first visit.

IN POLITICS, FILMS, THE STAGE—
YOUNG MEN OF MARK.

As occasion arises it is our policy to seize the psychological moment when a young man, hitherto unknown or hardly known to the public, rises from his surroundings and shows himself to be something out of the ordinary. Four of these newly "arrived" young men appear in this issue.

MR. J. HAROLD WILSON. *Aged thirty-one, he is the new President of the Board of Trade, and a Privy Councillor. Via Council schools education he won a grammar school scholarship to Jesus College, Cambridge. Had a brilliant academic career, and was Fellow of University College at twenty-two. Has held appointments in the Ministries of Supply and Labour; and comes to his new job from the Secretaryship for Overseas Trade. Has been Labour M.P. for Ormskirk since 1945.*

DIRK BOGARDE, *another British actor fresh to stardom, plays William Latch in the screen version of George Moore's "Esther Waters." Was destined for the Diplomatic, but preferred stage designing. Worked at the Embassy Theatre and the "Q" in any capacity; took over a rôle in Priestley's "When We Are Married," gravitated to the Amersham Repertory Company and to the West End. Was interpreter in Intelligence during the war; two of his D-Day drawings done in France were bought by the British Museum; two by America.*

KIERON MOORE *stars in "A Man About the House." Is saluted as a new British screen discovery of the first magnitude. He is twenty-two, an Irishman, whose performance in a Sean O'Casey play at Swiss Cottage eighteen months ago brought him a contract with Korda. Stars in "Anna Karenina" with Vivien Leigh; plays a schisophrenetic P.O.W. in "Mine Own Executioner."*

DEREK ADKINS

PETER DAUBENY, *London's youngest actor-manager, plays this part in "We Proudly Present"—written for him by Ivor Novello. Daubeny's last production, "Power Without Glory," is to be presented on Broadway, while "The Glass Menagerie," which has received more prizes in a year than any other Broadway play, will be his next London production. He lost an arm during the war.*

Elizabeth Taylor in the cherry orchard. Bendrose, 1951.

Jean Simmons and Anouk Aimée in a heat wave. Bendrose, 1951.

Kate dressed for a Sunday walk, 1952.

Beel House, Amersham, 1954, after demolition of the East Wing. The "Out-Patients Department" on right.

The Green Study, Beel House, 1955.

Tea in the "Out-Patients". Theo Cowan, Olive, Rex Harrison, Kate, Julie Harris and self, 1956.

With Elizabeth and my brother Gareth. La Napoule, 1954.

Natasha Parry and Lusia Parry on the beach at Tamariu, Spain, 1955.

set out tubs of white daisies and fuchsias, and dined by candle light nearly every evening at a small bamboo table under the bathroom built out on two iron columns, long before anyone had ever been to Spain and learned to call a yard a patio.

"Power Without Glory" closed at the end of May due to a lack of star names on the canopy and the excessive competition from the energetic Americans across the street in "Oklahoma". But I was not immediately worried, nor even sad. Everyone was moving on into Coward's new play, and I had my Contract. At the end of June the retainer money ceased and my salary began right away. I was to receive the unheard-of sum of three thousand pounds a year, with yearly options on their side to renew.

I bumped up the housekeeping, paid five pounds for an enormous 1938 Hepplewhite-style H.M.V. cabinet gramophone, with doors and lid, and decided to have a house warming party to show everything off. Including myself.

Lusia came, my catalyst from the Savoy; Freddy came, Forwood came, Chloe Gibson and all the cast came; Mr Daubeny even arrived, with a bottle of whisky and one of Vodka ("Gin is quite démodé, only sailors and servants drink it") which helped to swell the modest delights on my bar (Pimms No. 1, Pale Ale, and a bottle of Madeira from the wine shop at the corner). I wasn't that rich. Yet. My parents came from Sussex, and Elizabeth came with George from the RAF. And a bright-eyed, slender little woman came who looked rather like a blackbird with a hat and veil. Her name was Olive Dodds, the Contract Artists' Representative at Rank. My first real Official. This was the woman who was to push me, or steer me, whichever needed doing, through the Paradise-Hell of the Cinema Jungle. She it would be who would part the thorns and brambles and strangling vines, suggest new tracks, new directions, when to move, when to lie low. She would bring me to the very brink of chasms and then dare me not to jump; to catch me on the other side, breathless.

She raised her glass of Madeira, lifted her veil, and looked around the room with its family portraits from the junk shops, bowls of flowers, worn Persian rugs, and drank to my success.

"Not what I imagined; not a Film Star's House."

"A criticism?"

"No. A comment only. Meant kindly."

"What did you expect?"

"Oh ... off white ... chromium ... stripped pine ... a Utrillo reproduction ... Peter Jonesey."

"Well, it isn't And I'm not a film star . . ."

"Yet. I'm rather afraid that you soon might be." She cocked her blackbird head smiling gently. "I wonder if you'll like it?"

"Won't be for ages."

"You've got your name above the title on your first film. Technically you exist as a Star, my dear. Very good luck." She lifted her glass and sipped gently.

"Sounds like a threat."

"Another comment. That's all. Some people take to it like a drunk to drink, with much the same results." She fumbled for a cigarette, I lit it for her, she blew smoke into a steady high column. "Some others get hopelessly lost. It is not easy. Let me know if I can help. That's what I'm there for. I'm called The Shoulder. For weeping on."

★   ★   ★

Forwood arrived one morning for coffee and said that the lease was running out on his Mews Cottage and that he was going off on Tour for four months and had nowhere to store his bits and pieces. Nan instantly offered him the top front room with the bulging wall for a pound a week, storage rate, and a few days later he moved in his Medici print of the Amaryllis, his grandmother's petit point chair, books and boxes, and a set of silver forks and spoons which Nan shoved into the kitchen. My brother Gareth, picked to play my "son" in "Esther Waters" and presently at a loose end, moved into the small back bedroom next to it. I bought a second-hand Sunbeam Talbot, gold, with a drop-head, and acquired a chauffeur, since I would not drive, called Bond, ex-Coldstream Guards, very tall, very fast, from an ex-Serviceman's agency. My household, including Rose of the gull-like voice, was complete, and No. 44 was bursting at its seams. I was flying. Without wings.

Giddily, like a run-amok balloon, I sailed and swirled happily into the void, no pilot in my gondola, all tie-lines severed, the sand bags jettisoned, filled only with hot air and the false, delirious, sense of freedom. Up I flew into a sky so dark with storms and dangers, so fraught with stresses, rumbles of distant thunder and silent flashes of lethal lightning that anyone, but myself, would have had the wit to turn back, land safely and enter a Closed Order.

But that was not my style. My adventure had begun and I really rather liked it all. There was one gentle, worrying doubt, however. Just one. Who the hell was I? More important still, what was I? Like people of an immigrant race, I was searching for my identity, although I was not at all sure what I'd do with it when, if, I found it.

So who was I suddenly? I had known, to be sure, who I had been—the brave little Captain, the hopeful novice actor—but now there was a vast vacuum and in spite of a house, a car, all my family and possessions such as they were, I belonged nowhere. Unproven, except for one modest performance in a failed play, as an actor, and worse still, in the brand new life which I had entered, quite unproven as a man.

Old friends, such as I had, began to fall away. This is something one has to get used to: they leave you far quicker than you leave them. They go because you have moved ahead and they feel, usually correctly, that they are not able to keep up. As it happened I had very few old friends. Some, like Forwood, like Lusia, who had known me for many years, stayed close, because they understood the way the journey was going, and were unsurprised; but most of the others drifted away, even Vida. Uncomfortable in my new-found riches, embarrassed by my sudden new classification, so far completely undeserved, as a Film Star, they left me to get on with my new inheritance. The trouble was that I had no friends there either.

The people I had to mix with now were the established ones—they all were film stars—but they were proven. Their conversations were too hard for me to follow: I knew almost nothing of what they discussed. Having no experience of their world I desperately sought to establish myself in their eyes as someone they were sure to find interesting, delightful, clever and sophisticated. But I had no possible way of doing this except to chatter away about my war. The only thing I knew anything at all about —and no one in the world wanted to hear my stories and sagas and bragging. The war was over, the war was dead, and glazed eyes greeted my desperate efforts at self-assertion. Or was it only re-assertion? I can't be sure. But I knew that I bored them witless, and in desperation, and in fear, I started to drink too much, hoping that this would give me courage when all it gave me was a blinding hangover every morning and an over-exaggerating tongue the night before. I should have sat quietly, humbly, patiently, listening to them—they had something to teach me had I cared. Instead I beat about wildly in the seas of terror, and struck out like a drowning man at everyone who tried to come to my rescue. Including poor Nan, who was unmercifully clobbered simply because I felt I loved her well enough to do so.

A grave, and cruel, mistake.

Insecurity, that overworked word, swamped me. And swamped the new friends who leant backwards to make allowances and gave unheeded advice, which I desperately needed, and who finally moved away as determinedly as the old friends. I was very much alone for a great deal of the time. Which gave me, between beers, a good deal to think about. For thankfully, I did know that I was behaving appallingly, and I did know why. I just couldn't correct . . . or connect.

In the Studios, unable to join the top echelon, because of my own limitations, I graduated downwards in scale and made friends among the rag-tag-and-bobtail of the profession. People who would listen to my endless bleating for the sake of a double gin in the bar, or who would come to supper simply for a free meal and a shrewd feeling that they were being patronised, which most of them were.

At these suppers, which Nan prepared devotedly and constantly, after a long day's work at the office and at which she played an uncomfortable role as hostess, I happily played the role of host to my Court of small-part actors, extras, fifth-string hairdressers' assistants and noisy girls from the Publicity Pool at the Studio. I enjoyed their flattery, inaccurate gossip, false deference, and above all delighted in the respectful silences in which they patiently listened to my wild, improbable, theories about a profession of which I knew absolutely nothing. It's just that they made me feel Big. I laid down the law, in my own house, and all my trite little witticisms, if that's what they were, received bright laughter and heavy slaps on the back as someone reached again for the Vodka. Only Nan was distressed. And she did her best not to show it. Tight-lipped, but incredibly polite and charming, she served the food and drink and sought for some level of conversation in which she could safely join, in the intellectual desert of my drawing room on the second floor.

Her forced laughter, her worried eyes, her ill-concealed concern for me irritated constantly, and it was at those moments between us that I would start off on my Bore War and invent, and decorate, to astonish and gain support from my Court. My immodesty horrified her; and although I did, with little grace, assist her in the kitchen later with the washing-up, we hardly ever spoke, and indeed spoke less and less, for I would brook not the slightest criticism of my new friends. I needed their sycophancy and fed on it for my courage. And she knew only too well how dangerous this would be. I resented her wisdom, her cautions, and put it all aside furiously. I had been Small for too long, I thought. I enjoyed being Big.

So they fawned on me for my pathetic favours, borrowed money easily, invited me to grubby drinking clubs to which I went eagerly (anything now was better than sitting at 44 with the evening paper and Nan cooking a pilaff in the area), and all the time I knew that I was going the wrong way about things and desperately sought some form of balance. Even Freddy really couldn't help—he gave advice which was so sober that I immediately, and foolishly, rejected it—and Nan knew nothing of my profession, or how it worked or what it demanded. Her chief concern was that I should be happy, well fed, cosseted, loved and that she should be proud of me. Which she, blindingly, was.

Shyness has crippled me all my life; now coupled with a quite desperate desire to prove myself in my new profession, impatient for the results, I developed a cold arrogance to protect myself from the world of which I was now a part, but not truly an accepted Member. The worst, and most sickening part of each day at Pinewood was the lunch hour. I knew no one well enough to eat with. I had no set table. Like a new boy at school I sat miserably in my dressing room reading the script and not eating, or forced myself to go to the bar, which meant running the gauntlet of the great restaurant beyond which lay the bar itself and Eadie in shiny black satin who smiled at me and always talked about something. But in order to make this voyage I had to go blind and deaf and walk, like a robot, swiftly through the chattering, crowded tables, looking neither right nor left, eyes fixed in desperation on the wooden door behind which lay a temporary salvation to loneliness, with Eadie.

This caused concern among the diners. One day I was summoned by telephone to present myself at Earl St John's office at twelve-thirty. He was genial, quiet, polite. Olive Dodds was also present. Silent. My first encounter, since the days in South Street, with my Headmaster. He handed me a note wordlessly. It was a mild complaint, suggesting that perhaps Mr Bogarde might be asked not to walk through the restaurant each day as if he owned it. It was signed David Lean.

My mouth was dry, my hand shook. I apologised to Earl St John and Mrs Dodds and stayed alone in my room from then on. Until I found a way to get to the Bar through the gardens . . . which saved running the gauntlet.

One day there was a gentle knocking at my door. Two shining faces, the Attenboroughs. She with a white halo hat, smiling brightly, clutching a little purse. He with the alert, boyish smile, eager eyes, brimming confidence and infectious zeal of someone who had just seen a vision. For a blinding moment I thought that they might have been collecting for the Salvation Army.

"Hello! Just wondered if you were on your own; or simply not eating? This is Sheila, my wife. If you are on your own we just wondered if you'd like to lunch with us? The first couple of weeks are awful; like a new school. I mean if you need any help, want to know the teachers' names, where the class rooms are, that sort of thing, we'd be delighted to help you. Or just give you lunch?"

Their kindness winded me, their thoughtfulness nearly un-manned me, it was so completely unexpected and I have cherished it always. But it was, of necessity, an oasis only. I couldn't presume on them every day, and saw to it that I did not.

One evening Forwood came to dinner with his wife, Glynis. Although they had mutually agreed by this time on a full separation after all, they were still extremely fond of each other. Nan was tremendously excited and made a splendid meal. I bought two bottles of Hock, and we lit candles. But their visit was, as it happened, not entirely social. They came to instruct, to correct, to help. I sat frozen with shock at their gentle, considered, constructive advice. I was behaving badly, they both knew why and sympathised, but I had to pull myself together pretty soon or disaster lay ahead. "You talk too much, you exaggerate con-stantly, you are boring, rude and self-opinionated," said Glynis flatly. "And people don't like that kind of behaviour in this profession. You haven't done a single thing yet and yet you behave as if you knew it all and had nothing to learn. A little humility wouldn't be a bad thing at all. You are supposed to be a professional, try and behave like one."

Shattered by the truth, unable to defend it, I heaved an empty Hock bottle through the enormous aquarium full of tropical fish which stood at the end of the room. Cascades of water and weed, rocks and fish shot across the floor. Mixed with my uncontrollable wine-and-anger tears. They left shortly afterwards, picking their way through the wreckage of the fish tank and the shards of my ego.

Nan came clanking up the narrow staircase wearily with the buckets.

*   *   *

"What I can't understand," said Forwood a few days after this sorry episode, "is why you just don't be yourself Why this sudden determination to emulate Genghis Khan, for God's sake? It's a good role. I agree, but you aren't ready to play it yet . . . by a long chalk."

"I don't know who 'myself' is . . . I did once . . . you know that . . . but now it's got all muddled, and anyway being 'myself' in this business won't do. They want more than that."

"A lot of self-pitying twaddle. If you knew who you were once you can be it again. It got you through twenty-six years perfectly well. You seem to be going through a male menopause or something."

Glynis and he started work on me as if I were an unmade bed, stripped me down to the box-springs, turned the mattress, aired the blankets and, with my unconfident, but anxious, assistance, we started to put it all back together again. Not a moment too soon. Under their wise guidance, calm advice, among their own carefully-selected friends, who to my hidden surprise neither patronised nor ignored me, I began to regain the confidence within myself which I had somehow or other lost along the line. It had all been a case of too much too soon and not being able to carry corn.

Work started on poor "Esther Waters" proper, just after this, and that too helped to restore a sense of balance. I found that being myself, whatever that was, worked far better. I did my best to be pleasant, polite, humble and above all, with Glynis's terrible, and accurate, warning ringing constantly at the back of my mind, professional. Life became a good deal happier. At least I was just being me. And me seemed to be all right; if dull. I applied myself assiduously to the job in hand. Indeed I had to, for no one else was applying me. On the first morning of shooting on my first Epic, thirty years ago, I timidly (being myself) asked Mr Dalrymple, the director and my discoverer, what, exactly, I should do. I had never really seen a film camera before, apart from a few brief moments for make-up and costume tests in which no histrionics whatever were required on my part. Mr Dalrymple looked rather startled, and pushing his glasses high up on his nose, he said, very politely indeed: "My dear boy! I don't know. I'm the director, you're supposed to be the actor," leaving me nothing else to do but whistle hopelessly as I groped about for a lead line. It was the first time that I would hear this, but not the last. So, like the swimming baths at Maidstone, I held my nose and jumped, hoping that someone, or something, down in the dark water would come to my salvation.

It was fortunate indeed for me that after "Esther Waters" I was quickly bundled into another film, and then another, leaving me no time to panic and ensuring that if the first was a disaster, which it was, there would be a second and third chance coming up. Which there was. And Rank picked up the option after the first year, increased, very modestly, the salary, and hustled me off again on a second round. It says a great deal for their patience and belief in their investment. Totally miscast in "Waters" and lacking any screen personality whatsoever, I did not, as they hoped, come up to expectations. But by the time that this was discovered I had already played a slightly neurotic pianist in a Maugham short story, and was heavily involved in a love affair with a motor cycle for my role as a Speedway Rider. Which was nearly as dotty as anything I have ever been asked to do in the cinema. And that's saying something. I, of all people, with my horror of mechanics, machines and speed, was engaged to play the Speedway Champion of Europe. Or something. The director, standing beside a quite enormous copper and chromium bike, told me softly that he would like me to take it home, stand it in my bedroom, and love it as I would a woman.

I would have been happier with a ten foot boa-constrictor, and could have offered it far more love and affection than this harsh, gleaming, noisy machine on which I was to spend days and nights of agony, fear, and mounting hysteria. Hurtling round and round the track at New Cross Stadium, being towed by a very fast camera car, was as near as I had been to sudden death since the freedom struggles in Java. However, we got through all in one piece and the disaster of "Esther Waters" ebbed away; I was over the first hurdle and I was beginning to enjoy myself. But it had taken time, and toll.

Nan was not enjoying herself. In this new development of my life pattern, I gradually and naturally grew into a new world, and steadily away from my life with Nan.

I rose at five-thirty every morning and arrived back at 44 well after seven p.m. While I had spent the day with amusing, interesting people, enjoying very much my new-found confidence, and starting a mild flirtation with myself on the Studio Floor which was to last me all my life and become one of the great-love-stories-of-our-time as far as I was concerned, poor Nan, slogging away in a dullish office, coping with meals, the house, Rose (who now broke things daily), shopping and rations, laundry lists and my friends who came for drinks or supper and almost always ignored her, for she was completely lost in our intensely self-absorbed conversations, found that she was being edged further and further away from the life which had seemed so promising when she first arrived.

One evening I got home a little earlier than usual. I tried to tip-toe past her sitting room (it had reached that stage by now), but she was quickly at the door. Her smile steady.

"Your sherry's poured. I heard the car. Or there's Scotch . . ."

"Not now, I'm whacked. I'll have a bath."

"No. Not yet, please." She had moved into the narrow hall and blocked the way to the stairs.

"Be kind, Pip . . . it's important."

Her room was pretty, floral prints, the Meissen bowls on the mantelshelf, flowers, all her books, Cliff asleep on a chair, drinks on the little sideboard, a fire glowing.

"It's something I've been wanting to say for a long time, and I'm a little shaky, so be patient."

"What is it?"

"Well . . ." she fitted another cigarette into her long, black holder, "well . . . it's not working out, is it? Our arrangement here: it's got into a bit of a mess."

I knew what she meant and what she was going to say. I tried to swerve and avoid confrontation. "Nan! If it's money . . . I mean housekeeping, that sort of thing . . ."

She flushed angrily. "It's not that, Pip, don't be so damned insulting. Money! Hell . . . it's us, our attitude towards each other. Or rather yours to me."

"What have I done?"

"I'm just a housekeeper, aren't I? Nothing more to you. Oh, I know . . ." she waved her hand towards the pretty room, "I know I have all this; and more, I know that. But I also have pride, Pip. It's hateful of me to say so, but I have, and I'm rapidly losing it and I refuse to. There."

We sat silent.

"I know it can't be like it was in India, I know that. Your life has changed so much, and so quickly . . . and it hasn't been easy for you. I've seen how difficult it's been, and how you have managed. But you don't need me any longer."

"Nan! I do."

"You don't, dear. You avoid me as much as you can now; we hardly speak at supper . . . you never come down here for a sherry like the old days. I know that you try to tip-toe past my room, you'd rather be on your own. I do see that, I do understand it, but I can't really take it any longer. I don't fit in with your friends . . . my fault . . . but I can't speak the language, I don't know what half of them are talking about, and it's always the cinema or what you did today, and I don't know what you did today because I wasn't there and you never, ever, ever tell me, do you, Pip? You don't need me because I can't help you, and I can't help you if I don't know how to . . . and if you don't tell me, or even let me share your life; all you really need is a nice comfortable lady for three quid a week, who can cook and wash and tidy things up for you."

"Nan, Nan . . . for Christ's sake don't. It isn't like that at all, you know it."

"It is, dear, and *you* know it. I'm not utterly stupid. I may not know anything about scripts and lights and what the hairdresser said to the make-up man, but I do know, Pip, that I have a life of my own to live, and if I stay here like this for much longer I'll be lost and we will end up hating each other for ever." She smiled gently, and put her hand on my arm to soften the harsh truth of her words.

I was white with shock and shame.

"I wish, Pip dear, that I could say, cheer up, it doesn't matter, but you know that it does. Listen. I tell you what; you have said that you want to get out of London and live in the country . . . be nearer the Studios . . . I think that you should; it would be much wiser and healthier for you, and far less of a strain with that awful journey. But I couldn't come with you. And keep my job in Welbeck Square . . ."

The room lay silent. Cliff suddenly yawned and stretched his legs and dozed off again. I could hear the racing ticking of her little travelling clock on the table by my chair. She lit another cigarette from the butt already in her holder. Her hand shook.

"So I think that's what we should do." She pressed the old butt into her glass ash-tray.

"I don't honestly know what to say . . ."

"There is nothing you need say. We have had a marvellous time together, it was exciting and fun, really it was. No regrets. But we must be very grown up and sensible and not spoil what was so good. Odd, isn't it? When one gets to these moments in life they always sound like Marie Corelli. Sorry. I'll stay on, of course, if you want me to, until you find something out of town. It would be difficult for you to break in a servant at the moment; I know the ropes and you're terribly busy. As soon as you do, give me a bit of warning so that I can get packed up. I heard of a very nice little flat near Baker Street. There is no hurry. I was just poking about, you know, quite a lot of places I can get. And I'd take Cliff, if you wouldn't mind. He's got terribly fond of me. Used to me. He'd miss his mother, wouldn't he then?" She pulled him on to her lap and buried her face in his fur.

★   ★   ★

It was a modest sign-board in the front garden of an ordinary grey-brick villa, no different at all from its Victorian neighbours on the Green. Ealing Studios. A ragged laurel hedge and, behind the house, scabby turf and three elderly fir trees, beyond them the concrete blocks of the Stages spreading through suburbia.

Ealing, although affiliated to Rank, was regarded with grave suspicion by some of the impeccably tailored members of the Front Office in the Aberconways' house in South Street. They scented anarchy on the Green, distrusted the Young Directors and Producers who they felt sure were certainly all Left if not Communist, and even though the films made a great deal of money they had a Satirical Touch, an Intellectual Flavour, which was disturbing and against all Good Family Entertainment. Indeed I was once told that when the distributors, in a line north of

Oxford, saw the trade mark on the credits, Ealing Films set within a little wreath of leaves, they left the theatre in a drove and headed home. Without making a single booking. They didn't make films which the public wanted to see. So they insisted. And overlooked, conveniently, the fact that somebody somewhere wanted to see them because Ealing was extremely successful, and the cachet of working for them was very important to any actor. This point of view never changed.

However, Basil Dearden, one of the younger and brightest of the new school of directors, had sent for me, and since they, Rank, had no immediate plans to employ my services, I was despatched to the house on the Green.

Basil and I had worked together before the war when I was his rather inept Assistant Stage Manager at the "Q" Theatre.

"You haven't changed much, have you?" Raised eyebrows, cool regard, fiddling with a pencil on his desk.

"No. I should have."

"Yes. It's a pity. You've got a face like a baby's bottom."

"You haven't changed much yourself. Just as bloody rude."

"My trick. They love it."

"Who do?"

"Bloody actors. All so puffed up. Need a kick up the arse."

"Is that what I'm here for?"

"Could be. 'The Blue Lamp'; it's about the Police Force."

"I wouldn't think I was Copper material."

"You aren't. You *could* play the snivelling little killer. Neurotic, conceited, gets the rope in the end."

"That's me."

"That's what I thought."

"Have you seen my film work at all?"

"No. And I'm told that I am deeply enriched by that lack of experience."

"Then why send for me?"

"Liked the play you did at the New Lindsey . . . not bad. Do you think you could do something like that? Can you keep it up, I mean? Or was it just a one off?"

"If I tried very hard."

"You'd bloody well have to."

"Would you help me?"

"Not much. Why?"

"I don't really know how to act for the cinema."

"That has been made abundantly clear, I gather."

"So I'd need help, wouldn't I?"

"If you get the part."

"If I get the part. How do you do it . . . acting for the cinema?"

"You do the same as you do on a stage, for God's sake. Nothing different. It's a lot of bilge that you have to have a different technique for the cinema. Bilge. It's all acting. Do what you'd do in the theatre and I'll pull you down if you go over the top. All this nonsense about cinema technique! Bilge. People are trying to invent a myth. Act. It's simple. If you can."

It was the first time anyone had ever told me what to do: suddenly doors and windows opened all about me. Light came in.

He pushed a script towards me.

"The role is Tom Riley."

"Do you want me to do it?"

"I need a weedy type . . . and you're a Contract Artist. Rank insists that we use some of you from time to time, it's blackmail. So I haven't much choice, have I? Always on our necks to use someone out of their ruddy Charm School."

"I'm not from their Charm School."

"That," said Dearden rising and hitching up his pants with an ill-suppressed yawn, "is quite self-evident."

★   ★   ★

"The Blue Lamp" became a legend, so to speak, within its own lifetime, providing a welter of spin-offs for years to come in the cinema and, later, in television. The Documentary Police Movie. The first of its kind in England. It also altered, for all time, my professional life. Dearden pointed me in the right direction with his illuminating, over-simplified, approach to the camera. It was the first time I came near to giving a cinema performance in any kind of depth: I think it had some light and shade, whereas the work which had gone before was cardboard and one dimensional. I have never been an extrovert actor, always an introvert; instinctive rather than histrionic, and in this semi-documentary method of working I discovered, to my amazement and lasting delight, that the camera actually photographed the mind process however hesitant it was, however awkward. It had never, of course, occurred to me before, since I had very little mind of my own; but the people I played had minds, of some sort or another, and I became completely absorbed in trying to find those minds and offer them up to the camera. I was never to be satisfied again with a one-dimension performance. And neither was the camera, which now became the centre of my whole endeavour.

If my professional life had taken a turn for the better, the same could not be said of my personal life, which limped on unhappily and awkwardly, ever since Nan had taken up frail courage to throw down her gauntlet. The gentle challenge had to be answered. I was not very well equipped to reply. I tried a new approach to our existence—driving out on picnics at the weekends in the forlorn hope that a day spent by a river, in a wood, or on a hill, would break the tensions of life at 44. Petrol rationing was still in force, and our trips were of necessity limited. And in any case they didn't work; returning to the shadows of Chester Row with a bunch of cowslips, or aching legs from a climb over Ivinghoe Beacon, did almost nothing to conceal the lightly hidden distresses and frustrations which lay beneath our apparently happy exteriors like trip wires in a mine-field. I was trapped. She was trapped. I knew that I had to get out, away from London and away from the unhappy atmosphere I had, inadvertently, created. Trying, over-hard, to make her a part of my cinema life, as she called it, failed equally. It was not her world, and in no way possible could she join it. She was a sensible, loving creature, and the mounting pressures and demands of this new life, which took us both by surprise by the rapidity of its assault, overwhelmed her. And myself.

The Indian life we had both shared so happily had all but vanished, never to return. How could it? The people we had been then we no longer were now, and never would be, ever, again. Time had marched on us, catching us unprepared and woefully unarmed. All that remained was a deep bond of mutual respect and affection. Nothing else. And even that was now in danger. So, try to protect it.

"I've found a place in the country, near the Studios. I can move in about September."

We were down in the kitchen, she was preparing supper, her back towards me, at the sink.

"How splendid!" She took a cloth and wiped her hands. "Let's go into the garden. I thought we might eat out this evening, it's so warm . . . the food's cold so nothing will spoil yet. Have you got your glass?"

At the bamboo table under the bathroom, set neatly, we creaked into canvas chairs. The last of the sun slanted through the big limes.

"Where is it, far? A cottage or a castle? I know you."

"It's Forwood's family house actually, Bendrose House, near Amersham. It's empty, up for rent. He can't afford it all on his own, so if his family agrees we could go halves. He wants somewhere for his child, a sort of family base . . . seems a good idea."

She poured herself a gin and tonic. "Of course, there's the child. But it was a 'decent' divorce, wasn't it?"

"Very. They are tremendously fond of each other, just can't live together any longer. You know . . ."

The garden was very still. It trembled as a train rumbled beneath it into Sloane Square Station.

"So he wants somewhere for the boy in the holidays; they are going to share him, it's all very civilised."

"Sounds marvellous all round."

"Pretty big. Large garden. Unfurnished, of course."

"You'll manage. Think of all those lovely auction rooms and second hand shops, you'll be in your element. And you'd go in September?"

"If that's all right for you?"

"Fine for me. I can use my holidays flat hunting. I have my eye on one; a dear little place, quite reasonable, and a tiny bit of garden for Cliff . . . he'd hate a real flat . . . I'm glad you told me."

"Just had to do it, that's all . . ."

"I know."

"And you can come down at weekends. It's big. Masses of room."

"Lovely! And easy from Baker Street; the flat's just a few steps away. It is on the Bakerloo Line, isn't it?"

"Or Marylebone."

"Same thing really."

"So it wouldn't be a complete severance."

"That would be unthinkable! Never that! Of course not . . . I'm much too fond of you. It had to happen like this, you know. I suppose I was always aware it would, deep down. It's just life, as they say, it's all a matter of ins and outs I suppose. It is, isn't it?"

"But this is just a change of route, that's all . . . direction."

"Oh Pip dear!" She laughed gently and touched my knee. "You are a funny one: not awfully good at looking facts in the face, are you . . . still not yet? Well, never mind, just let's call this an entrance; does that feel better?"

She took up her glass and went up the steps to the kitchen; at the top she turned and looked back. "Such a pretty evening, that light in the trees. I had to give up two 'points' for a tiny tin of sardines this morning. Would you believe it? The peace is almost as bad as the war, in little things."

7

THE voyage on which I had embarked with Mr Dalrymple and "Esther Waters" in such light spirits was fraught with grave dangers. None of it, ever, was to be clear sailing, and there were moments indeed at the beginning when it looked as if it would be just a trip round the lighthouse and back to port, or, worse still, that I should be forced to founder with all hands on the hidden reef of economy. Rank was going through a very difficult period financially (and every other way) but I knew nothing of this until Olive Dodds took me quietly aside and said that owing to impossible financial problems they were going to introduce vast cuts in the economy, clear out all the dead-wood, see the wood for the trees, and try to start all over again with a neater, tighter, more manageable and less extravagant formula. To this end all the Contract Artists, to begin with, would be asked to take severe reductions in salary, otherwise, if they chose not to accept, they could annul their contracts and go free. For some, it was leaving prison.

She strongly advised me to take whatever cut was offered without question, since she felt that loyalty to the firm would not go unrecognised in the future, and that they would not forget the gesture. I was unsure. She also shoved me, against my will, into another cloth-cap and raincoat role in a film about the Irish troubles called "The Gentle Gunman". I said that I would certainly accept the cut if she advised it, for she knew a great deal better than I did what was afoot; but that I refused to be on the run yet again in another raincoat part. She was adamant. The film would start just as my Option Period was due, and if I was working, she reasoned, they would be less likely to chuck me out. And chuck me out, she hinted pleasantly, was just what they intended to do at the last Board Meeting. Could I afford that?

No one, as we have seen, was exactly ecstatic to have me from the very beginning; only Mr Dalrymple and she herself had felt any reason to hope that I would one day prove my worth. My record was hardly outstanding, no one was actually lighting candles to me. And worse than that, I had not made them much, if any, profit. My last effort, as she pointed out, a disastrous attempt at light comedy, had been as funny as a baby's coffin and although I argued that it had not been my fault, or my choice (the unhappy director, Val Guest, had wanted William Holden but had been forced to have me, as a Contract Artist, instead), Olive Dodds smiled her soft enigmatic smile and suggested that there were forces at work who really did want me out of the way. If I had the sense to accept her plans I might just possibly be saved from the humiliation. It was up to me.

So I accepted the cut, when it was offered, wielded with an axe rather than a penknife, accepted too the raincoated Irish killer, so that over the dangerous time of the Option Period I was to be found, had anyone so wished, being chased by more Coppers, nightly through the tunnels of Mornington Crescent Underground, and being bawled at by Basil Dearden once again.

Temporarily, at any rate, my skin had been saved by the advice of the one person in the Organisation who believed that I might, with help, one day pull it off.

It was a depressing time. Familiar faces slid away, in all departments, to fitful obscurity or television which, in those early fifties, was scooping up all the left-overs from the film industry and starting to build up a force which would eventually bring us to the brink of ruin. But for the moment the Organisation, having cleared out its dead-wood, found the land clear and open and with a little more money to spend bought the rights to a best seller called "The Cruel Sea". Here I thought, wrongly, was a chance for me to break away from the raincoats and caps and play an Officer and a Gentleman, for there had to be one or both, in a film about the Navy. But there was not the slightest chance. I implored, I begged, I grovelled. I offered to test for any part, even if I didn't get it, just so that I would have the chance to show them that I could speak "proper" and could therefore extend my range. I even offered to work for no money at all. Which didn't move them in the least. They insisted that I was best in working class roles, no one would believe me as a Gentleman, but that there was a nice little cameo, if I was *absolutely* determined on being in their epic, of an Able Bodied Seaman who had a "good little moment in a lifeboat".

Olive Dodds had done as much as possible and could help no more. I refused the Able Bodied Seaman in the lifeboat and went back to my uncertain role of Country Squire at Bendrose; but not for long. Ironically they cheerfully rented me out (they got half the salary) to a small company who offered me the part of a Wing Commander in a film about Bomber Command. He was an upper-class Wing Commander at that; never wore a raincoat and never saw a Copper. "Appointment in London" was the first time that I actually made any kind of impression for good on the screen. The *Daily Mail* suggested that I could act with my skin, *The Graphic* said it was my finest hour, *The Telegraph* welcomed me into the front rank of English screen actors, and *Picturegoer* threw all caution to the wind and hailed me as the foremost young actor on the British screen.

But no one from the Rank Organisation ever went to see it; nor did they make any comment whatsoever. As far as they were concerned I was still Working Class League. It was a crushing blow. It was made all the worse by the deep-seated knowledge, which I had always known but put aside in my usual way, that I had an enemy at court. Earl St John, for all his charm, and he had a great deal, had never been able to overcome the overcoming of his first edict, that I had no future for the cinema, and that I was not cinema material, and he never saw reason to change his mind. A few years ago, shortly before he died, at a party in the South of France at which I was the host, he came across the bustling, noisy restaurant, greeted me warmly, one arm round my shoulder like a loving friend, and said, with the implacable smile and eyes of a baby shark caught in shallow waters, "I said you'd never make it, kid. And you won't."

Whether he was right or wrong is neither here nor there at this particular moment. But I did make it, albeit briefly, with Philip Leacock and "Appointment in London". He, with Dearden, showed me that screen acting was more to do with the head than the left profile or the capped teeth. He made me more aware than any other director up till then that it was the thought which counted more than the looks.

And the fans found me quite acceptable without my raincoat, to such an extent that the mail trebled, a fact which could not possibly have gone unnoticed by the Organisation since it kept tallies on all the mail received by their Artists, but to which they never referred. Of the hundreds of letters which were received in the Fan Mail Department in South Street, only the most apparently private or personal mail was sent on to my home. Among them one day my secretary, Val, found a glossy picture postcard with an Amsterdam postmark. "This is something you'll have to deal with. I can't understand it." Gabled houses reflected in a sluggish canal. On the back the once-familiar printed writing.

"I saw you again at a cinema last night. You were in the RAF. Do you remember the cards? A different uniform, different badges, a bird, and lights everywhere? You see?" It was signed Harri. There was no address.

*　　*　　*

A great deal of my time, during the war, was spent, clenched-buttocked and white-knuckled, flying through German flak in lumbering planes which, as often as not, landed nose down in extremely unsuitable terrain. I never enjoyed these journeys, and was absolutely convinced that flying, for pleasure, or anything else, would not catch on in peace time. A serious miscalculation. So it took a great deal to persuade me back on board to fly all the way to Cyprus to make my first foreign location film. The persuasion was Lewis Milestone, a legendary director whose masterpiece, "All Quiet on the Western Front", stands as one of the ten greatest films ever made. He it was who would direct this film, and I was very happy and proud to be asked to participate. The fact that I had not much cared for the script didn't really worry me, for I felt sure that if Mr Milestone had agreed to direct it then he must also have liked what he read. Another serious miscalculation.

I discovered, far too late to cancel the flight, that he detested what he had read and demanded changes; these were promised, and he read the new material on the flight to Athens. Crossing the tarmac from the London 'plane, we were rather disconcerted to see him shredding the new material into confetti and chucking it over his shoulder into the cool Greek air.

"I don't mind," he said, "people carrying shit about with them in their pockets. What I do mind is that they don't know it's shit." Lewis Milestone was a man of few words; all of them effective.

The film was called "They Who Dare" (it was later dubbed by the Press, "How Dare They", but we weren't to know that for a time). A commando story, based on real events in Crete. There were eight of us in the cast. Eight commando packs, under the instructions of Mr Milestone himself, were packed for us by a combat unit in Malta. They weighed ninety pounds a piece. The first time we all struggled into them we fell flat on our faces before him; Moslems in Mecca. He suggested a week's training in the Troodos mountains, while he got on with the script and we got used to the packs. For some days we crawled, sobbing and moaning, up crags, ledges, gorges, cliffs and along the sheer edges of gaping ravines into which we plummeted, with astonishing regularity, to lie crumpled and groaning among the startled goats. No one was actually killed during these activities, but many of us longed for death as a speedy relief, for we expected every sortie to the mountains to be our last. Mr Milestone (we had by now actually overcome fear of him by fear of our exercises and called him Millie to his face) had a perfectly valid point. You cannot act weight. And neither you can. But actors we were, not commandos; and it is quite hard enough to act without a pack weighing ninety pounds let alone with one dragging you constantly towards oblivion. I pointed out to him that it might be wiser, should we ever start the film, to try and finish it, all in one piece and alive, than to have to abandon it because of a couple of random deaths somewhere towards the middle of things, when the insurance people would make things difficult. So, reluctantly, the packs were lightened to sixty pounds, and although we still careened into endless ravines, apparently for ever, we managed to give the impression, anyway, of a respectable band of brave desperados, tough, rough and bloodied. The only thing we hadn't got was a script.

We never actually got one. A writer was despatched from London to assist, but Millie took a dislike to him almost instantly, set him on a high stool in the middle of his room, and walked slowly round and round him dictating his notes, until the poor man, mesmerised, like the guinea fowl with a fox who makes slow circles round their roosting tree, was overcome by giddiness, slipped from his perch, cracked his skull on the stone floor and was jubilantly returned to London. Millie didn't like being bugged; as he put it quietly in the bar later. If I give the impression that he was a monster I hasten to correct. He was not. And we all worshipped him; he was funny, scathing, hated the Front Office, and was splendidly irreverent about everything. Except his work. Even though we had not much to go on as far as a script was concerned, we all worked together with him, as a great adventure, and did the best we could. And if nothing else, and there wasn't much else alas, we all enjoyed ourselves tremendously.

Anyway—I was back in the Army and consequently in my element.

He was a thick-set, heavy man, in his middle sixties at that time. And he never ever seemed to sit down, even on the roughest terrain or the highest peaks. I bought him a shooting-stick.

He accepted it gravely. His green, Russian eyes flicking about like a lizard's, suspiciously.

"What is it?"

"A shooting-stick."

"What the hell for?"

"For you."

"What do I shoot with it?"

"You sit on it."

His eyes flicked across my face, narrowed. His lips pursed doubtfully.

"This thing! This tin stick! I sit on it?"

"Yes . . . look, it has two little flaps which unfold, like this, makes a seat."

He closed his eyes thoughtfully. "Appreciate the thought. You see the size of my ass? You want this thing to go right through me? Upwards? Head on a pike?"

He used it as a walking stick, and viewed it with dull suspicion all through the work.

After two and a half months shooting we still hadn't really got much idea of an ending for our epic. He knew that I was worried, and took action to comfort me.

"Hell! I didn't have an ending for 'All Quiet' until the last minute. The Studio took the film away from me, said it was too long, too down-beat. They wanted to end it with some damned montage of thousands of marching soldiers singing some damn-fool patriotic song, flags waving, all that crap. Withdrew the money. I was sunk. There was just me and the camera crew left, in a car, coming away from the Studio with the bad news. I have never been so low in my life. A picture, and no ending. Stopped at an intersection. Rain so heavy you just couldn't see out the car. The windscreen wipers squeaking across the glass, back-wards and forwards, they made a funny noise. It seemed to me like Schmetterling, Schmetterling, that's the German for butter-fly . . . Schmetterling, Schmetterling, and suddenly I got it! I got the end. We turned right round and went to a butterfly farm, bought boxes of them. Found a building lot just off Sunset, in all the rain. No lights, so we used the headlamps of the car, turned them on a muddy bit of land, let the butterflies go . . . most of them flew away, but one little fellow, he just settled happily in the warmth of the lamps, flitting his wings. I reached out my hand, very gently to take him, and then he was gone. And that was the last shot of 'All Quiet on the Western Front'. Don't worry," he grinned and thumped my knee with affection, "we'll get an ending."

He made a cut of his version of the film and flew off to America; the producer made his cut and between the two of them we were a catastrophe. But it had been great fun and marvellous experience. And Millie taught me one of the greatest lessons to be learned in the cinema. "You can make a good script bad; but you can't ever make a bad script good. Never forget that." I was to be constantly reminded of his words for years to come. It is a lesson very few have bothered to remember.

*   *   *

While we were struggling to find an ending for a poor script in Cyprus, Miss Betty Box, on a long and tiring journey from Scotland, left her train for a few minutes at Crewe to purchase some reading matter, magazines and a slim book, to while away the remainder of the trip to Euston. She was quite unaware that this simple action was to switch the points, so to speak, not only on her own life, but on mine and the Miller's and his men as well. By the time she had reached London she had made up her mind to buy the rights of the book, and being the most far-sighted producer in the Rank Organisation at the time, did so, had a script roughed out, and sent it to me to see if I would like to play the young student. It was called "A Doctor in the House".

I was not, I remember, immediately impressed. It all seemed a bit light, the role a bit dim-witted, and every other character had funnier things to say and do. I was to be the simple Juvenile. Forwood, by now disenchanted with acting himself, although very successful, had generously renounced his own career and agreed to become my Personal Manager since I could now no longer handle my own affairs alone. He was in complete disagreement with me; here was a comedy, for the first time, which could well be an important success and lead me away from spivs and service heroes to which I was obviously becoming addicted.

He urged me to accept the offer immediately before it went to someone else. Impressed by his seriousness I telephoned Miss Box and said yes. But Miss Box, in her low and pleasant voice, confessed that there was, unfortunately, a hidden snag. Mr St John, she explained gently, was strongly opposed to her choice of myself for the part. He didn't think that I could play light comedy; my metier, he said, was action stuff. I did not have the necessary charm or lightness, and he reminded her that my last effort at comedy, at his own instigation, had been a complete and total catastrophe for all concerned; especially myself. It would be disastrous to play me in such a part.

Miss Box, happily for me and my future, disagreed with him. She had a hunch it would work. So fortunately did her director, Ralph Thomas, and together they fought a quiet battle to get me, and won. There is no question in my mind whatsoever that if they had not taken this courageous stand I should never have had a career in the cinema at all; it was the absolute turning point, and by their action they secured me in my profession. A debt it is impossible to repay.

It was one of the happiest times I have ever spent in a Studio, made all the happier when, one morning, I was taken in a great bear-hug from behind and a well-remembered voice said in my ear, "Caught you up at last!" Kenneth More. It had taken six years from the tatty dressing room in the New Lindsey Theatre to this splendid moment, made all the pleasanter eventually when he stole the picture from under all our noses. As Doctor Simon Sparrow I did surprisingly well. The film was a phenomenal success at the box office and Betty and Ralph immediately started planning sequels. Their hunch, and Olive Dodds's astute strategy, had paid off. It seemed that, at last, things were going to be all right for a time. I had proved my worth, if only modestly, and the dreaded yearly option could, more or less, be set aside. An immensely encouraging feeling, since my salary would increase comfortably each year. It was possible that I might even make the Seven Year Stretch.

No one, however, could relax, and no one did. I decided that it was perhaps now the moment for me to have for the first time in my life, a real bought-and-paid-for house of my own. I had my eye on one, not very far away, which was empty and for sale. However, it would of course mean leaving Bendrose.

The Bendrose days were the happiest; although there were to

be grander houses, greater riches, finer views, it is always to Bendrose that I look with nostalgia and happiness.

Perhaps it was because we were all so much younger then; because the calm of the countryside, after the depressed austerity of London, healed so well, or just perhaps it was because we were all content with so much less after the long strain of the war years so recently over, that even a shabby, still-rationed peace was better than anything which had gone before.

Bendrose House stood in three hundred acres of corn and mangolds surrounded by a vast cherry orchard. The estate belonged to the Forwoods, and they allowed me to rent the house and gardens at a very modest yearly rental.

Hardly to the delight and relief of the Studio Publicity Department who had already dubbed me as being uncooperative; along with the small head and the long legs and small trunk so despaired of by Earl St John, I also refused to play the game by attending premieres, escorting resting-actresses to night clubs, buying diamonds, fast cars, or fighting with waiters; I didn't even try to crash Society (a popular pastime then) by hobnobbing with minor Royalty, playing polo at Cowdray or trying to dance with Princess Margaret at Charity Balls. All the Publicity Department could scrape together was a sorry list of trivia, assembled by a harassed lady in a feathered hat one day, which stated, among other things, that I made my own lampshades, bred tropical fish, and was descended on my father's side from Anne of Cleves. Even I could see that this was hardly good news. Therefore the move from the shabby canyon of Chester Row to the elysian fields of Amersham Common was pounced upon with alacrity. I could now be given a Country Background; rolling fields, sunsets, a man of the earth, brooding solitude in the sombre plough of the Home Counties. A kind of anaemic Heathcliff. They dubbed me Lord of the Manor and only retracted a little when it was pointed out that Bendrose was not a manor nor mine, and substituted Country Squire, which anyway sounded better in a utilitarian, democratic, Socialist Britain. I was deeply relieved and brooded all over the place; anything so long as I was not forced into a black tie and the Orchid Room nightly, with a twenty pound bottle of champagne. I made the image stick.

It was not the most comfortable of houses—filled with icy draughts, twisting passages, floors on all levels and forests of dark-stained beams. The heart of the house, a modest sixteenth century cottage, stood smothered in a splendid muddle of Edwardian-Tudor extensions which ran in all directions. Forwood's grandfather, who had made it the family house, bought most of his material from builders' yards and the demolition of old houses throughout the county. Latticed windows nudged cheerfully at Georgian; four-poster beds were dismantled, cut to pieces, and formed ornate, if bewildering, fireplaces; walls were panelled with yards of cheap three-ply wood, bought in bulk from aeroplane factories after the First World War; and the kitchens lay miles from the dining room so that the food arrived frozen or spilled, since there were two floor levels to endure before arriving at the dining hatch, which fell down and jammed one's fingers every time it was raised to admit the chilling dishes. Forwood Senior bought and built expressively, and economically. One day at luncheon his wife had asked mildly what it could be she saw coming up the drive, and he replied that it was the railway station. It was. Shortly afterwards Chalfont and Latimer Station was re-erected opposite the dairy to house the hay and mangolds, proving to be a very economical barn.

On my arrival the house was empty and cobwebby, shabby, but loving, and with a van load of furniture which my father gave me from our old house in Sussex (which had been lying in store all the war) plus the bits and pieces I had got from junk shops for Chester Row, carpets and curtains bought at local village auctions, the house started to thrive again, and although it was always to be happily untidy and unplanned, it very soon became a home once more.

Bond, my driver, came from London to be odd job and handy man and to drive me to the Studios; Mr and Mrs Wally, from the Farm, came in daily, she to "do" and he to help untangle the wilderness of the gardens; and I sought and obtained a man-servant. Cook General was what I had asked for and is what I was told I had got when Catchpole arrived with his suitcase and a head of tight red wavy hair. He spent all his working time scrubbing out the kitchen and cooking cod steaks in heavy curry sauce. I don't think he knew anything else. His days off were spent entirely at the Windmill Theatre, from the first show till the last, and when he left, as leave he finally did, thankfully, glossy photographs of ladies arrived from time to time with polite letters regretting that, "We have no photographs of Valerie with Doves, but thought you might like to have these of

Clarice with Balloons." I couldn't send them on to him since he had left in a huff without a forwarding address.

Then came Philpot with a long record in the Merchant Navy, spick and span, and shipshape. He was carrying *The Economist* when he arrived for his first interview, so perhaps I should have been warned. Floors became decks, the twisting staircase companionways, the kitchen the galley, and he served meals, wearing a neat white apron and a Merchant Navy jacket. The meals themselves consisted mostly of corned beef in various disguises, mashed potatoes, and a rather ugly little pudding with a pink cherry on top. For the first week I let it pass, believing that I should soon wean him away from ship fare; even though rationing was still with us the diet could, I felt, be varied just a little.

Five days after he arrived I went to visit my parents, telling him to settle in and have a good clean up. Which he did. Following my instructions to the letter. On my return to Bendrose not a light shone, not a door was locked, no hens had been fed, and my open wardrobe doors revealed a softly swinging row of empty coat hangers. When they finally arrested him, in one of my suits coming down the steps of St Pancras Station, it was disheartening to discover that the nearest he had ever been to the sea, or a ship, was the Mersey ferry, and that he had spent most of his life in clink for pinching anything from a roll of linoleum to a hurricane lamp.

When I offered, rather stupidly, to stand bail for him he begged me, as one ex-serviceman to another, not to.

"I know you're a good Officer, could smell it as soon as I came aboard, but I'll only do it again, you see. It's my kick. Can't seem to get off it." He also added, confidentially in the cell at Chesham Police Station, that he had done a shocking deal on my Rolleiflex, my dinner jacket didn't fit him, or anyone else he knew, but that he had made a tidy bit on the silver lighters and the Chelsea figures.

Loyalty for my ex-service comrades gently faded, and indeed, need never have been applied in this particular instance. So I left Philpot to the Law and sought a well-experienced Lady Cook General. Mrs Walters sped down on winged feet, slim, trim, no nonsense, late sixties, umbrella and, instead of *The Economist* a thin red volume entitled *Get to Know Jesus*.

She said that she had very good references, and I said that I had no intention of being converted to anything. With a hearty laugh she said that she was just a seeker herself and that the only thing she wouldn't brook was women pottering in and out of her kitchen. When I assured her that she would be perfectly safe, she agreed to give me a try and said that the fee I was offering was too high, she could manage on two pounds less, and that I was too extravagant by far. We made a deal, on condition that there was something to help her with the trays. "I'm not about to carry trays from that kitchen, half a mile to the dining room, *that* I can tell you. Not at my age. You get me a nice little trolley with wheels and we'll all be as right as rain."

For weeks to come every meal was preceded by the rumbling of tumbrils; and the shattering of falling china. Her concern for my extravagance had touched me deeply, until it became apparent that it also applied to her cooking. Dead whiting we had; tails stuffed into glazed-eyed heads, smothered in sticky white sauce and buried, comfortingly, in wreaths of parsley; Lancashire hot pot, more pot than hot, shards of grey meat, swollen kidney, carrots, bullet-hard slices of blue potatoes swimming in a lake of thin gruel. One evening, returning late and hungry from London with Forwood and an old friend of his, Kay Young, she said all she could manage at that time of an evening was an egg. I lost my temper and my head and threw every tin I could lay hands upon in the larder at her. She ducked nimbly for ten minutes, while I shattered every plate and cup and saucer on the dresser, before which she was inconveniently standing.

After a glass of champagne, which she accepted cheerfully, we agreed that perhaps my irregular hours, and moods, might be tiresome for her and she left on a Green Line Bus for another post with a retired Colonel in Aylesbury.

A week later, a sullen couple of French people arrived from Lyons. They wore plimsolls, carried all their belongings in two paper bags, and took possession of the kitchen and the house which they filled with the just-remembered scents of garlic, thyme, and olive oil. Sullen they were, but cook and work they did. And Bendrose started to heave itself out of a rut and to run smoothly.

And so with excellent food at last, log fires, acres of fields in which to wander with the dogs, and assorted cats even, faded chintzes and a well-stocked drink-table, Bendrose was ready to accept its guests who came down every week-end and gave the place the feeling of a pleasant, if shabby, well-run boarding house.

We were always a mixed group; the steadies providing the solid background; these were the friends who had been summoned by Glynis and Forwood in the days of hysteria and who provided a safe and affectionate security without which I know that I could not have survived. Irene Howard, Kay Young, Michael Wilding, Jean Simmons, Michael Gough and his wife Anne Leon, Margaret Leighton and Olive Dodds; and they in turn brought other people who brought other people, and Bendrose Sundays became established.

Jessie Matthews did high kicks in the Oak Room; Gene Kelly danced up and down the staircase of an unfinished council house on a housing estate in nearby Bell Lane; Noël Coward asked me if I would like to revive his play "The Vortex"; Elizabeth Taylor, a constantly hungry eighteen, consumed endless portions of Christmas pudding; Ava Gardner warmed her naked feet against the dogs, all of them sprawled together before the big fireplace; and Forwood brought Kay Kendall down to tea and supper one Friday evening.

"I know you aren't mad on her; she can seem rather grand, but she really is lovely, and funny, and you'd like her and she is not grand at all. It's just her manner, she's a bit unconfident really."

I had met Miss Kendall once at the Studios and had been frightened out of my wits by her apparently Royal Manner, but as Forwood had worked with her on a film, and assured me that she was lovely I took his advice, and let her come.

She didn't seem to need confidence at all; she arrived dressed elegantly in the honey colours which she favoured and indeed she seemed as faintly condescending as before, patronising, and possessing the disdain of a Lama. It didn't really take long to discover that this was all a cover for an extremely soft centre. Forwood was right, as usual, but it was not immediately apparent.

After we had all had tea and done the walk round the gardens she thoughtfully settled herself into a deck chair and, nodding gentle approval all round, sipped her large gin and tonic. She decided to drop her Royal Manner for the role of Dorothy Adorable; which she played sickeningly well.

"What a sweet little housey pousey you have! Do you do it all yourself? So clever . . . such a lot of work . . . I've got a teeny weeny little flat in horrid London, too awful, and no dear little garden like this." (There were four acres.)

"I'm a bit square, you know. Country born and bred."

"I adore the country. So real."

"Yes . . ."

"How many rooms do you have here?"

"About, um, fifteen I think."

"Bedrooms I mean?" She was smiling sweetly.

"Eight."

"Oh poor little me . . ." Deep sighs.

"Only one bathroom though."

"That wouldn't matter." Wistful look.

"Frightfully cold in the winter, full of draughts . . ."

"But so near the Studios . . . those ghastly morning journeys . . . Ohhh . . ." More sighs.

"Twenty minutes about."

"Perfect." Eyes closing.

"And dreadfully quiet."

"I adore quiet." Eyes closed dreamily.

"So do I."

"I wouldn't utter!" Eyebrows arched like half hoops, finger to lips.

"Smelly from the farm though; cows, pigs, manure . . ."

"I have no sense of taste or smell."

"None?"

"None at all. A car crash." Suddenly she grabbed her nose and pulled it upwards like a wild Pinocchio. "This is all McIndoe; he only had two sorts of noses in those days, this and one other; squatter. I chose this. I look like a clown in a fright-wig . . . God knows why Rank ever signed me, they can't shoot my profile."

"But can't you taste anything at all?"

"Nothing, wifey. Someone gave me a red chilli last week somewhere . . ."

"But you tasted that?"

"Just. Divine."

"I don't believe you."

She thrust my finger into her face.

"Wheeee! You see? No bones, all cartilage. I'm Old Mother Riley in drag."

"He *is* in drag."

"Well, you know . . . in or out, oh dear, oh dear, what's to become of me, wifey?"

We sat there for a moment looking at each other seriously, and suddenly we burst into laughter, she laughed until the tears ran down her boneless face, and made her nose run which she wiped with the back of her hand helplessly.

"Oh dear! Poor me. I'm a ruin, a ruin . . . I need someone to look after me, wifey!"

Later, as the long evening shadows crept across the lawns, I took her round the farm to see the pigs, pick some raspberries and watch the dairy being hosed and scrubbed after milking. She got her feet wet and took off her shoes to plod cheerfully after me through the vegetables and down among the hens and ducks. She found it all "ravishing", and when we got back to the others sitting about on the terrace with their drinks, she announced that it was just what she had been looking for, and what on earth could I do with a huge house and all those rooms while she had a miserable little flat which made her depressed and lonely. Surely I could spare a teeny weeny bit of the house just for her at weekends? She'd be no trouble, she would knit a lot and do any mending, and help out with the drinks as a form of rent.

It was a bloody good act.

She moved into the double front bedroom the following Friday, with a bundle of old country clothes, her bottles of "ox blood for her anaemia", and a small white rug for the side of her bed. She stayed, on and off, for about five years. There had never been a happier decision ever made. And it was entirely her own. Kate always made her own decisions, I was to discover. That was Bendrose.

Beel House stood in the centre of a fifty-acre ring fence. Tudor by origin it now wore its Georgian façade, and later additions, with some elegance amidst sweeping lawns and herbaceous borders; it was ten minutes' walk from Bendrose, past the piggeries, and across Finch Lane. Empty and up for sale, it stood forlorn and uncared for, one great circular bed of Ophelia roses, shabbily scattering petals, the windows cobwebbed, the terrace greening with mosses. Standing in the shade of the two giant cedar trees which stood sentinel before its ivied West Front, I wondered how I could manage to buy it.

People who had wandered about its empty echoing rooms and dark, stone-floored kitchens, shivered at the gloom of it and said that it was a hopeless proposition. Too many rooms, nothing facing the right way, poor lighting and water systems, badly proportioned rooms and too much land to maintain. But the land joined the Forwoods' land and was excellent grazing; they thought they might extend their farm but didn't want the house. They bought the land, I bought the house and seven acres of pleasure gardens from them for the improbable sum of £4,000, and with the help of a local builder in the village and his two brothers ripped down a wing of eleven ugly rooms, tore out the kitchens, gutted the house and started from scratch, ripping down years of ivy, opening up long-blocked-in windows, and covering everything with layers of clean white paint. Beel House became manageable, bright, comfortable and my home, my first real home, for the next eight years.

We had one final family Christmas at Bendrose and moved out across the fields a week later with all my goods and chattels, the dogs, a couple of Bendrose rose bushes, but minus the sullen couple from Lyons who had become more and more sullen, refusing, on occasions, to serve at table if there were Jews or Negroes present. They went off in their plimsolls to a millionaire in Sunningdale at six times the salary and with a modest reference extolling the virtues of their cooking if not their racial charity.

We built a swimming pool, laid out a croquet lawn, turned the long-neglected tennis courts into chicken-runs and filled the enormous conservatory, which ran the entire length of the south terrace and was the only room in the house to receive any direct sun all year round, with palms, mimosa, geraniums, plumbago and heavily scented trumpet trees and an aviary of fifty tropical birds. In spite of its Victorian glamour, to me, Kate always called it the Out-Patients Department and so it remained. The sullen Lyonnais were swiftly replaced by Agnes and Hans Zwickl from Vienna, who brought a friend called Florian to tend the gardens and the vegetables, and every year, in September, we had the local gymkhana in the park when I, in tweed cap and cavalry twill, presented the cups at the end of the day. The Country Squire was fast in danger of believing his own image and changing to Lord of the Manor. It is an insidious business.

Christmas was still very much a family affair. We had a giant Christmas tree in the drawing room, my mother made all the pies and the puddings, as she always had done (except for the war years), fires blazed in every room, Hans and Florian smothered every picture, beam, and door with boughs of pine, holly and fir-cones, but the mistletoe, at my father's insistence, was hung from the brass lamp in the front hall just inside the front door so that he could smack a kiss on to the cheek of every woman who arrived. We had presents at tea-time which ran into drink time with considerable ease, and everyone dressed for dinner; candles winking on silver and glass, logs spitting, crackers, and reading the awful mottoes . . . and then there was the Loyal Toast, and the one which made everyone a little thoughtful: to absent friends. Afterwards, sitting about comfortably in the drawing room, a film show, or else a word game, dancing in the wide bay window, the tree shimmering with tinsel and golden stars. So much laughter; so much sureness.

All so long ago.

Now, here on my hill in Provence, that day is almost forgotten. Perhaps a chicken for supper, dogs snoring by the fire, the Mistral whipping and clattering at the shutters, stars hard and bright above the hills, the village clock clanging out the fading day, tinnily. The theatrical splendours of those past Christmases have all long since faded; the set has been dismantled, the cast dispersed, some older, some no longer here. Which is most probably why I now choose to ignore it. Stocktaking, especially on the edge of evening, is not very amusing.

*　　*　　*

One bitter, thin-sun morning, Millie Milestone telephoned to ask if I could sit an extra couple for lunch and dinner: "A sweet couple, just kids . . . they leave for the States tomorrow, and you know what a London Sunday in February is like. They'll walk round the Park twice and cut their throats on the second Martini." He was coming down with Akim Tamiroff and his wife Tamara, and his own wife Kendall. They all lived now in London, uncomfortable exiles from McCarthy.

The kids, as he called them, arrived in due time. Cold from the drive, pleasant, and as far as they were introduced by a vague Millie, their names were just Nancy and Alan. He was neat, tidy, dressed in a dark blue suit, glasses, and a sad nervous little smile. Nancy was bright, sparkling, blonde and pink, she laughed a lot and the day was brighter.

It was a quiet week-end. Kate was working in London on a film, and the other regulars had decided that the icy roads would be a hazard in the dark, so stayed in bed with the Sunday papers. After lunch came the obligatory walk over to the dell. We all started pulling on the old mackintoshes, scarves, gloves and wellingtons which were always kept in the downstairs bathroom, where years before the local cricket team used to shower and change after a game. It was, naturally, called the Cricket Room. Nancy said she was still frozen and preferred not to go. We stood at the windows and watched the Russians, Alan and Forwood plod away into the thin snow and failing sun.

"I don't know your names, you know . . . Millie was a bit vague."

"Well, my name is Nancy Olsen; I'm an actress, of sorts . . ."

" 'Sunset Boulevard'!"

"Right . . . I was the girl . . . and the little fellow all hunched up between Tamara and Kendall is my husband. And he's called Alan Lerner. J. He's a lyricist, he's really quite famous. Do you know 'Brigadoon'. 'Paint Your Wagon' or perhaps 'An American in Paris'? Well, those were his."

"Ah. It seemed to me that he was something rather good in a bank."

"A sort of clerk?" she smothered her laughter.

"Something like that. Modest, silent, good at figures . . ."

"He's that all right. But I think it's that awful coat he wears."

"And you leave for the States tomorrow?"

"Yes. Sadly. We've been here a week trying to meet with Rex Harrison, do you know him? It's very difficult . . . Alan's written a show and wants him terribly badly but he just won't take any notice. It's easier to ride a tiger than get a meeting fixed with Harrison." She shrugged sadly. "Oh well . . . we tried."

"Couldn't you wait a week? I know Rex quite well, he often comes down on Sundays, he's coming next week."

"You talk to Alan, if he ever comes back from out there . . . we're booked out at lunch-time tomorrow. He's fed up; you know?"

In the Cricket Room, in a swirl of damp coats, scarves and muddy wellingtons, Alan accepted my apologies for thinking him something in a bank, and we all went in to tea.

"What is the Show?"

Alan was spreading a crumpet with Gentlemen's Relish. He grinned a wry grin. "You'll disapprove, I know that."

"Come on; tell."

"It's Shaw. A musical of *Pygmalion*. We're calling it 'Lady Liza'."

150

Amidst cries of derision he calmly went on with his crumpet. Nancy looking a little anxious stirred her tea into a tempest.

"Disapprove! How could you! Shaw! Honestly you Americans pinch everything you can lay your hands on . . ."

"Well, why didn't the English think of doing it? It's been about for years? And it's all Shaw's dialogue, we haven't American-ised it; and we want Harrison for Higgins. Can you think of any other Higgins in the world?"

"No. Well, it's more than likely that he'll be here next Sunday, he said so. If you stayed on for a week; played it by ear, and just happened to be here for lunch next week while he was present. Very casually, you know. We won't say anything about you two at all, you'll just arrive, and then it would be up to you, wouldn't it?"

He looked across the table at Nancy doubtfully, his glasses winking in the candle-light.

"You want to risk it?"

"If you do; and I want to buy a Corgi, remember? And Dirk says he knows a kennels near Oxford, so . . ."

Tamara, sipping her tea comfortably smiled across us all: "I'm a witch; a Russian witch. You stay. You will see."

Rex was involved in rather a full Sunday without actually being told much about it. Millie and Kendall were there, the Tamiroffs, Peter Brook and his wife Natasha Parry (daughter of Lusia, my catalyst from the Savoy), Katie, Michael and Anne Gough. And Alan and Nancy. It was a perfectly normal Sunday. The only people absent from the obligatory afternoon walk over the fields were Rex and Alan. After tea, in the fading March light, we all gathered round the spinet in the Long Study, which was the only form of piano I possessed, and even though it was a full octave short Alan played the entire score, and sang, in a rather wavering voice, all the songs of his show, for the first time to a full audience.

Three years later, half an hour after the curtain fell on the First Night at Drury Lane, I, at Alan's request, introduced the music of "My Fair Lady" on television, sitting by the fire in the drawing room of Beel House where, as he pointed out, a small part of theatre history had started off. It was a graceful, if unde-served, gesture, for if I had not met Lewis Milestone in Cyprus all that time ago, would Alan Lerner have finally managed to meet Rex Harrison in Buckinghamshire? Tamara Tamiroff only smiled, her gentle witch's smile and, shaking her head, said that it was Fate.

*   *   *

At the time of this fateful lunch I had just, a few days before, finished my eighteenth picture, the second "Doctor" film. Although the option period was now almost forgotten, only Betty and Ralph seemed to have any idea of a plan for me and although I was handing out cups at gymkhanas and playing my Squire role to the hilt, I was still just hopping about from film to film wherever I was lucky enough to be asked. It didn't make for a settled feeling; I knew that as long as the Doctor films would be made I should probably be asked to be in them, but apart from that (and they could only happen now and again) there was a clear feeling of disinterest from Above.

Looking over the smooth lawns at Beel House, I had many moments of grave doubt at the wisdom of leaving the modest comforts of Bendrose just across the fields; at least the house had not been mine, Beel was. I had not only to support myself, but a large house and a busy staff of four, plus weekly gardeners. Stupid idiot. I had probably jumped too soon; I longed to be the proud possessor of an Oxo tin again, when I at least knew, to the last halfpenny, what I had in my bank. But there were also rumbles of doubt and worry, not only in my head, but in the Aberconways' Bedroom as well. The Studio writhed with rumours of changes to be made, heads to fall, and new brooms sweeping clean. A mounting panic almost choked me; after all, no one could prove that I had actually had anything very much to do with the success of "Doctor in the House": the film itself was the winner, and I had shown no definite signs yet to them that I was Box Office. So now that I had gone too far and attached myself to a large country house and dependants it was fate that I should be chucked out. There was trouble at the Millers, all right, and I was convinced that my time had come. Even Olive Dodds could offer little comfort; she too, who always smiled, was now looking fairly grim, probably worrying about her own job. I only hoped that when the blow came I would be able to weather it, and spent more time than was healthy wandering round the rooms of Beel House, an anxious Camille saying goodbye to them all.

The Blow was a summons to lunch at the Dorchester to meet

Mr Rank's Chief Accountant. At least that is what I understood at the time, and I experienced a slight flicker of hope; if I were to be dropped, surely Earl St John would have sent the news personally? And with pleasure. This must mean another tremendous cut in salary of such proportions that only the Chief Accountant could possibly confront me.

The confrontation with John Davis was so pleasant that I almost began to think that I might even be offered a raise in salary instead of a cut. He did, however, offer rather more than that. He started off by saying that certain changes were to be made generally, and that he was about to take a personal interest in the cinema section. He thought that I had worked exceedingly well over the years, had proved loyal and diligent, and that he was prepared to launch a campaign to involve me at the Studios for at least a couple of years, and that if I had the stamina to carry it through, he would make me into one of the biggest Stars, or biggest Box Office Attractions, Rank had ever had. How did I feel about that?

I felt fine. Could it be possible that I had, at last, a friend at court? He demanded complete loyalty, dedication and submission to the plan which he had in mind. There were already five films, in a row, some of which would be produced by the Box-Thomas team with whom I had worked so very happily and successfully. Successfully was what he really meant. It didn't matter much about the happiness: trade is trade, money is money. The commercial cinema is both those things. There was to be no room for anything else but success, and he wanted no excuses. Mr Davis was going to be extremely tough as a boss and very demanding; he would brook no failure on my part, but he was also very correct and just, hid nothing and asked only for total commitment and faith in him. I said that he would have them. He told me that he would be available to me, at any time, for any problem or worry which I might have, and hoped that I would dine with him privately the following week so that we could start to discuss, in detail, the first project he had in mind for me, A. J. Cronin's "The Spanish Gardener".

On the journey back to Beel House I was pardonably, in a state of mild euphoria. The signal was green. Weights had fallen from my back to such an extent that I was literally buoyant. Now someone else, apart from the ever loyal Olive Dodds, believed that I might have a potential at Rank.

Putting thoughts of Camille deftly aside, as we turned into Western Avenue, I hazily started a plan to purchase an extra two acres of paddock from the generous, unsuspecting Forwood family. I was a quick recoverer; a little encouragement went a long, long way. It always has. I knew that I had been taken in hand and was just about to be developed—manufactured would be a better word perhaps—like a stick of seaside rock with the lettering printed all the way through right down to the last little bit. And as sweet and sickly and forgettable as that product itself. I was to be a commercial creation pure and simple; that of course was the hidden message buried in the smoked salmon and the *poulet à l'estragon*. In return for loyalty, devotion, commitment, stamina and faith I should be raised to the giddy heights of a Box Office Attraction. I had promised all these. No one, however, had mentioned the word acting. Perhaps it really didn't matter in the commercial cinema, perhaps it took too much time, and time is money etcetera . . . but what of Garbo, or Tracy? I knew from Dearden, Leacock, and a tense, harried, perfectionist called Joseph Losey with whom I had recently worked on a cheapish, unremarkable, and now unremembered film, only a few months before, that it was essential and, more than that, it was exciting. I knew that there was much more to it than what some critics cheerfully call good facial expressions. Bob Thompson, the operator on "Doctor at Sea", had opened up unlimited vistas for me one day when he said, staring gloomily over his camera, that he didn't know how the hell I'd managed to get so far with so little camera technique.

"I know you can act all right, but you don't know how to act for the camera, do you, mate? Not much good you giving us your all with half your bleeding head off frame, your face in shadow and your back to the microphone, is it? You don't know a bloody thing about the camera, do you?"

For the rest of the film he had taught me the basics of cinema technique. Everything from lenses, to lights, to sound. I was a greedy pupil, he was a thorough tutor.

So now that all seemed safer and more secure for the first time, why not extend these lessons, work on a different plane, use a new dimension. Great opportunities to work for the camera, almost non-stop it would appear, were set before me; now was my chance to learn, and apply what I had learned: it couldn't possibly harm the box office potential because very few people would ever see what I was trying to do . . . having conquered the thin neck, small head syndrome, surely to Heaven I could conquer the acting as well? No one would stop me, for no one would know. I would be doing it for myself, so that when the miracle time had ended, as end I felt sure it must one day, I would at least be cast adrift fully equipped and armoured against a bed-sitter in Earl's Court, the pubs of Leicester Square, and supporting roles in plays for what Dearden once disparagingly called the medium of the mediocre, television. Grasp the nettle.

As we turned down towards Chalfont St Giles into the home stretch, I suddenly remembered the telegram which Noël Coward had sent me on the opening night of the revival of his play, "The Vortex". It was quite short. "Don't worry," it said. "It All Depends On You."

8

I SUPPOSE the greatest exit which we are called upon to make, or which is wished upon us, is our birth; that clumsy, uncomfortable, messy, bewildering affair which brings us often breathless into the long corridor of life leading directly, sometimes indirectly, but always inevitably, to our final supreme Exit, death.

The corridor is lined all its length with doors; some open, some just ajar, some closed. Closed; but seldom, if ever, locked. It is entirely up to us which ones we choose to try, and we are only given a certain amount of time in which to arrive at the inevitable door at the end. Nothing very original about that.

However, I have never been in too much of a hurry along the corridor. Indeed one might say that I have wandered down it over-cautiously, even reluctantly on many occasions, trying deliberately to avoid the doors so temptingly set along my path. I am in no hurry to reach the end, I have no fear of it, only of the manner in which I shall have to meet it, therefore a slow, wandering, lope, with as little fuss as possible has always seemed eminently desirable. But when forced, as I have often been, I have usually chosen the door which is slightly ajar rather than the ones which stand wide with blazing light, or murky with sombre shadow, always supposing, quite inaccurately unhappily, that if I approach anything with due caution and without making too much song and dance about it, I could in Lally's words, always retreat gracefully. Complete nonsense of course. Once you are in you are in.

The two matinee tickets which Rex sent for "My Fair Lady" seemed to provide me with a pleasingly just-ajar door. A trip to America, which I had never seen, two weeks of splendour in his house in the country, and a tempting chance to see Kate again for yet another Christmas together. The five years in which she had been a week-end lodger in Bendrose and Beel had made her very much part of one's life, her ups her downs, her sighs her moans, as Lerner so perfectly phrased it, were second nature to me now. I had grown accustomed to her face, and missed it badly since she had upped and left to go to America and join Rex, spilling with happiness and delight, to be with him on his Royal progression and become the Queen to his King of New York. Kate, with her wit, her elegance, her beauty, her fun, her rage, her laughter; Kate gobbling handfuls of her ox blood pills for her anaemia, sobbing noisily while Bruno Walter conducted his last concert, knitting endless yards of zig-zag woollen things, trailing my father through the house one evening when, to all our amazement, her sense of smell returned for a few brief moments: "Ulric! Wifey, I can smell your cigar! Quick, give me things to smell . . . a rose . . . the cheese . . ." in and out of rooms to find the scents so long lost, to the kitchen for garlic and lemons, burying her face deep in a great bowl of sweet-peas; in my mother's arms to savour her favourite scent, embracing us all to find again the traces of tweed, of wool, of soap, of self; tears of laughter and happiness streaming down her face. And then it was gone as suddenly as it arrived.

Her downs were as giddy as her highs. Once when I, unthinkingly, suddenly lost my patience (for she could be maddening in a completely feminine way) and sent her grumbling off to her room, Tamara Tamiroff, who was present, took my arm and chided me: "Be kind to that little one," she said, "she hasn't very long here, my dear." The constant nagging doubt, always suppressed, now so flatly stated, brought instant, and careful apology followed by swift reconciliation; with wild whoops of laughter and a most improbable Charleston danced through the hall: Kate had a fury for life.

No door, therefore, open, closed, or ajar, was difficult to enter if she was on the other side of it.

So to America I went. Forwood decided to come too. Alan Lerner had invited me to play in his projected film musical of Colette's "Gigi", but I had three firm projects lined up in a row for the following year with Rank; so delicate manoeuvring and diplomacy would be required before I could accept the chance to work with Dietrich, Chevalier, and Audrey Hepburn (the suggested cast at that time: in the event, dates on both sides proved inflexible, and I played Sydney Carton instead). Mr Davis paid the fares, the *Mauretania* carried us there, and as dawn broke one December morning, I stood on deck and watched the flat steel waters of the still Atlantic as the first thrusts of the New World rose inch by inch slowly into the mussel-shell light of the sky.

Skyscrapers glittering in the morning light, their upper reaches hidden by the clouds, dark canyons sliding past geometrically, cars and trucks speeding like toys, lights winking, gulls wheeling, bottles, crates and cabbage leaves bobbing idly in the oily waters, piers and jetties, giant cranes, steam drifting into the white air, Christmas trees in windows, sirens blowing, dirty snow, and Alan Lerner huddled against the bitter cold at Immigration to meet us in.

"You are mad! It's much too early . . ."

"I was writing all through the night . . . I never sleep. Welcome to New York!"

"I'm overwhelmed."

"American hospitality. And since you are god-father, it's high time you saw the child."

A low, long, black Cadillac to Rex and Kate's borrowed house on Long Island. A white clap-board, shuttered farmhouse, set among bare trees and snowy lawns, from which George Washington once watched a battle. Logs blazing, lights gleaming, dogs leaping, Kate laughing, polished wood and fat armchairs. Bacon and eggs, toast and Cooper's marmalade, scalding coffee, and legs still a little wobbly from six days at sea; later in the afternoon the House Lights dimming, the overture beginning, the gentle hush falling, filling one with all the long forgotten excitement of a first pantomime at the Lyceum; a long and exhilarating way to come to see a matinee . . . and Kate.

It was her Christmas. And she was determined that it should be one we would all remember. There were about eight of us, including Cathleen Nesbitt, Margaret Leighton, Forwood's son, Gareth, and Kate's ravishing sister, Kim. An enormous tree arrived, higher even than the room, decked in silver and sprayed-on frost. Holly wreaths, tied all about with scarlet ribbons and studded with candles hung at the front door and every window; boughs of fir and ivy were thrust into every nook and cranny; packets and parcels, brilliant in wrapping papers, spilled from every chair and table, the drawing room was the Fairies' Grotto in Selfridges. Music played all day, the record-player never seemed to cease, sending us all scurrying faster with yards of ribbons, evergreens, and boxes of glittering baubles for her tree. Cards were stacked on every free space, and food and drink arrived in such quantities as would have delighted Pickwick or Jorrocks and must have frightened the wits out of Rex at the cost. But he smiled bravely all about him, well pleased with Kate's delight.

She, in typical fashion, had just borrowed a large advance from the salary of her first Hollywood film which was to begin almost immediately, in order to buy everyone presents, her spending was so extravagant that one felt she must have had the entire salary plus overage in advance; not just a part. A Byron first edition in red calf for Rex, a mink-lined duffle coat, "not the best mink, it's only a lining." Cashmeres and gold fountain pens from Cartier's, for the rest of us, trinkets and jewels from Tiffany's to fill the stockings from Father Christmas. There was never to be such a Christmas; I don't believe there ever was. Sometimes in the hurry and rush there came a little pause. Suddenly tired Kate would crumple into a huge armchair, and legs and arms akimbo, her slow smile of pleasure lighting a tired wan face, she would ask for a drink and play, for the millionth time it seemed, her favourite record, Judy Holliday singing "Just in Time"

"Oh, wifey . . . I'm getting to be an old, old woman . . . oh! I am a lucky lady . . . it's Chriss'mus . . . Chriss'mus . . . and I've got all my loves about me."

★   ★   ★

If occasionally Kate seemed weary, then I was a wreck by the end of the week. The excitements and delights were exhausting, not a moment was wasted, and not a second left idle. Our daily walks together with Rex along Jones Beach beside the leaden, December sea, in a bitter wind, did much to revive me—and the scalding plastic cups of clam chowder from the deserted cafe on the beach tasted like negus—but the nightly journeys into New York, the constant round of parties, suppers, shows and conversation gradually took their toll of the pale Country Squire from the Home Counties, and by New Year's Eve I had decided that I would do no more for a time, and stay quietly in the company of the Late Show on television. Kate was anguished.

"You can't! But you can't! It's the most important party of the year . . . the Gilbert Millers are famous for it! People murder to get invited . . . Rex begged them to invite you and now you say you'll stay at home with Doris Day! You can't, Diggie, you can't. Please come?"

I refused flatly. No more opening of doors to unsuspected delights. I had had my fair share, more than, it had been marvellous, but enough was enough.

"No. I hate parties, I always get stuck with someone's aunt who is deep into Botticelli or something . . . usually in a corner or behind a door. And no one knows me and I don't know anyone there, and I hate New Year anyway. I'll stay here, very peacefully, and watch the telly, and go to bed early. I'm dead."

"Rex will be terribly disappointed, he went to such a lot of trouble."

"Well, bugger the Gilbert Millers . . . if they have half New York going they won't miss me."

"But it's so rude . . ." she wailed miserably off to change.

Forwood nobly stayed behind with me and I ate a light, sensible-to-sleep-on supper and settled down to watch the telly and it was absolutely appalling. After the hundredth commercial break for toothpaste, wrapped bread, shampoo, lavatory paper and Aunt Maude's Home-Baked Deep-Frozen Apple Pie I capitulated and accepted his advice that it *was* New Year, we *were* in New York, we were invited to the grandest party in town, a car awaited us and I was being very ungracious to my extraordinarily generous host and hostess. In black tie and a certain amount of suppressed fury, hopeless at the prospect of what lay before, we skidded into the city.

We all arrived at the party together and entered the elevator just as midnight started to strike. In a wild fit of joyousness Kate threw her arms around the lift-man and we all embraced and wished each other a Happy New Year. The lift stopped right at the open door of the Gilbert Millers' opulent apartment: the sound of Auld Lang Syne and cheers greeted us, and we pushed out happily, colliding with a tall, pale woman in a flowing scarlet dress who hurried into our vacated cage. As we reached for brimming glasses, Miss Garbo was borne silently from our sight forty floors to the street below.

And I was stuck with someone's aunt, a pleasant, rangy, white-haired woman of seventy, with wrap-around American teeth, who had just come back from a dig in Iran. We talked very pleasantly of shards, and artifacts, of sandstone and clay, of the total inability of the desert people to comprehend the excitement of finding a set of knucklebones, intact and in spanking condition, at a depth of fifty feet which could safely be dated to at least 44 B.C. "Time, as Plato said, brings everything," she cried happily. It also brought Kate speeding to my side. "Come with me, Diggie . . . there is someone in the next room who wants to meet you."

And there she was. Sitting in a bit of a lump in a corner, dressed in pink, hair very short, plump, jolly, laughing a great deal at something that Rubinstein was saying to her. She had a thin jade bracelet on one wrist, pearl ear-rings . . . the wide, brown, laughing eyes I knew so well. Kate introduced us and I kissed her quite simply on the lips. I said, "Oh . . . I love you!" and she laughed her extraordinary chuckling laugh and said, "Oh no! I love *you!*" and I burned a hole right through the bodice of her dress with the tip of my cigarette. Judy Garland. She gave a little scream, and then we laughed, and she pulled me down beside her and made me sit there on the floor and I stayed there, on and off, for almost ten years. Almost.

"It's so good to meet you. I've seen every movie you made . . ."

"I've only been doing it for ten years."

"I saw 'Stranger In Between'* five single times."

"I saw 'Pigskin Parade' . . . once."

She cried out with laughter. "I was awful, pigtails and cutes."

"I suppose I really went to see Betty Grable."

"I suppose you did. 1936 . . . almost twenty years ago."

"More. I'm loyal."

"You are? You'll come and see me, here, at the Palace?"

"I'm sailing on Saturday."

"You'll come Friday. I'll get you seats; now don't run away? We just met, and it's taken such a long, long time."

"I won't run away, I promise . . . Friday."

"And I want you real close; right up front. I hope you'll like me."

"I will."

She laughed, and threw her arms round my neck.

"You better, Buster. I'll be doing it for you, a Command Performance."

"Don't you do that for all your fans?"

She was suddenly grave.

"You're my friend. An old, old friend, remember that."

I was right up front for my Command Performance at the Palace, as close as she could place me. In the middle of the Brass Section. Rex's sister, Sylvia Kilmuir, was with us. Pale from jet lag, she had just arrived in New York that morning; I wondered how she would manage with the blasting noise. Stuffing her

* "Hunted" in Britain.

fingers in her ears she smiled a wink and shook her head in wry disbelief. The theatre was almost empty.

The first half was fearful: Hungarian ladies in red boots and sparkling gypsy head-dresses urged irritated dogs over boxes and through flaming hoops; a ventriloquist with a doll on his knee which talked animatedly while he consumed glass after glass of milk; two anxious dancers revolved endlessly in a Follow Spot on roller skates to the "Thunder and Lightning" polka. At the intermission we went into the street and smoked cigarettes.

The second half was Judy, and the theatre was suddenly full. Wise people had ignored the Hungarians and the Skaters. The lights dimmed and "Over the Rainbow" started. Anticipation mounted, twelve youngish men leapt on to the stage carrying sequined boards on the end of long poles. They did a shaky dance, in lamé jackets, and one by one spelled out her name with happy smiles and wiggling, pointed toes; the twelfth member came in on a late beat and threw up the exclamation mark. And then she was there.

Later, sitting hunched on the steps of the corridor outside her dressing room, we held each other laughing, while unrecognising people clambered over us to reach her room. She was drenched in sweat, a shabby pink candlewick wrap, her hair spiky and wet, like Gooley's years ago at Catterick, a wet cat. Her eyeblack had run, the lips were smudged, her small hands held my arm firm as clamps.

"Was I good? Did you like me? Did you really? As good as that! You're kidding? What's the matter with the dogs and the Hungarians? I don't get to see them, they just warm up the place for me, for chrissakes; but you really did like me? Was I OK? I was what . . . ? You're awful! I *couldn't* be that good . . . would it go in London? I want to bring it to London . . . how big is the Palace? As big as that . . . shit . . . the Cambridge? . . . Or they said the Princes? What do you mean you'll take care of it? You mean you'd bring me over and do the show . . . you'd take a theatre?"

"I'll take any theatre you like, but the Cambridge is a barn. Maybe the Princes would be better . . . I'll take the place and bring you over but without the Dancing Boys or the Hungarian Dancers. Just you alone."

Her eyes were wide with disbelief and laughter, people were still clambering over us to find her. She pulled off her ear-rings and shoved them into the pocket of her sagging candlewick and wiped her forehead on its sleeve.

"You are mad, and I love you . . . my new impresario! But I need the warm-up. I couldn't go it alone."

"The theatre was empty tonight until you came on . . . they were only there for the second half."

"I know . . . but that's the way it is. I couldn't do a whole show alone! For God's sake! What do you think I am? Aimée Semple McPherson?"

"Yes."

"You are one son-of-a-bitch. And I love you. Don't leave me now, will you? Now don't you leave me. People always go away from me, walking backwards . . . don't do that to me, will you? Promise? Just you promise me?"

Unthinkingly I made her the promise. She stared at me for a few seconds in silence and then, hugging me tightly, scrabbled to her feet and pushed through the crowd of people who had come to tell her how wonderful she was. And was. And I went into the street and joined the others and we went to the Plaza for supper.

★   ★   ★

In the deep leather chairs of the Oak Room Judy looked smaller than ever, and, rather crushed by an enormous black flat-brimmed hat, she poked about at her chicken fricassee tiredly. "Don't talk about you bringing me into London. Sid won't like it much . . . he's negotiating something there himself; he'd be furious if anything got in the way. We'll just leave it, huh? It was a marvellous idea, but he does all the deals, he always has, and he's very, very good at it . . . so let's forget it, okay?"

She raised her glass of white wine and looked steadily at me.

"But don't leave me, will you? You have to promise all over again."

"All right. I promise. You want me to cross my heart?"

"Yes."

"Cross my heart."

"And hope to die. I'll remember that."

★   ★   ★

We had taken Kate out to Idlewild (Rex had a matinee) to

start her on the trip to California and the despairs and miseries, she expected, of Hollywood. She was bitterly unhappy about leaving, but sensible enough to know that she had mortgaged herself completely to MGM and the film by the wildly idiotic advance she had borrowed against her salary in order to buy us all the presents which had so delighted her only a few days before. Now the house, stripped of its glittering frost-sprayed tree, the ivy and the holly wreaths, the ribbons and laughter, seemed empty and chill.

She was bundled into the car, a mass of expensive luggage, a black mink coat, and for some reason which I have now forgotten, Gladys Cooper's Corgi, June, whom she was accompanying on the flight to the Coast.

While Kate sniffed and hiccupped, slumped dejectedly in a corner, June whined and moaned in her smallish ply-wood travelling cage, and we fed her handfuls of tranquillisers all the way to Idlewild which merely had the effect of making her far more energetic and angry. It was a miserable ride. At the airport we shoved Kate through the barrier for her flight, clutching a furious June in her box, her boarding card, ticket, and a slipping bundle of hastily-bought magazines for the five-hour journey. She was still sniffing and teary, and looked pale and wan, dishevelled and weary, as if she had spent a week at sea in an open boat.

"Look after Rexie, won't you, promise me? And I'll try and telephone when I get there; I can't remember if we are ahead or behind . . . oh, it's all so confusing . . ."

Watching her tall, leggy, clumsy figure humping June along to the plane it never for one moment occurred to us that this despairing, hopeless exit was leading her directly to international fame, and that when we should all meet again together she would have become a World Star.

There was a good deal more which we did not suspect.

After the show we took Rex over to the penthouse on Park Avenue which he had chosen to rent so that he could rest between shows. He was, understandably, tired and rather strained, and, after some scrambled eggs and a pot of tea, decided to go and sleep until the Second House, asking only that we should awaken him in good time. We didn't any of us speak very much; Kate had taken all the fun away with her, and we were fairly subdued, talking about politics and books back in the Long Island house until the small hours when the telephone rang and it was Kate from Los Angeles in a state bordering on hysterics, partly tears and partly helpless laughter. The Studio had found her an apartment, she didn't know where, but in a dark street; the living room was filled with Tang horses, rubber trees and reproduction Modiglianis; the bedroom looked like an Amsterdam tart's parlour, swagged and buttoned satin, scatter cushions, an immense lilac nylon teddy bear, and the ice box was filled with everything from milk to Dom Perignon.

"It's like Golders Green High Street on a wet Sunday," she wailed. "Right opposite the window there's an Undertaker's place with a huge electric clock and it says, 'It's later than you think!' in bright green neon . . . Diggie, I can't stay a night here!" Tears had given way to laughter. "I'll slit my throat, wifey! Oh, I'se sick Miss Scarlett . . . help!"

Rex told her briskly to get a cab and check into the Beverly Hills Hotel even if it meant that she and June were to sleep at the pool-side, and we were all much relieved to hear that she had already contacted Minna Wallis, a much loved and capable, not to say powerful, friend of us all, who had wasted no time and had installed her there, with the cab already at the door.

We didn't know it then; but the clock opposite her window was correct.

*　　*　　*

A monstrous clattering and banging had awakened me on my very first morning in Beel House. It was barely dawn, and the sun had only just risen above the icing-sugar frost which sparkled on the wide lawns. The branches of the cedar trees black and silver against the lint-pink sky. A raven, seemingly the size of an eagle, was battering frantically at the dormer window of the upstairs hall. Wings wide, beak gaping, eyes brilliant with rage. Again and again he crashed and lunged at the diamond panes. The shadow loomed across the floor, flickered like a magic-lantern silhouette against the white-washed walls.

My theatrical mind instantly, and irrevocably, lined this simple moment of natural history with the supernatural, and bad omens and witchcraft proliferated all about the cold morning hall, and my head. I was convinced, on that first day, that my future in Beel House would be, as it were, cursed. Added to which I had most inconveniently been told that an elderly lady had died, quite suddenly, stuck irremovably in the guest-room bath. Here I now had proof of a lost, and indeed angry, as well she might have been, spirit come to haunt me in a most obviously Edgar Allan Poe manner. Ravens at the winter window, on my first morning. Of course it must be an omen. Of course it was perfectly absurd. Even I knew that. Somewhere. The raven was simply attacking its own reflection in the dawn light, the elderly woman could have died almost anywhere in the house; and in a house as aged as Beel it would have been most surprising if a great many other people had not died, here and there, in its rooms at one time or another. Reason tried to conquer superstition and theatricality; and succeeded. Almost. But I was never to be absolutely happy in my skin during all the years I lived there, even though they were among the most successful years of my career. If not my life.

Mr Davis's recipe for seaside rock, so lightly unfolded at a Dorchester luncheon, was speedily put into effect, and only his warning that stamina would be required caused me any great deal of surprise or worry. I needed the stamina of a vote-seeking politician coupled with that of an Everest Sherpa to survive, and to my astonishment, I had it. Film followed film, some even overlapping at times. Locations ranged from southern Spain to the Dolomites, from the Alps to Agra. I saw more of the Studios than I did of the raven-haunted house and tried, as often as was allowed, or demanded in these undemanding roles, to put all the learning I had had from the Dearden, Leacock, Losey and the Bob Thompson College of Arts and Crafts into practice. It was an exhausting if exhilarating time. My salary was increased, I celebrated my tenth year under contract, thereby allaying both my fears, and those of Freddy Joachim so long ago in the kitchen of Chester Row, and was given a private luncheon party at the Studio, a warm speech of congratulation from Mr Davis and a pair of Paul Storr sugar castors. I was almost undone.

At the same time I was now coming in for a certain amount of attention from the critics. Dismissed by a number as light weight but accepted by others, including Dilys Powell, Clive Barnes, Margaret Hinxman, and Paul Dehn, I was actively encouraged. Their criticism was just exactly that; constructive, caring, and therefore strengthening. They loved the cinema, willed it to flourish, to try to be better, and their obvious love for their craft made them notable teachers.

There was also, of course, even then the Sunday-Supplement,

New-Yorker Group. Schoolboys in 1939, they now emerged as an elegant shoal of piranhas savaging, on principle, practically anything which was not sub-titled. To be fair they did nod in the direction of Ealing Studios from time to time, but by and large did very little to encourage the British Cinema of the day which, with all its faults, and God knows there were some, was at least trying to exist. They offered neither true nor constructive criticism but, leaning heavily on M. Roget, provided jolly bon mots and epigrams for each other to read, filled with witty, if cruel, and often personal, observations. I accepted these attacks grudgingly enough and did my best to profit from those who gave encouragement; which is as it should be. Although I did have ideas above my station, I was quite content to bide my time for a little longer. There was still a lot to learn.

I now walked along the corridor of power (in reality a very ugly connecting link between the Admin. Block and the Executive Offices littered with junk furniture from a thousand sets, a sort of "Bridge of Sighs with a palace on one side and a prison on the other") beside Mr Davis himself, while Earl St John walked, very delicately, just behind us. Not the sort of thing to turn one's head, but the kind of thing for which a knife is turned eventually. Although I was now under the personal supervision and advice of the Big Chief, Earl St John was still very much a figure to be reckoned with, even from five paces behind in the corridor. He was still the Studio Boss: he had great influence on whether a film would, or would not, be made. He concealed his dislike, or dismay, I never knew which, but something, behind a very warm gentle, affectionate façade. Fresh red carnation, fresh-lit cigar, hidden feelings. Gently biding his time for a counter-attack.

Seaside rock, as one knows, is a sticky, insubstantial, unnourishing piece of confectionery. Meant only to be enjoyed at the moment, digested and soon forgotten. As such I prospered very acceptably. I felt that nothing more was expected of me by Rank, or would even be allowed; therefore it was with some degree of astonishment that I learned, in a very warm and personal letter from Mr Davis, that I had reached the top of the *Motion Picture Herald* poll both for Britain, my country, and also for the International Market, beating Bing Crosby, Humphrey Bogart and James Stewart. I had been top of the British Polls for the last two years, but this news was a tremendous surprise. My delight was nothing compared to the dismay and disbelief of the British Press.

The *Daily Mirror* took the trouble to telephone and ask me why I thought it could possibly be me who had reached such an elevated position? It was clear from the irritated, not to say scathing voice, at the other end, that such a result must have been rigged. Either I had bought it, or had cheated in some manner. It was apparently inconceivable that I could have just won it by hard labour.

I was a bit cast down, I confess. However, a Sunday newspaper, a day or so later, left no doubt at all in anyone's mind. Milton Shulman took a whole page to express his. Referring to the 4,000 distributors who had taken part in the yearly poll he writes, or wrote: "These experts have seriously voted Dirk Bogarde as the man who brings more money into British Box Offices than *any other Star in the world* (his italics) . . . If this poll really reflects the thinking of either the Cinema Managers or the British Public then few will mourn that cinemas have been closing at the rate of some 200 a year . . .", which seemed to place rather an excessive responsibility on my narrow shoulders. Forwood's wry comment that "today's reviews are tomorrow's wrapping at the fishmongers" gave me little comfort, even though I knew it to be true. I suppose that I had rather hoped that someone would have said, "Well done!" After all, they were all extremely busy flogging "British is Best" in relation to motor cars, woollens, whisky, tweeds and sundry pieces of hardware. But not, apparently, seaside rock.

I suppose, to be truthful, it was a matter of Quantity over Quality; nevertheless it had been a long hop from the hopeless, jobless vacuum of my demobilisation leave just ten years, almost to the month, ago.

It is only fair to say at this point that during all these years Rank had always honoured my contract and permitted me to return to the theatre from time to time.

I made these sorties in order to stretch myself and to make contact again with a living audience; they proved to be rather a mistake and they were not altogether happy experiences.

The plays I chose to do were not simple ones, being written by master writers like Anouilh, Coward, Betti, Boussicault, but they provided exhilarating escapes from the platitudes of so many of the film scripts of the day. The audiences, in the main, however, came to see the Film Star and not the Play, something which had never remotely occurred to me, and each performance became an exhausting, and extended, Personal Appearance, during which every entrance and exit was greeted by the hysterical screams and moans reserved today for pop singers; and the alarming chants, during the performance, of "We love you, Dirk!" or, if I was unwise enough to let exasperation show, even more threateningly, "We put you where you are!", destroyed the play, dismayed my fellow actors, and distressed me to such an unforeseen extent that every theatrical appearance became an ordeal.

Things finally reached a head during a matinee in Cardiff when the Scene Dock doors eventually gave way and cascaded a dishevelled, screaming, horde of young women across the stage hotly pursued, it appeared, by half the City Police Force. Helmetless.

In 1956 I lost my nerve and reluctantly abandoned the theatre for good. So deep was my fear of ridicule that later, in the summer of '61 when Laurence Olivier asked me to join him in the opening season at Chichester Theatre, suggesting that I might "do Hamlet or some such thing", I funked the honour and probably the greatest chance I had ever been offered really to learn my craft. Hoist by my own petard. So that to reach the top in the cinema did do something at least to alleviate my loss of the theatre.

I wondered if Gooley knew and was amused in his bar in Cork. If Kitty, Worms, or smug Tilly, cared. The only thing I knew with certainty was that Palmers Green, had he not decided to leave the scene so early, would have been very chuffed, as he would have called it; and that rather cheered me up. I was to stay there for the next four or five years, and in the Top Ten until 1964, presumably closing a further 2,000 cinemas in the process.

Mr Davis's recipe became ever more ambitious; a spectacular adventure story in the Canadian Rockies, a costly remake of "A Tale of Two Cities", later to be advertised in America as "Two Men and a Girl in Turbulent Paris", and a tragic love story all set in exotic India—all of them happily to be made with Miss Box and Mr Thomas. It was all very encouraging, and after them we would look even further afield. Any script I cared to do they would be willing to consider.

"You can have any Star you want to play opposite you from anywhere in the world," he announced one evening at dinner, "anyone you like. We'll bring them over."

I suggested Judy Garland.

"I meant a Star," he said kindly. She hadn't made money since "Summer Stock", in 1950 . . . too long.

Finding the scripts was bad enough; they had to conform to Family Entertainment which made choice limited. When a very young John Osborne shyly brought me a copy of his play "Look Back in Anger" down to Beel one wet Sunday afternoon to see if there was a possible film in it, the Studio returned it a week later with a polite, if strained note, stating that I should try to remember that the cinema was a Visual Art and that there was altogether too much dense dialogue in the enclosed manuscript. When I hopelessly submitted a book called *Saturday Night and Sunday Morning*, Earl St John gave me a splendid lunch in his private, pine-panelled office, and, after he had lighted his cigar, asked me, gently, how I imagined that anyone could consider making a film which began with a forty-year-old woman inducing an abortion in a hot bath?

So off we all went to India and made a "never the twain shall meet" kind of film during which I broke my foot and fought a long and bitter battle to prevent the Studio tacking on a happy ending. Eventually after a good deal of strained politeness, a play-safe compromise was reached. It made a great deal of money and suddenly, out of the blue, Anthony Asquith arrived with a beautiful script by Rattigan on Lawrence of Arabia.

Although this could, under no circumstances, be termed Family Fun, to my delighted astonishment the Studio agreed. (Looking back from this distance it might just have been a ploy to shut me up.) This was to be no monumental epic, rather the straightforward, if there could be such a term applied to such a man, story about Lawrence, starting in Uxbridge and ending with his still-unexplained death on the lonely country road to Clouds Hill. I had never, in my life, wanted a part, or script, so much. Asquith spent a lot of time helping me to put aside my very serious doubts about my ability, my physical resemblance (nil) and my acceptability in such a role. Locations were found and King Feisal offered us his entire army.

Mr Davis insisted that an hour should be cut from the three-hour running time; this was reluctantly agreed to, and Script Conferences started daily, almost hourly. Wig fittings, costume fittings and intensive research now occupied my time entirely. I thought of nothing else but the man I was to represent, which was a word that Puffin Asquith and I agreed on mutually rather than the word "be". I could never "be" Lawrence, but we both felt that it could be possible to offer a portrait of the man to a public generally in ignorance of his stature. I read every book available on his work and life, wrote to his friends, received warm and encouraging letters in return, especially from Geoffrey Woolley who even sent me unpublished letters and a mass of deeply considered information, and quite lost my own identity in what the Americans call a period of total immersion.

So lost was I in preparation and absorption that I took little, if any, notice of what was going on around me: all I could think of was the strange blond wig which was slowly, and carefully, taking shape in Make-Up, and the probable starting date in the desert of April 7th. I didn't take any notice at all of what was happening about the Studios, which is why I was so completely unprepared for Olive Dodds's cool, impersonal, business-voice on the telephone on Friday, March the 14th at six-thirty precisely to announce that "Lawrence" was now off. And please would I report to Mr St John's office at the Studios on the following Monday morning at eleven am promptly. She could say no more, she regretted; the Office was closing for the week-end.

Puffin and his producer, de Grunwald, and all the production team were still, at this moment in the Middle East with the King. They returned the next morning, happily unaware of catastrophe until they met it physically in the form of Earl St John himself at the airport as they arrived in and he was busy meeting a flight from New York. Across the crowded hall he told them casually that the film was no longer operative and would they come to his office on the Monday morning at ten o'clock.

At the meeting they were each accorded half an hour, told it was definitely off but, as far as I know, were never ever given a reason. When my turn came, just as de Grunwald had hurried out past me with an ashen face and without a greeting, Earl St John, beaming pleasantly, offered me a chair and a book which he placed in my unresponsive hands and asked me, earnestly, to consider as an alternative to "Lawrence". He gave no reason for the cancellation whatsoever. I looked at the book. It was a jolly comedy set on board a Cruise Liner.

"But, Earl . . . we turned this down a year ago."

"I'm aware of that. But we still own the rights. You could change your mind."

"We've made it already, it's the same formula as 'Doctor at Sea'."

"And that made a tidy fortune; you can't beat a well-tried formula, kid. Girls, lovely locations in the Mediterranean, a comic cook, there's a Dowager too. Can you imagine Maggie Ruther-ford in a lifeboat with a tiara?"

No one ever mentioned "Lawrence" again. I never knew, and still do not know, what stopped the plans so suddenly a few weeks before shooting. Neither, if I remember, did Puffin or anyone else connected with the production. Was it a matter of politics? Did someone somewhere object to the exposing of a very private man? Was the strange, still unexplained, ending to his life a forbidden area? The lonely road, a black car, two school boys, skid marks . . . was this a silence to be kept for ever? Or did someone know that the situation in the Middle East at that moment was to lead to the assassination of King Feisal, his heir and his Prime Minister in the middle of July? Or, simply, did the Studio go cold, fearing the high cost? Mr Davis kept firmly out of it all and only in a letter, months later, confided that he himself had been too distressed to even speak of it at the time. Whatever happened, "Lawrence" did not go as a film, although Rank, who still owned the copyright, permitted Rattigan to re-work it as a play, which opened subsequently under the title of "Ross" with Alec Guinness giving a moving performance. But my door, pushed at, closed sharply. It was my bitterest disappointment. However, Puffin was not one to be downcast for long. We had worked so hard and so long together on the project that the idea of full abandonment was unthinkable, and he set his mind towards another objective which could serve us well enough, Shaw's "The Doctor's Dilemma", which an American Studio, MGM, offered to finance and distribute.

Mr Davis gave me the necessary permissions, and the saddened team who had fought so long to bring "Lawrence" to the screen swung back into business on a very different level. It was not, however, thankfully, a jolly romp on a Cruise Liner; someone else did that while I steered myself, with Puffin's help, towards the despised Art Cinema circuit, much to Earl St John's amusement.

"The public," he said one evening at dinner in my house, "will confuse it with one of the real 'Doctor' films you made for us, kid. They'll feel cheated, you wait and see. They don't want to pay good money to watch you croaking about with TB in an attic! Who does, for chrissakes? And once they find you've cheated them it'll be downhill all the way."

Later on, just as Hans brought in the coffee, he rose a little unsteadily to his feet and turned towards the fireplace.

"Earl, dear!" cried his pretty wife helplessly. "Whatever are you doing?"

He rolled his cigar slowly and deliberately to the other side of his mouth. "Trying to put my host's goddamned fire out, that's what," he said.

*　　*　　*

But he was right. The British public did feel cheated, and as soon as they found out that I was not playing the adorable, twinkling Dr Simon Sparrow, they stayed firmly away from Shaw, and apart from some kind comments from a few of the critics, the film slid into obscurity. Not, however, in America, where they were ready for the Art Theatre Snob Stuff, and MGM, delighted with their modest investment, financed us all again to do another subject together. I was invited to go and work in Hollywood, which this time, after many refusals in the past, I accepted. I realised, almost subconsciously, that the recipe for the manufacturing of seaside rock after two or three years was wearing thin unless I agreed to continue in the old formulas which, as Earl had pointed out, were well tried and seldom failed. It seemed the right time to make a change. I was nearly forty.

*　　*　　*

"The one thing that you simply have to remember all the time that you are there," said Olivia de Havilland just before I left, "is that Hollywood is an Oriental city. As long as you do that you might survive. If you try to equate it with anything else you'll perish."

There was a scatter of photographers wearily popping flash-lights at the airport, the smog, through diluted white sun, stung my eyes, a girl with red plastic boots, a tall hat with a plume, a braided satin jacket tight across her enormous breasts and a smile like a silent scream, offered me a cellophane-wrapped basket of oranges and said, "Hi, Dirk! I'm Mary-Paul-Jayne, welcome to California!"

The hotel was a scatter of pseudo-Spanish bungalows around a vast kidney-shaped pool, amidst hibiscus, banana palms, carmine bougainvillaea and a constant soaking mist from thousands of water-sprinklers buried in the plastic grass. There were also humming birds, two swans on a stream, and the street on which it was set was called Charing Cross Road.

The bungalow allotted to me was filled with flowers, baskets of yet more fruits in stiff yellow cellophane, packets of nuts, pretzels, bottles of drink, and a deep canyon-like gloom. Everything was off-white. Chairs, carpets, walls, lampshades even the logs in the fake Louis fireplace. There were screens at every window to keep out the bugs, and the lintel between my bedroom door and the lounge was splintered violently down its entire length, ripped into jagged pieces, as if someone had used a dagger or an axe to force an entry. A four-inch shard of wood rammed into my hand and I bled like a stuck pig.

My fist wrapped in an off-white towel I dialled the desk clerk.
"Yeh?"
"Um . . . it's about the bedroom door here."
"So?"
"It won't close. The lintel is smashed."
"The what?"
"Lintel."
"Where are you?"
I told him.
"Who are you?"
I told him my name. A long silence . . . rustling sounds, eventually a tired voice. "We don't have you listed here."
"I must be listed here. I'm here. In your bungalow."
"You with a firm? Colgate or something? You with Sunkist-Krispies?"
"Columbia Pictures."
"Oh . . . you the British actor, right?"
"Right. And the lintel is smashed . . ."
"Yeh . . . I don't rightly know what a lintel is; what number did you say?"
Again I told him.
"Ah. Yeh . . . okeydokey . . . that's the Lana Turner Suite . . . you say the door's smashed?"
"That's right, can you fix it or move me?"
"Can't do a thing; Sunday, you know. How about a coffee or juice or something? We'll get it fixed Monday morning for sure."
I sucked the wound mournfully; staring across the room through the cellophane fruit and bottles of imported gin. Under a plastic rubber tree, a wide dummy piano keyboard glistened.

Beside it a foot-high pile of records in neat, crackly, orange covers.

"What do you suppose that all is?"

Forwood picked up a disc and turned it to the light.

"Concerto No. 1 in E Flat. Liszt." He placed it neatly back on top of the pile. "Your music, I imagine."

"A foot high? All that . . . they said they were using a double."

"Well, you'll have to know the music, even if they do . . ."

The telephone rang.

"Hello? Hello?" a breathless, whispering voice.

"Who do you want?"

"You're British, aren't you?" the voice gasped softly.

"Yes."

"I heard you talking by the pool a while back . . . I'm British, I need help. Help me."

"Where are you?"

"It's my feet, oh God! My feet . . ."

"What do you want?"

"I'm next door, across your patio . . . help me. They've strung me up by my feet, from the ceiling . . . my feet . . . I'm hanging here; help me, please help me."

I hung up swiftly.

Forwood looked curious. "Who was it?"

"A man hanging by his feet in the next bungalow."

"Call the desk clerk."

The same tired voice. "Can't do anything about the lintel today, I told you . . ."

"There is someone in the next bungalow who needs help urgently."

"Which bungalow?"

"Across from mine. He just called. He's British."

"Oh God, again . . . they're crazy in there. Was he drunk?"

"Strangling."

"Okeydokey, we'll take care of it."

We looked at each other dully across the off-white room. "I think," I said, "I'd like to go home."

A week later I was more determined; I had done costume tests, make-up tests, acting tests with sundry people hoping to be cast as Countesses, George Sand, Chopin and my Mother. I had also been faced with the prospect of having to learn eighty-five minutes of piano music accurately enough for my hands to be examined by the giant Cinemascope camera, within five weeks. Since I couldn't even play a Jew's harp with any degree of confidence this was a severe challenge. My music coach, a gentle, gifted, Russian with rimless glasses and thirty years experience of music, called Victor Aller, sadly shook his head and pronounced it impossible.

An urgent meeting to request my immediate withdrawal from this débâcle was demanded and resignedly agreed to. The cast was all assembled, Charles Vidor, the director, Victor Aller, Mr Goetz, the producer, Forwood, and my extremely gentlemanly, calm, and pleasant American agent, Charles Feldman. And all the Top Brass. I was assured that it had never happened before in Columbia, and was I sure I knew what I was doing? I knew all right; I was going home as soon as possible. Before the meeting Vidor asked me to go to his office to have a "final little chat, just to see if we can't come to some arrangement . . . this is a desperate step you're taking."

Rubber trees again, a small Renoir, a Manet with poppies, air-conditioning, Mr Vidor, a symphony in grey and cream, cashmere and silk, alligator shoes winking like glass boats. His desk neat and tidy. A copy of the script, a telephone with fifty extension buttons, a photograph of Liszt aged twenty-five, a swatch of red and yellow suede, an onyx pen holder.

"This is a terrible state of affairs, kid . . . terrible." He shook his spiky white cropped head and pulled out a deep drawer on his right. There were four, chilling, Martinis, each with a twist of lemon. He offered me one, and when I refused sipped his own with worried eyes fixed on Manet's poppies.

"I hope you'll be reasonable . . . just think of all the people who have been working so hard for you for months. Researchers, musicians, writers. The little people who work on the sets with such care and love. The costoom people, hours and hours they've spent designing just for you . . . 35,000 dollars worth of costooms we have, all authentic, all his stuff . . . so dedicated, so devoted . . . all for you." In my silence he took another Martini, dribbles of condensation puddled his grey leather desk-top. "You know we have five million dollars invested in you, kid?" The question was gentle, mild, there was no rebuke.

"Yes. I know."

He was startled, but only showed it by the trembling of his glass. "You know?"

"They told me in New York. They said that five million dollars was on my shoulders."

"They said five? Not three?" He was anxious.

"No. They said five."

He finished his Martini, a hint of satisfaction.

"Just because of a little bit of music, you know, it doesn't seem fair to throw all this away?" He waved the empty glass gently round the air-conditioned room and the grey leather desk.

"Everyone told me in London we'd use a double. I simply can't do what you ask me to do. You must re-cast and let me go back to Europe."

"Be reasonable, please. So many heads could fall . . . you want that?"

The Executive Office was on the top floor. The cast assembled, uneasily, all in dark suits, a convention of coroners. A *Fiscus Benjamina* wept motionless in one corner, an iced-water machine bubbled occasionally. Papers were shuffled, seats creaked, Victor Aller stared dully at the deep pile carpet, his lips pursed, glasses winking. Someone behind a vast desk cleared his throat comfortably.

"What seems to be the trouble, Mr Bogaarde?"

"I'm here under false pretences. You engaged me to play Liszt and presumably play a piano. I cannot do this. At the first meeting I had at the Connaught in London I explained this point carefully, and it was accepted, it was agreed then that a double would be used for the piano work and what I would merely do my job as an actor. Since it is now deemed necessary that I must do both, I must ask you to release me from the contract, and re-cast. There has not been very much publicity so far; at this stage I can simply announce that I was not able to perform my duties and so have withdrawn. It is very simple . . ."

The man behind the desk smiled a cosmetic smile.

"I suggest it is more than that. I suggest that you are not too happy with your Co-Star . . ."

"I refute that. I am extremely fond of Miss Capucine, she is absolutely charming."

"Then you dislike Mr Vidor . . ."

"Not at all. He has been very kind and sympathetic . . ."

"The script then; you say you don't agree with the story line."

"Not true."

He leaned across the desk and killed the smile.

"There has been an item to this effect in the last five editions of the *Los Angeles Times* . . . we have already bought out two whole morning editions . . . how do you account for that?" His eyes were lasers.

"I can't account for it at all. I have never spoken to a member of the Press."

He turned to the room at large, expansive hands.

"Gentlemen, didn't Mr Goetz here have to buy out two entire morning editions of the *Los Angeles Times* because of some very, very unattractive comments made by Mr Bogaarde about the script, Mr Vidor and Miss Capucine's height being too tall for him by a good ten inches. Isn't that a fact?"

Mr Goetz agreed. "But I do not think that Mr Bogarde voiced those opinions."

"Then who the hell did? Khrushchev?"

Mr Feldman now leaned forward quietly.

"We have been very distressed by these paragraphs, we have checked on them, and it would seem that they were all written, and despatched, by the Front Office in New York. My client has had no contact whatsoever with any member of the Press since his arrival here in Los Angeles. Front Office do not wish his participation in this motion picture, they would prefer he be replaced by a Contract Artist from Columbia, as you well know; Mr Goetz and Mr Vidor have fought long and hard to have him for their project, because they believe he is emotionally capable of such a role."

The man behind the desk took the top off his fountain pen, and snapped the clip nervously with his fingers. He swivelled suddenly like a bird of prey on the hunched figure of Victor Aller.

"You are the music coach on this production, right?"

"Right."

"You coached Cornel Wilde to play Chopin, right?"

"Right. But Cornel Wilde could play tennis."

An aching stillness.

"What the hell has tennis got to do with the piano?"

"A matter of co-ordination. Cornel Wilde could swim, ride horseback, play tennis and squash."

"So?"

"So my pupil here can't even play 'Happy Families'."

"He lacks, er, co-ordination, I take it?"

"Completely."

"How long will it take you to teach him to play piano?"

Victor Aller sat upright; courage flooded his weary, stocky, frame. "If my pupil had just one degree of co-ordination, which he has not, if he had one iota of understanding for the piano, which he has not, I could probably get him to learn, and to play, the first eight bars of the Moonlight Sonata, the very simplest piece in the repertoire chosen for this motion picture—if you gave me one thousand years."

I heard an ambulance bell far away on Hollywood Boulevard, the elevator rattle down to a lower floor; the man at the desk stared worriedly at Mr Vidor.

"Charlie . . . say, can we compromise? We are too deep in. He can fake the long shots, you come in close over the keyboard for the rest, we use a double for the hand inserts. OK?"

It was agreed. My heart plummeted. We left in a draggle and stood in silence waiting for the elevator. I said I'd walk down, Victor Aller came with me. He mopped his brow with a handkerchief.

"That's the first inquisition I ever attended in this town in over thirty years; I feel sick to my stomach."

"You were very brave, thank you."

"You shouldn't bring your good British manners here; they don't want 'em."

"Anyway, thank you for speaking the truth."

"They don't like the truth here, that's another thing, the truth's dangerous."

"I know . . . it could have meant your job, that's why I said 'thank you'."

"Shit. Sometimes it's nice to tell the truth once in a while."

"You are a very good friend."

He laughed mirthlessly, paused and removed his glasses, and wiped them carefully on his tie.

"Well, you got plenty of time to find out . . . plenty of time . . ." he settled the glasses back on his nose and hurried on down the concrete steps, ". . . like one thousand years."

9

BACK in the Lana Turner Suite with its squashed porridge carpet, Forwood steadily played through the entire foot-high pile of records required for the film, while I sprawled, numb with misery and full of Hennessy and self-pity, half in and half out of one of the porridge tweed armchairs, staring hopelessly at the splintered woodwork of the unmended lintel. After an hour and a half of sonorous organs, crashing cymbals and a run-amok piano, I slid into a heap on the floor and begged most earnestly to be carried to the next flight for London.

Forwood carefully replaced "Fantasy on Verdi's Rigoletto" in its crackly new orange paper sleeve, and took my empty glass; and bottle.

"Come on. Stop whining. They've made a compromise . . . you only have to play from the back. And it's a dummy keyboard, not a real piano . . ."

"Oh God help me . . . but I still have to play the exact keys . . . it's got to be musically accurate."

"No one has ever done it before, of course, you know."

"Done what?"

"Played eighty-five minutes of piano music *without* a double."

"Oh shit! Who'll know? Who'll even care?"

"You will."

"I can't do it! I have no co-ordination; you heard what Aller said. He should know, he's been teaching the piano for years and years . . ."

Forwood blew some dust off the plastic rubber tree.

"Seems a bit undignified finally coming all this way to a place which you have avoided for so long and letting it beat you; a kind of Dunkirk retreat; without valour."

*　　*　　*

Victor Aller and I worked together in a dank brown sound-proofed room with a picture of Myrna Loy on one wall and a view of Naples on another for twelve to fourteen hours a day. Every day, with Sunday afternoons off for rest. By the time we

The twenty-first anniversary of Pinewood Studios. J. Arthur Rank and John Davis, and myself as Sydney Carton, September 1957.

The bar of the Hotel Terminus, Bourges, during "A Tale of Two Cities", 1957.

A. Armstrong Jones

Christmas day, Westbury, Long Island. Self, Rex, Kate, Tony Forwood and "June", 1956.

With Betty E. Box and Ralph Thomas on location at Cortina d'Ampezzo, March 1957.

Victor Aller, my loyal and devoted music coach, on "The Liszt Bio". Vienna, 1959.

Columbia Pictures

Capucine and the dogs. Christmas day, 1960.

With Elizabeth in a mistral at Cannes, 1961.

My mother and my father. Cagnes, 1965.

The Palace near Beaconsfield, Buckinghamshire, 1960.

Hans and Agnes Zwickl: my cook and housekeeper for ten years. With the Corgis and the English Mastiff, Candida.

Rank

A courtyard at The Palace, with Sinhue and Bogie.

got to Vienna, one month later, I played my part of Liebestraum No. 3 before "all the Crowned Heads of Europe" including half the Court and many hangers on, in the ballroom at Schönbrunn Palace. With the camera on my hands. It had not, as Aller had predicted, taken a thousand years after all, and although it was a slow piece we had made a start, and with his patience and devotion, Forwood's unending encouragement and Capucine's constant loving support (she was never to miss a single performance all through the weary seven months of work), plus ten to twelve hours work at the keyboard daily, including all day on Sundays latterly, I lost three stone in weight but managed to get through all the pieces selected for me to play, ending up eventually with the major chunk of No. 1 in E Flat with entire orchestra in the Cuvillies Theatre, Munich, accurately enough and with some degree of Lisztian panache; it brought the house to its feet voluntarily, and the orchestra applauded beaming brightly. Aller turned his back and burst into tears. I had no retreat without valour; and although I frequently choked to death on the dialogue, I almost began to enjoy my steady walk to the piano in every palace, church, concert hall and drawing room from Bayreuth to the Hungarian border.

How I did it I do not know nor ever will. I invented a private code for the keys which only I could comprehend, leaving Aller mystified but pleasantly amazed as he corrected posture, wrists, thighs, back, feet, head and every form of musicianly behaviour. One piece of behaviour which vexed us considerably was the blood. After so many days, weeks and hours of practice, my fingers were inclined to split from time to time, leaving sensationally blood-splattered keys for the eager eye of the Cinemascope camera to delight in. During the Campanella there was a veritable cascade, which although quite inaccurate for a pianist, even one as passionate as Lovable Liszt, pleased the Studio Chiefs enormously since it proved that I had worked hard for my money and that audiences would be quite electrified by such intensity. I very much doubt that they were. However, I had done it; that is what mattered to me. Capucine and Aller both felt that God had leaned out of Heaven for a while, and although I seriously doubted that He had the time to spare, I was bound to agree, in private, that He might perhaps have sent a friend along. It was the nearest thing to a miracle that I have ever personally encountered.

The full story of the making of this unhappy epic is so distressing that it cannot, yet, be written. Although I managed, eventually, to overcome my lack of co-ordination, it was a grinding and profoundly unhappy experience. After the first three weeks of shooting, Charles Vidor died of a heart attack in his hotel bedroom and the film foundered like a holed galleon. Capucine, Aller, Forwood and myself, now a solid block of four, were overwhelmed with relief. Not so much at Vidor's untimely death—although his apparent illness before made all our lives unbearable, particularly Capucine's whose first film this was—as the fact that everyone was convinced that the whole sorry mess must surely be abandoned before any more money was spent, any more tears were shed, or any more people were humiliated. Surely now there would be calm and a chance for the survivors to move quietly away from the wreckage. No more candy-floss hair styles, no more appalling dialogue to struggle with, no more oaths or yells sent ripping across the bewildered Austrian technicians and small-part actors. "Don't give me that goddamned 'lampshade' look, Kraut!"; above all no more endless piano practice long into the night in the Bristol Hotel room which had seemed now to become my tomb.

For the first two or three days, while a shattered Hollywood decided what to do, Cap, Aller, Forwood and myself drove into the countryside, walked in the woods, dined nightly at Sacher and, arms linked in delight, sang our way through the spring streets of Vienna. We did not, I regret to say, behave with the respect normally reserved for sudden death, although Cap and I did at least go to the lying-in-state of our late director in the mortuary, taking flowers (one could hardly take champagne), and were about the only two to do so. But relief was short-lived. Almost as soon as Mr Vidor was freighted aboard a K.L.M. flight to Los Angeles, another flight arrived bearing a tired, but encouraging, George Cukor who arrived determined to hold the sagging epic together, bearing Osbert Sitwell's *Life of Liszt* firmly clutched for us all to see in his hand. A flicker of hope dawned amidst our well-concealed despair. Perhaps Mr Cukor could make some changes in the script? Perhaps he could even read? He could do both. And did.

Mr Cukor had dealt with the very greatest all his working life, the Barrymores, Hepburn and Tracy, Garbo, Garland and many others: he was not about to be dismayed by taking over a shipwreck with an almost, to him, unknown crew. He was a working professional from the tip of his fingers to the crown of his splendid head, and he expected and demanded no less from us. He rallied our forlorn band together swiftly; giving each one of us a private pep talk outlining the way that he would now steer our drifting barque. He was rightly appalled by my own performance, "a mincing tailor's dummy" he cried furiously, and sent my heart soaring by the detailed ideas he had for a complete re-working of Lovable Liszt. He also, as it happened, had a total love of, and dedication to, Kate Kendall with whom he had recently worked on "Les Girls". This slender bond of mutual love and respect was a great asset at the uneasy beginning of our partnership, and the laughter we shared together talking of Kate's idiocies eased him into wary confidence and me into total trust.

Under his determined authority we all began to come alive, costumes were altered to the correct period, actors re-cast where needed, sets modified, a general feeling of enthusiasm began to flow and Capucine found it possible to laugh again. The only thing he couldn't do much about was the script, although he did manage to clear up quite a number of "Hi! Liszt . . . meet my friend, Schubert, he's a pal of Chopin's". Which was a relief. However, none of us was under any illusion that we were making anything more than a big Hollywood standard. We just tried harder to make it work better, and Cukor was even able to make me realise that a line like "Pray for me, Mother!" was possible if you managed to believe it, and that nothing whatsoever should be done on a screen unless you made it interesting, from closing a door, crossing a room, to reading a letter. And so, finally, we ended the location work in the Cuvillies Theatre in Munich, I now weighing seven stone with bleeding fingers and eighty minutes of piano music behind me and a lasting and binding friendship with Cukor and gratitude for his teaching.

The modest house I rented in Hollywood had a swimming pool, two eucalyptus trees and a staggering view of Los Angeles swarming across its dusty plain below. Life was more tolerable here than in the Lana Turner Suite and seemed all the better because the light was now glimmering softly at the end of the long, long tunnel. I still spent hours at the piano, but Aller often sat by the pool reading a paper in the sun, tapping his feet, and the pressure was not nearly as great as it had been before; I was working up for my final concert, the 6th Rhapsody—it had originally been cut out as being too complicated, but after the successes of the European tour it was reinstated. After that nothing bad could happen again, I felt sure. I was nearly through; the Studio were very pleased with me, it had even been said that the moment the film opened in New York, the following July they planned, I'd be a World Star, and the Coroners, whenever I met them, actually put their arms affectionately round my shoulders, and said I was doing just great, kid. Which was very comforting, knocking forty. I even allowed myself to think, for the first time, of Beel House, and wondered what the new dahlia beds which Florian and Hans had planted by the pool must look like now, since this was the first week of September. I realised wistfully that I'd not see them before the frosts came; however, maybe next year. There was always time.

It was almost dawn when the telephone rang, that urgent, desperate sound which drags you from the deepest moment of sleep. In the dim room I groped about for the thing, heard the bell stop and Forwood's voice from his room down the long corridor. I lay very still. In the flint sky beyond the eucalyptus trees a thin wavering thread of crimson in the east. I knew what had happened even before he had opened my door.

"It's Kate." He was a silhouette.

"When?"

"A few hours ago."

"I see."

"Leukaemia."

"Yes."

"Rex was with her."

"Who called?"

"Annie Leon. She and Mike have been at the hospital with him."

"How good of them; good friends . . ."

"She never knew . . ."

"No."

He closed the door quietly. The crimson thread in the sky gently split and became two, then three and then a whole shimmering mass, tangled silks spilled into the sky above the hazy sprawl of the city far below. The leaves of the tree hung still, thin fingers; no point now in thinking about Beel, or dahlia beds or frost; the bright one had gone, and another day, but without her, was breaking.

*   *   *

Her death was not unexpected. For some time a small group of us, Kenny More and his wife Billie, the Goughs and others had been growing increasingly alarmed and distressed by the subtle and insidious changes in her health. One day, the summer before, playing croquet at Beel she quite suddenly collapsed and sat shivering and pinched, humped into a corner in the Out-Patients Department.

"I'm so cold, wifey . . ."

"There's a cool wind."

"But it's June."

"Unpredictable weather in England, darling." I wrapped her heavy mink round her.

She smiled wanly: "I'se sick, Miss Scarlett . . ."

"I'll get your medicine."

As she sipped slowly at her large glass of Guinness with a double Port, the only thing which ever seemed to bring some immediate energy back, she stared with wide troubled eyes out across the sun-flecked lawns.

"Do you think I've got something dreadful, Diggie? And they won't tell me."

"Balls! Of course you haven't, don't be such an idiot . . . you've probably got the curse or something."

She laughed a bit, and shook her head gently. "I've got something . . ."

Our mounting distress was compounded by the fear that Rex did not know that something was gravely wrong. But he did know. He had known, for certain from the doctors, on that unhappy day long ago, when we had bundled her off to Los Angeles with Gladys Cooper's Corgi and had made him scrambled eggs between the shows. He had decided then with extraordinary courage to keep the facts to himself, and that on no account was Kate ever to get the very slightest hint that her life was measured out to the very last day. It was never mentioned by any of us, and the only cause for doubt which she might have had was when the *Sunday Express* decided to print in a banner headline on the Entertainments page after her last important work, "Will Kay Ever Film Again?" Proving that there is always a market for private grief.

Rex asked us to arrange a memorial service for her in Hollywood at the same time as one was held in London and New York. As a mark of respect, three major studios closed down for two hours in Hollywood so that people could attend the service in the little English church of St John's, an extraordinary gesture of love and respect for a woman who had only ever made a single film in that Oriental city. Gladys Cooper read the eulogy, I funked it I regret to say, and George Cukor had a splendid magnolia standing by the altar, which was planted later on in the gardens of the Actors' Home in North Hollywood as a green and flourishing memorial to a vivid, joyful, all too short, life.

A few weeks later "Liszt" finally ended and I accepted to replace Montgomery Clift in a film which was to be made in Italy opposite Ava Gardner, almost immediately. I had no urgent desire, now, to return to Beel, in fact I was not even sure that I wanted to see it ever again and resolved, on the long flight over the Pole to Europe, that I would put it on the market and find somewhere else to live.

I had only been on the Italian-Hollywood film a very few days before I realised that Mr Clift had shown remarkable sagacity in withdrawing from the production. Spanish Civil War and Gentle-Priest-Loves-Tart-With-Heart etc. We started off, mercifully free from Studio interference, in a semi-documentary style, no make-up, grainy, real—which pleased me after the theatricalities of Liszt, and Ava, burdened by the absurd label, "The World's Most Exciting Animal", was equally happy. Hair scraped back, skin shining, in a cheap floral dress, she made a perfect foil to my shabby cassocked Priest. For a little time we thought we could be "bucking the system". But after the first ten days' rushes had been viewed by an astonished, not to say shocked, Hollywood, we were ordered to re-shoot and gloss everything up. Ava was bundled into a wardrobe by Fontana and I was tidied up generally. The title "La Sposa Bella" was suddenly altered to "Temptation" and finally, incomprehensibly, to "The Angel Wore Red". We spent a considerable time freezing to death in a Catania slum. Nunnally Johnson, our gentle director, grew sadder by the day, and finally Ava and I lost heart and threw in the sponge helplessly; you *couldn't* buck the system. As far as I know the film never even got a showing on television. Our attempt at realism had angered the bosses who wanted passion and sacrifice in blazing Madrid and our desperate attempts at a compromise failed miserably. However, we were handsomely paid, because of all the retakes they kept on insisting upon, and

Christmas found me finally released from the burden, exhausted, but moderately rich, in Rome.

I decided to have an enormous family Christmas to obliterate at least some of the disappointments which had enabled me to afford such a gesture. My father and mother flew in from London; Capucine and my gentlemanly agent, Charles Feldman, of whom she was exceptionally fond, flew in from Los Angeles; Glynis, ever loyal, came all the way from Sydney where she was filming; and her son Gareth came from Prep School with Irene Howard as a chaperone. It was a splendid family effort. Turkey, holly, mistletoe, presents galore, and the loyal toast proposed by my father at the end of dinner. Afterwards we all went on to a night club and danced until four in the morning. Kate, we all felt, would have approved enormously.

"Well! Would you believe it!" said my father when we all arrived back at the Hassler. "The bar is still open. I think we should have just a little night cap after such a strenuous day."

Charlie Feldman, Forwood and I, led by my determined father, headed for the empty bar, leaving the women to go on up to bed.

"A most successful Christmas, I think," said my father chucking a log on to the dying embers of the fire. He raised his glass towards me: "I drink to your continued success, my dear."

"Depends what you mean by success, but thank you."

"Well . . . twelve years must count for something, surely?"

"Quantity rather than Quality. I've made thirty films and a lot of money."

"You've made more money than I have ever seen in my life. I brought you all up on two thousand five hundred pounds a year. I never earned more. On *The Times* one is supposed to have private means, only I didn't; it was a struggle but I think it was a success in the end."

"But, Pa, you had personal satisfaction from your work, didn't you?"

"Of course!" he looked surprised. "Don't you?"

"Not much. I've done an awful lot of junk over the years; and this last year has been even worse. They may be successful in terms of money at the box office, but they don't actually fulfil anyone much, apart from the producers."

"I think," said Charles, "that he's kicking against entertainment movies. But that's what the cinema was invented for, you know. To entertain."

"And what do you think they should do?" said my father, stretching in his chair.

"Disturb, educate, illuminate."

My father snorted cheerfully. "We get quite enough of that in the newspapers and things. I like a good flick. I don't think I want to be disturbed, as you call it; but perhaps that's a question of age. I must say I like a good comedy you know; Charlie Chaplin, Laurel and Hardy, Will Hay, that sort of thing. Don't you think that people should have a laugh sometimes? You sound very worthy to me."

"No, of course I do! I'd love to make a good comedy; Cukor, Billy Wilder, Lubitsch, Robert Hamer. I enjoyed the 'Doctor' films, but there isn't much scope in England for sophisticated comedy nowadays."

"Oh well. That doesn't go down very well in Uckfield or Burgess Hill, I'm afraid. Your people must know what they're up to surely?"

"Anyway I have a nasty feeling that it is all going to change quite soon; the kind of films I've been making are going to be swept away by television and by people like Bill Haley and Elvis Presley. There is a new audience on the way, and not for the stuff I make."

"You do sound depressed! And after such a splendid day!"

"Look; if these two epics fail, which I personally think they will, then I am in serious trouble. They are old-fashioned movies, I don't believe that the kids, as they call them, will give a tuppenny damn about them. I think that my days of success, as you call it, are numbered. It's been a good innings; but if I don't catch the trolley I'm for it."

My father looked very bewildered indeed. "Tote!" he said to Forwood, his eyebrows raised in disbelief. "Is that really so? You're his Manager, what does he mean?"

"What he means," said Forwood slowly and carefully, "I think, is that he has never given a great performance in a great film; good ones in bad films, excellent ones in medium ones, poor ones in appalling ones, but never a spell-binding, commanding performance in anything. He's worked hard, is highly competent, sometimes interesting, often watchable, but really nothing more than a very successful film star; and he wants more, and feels that he can be more. But the subjects haven't been there; the climate isn't right yet. But it is changing, and when it comes he is frightened that he may not be able to convince the new directors that he is anything more than just a pretty face . . . and perhaps he's not . . . do you follow me?"

"No," said my father shortly. "It sounds quite like one of his reports from school: not very encouraging. But in spite of that he has made something of his life, isn't being a successful film star enough?"

"No," I said.

"Well . . . I think you're all taking it much too seriously. It's been a very successful time, I'd have said. I don't know what anyone could possibly want more." He set his glass carefully on the table and got to his feet. He leant down and kissed the top of my worried head. "It's been a splendid time, splendid day too; I'm off to bed now. As far as Mother and I are concerned we are very proud of you, and I think that you have been a very lucky fellow indeed."

I watched him thread his way carefully across the empty bar; suddenly he stopped and patted his pocket. "My key isn't on the table, is it?"

"Mother's got it."

"Of course! You've really made me quite muddled." He went on towards the lift.

★　★　★

A cat ran hurriedly down the Spanish Steps, shadowy, deserted under the pale lamps. The wind was soft and cool, traffic lights winked red, amber, green unheeded on the empty Via Sistina, below me a giant Christmas tree shimmered and rustled in the hush before morning, the golden star at its peak, nodding and swaying gently. A star. How could I explain it to him? No wonder he was muddled, I was as muddled myself. I now lived in an alien world, as unlikely and unfamiliar to him, and the rest of my family, as a walk on Mars. A world in which all the standards and beliefs we had been brought up to respect as right and honourable were almost completely redundant and which, if one did try to observe them, tripped you up more often than they ever secured you.

"It's rude to point!" Lally used to say, rude to stare, to laugh or to comment on someone else's appearance or disabilities, at all times and with no allowable exceptions; it was right and proper to consider other people's feelings above one's own no matter what. This we had had drummed into us from the very earliest days, and it was so ingrained in me that it came as a major shock to discover on my rise towards the giddy elevation to the canopy of the Odeon, Leicester Square, that these rules did not, seemingly, apply to public property like politicians, jockeys, footballers, boxers, murderers, the entire Royal Family and its appendages, and above all to film stars. We, I understood fairly quickly, were immune from any form of respect, like the clown who gets water squirted in his face, or the polar bear in a tutu dancing in the ring to a whip. By placing ourselves from choice, apparently, in the glare of the spotlight we had automatically forfeited our privacy and, for the most part, our lives. We belonged to the mass just as much as their three-piece suite belonged to them, and were treated, for the most part, with the same easy familiarity. Stage actors, one gathered, were a little more distant, due perhaps to the saving distance between audience and player created by the proscenium arch. The cinema, however, threw you right into their laps, and hopefully, for some, their arms. The intimacy of the close-up destroyed any possible illusion of apartness, and only the excessive riches one was supposed to accrue—yachts, servants, swimming pools and mansions—made one in any way different. In fact they merely created something more desirable, desirable because, in fact, deeply concealed beneath the cosy owning was a constant longing for the unattainable. The Dream.

It had never at any time remotely occurred to me that one day I might become part of the Dream, that for a number of years in fact I would be the Dream. It was the last thing I had wanted, and the last thing that my father, or the family, could come to terms with.

"Can't understand it at all, my dear," he had said, his eyes bright with amusement. "They must all be bonkers!" Some of them were. But by the time I had really discovered that, I had succumbed to being bonkers, as he put it, myself.

Audiences, one gathered, liked the performances I gave, even if they left me dissatisfied and keenly aware that I should do better, and so I was a success. Rank were pleased because I made money with the films, most of them, and that was their yardstick to everything; the cinema was big business. So. If this success secretly caused me distress, despair and disillusion at times, the reaction of my family had been comforting, for they simply didn't believe it and, apart from being slightly bewildered and amused, accepted it calmly with a vague sense of disbelief. Which had a very stabilising effect on me. My family life, which I cherished above all things, was never in any way altered; they and it were the ballast which had helped to carry me on a pretty long journey. We all went on much as we had done before my gentle climb upwards, except that I had made something out of my life and this gave them all the greatest pleasure. But my father was too wise a creature to come to terms with it seriously. It in no way diminished the pleasure he took in the modest perks, as he used to call them, which came his way. Trips to Venice or Malaga, St Moritz or New York; lazy afternoons sketching on Long Island, or surfing at Biarritz; choosing the best clarets and burgundies he could find in hotels and restaurants all over Europe, and even tonight he had made his toast to the Queen in Rome. But he simply brushed aside the reasons for these pleasures. As far as he was concerned it was all really nothing but a bit of a lark.

My mother, on the other hand, had taken it rather more in her stride, as she takes most things, eagerly and unthinkingly. After all, she pointed out, it was all perfectly natural since I took after her, and had she not married so young and decided to have me, she herself would have been a famous star, for had she not been on the point of going to Hollywood when my father shattered her dream for ever by explaining that she had made a contract with him, and not Mr Lasky? Wistfully she languished in England bringing up her family, doing her best to hide the disappointment. Not altogether successfully. So when the time came she delighted in fluttering about like an elegant dragonfly, in the warm periphery of my spotlight; it was as near as she ever got to the silver screen which she had so coveted.

Elizabeth, now married to George and a mother of two, was altogether less sure. We had grown up so closely together, shared so much of life, that she could not be so easily swayed by screaming fans in the streets, police escorts, and the curious fact that on some occasions during public appearances it had been deemed necessary at times for me to have my flies sewn up as a protection from my more ardent followers.

"My dear, I just can't take it seriously, that's all. I'm awfully sorry if it sounds rude or something . . . you know . . . but it's all so dotty, isn't it? I mean why you of all people? Really! It doesn't make sense to me at all. It's really rather disgusting, in a way, I mean when you think of it."

"You mean like being sick on a bus?"

"Well . . . not as awful as all that . . . but pretty vile really. It isn't even as if it was a very important thing to be, is it? A film star?"

"It isn't."

"Well then; like a surgeon, or scientist, a composer even, you know. Goodness; you must feel *awful* really."

But generally we had managed, over the years, to weather this strange metamorphosis together, although I could only guess at the silent stresses and strains they must have endured; for it is no great pleasure to be on the fringe of the famous; and their privacy and anonymity were constantly invaded by idle chatter and envious gossip which inevitably, it seems, surrounds what is euphemistically called today a celebrity.

To a closely-knit, loving family who wished and indeed expected to keep their lives quite undisturbed and above all private, it sometimes came as a bit of a jolt. But I was never reproached. Lally, however, with her usual excellent sense and awareness of what was what, kept out of it all entirely; she was delighted for me, if what I had was what I wanted, but she wished no part of it herself. She preferred to carry on with her own life, her own family, and her own affairs, and as always kept herself to herself. Very wisely.

I envied her her wisdom and tidiness of mind. How could I be wise? Know when and how to make the jump. To have less, like my father, but to have more, as he had in self-fulfilment and pride in his work. I knew that he was right. I had been very, very lucky in the twelve years. It had been a totally unexpected achievement, if achievement it could be called, it had even started off with a mistake that cold, snowy day in the Aeolian Hall, but I couldn't kick against that. Here I was, thirty films behind me, popular, highly paid, and constantly in work, something most actors would willingly give up everything in life to have. And yet I was deeply unsatisfied under all the glitter and gloss, unfulfilled, and almost, it had to be faced, ashamed of the position I had reached.

Why? I had been manufactured to entertain people, that was all, and apparently I had done just that. I should have no pretensions. That was my function. So why go on trying to prove things? Was there anything left to prove really? Only the one nagging doubt that I could act. But since no one really cared much about that except myself, what did it matter? And if I cared all that much, all I had to do was to get my release from Rank, clear off back to the theatre, and start all over again if I could.

All I wanted, I supposed, was respect in my work, but how could I possibly achieve that by playing spaniel-eyed priests or Liszt in a fright-wig? The theatre, I knew, terrified me and could not satisfy me now; I had fallen completely under the spell of the cinema, the technical work. The camera excited me by its apparent awareness of anything which I wished to impart to an audience mentally; it was my friend never my enemy, for some unexplained reason; there was a rapport between us which exhilarated me. Dearden had seen this, Losey and Asquith, so too had Cukor, and I revelled in the intensity of concentration which it demanded and I gave it until I was almost ill with exhaustion; and because I very often fell desperately short of what I had hoped I was doing, I wanted to go on and on until one day I would be able to sit down and say, "Ah! That's it! That's what I meant it to be."

But how long would my opportunities hold out? Where could I find the subject which would really allow me to apply everything I had so far learned? I leaned my head against the cold glass of the window watching the light rise on Rome. St Peter's, a tin jelly mould shimmering in the first glow of day. A sudden flight of starlings swirling into the grey sky, a soaring comma . . . below me the day staff were beginning to arrive, *prego*-ing themselves cheerfully up the hotel steps. I pulled the shutters to and went to bed. Next week a new decade would begin; perhaps things would change.

*   *   *

But they didn't; at first. I was sent off to Spain to play a Mexican bandit sheathed in black leather, riding a white horse, carrying a white cat, and belting everyone in sight with a silver-topped riding crop. It wasn't much fun; it was the last picture in

Mr Davis's recipe, and the last I was to make for Rank under his protection.

Shortly afterwards the Liszt Bio opened in America and, after seven excellent weeks in New York, died the death everywhere else. The same thing happened in London, and in spite of a great publicity campaign in which Columbia discreetly suggested that Capucine and I would announce our engagement at the Press Reception, of all unlikely places, it floated down the river of no return. The Spanish Priest and Tart With Heart film, as I said, never even got shown on television. One way or another a depressing start. What it all proved, without much doubt, was that I had failed in America. My work, or personality, or whatever you care to call it, was unacceptable to American audiences. The American audiences like meat and potatoes, one lady critic told me in New York, which, unhappily for me, I was not. A piano was not, obviously, quite enough. The blame was neatly laid on my shoulders. But never, at any time, by my producer Bill Goetz, who with his enchanting wife, Eadie, remained staunchly loyal and undismayed. A rare and heart-warming event in Tinsel Town.

But everything which Dolly Rubin had warned me about during a supper at Sardi's in New York, months before, came to pass.

The telephone, which had rung almost daily from California asking me how it felt "to be a Star" after the first seven weeks at Radio City, stopped abruptly. Columbia, who had eagerly been negotiating to buy out my contract from a delighted Rank Organisation, just faded gently away like a dispersing morning-fog. And two producers of repute, to whose children I had very happily become god-father, were suddenly no longer available when I called.

Dolly was a tough, bright, rather short Estonian with an accent which could crush rocks. She was something important to do with Publicity for the Liszt film. After a hellish day of interviews with the Press, which was known as "Total Exposure", we had gone for Eggs Benedict to Sardi's.

"How do you think we're doing?" I was really too tired to care.

"Fine. Just great." She snapped a pretzel. "Wanna know what I *really* think. Off the rekord? It's old fashioned. The movie. I don't think the kids'll go for it. It's pre-war, for God's sake. Know what I mean?"

"And if it fails at the box office?"

"You'll fail too. Remember this, honey; it isn't great acting that gets you up there as a Star, it's great grosses. Nothing more and nothing less. That old chestnut about being only as good as your last movie is absolutely true." She leant across the table and tapped my hand. "*Absolutely*. If this movie makes it you'll be offered every role from Mary Magdalene to Stalin . . . never mind you don't look like them, they'll fix it so you do because you'll be bankable, they can sell you. This is a Consumers' Market. When you don't sell they don't buy, not the Prodoocers, not the Exhibitors, not the goddamned audiences. Maybe one near-miss is allowable, but two is curtains. You can be the greatest god-damned 'King Lear' Broadway ever saw, but if you don't come off the screen and bring in the shekels they can't give you away with a packet of Mary Baker Cake-Mix. I bin here a long, long time, sweetie; I know. It is a mathematical formula you could remember from Aunt Dolly, and it all starts with the letter B. Box Office equals Big Name equals Bankability, anything else equals Brankrupt." She forked her frozen spinach into a neat green hillock.

"Get it? The facts of life."

So, to be fair, I had been expecting this all to happen, but when it did it was not the most agreeable of feelings. However, as George Cukor said, when a thing doesn't go, then the hell with it: just say, "Well; it didn't go" and get on with life. Much easier said than done. A door had closed for me rather firmly. I had made my exit from the Hollywood scene with as much dignity as possible, and I was comforted by the fact that every exit has to have an entrance, although I was not absolutely sure now where this might be. Well aware of Mr Presley, of James Dean with his sullen youth-identification, of Brando with his power and force, of the new generation who were now following a different piper in Hamelin, I was supremely aware that the kind of work I did, and the kind of actor I was, was doomed. I had to take action pretty soon, and drastically.

To this end I sold Beel House, which I had come to dislike more and more since Kate's death, to my other catalyst, Basil Dearden, and moved into a vast stone and marble edifice near Beaconsfield which I got cheap since it had been a Children's Home for years and no one knew what to do with all the partitioning, frosted glass, and red crosses everywhere.

But just before I left Beel for ever, Kate's bedroom had its final guest. Judy Garland arrived unexpectedly, slightly amazed herself at her own daring, since she had come from Los Angeles quite alone for the first time in her life, with, as she said, "a real purse with real money in it! I'm so excited." The last time we had met was in my house in Hollywood; then she was fat, ill, moved in a trance, and those wide brown eyes were almost buried in a white puffy face. But now here she was eating a vast breakfast, laughing and giggling, pretty, plump I suppose, but no longer fat, and back on form and ready to go.

"I'm planning a concert, just two nights, at the Palladium, and you'd better be there, but first of all I'm going to Rome . . . can you imagine? All alone, no Sid, no family. I'm having such a ball! And I'm going to look about for a house in London to live in for ever. We are all coming over; no more Hollywood, no more Hell. I'm better now, cured by a wonderful doctor, and I know just where I'm at."

It was a wonderfully happy time. We went for long drives into the country, Chipping Campden, Burford, Lechlade, King's Stanton, Oxford, places she had never seen and most times had never heard of. We walked with the dogs; sat in the sun; talked and laughed. She was without doubt, I suppose, the funniest woman I have ever met. We seemed, in that July, to laugh endlessly.

"Oh! I'm so happy, you know that?" She put her arms round my neck.

"You sound happy, I know it."

"You want to know why?"

"Why?"

"Because you are my new friend, Kate brought you to me, that night ages ago . . . you made me a promise, remember? You'd not leave me, remember that promise?"

"I do."

"And I trust you."

"That's a very serious statement."

"It's supposed to be goddamned serious, trust is. I don't have too much of it in my life, you know that. I spend most of my time groping about in the dark like Helen Keller, feeling faces to find someone to trust, to be safe with."

She ran her fingers lightly over my face. "I found you. Now don't you go and leave me; all I have in all this world is Sid and my family, I love them and I trust them, but no one else in all this stinking world, except you."

"That's a heavy burden."

"You can carry it. I'll help you along."

"All right; you promise me that. You'll help me along."

"And you be at the Palladium."

"Same show? Hungarians with dogs and ventriloquists?"

"Oh you! Now just you stop that! I need the warm-up."

"You don't. And you don't need those Dancing Gentlemen to spell out your name. They all know who you are."

"I need the warm-up, I've always had a warm-up . . . I know this part better than you do, Buster."

"How many songs do you know by heart?"

She looked vaguely round the Out-Patients Department, playing thoughtfully with a pearl ear-ring.

"Songs? You mean words of the songs, lyrics?"

"Yes . . . how many?"

"Oh . . . I dunno . . . maybe two hundred, could be. Why?"

"Just sing them all."

She looked up in amazement and burst into laughter. "All of them! Are you out of your mind?"

"Just you and a whopping big orchestra and just go on singing."

"Until the cows come home?"

"Until they let you go; as long as they ask for more."

"You mean start cold? Cold! And just sing?"

"A tremendous overture, and just you in a spotlight. Cold."

Her eyes were suddenly interested.

"Not a spotlight . . . a pin spot . . . maybe a follow spot crossing the stage . . ."

"Whatever kind of spot you want. And take a big place, a huge place, Madison Square Garden, a football stadium."

"I know!" she was laughing now. "I'll take the Metropolitan and be like the wife in 'Citizen Kane'! You want to kill me for ever?"

"You said that you trust me? Well, I tell you it would work."

"Honey," she poured out a small glass of Blue Nun, poked the ice cubes with her finger. "Honey, I played the Met. I played every goddamned Opera House in the U.S.A.; and I filled them, I am always a sell-out. But I've been terribly, terribly sick. That hepatitis nearly killed me and I have to go back to work and earn some money, I can't take any kind of risk, believe me . . . I do the show-I-know-how."

"Then make a change, do it alone."

"I'm not Samson, for God's sake! I'm not that strong. I'm Fay Wray in 'King Kong', remember? I just holler. And I can't holler for two long hours."

"Try."

"You are a shit. My best friend and you want to ruin me . . . I'm going to see Kay Thompson in Rome, I love her and I trust her too. I'll maybe kick it around with her."

She moved into a pretty house in Chelsea with the family, and started to settle down to what she called just being a housewife; and although she was often to be seen shopping for her groceries up and down the King's Road, the food she served was mainly from Fortnum and Mason; if she was worried about anything as sordid and incomprehensible to her as money, she never showed it, and the time was happy.

At the Palladium at the end of August she did her show alone. For the first time. Halfway through she had a spot turned on me, to my misery, and forced me to go up on stage and sit at her feet while she sang a song which she knew I loved above all the others. "It Never Was You". It was a calculated piece of show business . . . and she knew it. I sat humbly at her feet, she sang softly and sweetly, one arm round my shoulder, but when she finished, and while the crash of applause brought down the plaster, she kissed me and said: "You see, I can; thank you."

That show and the second one she did were triumphs. She was radiant, reborn, sure. Once she said to me: "You know something? It's so damned lonely up there. I'm so alone, so afraid. Just before it starts you have everyone around you, telling you you're great, doing your hair, making up your face, mending your pants, kissing you, telling you they love you, touching you (I hate to be touched), building it all up for you, giving you wine, giving you pills, getting you on to your feet so you'll be ready to go on . . . they take you right to the side of the stage, all touching, kissing, whispering, encouraging . . . they have the towel, the glass of water, the hair spray, all the goddamned paraphernalia, and they know the 'Take'. And then you go out there and you are absolutely, absolutely, alone. Suddenly you are *alone*. It is the most awful feeling in the world. And that's how it's always been, and that's how it always will be . . . alone."

"But then it gets better?" I said.

"Sure it gets better; the moment I open my mouth. You know once at the Hollywood Bowl a damned great moth, yes a moth!, flew right in there!"

Her eyes were wide with remembered horror.

"What did you do?"

She shrugged slightly. "Oh . . . I parked it . . . what else? But I'm so sure, you know, that one day they'll find me out." She suddenly burst out laughing, shaking her head. "You know, I can't really sing, not really; I holler, like I said. Oh sure, I'm no Deanna Durbin, now she really can't sing, and that silly horse, Jeanette MacDonald, yakking away at wooden-peg Eddy with all that glycerine running down her Max Factor! I have a voice that hurts people where they think they want to be hurt, that's all . . . and I can't act a row of beans either; I'm just me. And I'm so damned scared they'll all find out one day. Can you imagine the pleasure everyone will have? But just now I feel what the hell! I feel good! I feel great! I am great, and I love you."

For Judy then, another start, for me, at that time, another move from Beel House to the stone and marble Children's Home, now gutted, redecorated, and far too opulent and rich for my present position of almost complete limbo.

It was Christmas again, another house full, the same cast as the year before in Rome, and my gloom and foreboding of that Christmas were in no way relieved. However, there were presents to wrap, a tree to decorate, a job my father had done every year since I was born and which he still took extremely seriously. Wreathed in yards of tinsel he sat on the top of a ladder fixing glittering balls among the branches, and fitting barley sugar candles into holders. The telephone rang, it was Basil Dearden. My heart sank, I thought he'd found something wrong with the plumbing at Beel.

"No . . . nothing wrong, thanks, we're very comfortable. Melissa is spending a fortune, of course, putting in a new bathroom, stripping the panelling all over the house . . . and planning an Italian Garden where the old tennis court was."

"Oh good. I thought the central heating had blown up."

"No, it's working. I gather the Liszt epic did though?"

"You gather correctly."

"And the other two. My spies tell me the bandit thing is a sod."

"Could be. I haven't seen it."

"Getting a bit old for leather knickers, aren't you?"

"I'm beginning to think so."

"A bad run really . . . anything planned for next year?"

"Nothing . . . you got anything planned?"

"Sent you a script over this afternoon, by messenger. Might interest you. Read it over the holiday and let me know, OK?"

"I'll try . . . got a full house here, family."

"You may not like it. No one else does. Everyone we offered it to has turned it down. You're our last chance."

"Thanks. What's it about, paedophilia?"

"No. But our first choice said that it would prejudice his chances of a Knighthood."

"What is it? The October Revolution?"

"No. Homosexuality, actually. Middle-aged married man with a yen for a bloke on a building site."

"Can you make a film about that?"

"Rank have said they'll distribute, the lawyers say there's nothing wrong libel-wise; just wanted to wash their hands after reading it."

"It gets better and better."

"Better still. An accountant read it for costing and said he felt he should have a gargle."

"Must have read it aloud."

"Must have. If it's any comfort we don't call anyone a queer, homo, pouf, nancy or faggot."

"What the hell do you call them then?"

Basil's voice was silky.

"Inverts."

My father was struggling at the top of the tree trying to fix the fairy on top. A little pink angel with wings and benevolent wand. He came slowly clambering down the steps, puffing a bit. "Jolly hot work this tree business. I think a nice little sip of one of your Worthingtons would be just right now. What's the matter?"

"Pa . . . would you mind if I made a rather, difficult film . . . I mean difficult in the moral sense; serious stuff?"

"I don't think I quite follow you. Political do you mean?"

"Homosexual."

He pulled out his handkerchief and mopped his brow gently; had a sip of his beer. "Oh my dear boy, we get so much of that sort of thing on television. Mother and I find it dreadfully boring, all those doctors and psychiatrists bumbling on. Now if you want to do something really serious, why on earth don't you do *The Mayor of Casterbridge*?"

"Well, you remember what I said in Rome last year?"

"Yes, I do. I do. Something about disturbing. I can't really remember . . ."

"Yes, disturb, educate, that sort of thing."

"You know I must confess that I really didn't understand what you were talking about. Got into a bit of a muddle, I seem to recall. Personally I think there are quite enough people doing that all over the place without your having to do it in the local flea-pit, but that's up to you. Just remember that mother and I live in a small village, we have to get on with our neighbours, not always easy. Try not to do anything which would embarrass *her*, people are so narrow, you know. That's all I have to say."

Forwood and Capucine were laying cloths on the long tables in the hall ready for the evening party. He looked up.

"Who was on the telephone?"

"Dearden. He's sending a script over. It's a bit of a problem one."

"Oh. Why?"

"Married man with a secret passion."

"What's the problem there?"

"The passion is another bloke."

"I don't see the problem," said Capucine. "My God! You English. You think that nothing happens to you below your necks."

"And in any case," said my father settling comfortably down into his chair, "I've told him that I think he ought to do *The Mayor of Casterbridge*."

But I did "Victim" instead, and played the barrister with the loving wife, a loyal housekeeper, devoted secretary and the Secret Passion. It was the wisest decision I ever made in my cinematic life.

It is extraordinary, in this over-permissive age, to believe that this modest film could ever have been considered courageous, daring or dangerous to make. It was, in its time, all three.

To start with, very few of the actors approached to play in it accepted; most flatly refused, and every actress asked to play the wife turned it down without even reading the script, except for Sylvia Syms who accepted readily and with warm comprehension.

The set was closed to all visitors, the Press firmly forbidden, and the whole project was treated, at the beginning, with all the false reverence, dignity and respect usually accorded to the Crucifixion or Queen Victoria. Fortunately this nonsense was brought to a swift end by one of the chippies yelling out, "Watch yer arse, Charlie!" to a bending companion, and we settled down to work as if it was any other film. Except that this was not.

Janet Green's modest, tight, neat little thriller, for that is all it was fundamentally, might not have been Shaw, Ibsen, or Strindberg, but it did at least probe and explore a hitherto forbidden Social Problem, simply, clearly, and with great impact for the first time in an English-speaking film. It was refused a Seal of Approval in America for being too explicit and it was many years before Hollywood even dared to tread the same path with any truth or honour. Some critics complained that it was only a thriller with a message tacked on rather loosely; but the best way to persuade a patient to take his medicine is by sugaring the pill—and this was the only possible way the film could have been approached in those early days. Whatever else, it was a tremendous success, pleasing us and confounding our detractors. The countless letters of gratitude which flooded in were proof enough of that, and I had achieved what I had longed to do for so long, to be in a film which disturbed, educated, and illuminated as well as merely giving entertainment. I had been fortuitously pointed in the right direction again, just in time. This time the door I had chosen to enter was not just ajar . . . it had been wide with a blaze of light and I was not to retreat ever again.

Incredibly, the fourteen-year-old image was almost instantly shattered. The fans, that is those who thought that being queer meant having a head cold or the belly ache, whirled away like chaff in a gale. They were bored by the subject I had chosen, felt betrayed that I had, as they said, gone serious, and had admitted my age; and in any case they had heard a different sound on the wind, the sound of the sixties—Youth. Elvis Presley led a whole generation away from my kind of old-fashioned cinema; television gave them all they needed in the way of visual entertainment. What they wanted now was music, a new beat, a new sound, a new believing and new identification with themselves, and they got it from him . . . and while he was leading them out of the fifties, four young Liverpudlians in Hamburg were waiting to grab them and remove them from sight for ever. The kids were leaving Hamelin, and although half-hearted attempts would be made to lure them back they would pay no heed, and I would have to learn to play my new pipes and go off on my own.

It would be a great deal easier, I thought, than learning to play a piano.

IO

ANOTHER serious miscalculation on my part. It was far harder. After the failure of my Hollywood ventures, and the equal failure of my attempts as a Mexican bandit on a white horse, a cool, not to say chilling, wind rustled down the long corridor of power which I had once so blithely walked in august company. Now I was alone there; not often accompanied. No longer by Mr Davis at least, of whom, sadly, for he had been a good friend, I now saw very little. Dolly Rubin's words echoed in the solitude. Bluntly, Rank had no plans for me in the foreseeable future, and suggested that I have a look round for subjects myself which might be of interest to us both. Which I knew would be extremely unlikely.

I owned, at this time, the rights to John Osborne's play, "Epitaph for George Dillon", and had spent a considerable sum of money having it scripted as a film. This I carried to Earl St John who pronounced it downbeat and negative and that was that. Despairingly I asked for release from my contract, not out of pique, but from a steadily mounting sense of hopelessness. I was determined to break into a new kind of cinema, they were equally determined not to.

Freddy Joachim, after a long and happy partnership felt that I was being both impetuous and childish. Which perhaps I was, but his very gentleness and caution and innate sense of fair play were paper swords in a duel with an adversary, for this is how I now openly considered St John, armed with steel. My release was refused, but I heard growing rumours that plans were afoot to sell the remainder of my contract elsewhere. Which they had a perfectly legal right to do if they wished. I was in a state bordering panic, and bitterly resented the idea that after so many years loyal work I should be offered up like a packet of the Miller's own flour. Freddy and I agreed to differ on the subject, and after fourteen happy years we parted company in a warm and friendly manner.

I was still determined to obtain my release but neither Forwood nor myself was capable of negotiations which were, to say the least of it, strained and dangerously fused. Robin Fox and Dennis van Thal, who had a thriving agency, agreed to take me on and help me in the uncomfortable struggle. Eventually, under pressure, Earl St John agreed to let me go, immediately, on condition that I surrender a large amount of money due to me by contract which I could ill-afford. John Davis, in a final gesture of goodwill overruled this and in return I offered to make a film for them at a later date at a much reduced salary. Accordingly a handout was drawn up for the Press, which merely stated that "at the request of Dirk Bogarde, the Rank Organisation has not exercised the option on his contract with them". After fourteen years, twice the amount of time I had expected even in my most optimistic dreams, I was released. Nobody waved goodbye. Nor did they telephone any more. It was like a protracted armistice, except that it had finally been a compromise rather than a battle. But I was free at last.

For the time being I rattled round my vast stone edifice like a glass marble; Elizabeth's husband George, now running a very successful business as a tree surgeon and garden consultant, spent hours with his team of men laying out the long-neglected borders, making a vast lagoon with water-lilies and fountains, wrenching up brambles and overgrown rhododendrons and planting walks and alleys; I was very busy hunting for specimen plants, costly shrubs, and old-fashioned roses, spending capital with nothing coming in; if I felt optimistic, Forwood felt the reverse.

"It always amazes me that just when you should be pulling in you expand. Every time there is a crisis you buy a palace; you have no savings, no work in the future and there's George hacking about out there like Capability Brown, and you playing a latter-day Linnaeus."

"That's what I have always done. Something will happen."

"You'll end up in a debtors' prison, that's what'll happen."

"I'm spending my own money, for God's sake."

"You're spending your tax reserve money, my boy."

"Well, they can bloody well wait . . . they've taken a hell of a chunk of my loot already."

"They don't wait, they sit in their bungalows in Hillingdon and Edgware planning how to give you the chop. Their wives haven't got a mink coat, so why should you?"

"I haven't got a mink coat."

"Don't be so bloody dense, you know what I mean. If you

don't get a job in a couple of months you'll have to sell up. Right away."

*　　*　　*

Judy arrived suddenly one morning, pale, tired and under stress, a few weeks after the end of a marathon concert tour of America ending with a final show at Carnegie Hall which had proved to be one of the greatest peaks of her career.

She came alone *again*, no Sid and no family. There was a tighter edge to her now; sure, trim, confident, harder, but exhausted.

"I want to sleep for days. Unwind. Heal. I'm dead. I've come to hide. No one knows where I am . . . I had to get away from them all, they try to tear me apart."

The healing started after lunch. She refused to go to bed and instead insisted on a drive into the country which always seemed to relax her better than almost anything else. To Pangbourne, Henley, along the river as far as its source. She sat curled in the back of the car, in slacks and a sweater, impracticable little taffeta boots, her face pale, hands trembling but her eyes delighting in the tumbling blossoms of the orchards, lambs in the fields, the "houses with hay on their roofs" and the soothing peace of May in England. By the time we had got back to The Palace, after tea by the river at Sonning, she was nothing to do with the harassed, pale, tired woman of the morning. In the evening, round the fire in the Study, she handed me a packet almost shyly.

"This is what I really came to do; to bring you this. I hope you'll like me. No dancing boys, no Hungarians."

Two blue transparent records. No labels. Side One, Side Two. The matrix of the Carnegie Hall concert. "You wouldn't come, so I brought it to you . . . you know there were two empty seats waiting there for you until the end of the overture . . . just in case you made it." She sat on the floor beside my chair, her head on my knee, the dogs sprawled beside her, once or twice she squeezed my leg hard during key moments, or clapped her hands and cried with laughter at her own version of "San Francisco". Just before the final number, "Chicago", she stopped the record.

"You hear my voice? I had almost gone. I was dead beat . . . they wanted more and more . . . they wouldn't let me go, you can hear? And then when I got to this last song I knew I'd not get through, I couldn't get the breath . . . and then something fantastic happened; I want you to listen. Right after the first verse, when I sing . . . 'And you will never guess where' . . . right there, in the silence, one voice from way, way out in the dark, called out 'Where?' . . . right on beat . . . and he saved me. I took it from him and I went, brother I went! I have tried ever since to find out who he was . . . where he was . . . to thank him. Do you believe in God?"

"Sometimes, not often."

"Well . . . God sent this voice . . . you listen."

Although she had said that no one knew where she was, the telephone was almost constantly busy, and one afternoon there was a call for her from California. We were all sitting on the terrace having tea, I saw her come through the study windows, her arms outstretched; she beckoned, and I went to her. She put her arms round me, eyes smiling, tears brimming, lips trembling.

"It was the Coast. Stanley Kramer. He wants me to do a movie . . . with Burt Lancaster."

"And?"

"It's about retarded children; I said yes. Now do you believe in God?"

"No. But I believe in Stanley Kramer."

She punched me, and laughed. "Oh you! You are so damned British, I hate you!"

"When does it start?"

"I have to leave at the end of the week."

It was a good, happy week. Although she was still tired, still restless, not yet able to sleep, she was happy, funny as always and above all excited at the near prospect of the film. On her last evening we gave a great party for her; she made out a list, and everyone she asked accepted. She had never looked prettier, never been in such form, she was having a really magical time and was the most immaculate hostess. After supper, in the fading light of the summer sun, everyone sat round the grand piano and she and Noël Coward sang for their suppers. She knew all Noël's lyrics, which pleased him greatly, from "Mrs Worthington" to the entire score of "Bitter Sweet", and "If Love Were All", which they sang as a duet, brought the packed room roaring to its feet. It was a shimmering evening; and Noël was the last to leave sometime in the very early hours. I got into bed about five, just as the first light was rising above the trees, under my pillow a note from her. It read in part:

". . . What you have given me is something I will never be able to explain to you, ever. I honestly don't know what I would have done without you. You always give me pride in myself and belief in myself . . . and that's the loveliest gift of all. How I will ever repay you, Heaven knows!

Thank you for my shining new life. I won't fail you, and you have made it impossible for me to fail myself. God bless you.

for ever,

Judy."

Alas.

*   *   *

If the telephone rang constantly for Miss Garland it now hardly ever rang for me. Sitting slumped with a Guinness amidst my playing fountains and tossing rhododendrons I became very well aware of the sudden shift in my status. Rank had been a superb umbrella; however much I might have railed and complained against it. Now the elements hit me full on the head. No weekly cheque, no future plans, no capital. Apart from the tax reserves which I was steadily eating into like a termite.

One morning Hans and Agnes announced, in floods of tears, that The Palace was far too big for them to handle on their own and that after ten happy years in my service they now felt it was time to move elsewhere and in consequence had accepted the offer of a job with a millionaire in Florida. We were all suitably distressed . . . but Florida was Florida, and Beaconsfield and no capital was, to say the least of it, alarming. I was dragging my anchor; clearly The Palace had to go.

I made a brilliant decision on the third Guinness, staring into the night-scented-stock and bee-ridden lupins; I would sell up, and with the capital hopefully obtained, purchase a small farm and retire to work on the land for ever. No more cinema, no more theatre, peace and self-containment. I would, I thought, get Elizabeth and George (he was obviously good at land and farms and that sort of thing) to join me; give them a cottage, and together we would run the Elysian fields, and go to market, milk, collect eggs, plough, reap and sow, and lead the simple unrushed life of the land. I was immensely cheered by the idea of Elizabeth already in a gingham poke bonnet churning the butter; of the children, Mark and Sarah, on the hay wain, of ample teas and suppers round the scrubbed table in the lamp-light: the simple family life.

I took up a bundle of old *Country Life*'s and started to thumb through them in a happily bucolic state, secure in having made a firm decision at last. And Dennis van Thal called, almost at that moment, to say that he had managed to get me a film, at a much reduced salary, and that I'd better grab it while I could. Poke bonnets and hay wains slid from my grasp and I was shortly bobbing about off the coast of Spain in a three-masted schooner, being beastly to my crew and ordering everyone in sight to submit to the cat-o'-nine-tails, while Alec Guinness slapped his thigh from time to time in a grey wig which looked remarkably like a tea-cosy.

It was not a very distinguished affair, and apart from the enormous pleasure of being with Alec, a patient and generous actor if ever there was one, it was nothing, I think, which either of us greatly enjoyed. But it brought in a little loot, and thus, secured temporarily, a breathing space which I spent trailing about Kent and Sussex searching for the farm which would provide me with my kind of Mary Webb-Stella Gibbons-Thomas Hardy existence. Elizabeth in her poke bonnet simply would not leave my mind, although her immediate reaction to it had been less than exuberant.

"We are really very comfortable in Rustington, dear. I mean, what *sort* of farm, and where? It's very flattering of you, I'm sure, but George has got quite a big firm now, he's pretty busy; and I don't know anything about butter or cows . . . and the children can't ride about on hay wains all the year through, can they? Isn't it only in June or something?"

However, I would not be daunted and found a farm in a perfect setting not far from Edenbridge, which was up for auction. It had a tumbled-down timbered house, five cottages and four hundred acres with a river running through, starred by marsh-marigolds. I was determined to have it. All the money which I had spent on restoring The Palace, lagoons, fountains and smooth lawn walks, paid off, and I sold it privately, extremely well, and thus armed with a comforting cushion against immediate disaster sent poor Forwood off to the auction for the farm which he speedily obtained for me but without the five important cottages, which were all sold for enormous prices, singly, to stockbrokers and junior architects who would, in due time, smother them in high-gloss paint, William Morris papers, London lampposts and wishing wells and sell them at vast profit. I was left with a derelict farm-house, a huddle of barns, and four hundred acres. Ruin stared me in the face, and Elizabeth in gingham faded swiftly from sight for ever. I put it straight back on the market and sold it for the price I had paid to a neighbouring farmer and with a deep sigh of relief came sadly down to earth; homeless.

Although The Palace was technically sold, I did not have to give possession until April, and by the grace of God and Irene Howard, who was then casting at MGM, I found myself in a modest little Army-Comedy-Drama and stamped through the coldest winter for years with army boots and a cockney accent. It was a fortuitous move. The film was made entirely on location all over Essex, Surrey and Kent; each time we reached an area it was desperately combed for an alternative to The Palace. Day after day, as I slid and shivered through snow drifts rallying my brave soldiery, Forwood trailed wanly about with Estate Agents and too-eulogistic catalogues of Home Counties Tudor, until one morning he found me lying, frozen, in a barn near Ewhurst buried in straw eating a hard-boiled egg at the lunch break.

"It's not a farm; but it's pretty marvellous."

"Where is it?" I was numb with cold and past caring.

"Just up the hill there, staggering view. I can run you up in the car now."

"I can't come and see a house like this, covered in mud and plastic blood . . . this filthy uniform . . ."

"I think you should. It's exactly what you want . . ."

It was. And I moved into Nore six weeks later.

★   ★   ★

Judy had been in a cinematic limbo, so to speak, since "A Star Is Born" which she made in 1954 with George Cukor. Apart from a small role in "Judgement at Nuremberg", and the recent film with Kramer, she had not faced a camera for seven years. Now, with her shining new life, the stresses and strains were once more appearing like cracks in a patched-up wall. She was finding life difficult to handle and telephoned three or four times a week from New York, always about four or five in the morning my time. She couldn't sleep, and feared the dark; she wanted, and often got, constant reassurance, although I can't believe I ever made a great deal of sense blurred with sleep as I was. Sometimes she was on form and happy, but mostly she was depressed, worried, or planning wild All-Star-Concerts for the Kennedys, whom she much admired, or earthquake victims in Peru or Persia; these problems were harder to deal with at four in the morning.

"What time is it with you?" her voice careful, worried.

"Five am, you beastly woman."

"Oh! I waked you!"

"Doesn't matter . . . I have to get up soon anyway, it's a Studio day."

"Have you ever heard about a script called 'The Lonely Stage'?"

"No . . . why?"

"Well there is one and they want me to do it; in London."

"I heard rumours, didn't know the title. So?"

"It stinks."

"Well, say 'no' then."

"But it's a good idea. The idea is good. The dialogue is just yuccky."

"What's it about if it's so good?"

There was a pause, she laughed ruefully.

"This big, big Star goes to London to do a concert at the Palladium and finds the man who got away . . . It's about me; I guess someone has read my lyrics."

"Well, get a new writer and see how you feel then."

"Would you do it with me?"

"Play the one who got away?"

"Sure."

"Of course I would. You know that. But I know they want an American star."

"Why for chrissakes! He's supposed to be British."

"Box Office."

"Don't give me that. I'll do it if you say yes. Yes?"

"Yes."

There was a pause again, crackle noises: "I love you very much," she said. And hung up.

She got to work pretty quickly, for a very few days later I was asked if I would care to do a film with Miss Garland. Although there was no script ready yet, would I take it on trust? I agreed, providing that it did not interfere with a film I was discussing with Dearden for July, "The Mind Benders". The spokesman assured me warmly that the Garland film would commence in early May and that I would be well finished by June, since my role was not long. Miss Garland was the star. I would have plenty of time. Little did he know.

We all embarked, unwittingly, on a brakeless roller-coaster which, reaching its final peak, roared down ricketing and racketing, exploding us all into smithereens at the end.

Although the script, when it arrived finally, was a professional workmanlike job, well constructed and not quite as bad as Judy had led me to believe, I knew from her present state of depression and indecision (for she now telephoned me nightly, filled with doubts and fears and an unreasoning dislike of her part as written) that something would have to be done quickly or we would all be in for a very bumpy ride. I implored the producers not to show it to her when she arrived in England.

"But we have made a number of changes according to her wishes."

"If you show her that she'll turn right round and go back to the States. I know Judy, and I know her present mood."

"Well, what do we do? This is the script she agreed."

"I think she agreed only the story line. If you let me have a day or two I could try and re-write some of the stuff she has to say; but don't show it to her until I have talked with her."

They agreed, worriedly. Her present mood was frantic. Panicked by marital trouble in New York, she was in terror that the children, Liza, Lorna and Joe, would be forcibly removed from her, so she shoved them on to a flight in such haste that Liza arrived in London in slacks and a shirt with a bundle of odd garments clutched in her arms and Judy immediately sought to have them all made wards of the British Court. It was not the calmest way to start a very difficult assignment. To compound the problems which she had to face she was hurried to a foul little house in Sunningdale which the Company had rented for her for the duration of the film, adjacent to the golf course, because they thought she liked to play golf. This was a grave error and only served to make her feel that they were amateur idiots, since her affection for golf at a time like this was nil to say the least.

"Who do they think they've hired? Babe Zaharias?"

She eventually found a house in Hyde Park Gardens and moved in just before we started work. She was tired, frightened, and quite alone. Now at the top of her career again, after years in a limbo of illness and despair, and box office failure, she was unsure and unequipped to handle things for herself; van Thal willingly took over her domestic problems which were many, while I tried to assist her with the professional ones. The script was the first. Someone, idiotically, had already shown it to her and it caused immense distress. She was trusting no one from now on in. The storm was in the wind.

The first day at the Studio, make-up tests only, was not so bad. The crew, handpicked for such an august Star, were delighted and proud to be working with her. She was charming, funny, easy, and almost gay. It all seemed, on the surface, as if things would settle down. In her dressing room, later, massed with flowers and crates of Blue Nun, cards of good wishes and boxes of Bendicks chocolates, she shut the door firmly and announced that she was leaving . . . immediately . . . and slammed into the bathroom.

"You can't leave. You have a contract, darling. We're in."

"I'm not in . . . it won't be the first contract I've broken. I can't play this crap. They promised changes: they failed."

She was sitting on the closed lavatory seat, always her place of refuge in moments of shattering panic, a glass of Blue Nun clinking in her hands, her face pale, drawn, body shaking, looking small, ill and hopeless. For an hour I sat on the edge of the bath and reasoned with her; she wouldn't budge. Just shook her head slowly at every suggestion, at every gentle argument I brought forward. Finally, in desperation, I read her the first scene which we were to play and which I had entirely re-written. She stopped her head-shaking and sat listening; then reached out and took the pages and started to read them aloud with me. She laughed a couple of times, put down the Blue Nun; we went over it two or three times... she was suddenly, immediately, worryingly, happy.

"Hey! It's good . . . did you do all this?"

"Yes."

"It's really funny . . . don't you think Atlantic City would be funnier than Wilmette? They're both *awful*, but Atlantic City . . . I can make that funny . . . let's do it again. With Atlantic City instead."

We started shooting a day later at the Palladium. She was happy, in marvellous voice, nervous, excited; it was her first big number in the film, "Hello, Blue Bird". I had given her a blue bird brooch in sapphires; she was in her familiar dressing room, surrounded by an adoring company of Make-Up and Hair people; she was literally, at eight in the morning, bubbling with pleasure. She held the brooch tightly in a small closed fist.

"We'll be a new team, you and I. Won't it be great!" She was sparkling.

"Gaynor and Farrell!"

"MacDonald and Eddy!"

"I don't sing . . ."

"The Lunts!"

We held each other laughing, promising each other our futures.

At twelve-thirty she was on her way to hospital in an urgently clanging ambulance. We had started as we had, obviously, intended to go on.

"But why? Why, darling? What did you do it for . . . it was such a good beginning."

"It was a lousy beginning." Unrepentant, unashamed, pale, two days later.

"What went wrong? Was it me? Something I did?"

"No . . ." She twisted a spit-curl into place in the mirror and stuck it to her cheek. "Something *he* didn't do."

"Who?"

"Neame, our so darling director. He didn't even say 'thank you' when I finished the number, he didn't say anything. Just 'Marvellous, Judy darling'." She mocked a very British accent. " 'Marvellous, Judy darling'. Christ!"

"That's not so. He was thrilled by what you did, we all were, everyone was, you must know that, you must have felt it?"

"I don't 'feel' things. I need to be told; OK? Confidence. Who the hell does he think I am, Dorothy Adorable? I'm a goddamned star . . . I need help."

"Darling, you'll have to get used to the way we all work here. It's not the same as the States, we don't use the exaggerations, great, greatest, the best. It's all a bit cooler. If you don't understand that you'll get hurt; we don't get hysterical very often."

She shrugged and pulled on a shoe angrily. "That damned British understatement, the stiff upper lip . . . well, it won't do for Frances Gumm."

"Who the hell's that?"

For a moment she looked at me in the mirror with a face of white stone. Then it cracked, and she started to smile a little, she reached out her hand and took mine. Not facing me directly. Ashamed suddenly, aware of bad behaviour. In the wrong. I pressed her hand hard. She lowered her head.

"It's me. Frances Ethel. Isn't it awful?"

"Well, Frances Ethel, just remember that Neame had one hell of a day . . . he had to clear the Palladium by four-thirty for the evening show there . . . he was under pressure and first days shooting are frightening for everyone."

She withdrew her hand gently. "Just you tell Neame he'd better watch out for me. *I* get scared, he think he's the only one? I need help and trust. I don't trust him. I want him off the production."

She didn't have him off; but she never trusted him again and the first serious crack was opened, never to be more than very temporarily repaired. It was a very uncomfortable situation for Ronnie Neame, and he behaved impeccably with the patience and care of a saint. He was helpful, enthusiastic, and agreeable to all the re-writes I did for our scenes together. He did everything possible to make her happy and secure and lavished her with praise, justified always, but she never quite bent towards him again, even though after our first few scenes together she was patently thrilled by her work and was giving a quite superb performance. For a little time we settled down; writing every evening and every week-end. Sometimes she came down to Nore and made brilliant suggestions, funny, real, moving, and although she never wrote a word herself, she sat in my office all the time, smoking, sleeping, keeping close, awaiting each page as it came off the machine, reading it aloud, rejecting some words or phrases, offering better alternatives. It was a marvellous, happy combination. We honed and polished and rehearsed continually, avidly, so that when we eventually got to the take it was smooth and precise, spinning along on ball bearings. Spirits everywhere rose; her work was proving to be the best she had ever done, and she knew it.

"I'm good, aren't I?" She was humble, happy, sure.

"Gooder than you've ever been."

"You didn't see 'A Star is Born' . . . not really, they hacked it to bits, George Cukor and I have never ever seen it . . . do you know that? They mutilated it. Do you remember that scene I did in the dressing room with Bickford, about a ten-minute monologue? Remember? Well . . . could you write me something like that for the end of this thing? A long scene, all about . . . all about . . ." she fished slowly in the air seeking words, "all about what it means to be Jenny Bowman." Her name in the film.

"I'm not sure that I know all about what it means to be Jenny Bowman."

"Sure you do . . . she's me. You know that, don't you? She's really me. And you know me all right, Buster. That line you wrote that you say to the kid . . . remember? 'Jenny gives more love than anyone but takes more love than anyone can possibly give.' Remember that?" she chuckled happily, wickedly. "I reckon you know; and I'll always help you out with a real Garland-line when you get stuck. I'm full of goodies!"

But the good times grew fewer and fewer as Judy got later and later, or sometimes didn't even arrive at all for work. We used to sit about from eight-thirty, in dull, depressed heaps; the crew played cards and drank endless cups of tea; the guts were slipping out of the production. We were losing so many work days that I realised that the film I wanted so much to make with Dearden, and to which I had wholeheartedly committed myself, was in jeopardy. I would never, at this rate, make the Start Date and they would probably have to recast.

"Judy . . . you know I have to start another film in July?"

"So?"

"Well with all these delays . . ."

"Don't you start blaming me! I've been sick . . ."

"I know, but just remember that I only have seven weeks' work on this . . . you have ten, if I can't finish my part in that time I'll just have to leave."

"You can't."

"I have a contract with the other people. Signed."

"Break it."

"I don't want to. I want to do the film desperately."

She turned from the mirror, we always seemed to have these discussions in her portable dressing room on the set, and looked me straight in the eye.

"When you leave, lover, I leave. Finish. Right?"

"But you can't . . . for God's sake . . ."

"Don't tell me what I can't do! Everyone tells me what I can and can't do . . . I do what I want to do . . . and I don't want to shoot one bloody frame on this stinking mess after you have gone. When you leave for your oh-so-marvellous movie, I leave on the first flight for L.A. . . . don't you forget it!"

"I've always promised I'd never ever lie to you, right?"

"Right."

"But I'm leaving at the end of my seven weeks."

"Then we won't have a movie, will we?" She pulled off her ear-rings slowly and put each one carefully on the tray before her.

"You won't have a movie. This is your movie, no one else's. We've got the big scene to do; you want to do it, you know that, so far this is the best work you have ever done, better perhaps than 'Star'. It's your time; your career, I promise you I'll never fail you, but you must promise me to not fail yourself . . . please? Darling, be a good girl and come back again . . . please."

"Don't you good girl me, for godssake! They hate me out there. Have you seen those loving Cockney faces full of 'good girl'; they hate me. I feel the hate."

"They don't, they don't; they're working for you all the way . . . you know that."

She swivelled round on her chair and took my hands suddenly. "You really, really want to do this damned movie of yours?"

"I do."

"What's it about?"

"Deprivation of the senses."

"In English?"

"Brainwashing. It's a new, terrible weapon."

"Someone used it on me."

"They used it on the American troops in Korea. No one knows much about it yet."

"I do, all about it. I invented it; Louis B. Mayer invented it. My loving damn agents 'Frick' and 'Frack' invented it. There is nothing I don't know about it, do you hear? Nothing I don't know about your terrible new weapon. *I've* been so brainwashed I'm Persil White all through." She burst into tears and I held her very tightly. Above her shoulder I saw my own face reflected in the mirror; it was Persil White as well.

* * *

At Canterbury; a one-day location at the cathedral started well. She met the Red Dean and made him laugh, posed for the Press. At the lunch break an ashen faced wardrobe-mistress hurried from her caravan, her costume bundled in one arm, shoes in the other. "She's not working any more; you never heard such language." Grim-faced producers, the director, a covey of assistants; one or two blazered choir-boys hoping for an autograph. Despair wafting like smoke from a dying bonfire.

In her caravan, curtains drawn, light filtered, a litter of clothes, papers, a fallen vase of carnations, water dripping on the cheap linoleum. Judy hunched at her dressing table in a green silk kimono; hair a ruin, make-up wiped roughly off a white, anguished face. In front of her a tin tray with a wrecked salmon mayonnaise.

"What's wrong, pussy cat?"

"Get out . . . get right out."

"You were so happy this morning."

"Now I'm not."

"My fault?"

"You know damned well . . ."

"I don't . . . what is it?"

"I wanted you to stay tonight in Folkestone . . . I booked you a room; Liza, Lorna, Joey, all of us together. Just one night, one happy, lovely night . . ."

"I can't, darling, I told you. I have to get back by eight."

"You told me. The only thing I have ever asked of you." She started to weep silently. "Tonight, there's a full moon, did you know? A full moon, we could have all gone along the beach together, along the shore, in the moonlight, peaceful, calm, I need calm. The kids want to go. I want to go. Just one time and you refuse."

"I told you why."

"They were all looking forward to it . . ." she suddenly took her knife from the tray and stabbed me in the arm. I grabbed her wrist and we fell, in a sprawling heap together among the sodden carnations and the tumbled tray of salmon mayonnaise. "I hate you! I hate you!" She struggled and heaved, the knife still tight in her fist, I twisted her wrist and she cried out suddenly. Somewhere the knife clattered. I was across her, heavy; she fought for breath.

"Say you hate me . . . say you hate me."

"I don't." I still held her twisted wrist firmly. She moved under me, her free hand scrabbling in the debris. A fork suddenly thrust against my cheek, under the right eye.

She stared up in the gloom. "This can do as much damage. Say you hate me, I know you hate me, they all do, hate me . . ."

Gently I leant down and kissed her face; she crumpled, sobbing

218

uncontrollably, her arms around me, clutching like a drowning child. I helped her up and we stood in the ruins of her lunch and the water from the fallen flowers, standing together until the pain had eased, then I gently put her from me, smoothing her straggling hair, wiping her nose with my finger.

"You are all snotty . . . disgusting."

She half laughed, pushed the hair from her face, her eyes wide, streaming, filled with pain.

"How long will it take to make you presentable; an hour?" She wiped her mouth with the back of a hand, shrugged the kimono over her shoulders. "About; wheel them in."

Outside the sun was so brilliant that I could only just see the anxious huddle, a few discreet paces from the caravan; Neame was twisting and untwisting a white plastic spoon.

"She'll work," I said. I suddenly realised that I was still wearing my hat, that there was a splatter of mayonnaise on my tie. Wisely they stood aside and no one followed me, blindly I walked into a tree; and knocked myself out.

*　　*　　*

We had one week, one final week which she did for me, of complete, unforgettable magic. She was on time every day, her work was brilliant, we tore into the scenes and she blasted off the screen. My final day was our big scene. We started together rehearsing in her dressing room at eight-thirty. No one came near us. She had wanted to play it sitting down, not to move; I wrote it so that she had sprained an ankle and was carted, drunk, to St George's Hospital. She sat in a chair, I knelt at her feet. We rehearsed for six hours, with half an hour for a sandwich, in the cramped little caravan. At four-thirty we went on to the floor and shot the entire scene just once. It lasted eight minutes and was one of the most perfect moments of supreme screen-acting I have ever witnessed. I shall never see its like again. She never put a foot wrong, not an effect was missed, the overlaps, the stumbling, the range, above all the brilliance of her range. The range was amazing; from black farce right through to black tragedy, a cadenza of pain and suffering, of bald, unvarnished truth. It had taken us three days to write; she passed every line as I set it down, "warts," she said, "and all"; it took six hours to rehearse, eight minutes to shoot, and when it was over one of the crew walking across from the stage was stopped by one of his fellows.

"What," said the man, "happened on your stage today?"

"A miracle," said Bob.

* * *

A miracle it was indeed; in that last week of June, we shot twenty minutes of screen time and, more or less, finished off the main bulk of our work together. Judy was quite aware of what she was doing. She gave me the week in order that I could go off to do my "damned movie" as she called it, knowing full well that she would then be on her own to finish off the film which she so detested. The following week only a few seconds were shot, and she behaved unkindly and uncontrolledly, falling, in one instance, in a bathroom, cracking her head badly, necessitating, yet again, hospital treatment. Once more she tried to fire the patient, unhappy Neame, and finally, on Black Friday the 13th of July she walked off the film and that was that. I still had one or two small pick-up shots to do with her, and was forced to do them with a double, wigged, and dressed in her clothes. The miracle, though gigantic, was finally over. With my completion of the seven weeks' work, in my acceptance of the film with Dearden to which I had been fully committed, I could no longer stay at her side and she felt completely rejected. In a hostile atmosphere, untrusting and by now quite unloved, she was unable to contain her terror and her unhappiness; her private life lay about her like a pillaged room, there were court cases, and a bitter struggle to retain her children whom she adored above all things, but I could no longer heed the urgent summonses by telephone, nor could I make her understand that my duty, if one dared use such a word, now lay with Dearden and a new, extremely involving film.

"You are walking away from me," she cried in anguish, "you are walking away, like they all do . . . walking away backwards, smiling."

Useless to try to explain; there was no way now that I knew to help her. All I did know was that being with her, working with her, loving her as I did, had made me the most privileged of men.

* * *

220

And later, when one had added up the total of this unhappy summer's sum, the result was, tragically, a loss. "The Mind Benders", the film with Dearden, was too far ahead of its time. No one knew very much about brainwashing; no one really believed that it was possible, nor, apparently, did they wish to. If they had ever heard of Gary Powers, or had known the appalling effects on the GI prisoners in Korea, if they had known then, what they know today, about psychiatric treatment of political dissidents, maybe we might have fared a little better; but they didn't, alas, and one headline which blared, "Bogarde Thriller Is Shabby and Nasty" summed up the general reaction. Another thumping failure in my brave new effort to disturb, illuminate and educate. Someone was on the wrong track; it depressed me deeply that all the signs pointed towards myself.

And when finally the stuck-together, patched-up version of "The Lonely Stage" opened it was, in the main, received with superlatives by a loyal, loving, Garland Press. Although they all disliked the woman's-magazine story, which we had always known it to be, they praised Judy unstintingly, deservedly. One of the, at the time, leading critics, awash with what Judy called "spastic Garland mania" overstepped himself slightly: "There is one drunk scene," he wrote, "with Bogarde which mixes laughs with tears with such expert timing that I felt like raising my hat to the script-writer. I am told, in fact, that this was one scene which did not go according to the script. Halfway through it Judy suddenly realised that this might well be a moment from her own life. The real Judy took over from the cinema heroine. She started to make up her own lines. Just you listen to them," he sagely counsels his readers, "they are spoken from unhappy memories. Bogarde could only lean back, feed in a word here and there and let the camera move in on someone re-enacting an experience of her very, very own." Three days writing, six hours rehearsal.

"Golly!" she said, laughing with pleasure at the idiocy. "It only goes to show they don't *really* know . . . but we must have been very, very good." She had flown in from New York with a vast entourage of hangers-on, American Press and our now ebullient producers. It was the most amazing First Night I have ever witnessed. I picked her up at the Savoy, pushed her into the car, leaving her Empty Suits and Frilly Shirts aghast on the pavement, and together, quite alone, we drove slowly round London, all pain forgotten; all happiness ahead. At the cinema the crowds were dense, shouting, cheering, loving her, rocking the car with wild abandon, grabbing to touch her, tears streaming, voices screaming, hands outstretched as if to heal . . . to touch . . . to be healed. She was radiant, moved deeply, in tears herself. Afterwards we danced together at the reception; "We were good, you know that? Really good . . . we are a team."

"Gaynor and Farrell."

"Garland and Bogarde." She laughed and hugged me.

"Do you mind if I take first billing?"

"No . . . your privilege, ladies first."

"G is before B, isn't it?"

"Now it is."

"Oh! I'm so happy . . . and you were such a bastard to me all the time . . . so mean! How could you have been so mean when I love you so much; you better be sweet to me the next time around, Buster!"

But there was not to be a next time. If the film was a critical success, it was a public disaster, crumbling away like a piece of old lace. In Guildford, three days after it opened, they ripped down the posters and announced the revival of a well-tried British comedy about vintage cars. We were off. It is hard to tell why. Maybe the story was too sickly, maybe the new awful title, "I Could Go On Singing", which the producers changed in a fit of panic on the day of the Press Show itself, misled audiences into thinking that it was a straight Garland musical which it obviously was not. Maybe Judy, playing so close to the truth of herself, distressed her fans. Whatever it was, it sank without trace. But she, happily, was unaware of this at the time. She flew back to America after the premiere to be present as her daughter, Liza, set her own course towards the dizzying roller-coaster of the lonely stage.

*　　*　　*

It is almost extraordinary to discover that a great many other things were taking place in 1962, one was so hermetically sealed in a globe of self-absorption that they passed almost unnoticed or not even noticed at all. Algeria and Uganda became independent, the Russians sent arms to Cuba, Charles Laughton died, someone tried to assassinate President de Gaulle, they built a Hilton Hotel in Park Lane, France and England decided to build Concorde and, somewhere in April a much-loved and respected friend from many years, Daniel Angel, telephoned from Rome. It was a pleasant surprise, but so apparently ordinary that, like the rest of events, it too almost might have gone unnoticed. Almost.

"Enjoying your new house then?" He was laughing.

"Only been in a week or two. It seems fine."

"You move about more than fleas on a dog . . . who are you dodging? Creditors?"

"Any time now. Where are you, Danny?"

"Rome. . . trying to set up a deal, usual thing, know what I mean? Got a very old friend of yours here, wants to say hello. Hang on . . ." There was a pause, then a weary, well-remembered voice.

"Hulloo . . . how are you?" No interest in the question really, barest good manners.

"You don't sound very happy, anything wrong?"

"No. Just bored. Bored and tired and not working. It's been a long time since *we* worked; about ten years?"

I had first met Joseph Losey ten years before, on a bitter winter afternoon at the Studio. I knew nothing about him save that he was an American refugee from McCarthy, a director of talent, that his assumed name, for security reasons was Victor Hanbury, and that he was setting up a small budget film and was hopeful that I could be interested to play in it; my presence, it was explained, would help him to increase, if not double, his budget. I was not truthfully interested. Tired after making three films in a row, uncertain of this director with an assumed name and a not very good script I agreed, at least, to let him show me some of the last film he had made before he had had to leave Hollywood and the witch-hunt. I hope that I was not patronising; I know that I was not enthusiastic at the time.

It was freezing in the small theatre where the film was projected. I was alone, since he preferred to walk about outside in the slush like an expectant father, and quite unaware of the importance for him, then, of my acceptance or not of his work. After twenty minutes I knew, without any doubt whatsoever, that the one person I wanted to work with most was kicking his heels in the car-park in a long blue overcoat waiting for my verdict. We watched the rest of the film together in silence—it was called "The Prowler"—and after, in the Studio Bar, he started to outline for me the ideas he had for the hackneyed little thriller which neither of us liked but which he knew we could use as a base to move from. Alexis Smith willingly agreed to join us, taking an incredible risk for an American actress in those days of McCarthy, and so became my first Hollywood leading lady. The modest budget was therefore, predictably, doubled, and in high heart we all set off.

The result, after weeks of uncomfortable work in a run-down little studio where we had to fire a gun to frighten away the sparrows from the Sound Stage before every Take, was not, perhaps the greatest of our careers, but it had served to form a bond of respect and affection which was to last a lifetime. And it taught me, very early on, in line with Dearden and Leacock, that there was a magical, untapped, untrodden world awaiting in the cinema. I had managed in my Corridor of Power years, and with the willing assistance of Olive Dodds, to get him a contract with Rank; for which he eventually forgave me; his stay there not being of the happiest or most successful, although it did help a little to settle some problems for him, we unhappily had never worked together again. His weary, flat, affectionate voice, that morning from Rome, was sunlight through fog.

"What are you doing in Rome?"

"Finishing off a job."

"Happy with it?"

"I think so. Can't tell. It was a sweat. Good, ultimately."

"What next, something fun?"

"What the hell is fun? Do you know?"

"Just asking. Nothing then?"

"Nope. You?"

"A film with Judy Garland. Then something with Dearden."

"You'll never get rich that way."

"I'm trying."

He laughed gently. "So you're unavailable then, I take it?"

"Not after the Dearden thing. Then there's a big, big void. I'm on my own now. No Rank . . . free . . ."

"Happy?"

"Chilly. I wish we could find something to do together again . . ."

"And I. But what?"

"Joe. Joe, remember that book you found, ages ago? A slight thing, novella more than a novel. You thought it might make a film when we were doing 'Sleeping Tiger'."

There was a long pause, when he answered his voice was not quite as flat.

"You mean the Robin Maugham thing? About the man-servant?"

" 'The Servant'. That's it. What about that? Do you think it's still available?"

"I don't know, let me check it out. But Christ! You're too old now to play the boy."

"I know that, but I could produce it or something with you, couldn't I?"

"Producers have to be bright. Anyway . . . let me check it . . . I'll call you later."

When he called it was to say that the book was still available, that it had been bought by someone, scripted by Harold Pinter, abandoned, and that for a certain sum we could secure the rights; he didn't like the present version, had had long discussions with Pinter and they had found a new formula together. If, he said, I was really serious he would start negotiations right away.

"Of course I'm serious; could I produce it with you?"

"God no. I've got a producer, you can play the servant."

"No, we need someone like Ralph Richardson . . ."

"I need a movie name; they tell me you are what is laughingly called 'hot', so you play the servant; we won't get finance otherwise, yes or no? There's a lot of work to do."

"Yes, of course. When will there be something to read?"

"Not in time for you to change your mind. Late summer, after you have gotten through with being a movie star. I'll keep in touch."

The bay of Cannes lay before me, blue, still, calm in the September sun. The sand was hot, the beer iced, the rattan shades slatted shadows across the pages and made it difficult to read; it was difficult enough anyway (I had never read Pinter before), but I knew instinctively, which is how I have always worked, that what I presently held in my sandy hands on the hot morning beach, was not merely a script, but rather a key. The key to a door in my long corridor which only awaited the courage of my turning; and keeping to my dangerous track.

11

ELIZABETH came and squatted down beside me, spilling a handful of bulbs into my lap. "Those are the last, no more. November is a bit late for tulips, isn't it? Shouldn't it be October or something?"

"Better late than never; didn't have the time. Actually I forgot really."

She got up and stretched, swivelling to look out over the fish pool through the bare chestnuts. "I'm so stiff. Getting old. I do think it's pretty here, the prettiest house you've ever had. The last place, The Palace, was a bit film starry; not really you, if you know what I mean."

I pushed in the last of the bulbs, raked the earth over them, wrote "Carrara" on the wooden marker and got up.

"Everything is white."

"It's the White Garden, that's why."

"I expect you forgot them because of all that business in Cuba. I was so frightened, I wouldn't even listen to the News."

"Perhaps that's why."

"It really was nearly war, wasn't it? I don't think I could have managed another one, could you? I mean so soon after."

"No. I had enough last time."

"I was thinking of the children, and George, not so much myself this time."

We stood together and looked down across the Weald. To the right Chanctonbury Ring; far, far away, like a slit in the canvas of the sky, Shoreham Gap, glinting. Magpies stalked importantly, like judges, through the stubble across the sunken lane. It was cool, still, white doves clattered down in a covey and bobbed gently to each other.

She sighed; almost a laugh. "I don't think I could have. Do you remember how worried we both were about growing up; after ours? I didn't think I'd know how to do it."

"I remember. Took me a long time."

She put her arm round my shoulder and scuffed the November leaves into flurries. "Do you think we have now? Oh, I know I have. That hotel in Hove we ran, for Allied ex-Service men, a sort of rehabilitation centre really; our first job after we got married. You know how hard it was to start again. George and I did all the cooking, and the boilers: we couldn't get help, one old woman who came in sometimes. We were doing the beds, cleaning, cooking, washing up. I'd never ever had to do anything like that before. Sheltered little thing. I grew up all right. I felt so old at the end of it that I was just like that lady in the Shangri La thing; you know, the one who turned to dust in the end . . . she was so terribly old really? That was just how I felt. Dust."

I pulled her down the steep bank, among the leaves and we started up towards the house through the chestnut walk.

"I was so thick," I said, "that I tried to be an adolescent all the time; to recapture what I had never really had. Very boring for people who had to deal with a twenty-six-year-old eighteen. Do you know what I mean?"

"No. Not really. You were pretty awful sometimes; isn't it funny that we didn't actually grow up in the war, just when you'd expect it, with all the killing and bombs and things. It all happened in the peace; not what you imagine really." She stopped suddenly and scrabbled about in the leaves for some conkers and put them in her pocket. "They're for Mark, champion conker killer . . . or something idiotic. Conkers on a bit of string. Isn't it silly? We grow up but we don't much change do we, inside I mean. I'd quite like to play conkers again; you were awfully good, weren't you? Champion as well. I look at the children, I look at George, look at myself in the mirror and I know I've only got older. I don't suppose we'll ever really grow up truthfully, I mean like real people, do you?"

"Don't suppose so. Don't know, don't care now."

We reached the oak gate leading on to the ribbon-smooth lawns, worm casts like Pontefract cakes, neat box hedges, the house glowing in the winter sun. She clambered on to the gate and sat there, brushing dried earth from her hands; I heaved myself up beside her.

"I was saying to Pa the other evening that I think I could put my roots down here, you know."

She looked vaguely across the lawns. "Your roots?"

"Yes . . . for good."

"Have you got a super job coming or something?"

"In January, perhaps. A film by Pinter; with Losey."

"The Red Indian-looking man?"

"Yes."

"Will you get lots of money?"

"No. Nothing really, it's a small budget."

"How much?" Always deadly curious.

"Seven thousand pounds, about."

She looked at me with surprise, her eyes smiling. "Seven thousand pounds? That's all you'll make?"

"About . . . it's a difficult film, no one wants to do it, you know."

"Do you?"

"We all do . . . yes, of course . . . more than anything. But the money-men don't want to."

"Why don't they want to make it then?"

"It's not commercial, they won't risk the loot."

"Will anyone ever go to see it, if you do make it?"

"Not many perhaps . . . it's difficult, you know."

"Don't keep on saying 'you know'—I don't."

"Sorry."

"You must be dotty."

"Why?"

"Well . . ." She polished a conker briskly on her sleeve. "You say you think you can put your roots down here. How can you for seven thousand pounds in a film no one wants to make and no one will go to see? Of course, you're dotty! Why don't you do something like, oh I don't know, 'Cleopatra' or something." She laughed and her breath wisped into the still morning air. "It really isn't very sensible, is it? I mean if you do want to put down roots or whatever you call it."

I slid off the gate and it wobbled, she dropped her conker to hold on.

"Don't do that! You are vile! I could have fallen off easily. Now I've lost Mark's best conker." She clambered down beside me, searching for it in the cropped grass. "If you want to be in that kind of film you ought to live in a little flat like the one you had in Hasker Street. With two suitcases." She found the conker and caught me up walking towards the house. "You shouldn't have all this. It's silly." She waved her arms wide, embracing lawns, hedges, dovecote, house.

"Shut up!"

She threw the conker high in the air, waited for it to fall, caught it.

"I don't think you have grown up," she said flatly.

*　*　*

But I did, I think. The four films which I made with Losey between '62 and '66 saw to that. Each one was a bitter, exhausting, desperate battle. It never got any better; only Losey's obstinacy, determination, belief, optimism and unflagging courage managed to get us through; that coupled with a crew who also believed and a growing company, as he called it, of actors who were also prepared to put money second to career. In order to get any of these films made we all had to work for very modest salaries with the vague promises of percentages which we were seldom to see. No one got rich, in any possible degree from these enterprises. But we were enriched in our values; and that is what mattered most to us all; however, our values at no time matched the values of the Distributors or the Money. As Losey said, "The Money isn't even smart, even about money." But we fought, and we fought, until eventually they beat us in the battle between Art and Profit; and Art is the ugliest word you can use in their limited vocabulary.

We wrestled "The Servant" to the screen. It was on and off with the frequency of a conjuror's hat. If I had found Pinter's script difficult to read, then the Distributors and Money found it utterly incomprehensible and shied away from it like frightened horses, but a series of odd coincidences gave us courage.

With myself set to play the servant, Losey knew that he must bolster my name in such a delicate enterprise with a sound female one. He had in mind a new and very exciting girl called Sarah Miles. She, we both knew, was the ideal choice. But, it appeared, others had the same ideas about her, and she was greatly in demand. It seemed unlikely that she would accept such a modest assignment. She read it, said she liked it, but . . . One night I switched on the television to watch the News and, quite by chance, tuned into the wrong channel. A small one-act play of not much interest except for the sudden astonishing appearance of a young man who was instantly, beyond any shadow of doubt, the one actor we had to have for the third, exceptionally difficult part. I had never seen nor heard of him before. His name was Maurice Oliver. I called Losey, who hung up to watch, and our mutual agent, Robin Fox who was, as it happened, watching already. Since Maurice Oliver was in fact James Fox, and his own son. Losey agreed that Oliver-Fox was ideal-looking, but was worried that his inexperience (this was his first acting role as it happened) might be a strain on such a complicated, subtle, part.

We were starting. And then the slender hopes were dashed when we learned that Sarah Miles was now committed to a more commercial project for a great deal more money than we could ever hope to pay her. Even though, at this juncture, we had no money; only high hopes. Not quite enough. Once again the conjuror doffed his hat, the film folded its timorous wings, and settled down with a dull thump. Without her we were lost. Not only was she the only conceivable actress for the part, she was also the only bait we had to offer the Money.

Some days later, much against my wishes, and only under constant prodding from Forwood, I was forced, and that is the word, to attend an important premiere and go to the supper which was to follow. Something which I absolutely detested. I found my own premieres bad enough but someone else's intolerable. Forwood insisted that it would be the gravest of ill-manners not to accept the invitation which came from an extremely powerful producer who had, quite recently, been making polite overtures about a couple of not-very-interesting but commercial subjects. I was made to see, eventually, that I was not in the position to play the role of recluse at this juncture, nor to refuse the offered hand. So I went. It was a tedious event except for one fact, which made it depressing as well. In the seats in front of me were Sarah Miles and the golden-haired Fox boy. Together. Coincidence of a saddening kind. The supper which followed was the usual affair of many round tables and rounder producers and money-men, but at the table to which I was bidden I found myself, surprisingly, beside Joseph Losey, more of a stranger at this kind of junket than I myself. We smiled wanly, and spoke little. Both of us depressed. Forwood on the other hand was sitting at a table some distance away and found himself beside Sarah Miles, whom he did not know, except by sight. Across from him, to his mild astonishment, was Fox. He decided to meddle.

"It's awfully sad that you can't do 'The Servant'," he said. "You'd be marvellous."

Sarah looked vaguely surprised. "I simply long to do it! What do you mean?"

"But I hear you are committed elsewhere?"

"No . . . no that's all nonsense. I love 'The Servant', I'm mad about it, really." She nodded her head across the table to Fox. "And wouldn't he be super as 'Tony'!" she said happily.

"That's who we want for Tony."

"I don't believe it! How marvellous! Oh! Goodness . . . he's my very best friend."

"I think," said Forwood, "that we ought to go and have a word with Mr Losey . . . he's sitting over there."

The next morning, at half past ten, we all met together in my apartment at the Connaught, and over coffee and Bloody Marys "The Servant" unfolded its wings again, Losey was back in battle, successfully tested the boy, and I had once again been steered towards another door.

*   *   *

With Sarah we eventually got some money; not much, but a start. We also had, therefore, a distributor. One important part remained to be cast, and I suggested a much underestimated actress called Wendy Craig who had played a very minor role with me in the ill-fated Dearden film, "The Mind Benders". Thus we had the cast. But not the final, ready-to-shoot-with money. Robin Fox, now rather heavily committed in the project, much to his surprise, with a son and three clients busting to start, one memorable afternoon at the Connaught, made a swift, desperate, and final telephone call to Leslie Grade; who came to the rescue and provided the necessary cash. Losey has called Mr Grade noble, I cannot better the word. After the weeks and weeks of battle and strain, of high hope and shattering disappointment almost hourly, Losey was a weakened man, and exactly one week after we started shooting on our film he collapsed, in the coldest winter we had had for years, with pneumonia.

"It's a bitch. Got to stay put until I'm better. Maybe three or four weeks: and that's that. I'm sorry." His voice was weak, whispery, agonised.

"But, Joe . . . surely we can do something?"

"Nothing. What can we do? They'll abandon; never wanted to make it in the first place, this is an excellent chance; collect the insurance money and forget all about it. It often happens." He was so weak that he could hardly speak, and I could hardly hear him, but I did hear the softest word which he managed to add.

"Unless . . ."

"Unless what?"

"Could you take over?"

"And direct?"

"Yes . . . I could give you instructions by telephone. I've worked a lot of it out."

The next day, with a thudding heart and a willing, loyal cast and crew, I nervously picked up his baton, and we were off again.

For ten days, with almost hourly calls to Losey's bedside for explicit and detailed instructions which he never failed to give, however ill, we carried on with the film. My authority and decisions were never doubted, my suggestions examined and either accepted or, otherwise, discussed and modified, I never strayed from Losey's style, and the work went along at a good pace. They did not abandon. I was immeasurably proud, not of myself, ever, but of the crew and cast who so eagerly moved to help a man they greatly respected, almost revered in fact, who lay so despairingly ill and whose super-human efforts and beliefs now seemed to be in jeopardy. It was one of the most extra-ordinary expressions of loyalty and devotion that I have witnessed in this sometimes tawdry profession; and when he broke the rule, yet again, by staggering back to the Studio far too soon, gaunt, grey, painfully weak, the heartfelt applause which greeted his arrival was deeply moving. He is not, however, a sentimental man. Lying on an iron bed, wrapped in blankets and a long woollen scarf which Wendy Craig had bought for him, smothered in hot water bottles and attended by a slightly bewildered, and ignored, nurse, he got on with the job. The only concession he made to his state of health was that we were asked to refrain from smoking since it made him cough. That evening, again breaking doctor's orders, he attended, with me, a full running of all the material which I had shot during his absence. He made no comment, other than hoicking and spitting into a steadily mount-ing pile of paper handkerchiefs, and was eventually led by his worried nurse through the bitter February wind to his car. "See you tomorrow," he croaked, and was driven away.

Every film which I had made before this, with very few exceptions, was timed by a stop-watch. That is to say, every look, every move, every gesture even, every speech and even a run-along-a-busy-street was ruled by the vicious, staggering move of the stop-watch hand. Films cost money. Time is money. Waste, even intelligent waste, was not tolerated. I remember being politely taken to task by a producer because I had made a move (crossing a room and looking from a window, merely that) last one minute four seconds instead of the laid-down time of thirty-six seconds which had been allotted me. I had overrun time . . . if I continued to play in this manner, he explained kindly enough, the film would run another fifteen minutes, which would mean serious editing problems, something else would have to be cut, otherwise the film would run too long and not fit its time-slot which had all been carefully worked out, I gathered, by a lady called Barbara-Jo in an office in Hollywood, California, some months before. Barbara-Jo, sitting at her desk, reading her script, decided with a press of her steel button, just exactly how long a totally unknown person would take to do the things required of him or her set down by the script. There was no time for human error, for a developing emotion, for inspiration. It was all set down and sealed. Timed to the last split-second. Pre-packaged behaviour. So we speeded things up a little, and any time required for thought was neatly erased. One developed the habit and tried to accommodate to it as best one could, playing against the text sometimes, walking with the lines, to save time, and so on. It was a soulless piece of machinery, but it fitted the film into its slot in the programme and allowed the audiences to catch the last bus home.

With Losey there was none of this. No frantic cry from the Script Girl that a scene, a speech, a move even, had overrun its time; it was a sublime luxury. Not a form of self-indulgence (that is to be avoided at all costs, it is both false and ugly to watch) but an exhilarating form of developing someone else, of letting another person, so to speak, inhabit the empty vessels of one's body and mind. Under Losey's shrewd, watching eye, and with Bumble Dawson's simple, brilliant, designs for the clothes he would wear and live in, we started together to build the character of Barrett.

It is important to make it clear at this juncture that a brilliant designer, and Bumble was one of the very best, has a great deal to do with an actor's performance. I am an actor who works from the outside in, rather than the reverse. Once I can wear the clothes which my alter-ego has chosen to wear, I then begin the process of his development from inside the layers. Each item selected by her was carefully chosen by Losey, down to the tie-pin: a tight, shiny, blue serge suit, black shoes which squeaked a little, lending a disturbing sense of secret arrival, pork-pie hat with a jay's feather, a Fair Isle sweater, shrunken, darned at the elbows, a nylon scarf with horses' heads and stirrups. A mean, shabby outfit for a mean and shabby man.

For me the most important element of the wardrobe are always the shoes. From the shoes I can find the walk I must use; from the walk comes the stance, since naturally the spine is balanced on the feet. From the stance the shoulders may sag or become hunched, the neck might be thinly erect, or slip suggestively to one side or the other, the arms hang or are braced. In the chosen clothes one's body starts to form another's; another person walks and breathes in the shabby, serge suit. The whole is carried by the softly squeaking shoes. Thus the shape is arrived at; the physical frame.

Next the detail. Brylcreemed hair, flat to the head, a little scurfy round the back and in the parting, white puddingy face, damp hands (arms which hang loosely often have damp hands at their extremities, I don't know why). Glazed, aggrieved eyes, and then the walk to blend the assembly together. These details are always obtained from observing other people; an extension of my father's childhood game of "Pots and Pans". Always examine, question, the little things which go to make up human behaviour. The nervous ticks, the throbbing vein, the sudden flush of pleasure or anger, the unaware habits under stress. Ask what makes a man use this behaviour, analyse why he does, try to trace it back to a source. A complicated game; but one which has proved invaluable. Barrett's hair came from poor Philpot who ransacked Bendrose and went to clink. His walk I took from an ingratiating Welsh waiter who attended me in an hotel in Liverpool. The glazed and pouched eyes were those of a car-salesman lounging against a Buick in the Euston Road, aggrieved, antagonistic, resentful, sharp; filing his nails. No make-up, ever.

With my paraphernalia assembled under Losey's approving eye, with a superb text from Pinter handed to me as a gift, Barrett was ready to exist, there was almost nothing left to do but wind him up and set him off to work.

Like all the greatest directors, Losey never tells one what to do, or how to do it. Ever. Only what not to do. Which is very different. You give him your character and he will watch it develop, encouraging or modifying, always taking what is offered and using it deftly. You only know that you have done it to his ultimate satisfaction when he says, "Print!" at the end of a take. There is no waste of chatter, no great in-depth discussions about motivation, no mumbo-jumbo about identification, soul, or truth. You get on with it. Coward's famous advice years ago to an actor still holds good. "Just learn your lines, dear," he said, "and don't bump into the furniture."

With Pinter the same applies. We never, at any time either on "The Servant" or on the later, and far more complicated "Accident", sat in huddled readings of the text having it explained or trying to find what was "meaningful". Pinter's scripts are honed and polished long before they reach the actor's hand, and what he intends, or doesn't intend, becomes abundantly clear and lucid the instant one starts to work. His writing, at least as far as I have personally been privileged to experience it, reminds me of a beautifully laid-out scenic model railway. A start and an end. Tunnels and level-crossings, gradients, cuttings, little stations and smaller halts, signals all the way. The whole track laid and set out with the precision of a master jeweller. Pinter doesn't give you instructions like a packet of instant minestrone. The instructions are implicit in the words he offers so sparingly for his characters to speak. There is a popular and far too widely-held belief among many actors, and directors too (not to mention critics) that Pinter writes pauses. I don't think that he does. But I do think that he is one of the few writers who are brilliant in the text they *don't* write. His pauses are merely the time-phases which he gives you so that you may develop the thought behind the line he has written, and to alert your mind itself to the dangerous simplicities of the lines to come; it is an exhilarating experience, and given all these factors it is almost, and I repeat carefully, almost, impossible to go wrong.

As well as discovering the time for thinking or thought, with Losey one also discovered the values of texture. The textures of things; of wood, of metal, of glass, of the petals of a flower, the paper of a simple playing card, of snow even, and fabric. Plaster wood, however well combed does not feel like wood, neither does it photograph like wood; nylon is not silk, fibre glass is not steel, a canvas door does not close with the satisfying sound or weight of mahogany. All these apparently trivial items, or obvious if you like, add up to an enormous whole. Even if the audience is not immediately aware, it is subliminally aroused and its emotions feel the truth. It is real. And the actor feels the reality. It is, of course, totally cinematic not theatrical. In the theatre almost nothing must be real. It is reality extended; an actor must act the weight of mahogany when he closes his canvas door, his style is larger than life and must be of necessity, for he has to reach both the man in the Stall seat as well as the man in the back of the Gallery.

Because of the distance between himself and his audience the stage actor must project reality. Reality itself seldom reaches beyond the Orchestra Pit. The camera is a magnifying glass, and it betrays the theatre technique cruelly; a number of theatre actors, either out of fear or ignorance, despise the cinema and all its technicalities. And it very often shows. I committed the same error all those years ago when I got that one day's work on a film with the Attenboroughs, and derided a job which earned me three times the amount I was paid in the theatre for just sitting about looking like a policeman. Nothing to it, I thought cheerfully, any fool can do it. Any fool can. But not any fool can make it work. One just has to go on trying and proving, sometimes for years. For the intense love of it.

It was the intensity of this love which started us all off on the battle to get "The Servant" off the ground. And we managed. It was, however, quite another thing to get it shown when we finally finished. No one wanted this effort, no one was even prepared to give it a single showing. Obscure, obscene, too complicated, too dark, too slow, and naturally too uncommercial. Even the slight of obscenity didn't help it; it was removed from our hands and placed on the Distributors' shelves to gather dust like a poor wine. It seemed that the whole endeavour had not paid off, the courage had been in vain, the money, such as there had been, was lost, written off as a company loss. We set it aside as experience. It was to be the first example only.

*   *   *

Elizabeth was no fool; what was the point in making films which no one would show and to which very few people would come if they did? This *was* a form of self-indulgence which I could ill-afford. Surely, if my dedication was so intense, I should behave like a novice Buddhist, crop my hair, clothe myself in saffron and sandals and offer my begging bowl for physical sustenance. Or, less romantically, clear out of Nore, take a small flat and move in with a couple of suitcases. In that way I could just about manage to sit it out and wait for the Art Film of my heart to arrive, if it ever did again, instead of facing ruin sitting amidst a splendour of exposed oak beams, Meissen china and the best collection of dud eighteenth-century paintings the man from Christie's said he'd ever seen. But I had, I discovered to my shame, become very attached to the better things of life. The distance between Chester Row and Nore was an ocean. I liked my exposed oak beams and dud collection; I liked the life I lived. I liked travelling first class; and what was more, both my friends and my family liked it too.

The same old group from Bendrose had now come deeper into Sussex, bringing with them the same sense of security and affection. I had lost no one on the way and had gained many. Irene and Glynis, Margaret Leighton, David Oxley, the Goughs, and Gareth Forwood who rightly considered every house as his home in between terms at Ludgrove or Millfield, Daphne and Xan Fielding, Moura Budberg and Bumble Dawson, who were now joined by a younger, newer group who joined the team on Sundays. John Standing and his wife Jill Melford, Sarah and Noel Harrison and all their children, James Fox and Sarah Miles, Sybil and Jordan Christopher, Boaty Boatwright and others. No one tremendously grand; real friends to provide real stability.

Every month, for two or three days, I moved into the Connaught where I had a more or less permanent suite, and from there the business and the more social life was conducted. It was altogether a more elegant, and convenient setting for the other side of the life I chose to live. Here the deals were made, here the contracts were argued, here the Americans were feted as they preferred. Here status was symbolised. At Nore we sat around the fire, ran movies in the cinema at nights, read the papers, talked endlessly and walked miles across the fields with dogs and raincoats and a varied assortment of boots and stout sticks. At the Connaught it was dark suits and head waiters; duty in an elegant form.

This, if I altered my life to accommodate the Art Cinema, would all have to go. So too would the travelling which both I and my family had now grown to enjoy so well: Venice, Rome, New York, Vienna, Athens, Paris—they came with me to all points—and even Elizabeth willingly left her sink, family and the Hoover for the wistful pleasures of Budapest or the more obvious ones of Cannes, and my brother Gareth, the late arrival in the family, presently a trainee cutter at Pinewood, joined us for holidays. In those days we drove many thousands of miles across Europe, flew and sailed across oceans, and forged a pattern of discreet, one hopes, luxury all the way. The Gritti in Venice, Hassler in Rome, the Lancaster in Paris, the Bristol in Vienna, the Plaza in New York, car to the gangplank of the *Elizabeth*, flowers in the State Rooms, the one particular table reserved always in the corner of the Verandah Grill. It was the Grand Life and I enjoyed every moment of it. The only problem was having to earn the money which this sybaritic life demanded. And it demanded a lot.

So I compromised. Reluctant to let slip these undoubted pleasures, I decided on a sort of sandwich existence: Commercial Products which would provide the money to enable me to make the uncommercial Art film if and when it arrived. I saw no other way out, for the pickings, on both sides, were now getting thin on the ground.

In accepting this deadly weapon, compromise, I knew that I had once again broken one of the rules which Noël Coward had brandished at me like a stick, sitting in the Oak Room at Bendrose, just when the first flickers of success were beginning to kindle my wood. He had waved his finger angrily across the room and said, "Whatever you do, theatre or cinema, never, never, never compromise!" But there was no other way that I could see? "The Servant" lay in its dust. Surely therefore it was wiser to accept the chances which were being offered here and there to raise yet another eyebrow, a trademark with which I seemed to have saddled myself, as the cheerful, commercially acceptable "Doctor" . . . and a long line of semi-romantic heroes which I knew I could play on the top of my un-Brylcreemed head? In any case I was existing at that time in a compromise world in the cinema. No one knew which way to jump. Aware of those pipers in Hamelin, frightened by declining box-office receipts, the directors and producers themselves were compromising. Trying to add serious undertones to perfectly ordinary subjects and nervously congratulating themselves that they were keeping abreast of the new trend. Although their roots were far too deep down to alter anything; they knew almost nothing of the new trend, and were unable to implement it even if they did. Wallowing in compromise we steered a desperate course for the rocks. I was unhappily a passenger; I could not complain since I had purchased my own ticket.

Losey, on the other hand, was not prepared to let his work lie on shelves, or to compromise. From time to time he rescued his stack of tins and we had showings of the film for selected people in private screening theatres for which he, or we, paid the rent. Afterwards the reaction from these groups gave him so much confidence that he grew bolder and carried his packages to Paris where Florence Malraux set up screenings for influential people, and people began to talk; favourably. Eventually, after eight months of battle and trailing about like commercial travellers selling a brand of soap which nobody, including the owners, believed in, fortune came in the shape of Arthur Abeles, then head of Warner Bros in Europe. With a spare week to fill at his vast theatre in Leicester Square he ran a pile of rejected films to try and fill the gap. "The Servant" was the one he chose. A gentle man, more like a writer or an artist than a hard-headed American film tycoon, we could not have fallen into more sensitive hands. Amazed at the stupidity of his fellows, passionate about the film, he announced that we were to open after all. It was an unbelievably lucky chance.

I was in my Dressing Room, changing out of my costume to go and lunch, when Arnold Schulkes, my Stand-in for many years, banged at the door with the entire London Press in his arms.

"Brought you these; the first reviews." He never gave anything away.

"All right? A slating or what?"

"Not a slating, no. Bloody fantastic."

"All of them?"

"All . . . every one. Good, isn't it? After all this time? *The Times* is on top, read it first I would. After all you are family-connected, you might say; right?"

They lay before me, the verdicts on our work. A jury returned. I locked the door and leant against it with *The Times* and read slowly and carefully all the way through, slowly sliding down until I was squatting on my haunches, my back hard against the primrose paint. The last two paragraphs of John Russell Taylor's review were difficult to read because of tears. But I got the point. The moment which I had never thought would come had come at last. The moment when, sitting down, albeit squatting on Mr Rank's brown Wilton, I would be able to say, "Ah! That's it! That's what I meant it to be." And I said it aloud to relish the sounds of the thought-of words; not only for myself, indeed not that, but for all of us. Blearily I got to my feet and clumped across to the dressing table where Arnold had left the rest of the papers. The large lamp-framed mirror reflected a woeful image. Tall boots, green tights, frilly shirt, pink-smeary face, neatly waved hair on top of which coyly rested, at a jaunty angle, a Robin Hood hat stuck with a fistful of black cockerel's tails. What the hell did I look like? What was I doing? Compromising, said the reflection. "Right!" I said aloud. "Compromise comes to a full stop. Whatever happens. From now on."

Brave words. And they were brave words which blazed, in scarlet neon, from the façade of Warner's Cinema that night. Finally we had all made it; it remained to be seen how long we would stay, but at least we had got there. A far cry from the times when I had waited for Vida, or she had waited for me, outside this very same building, during the blitz when we would march off together through the crumping bombs to toast and beans at Lyons Corner House or, if we were better off that night, to the Café Royal for unrationed venison and steamed cauliflower. An equally far cry from "Rope" in Catterick and thimble-gins-and-limes in the officers' messes; I had pushed open a great many doors along the way since then. But time, as they say, is all relative and this was only one battle won.

At the big party later which I gave in the Connaught drawing room, the air was splendid with the scents of success. The Press had hailed the film as nothing other than a masterpiece, James Fox as the star of the future, and Losey no more nor less than a master. Standing watching him across the crowded room he looked, I thought, more like a weary don at a Speech Day. Surrounded by congratulating students, glass tightly in both hands, head bowed to listen to constant questions and praise, flushed with the pleasure he was so good at concealing. My heart rose with delight at his quiet triumph.

"What chances do you think it's got outside London?" I asked Theo Cowan, who, as always throughout my long career with Rank, had never left my side at receptions of this kind. He was Head of Publicity when I had started off with "Esther Waters" and had steered me through the early days of Image

Building, skilfully getting me through the inanities of judging Beauty Queens, opening swimming pools in civic centres, giving bouquets to the Most Glamorous Grannies of Hull or Gipsy Hill and helping me to deal with the not-always-enthusiastic Press at innumerable press-shows after innumerable near misses. Always genial, always alert, always the kindest of men and the shrewdest, he had finally left Rank when I did and started out on his own. "The Servant" was his first assignment, so he too was in at his own form of baptism. His opinions, when sought, were always honest, usually devastating in their accuracy. Losey trusted his judgement implicitly.

"Slender, I'd say." He had almost finished an entire plate of smoked salmon sandwiches.

"That's what worries me, and worries Joe. If this fails outside we won't ever get another penny to do anything again," I said.

"Well, it's difficult to say, you know; audiences are changing quickly now . . . it's exciting, the film, sexy enough, good exploitation stuff there; but it's a fickle world, what pleases the critics usually bores the provincial audience stiff. Just have to keep our fingers crossed; at least we did it, didn't we?"

I embraced my parents and took them across to meet Losey. His glass was empty. I refilled it and he took it automatically raising it only for a moment towards me in a silent toast just as Basil Dearden slowly, and gracefully, knelt at his feet.

"I am kneeling," said Dearden, "as you will note, in respect and homage to you."

Losey looked slightly embarrassed and smiled his gentle smile. "I really wish you wouldn't, Basil, you are too far away . . ."

"Just tell me, I ask in all sincerity, how can I make a film like this?"

"Oh for God's sake! You could . . ."

"How would I go about it? How should I even start?"

Losey took a slow sip of his vodka. "I can't answer while you are down there."

Basil rose and faced him squarely. "Well, how would I? How should I start . . . you must know?"

Losey grinned happily. "Sure I know. Shall I tell you? Well; first of all you take your son away from Eton, sell all Melissa's furs, get rid of the house and the pool, get rid of the cars, pack a couple of suitcases and move into a small flat and think things over. That's the only way I know, Basil . . . no overheads; just the film."

"Uncompromising chap," said my father as we went across to the bar-table. "I suppose that's right; takes a lot of courage, I should think."

"Too much for me all at once. Elizabeth said the same thing . . . I know they are right, of course . . ."

"You told me, my dear, that Christmas in Rome, that you wanted to be more than just a film star, didn't you?"

"Yes."

"Well, isn't this the chance you wanted? You said something about catching a tram-car or something, I didn't really understand."

"No, Pa, trolley."

"Oh well; whatever it was, it seems to me that you have caught it now, surely?"

"Not surely, no."

"What's the difficulty?"

"Staying on," I said.

* * *

Hanging on would have been more accurate, for hanging on it was. Although we were swamped with awards and prizes and an enormous amount of Press coverage on both sides of the Atlantic and in Europe too, the film was, eventually, only a satisfactory success commercially, and the struggle to make the kind of films we both wanted to grew harder than easier. "King and Country" was made in eighteen days for a total sum of £85,000. This Daniel Angel, who had been responsible for the telephone call from Rome with Losey which had sparked the whole thing off, guaranteed us and, presumably lost, for although we once again reaped a generous harvest of accolades and awards galore everywhere, and even sold it to television all over the world, it never made a profit and the film is, to this day, apparently still in the red.

Prestige doesn't pay the rent; not even on a small flat.

"This is not going to be a prestige picture," said John Schlesinger at lunch the first time we ever met. "By that I mean there is no money, and really no one wants to make it much except me and the girl and Joe Janni. We're calling it 'Darling' . . ."

"Who is the girl?"

"Oh, you wouldn't know her, just starting; brilliant, that's been the problem. We can't find a man to play the second role. Gregory Peck's turned it down already. They all have. Everyone we wanted."

It was almost a repetition of the conversation I had had three years ago with Dearden about "Victim". I was to be last chance again.

"But who is the girl?"

"Called Julie Christie, she's marvellous; huge future."

"Well, do you want me to do it or not?"

He looked at me thoughtfully across his vichyssoise, spoon poised. "You're so frightfully *soigné* ... you know ..." He waved the spoon worriedly, not very much liking what he saw.

"Well, it's only because I'm wearing a suit, for God's sake. And I've brushed my hair. I can be quite un-*soigné*, or whatever you call it."

"But this character is a telly interviewer; rather intellectual; Hampstead, baggy flannels, a couple of kids. Shaggy, brilliant. A sort of Robert Kee; he's also supposed to be Jewish but we can give that a miss."

"Well, I'll do it. I want to work with you and I want to work with Christie."

"Have you ever seen her?"

"On telly, in a space fiction thing. But she's The Young. I want to be with the young." He looked mollified and took the compliment for himself. "Well, thank you . . . we'd just have to tweed you up a bit. We've got to have *someone*."

"I like the script and I'll do it; what more do you want, if I'm last chance?"

He shrugged sadly and went on with his soup. "We really did need a *big* name to bolster hers at the box office. Unknown, you see. An American name would be perfect. If you do it we won't, of course, get the backing we'd need. Never mind. If you want to we could do some tests next week."

"Not acting tests? For God's sake! Surely I've done enough."

He waved his spoon across the table again. "No. No. Not acting . . . we'll manage that somehow. Tweedy tests. Try to make you look . . ." He paused and took a sip of his wine. "Well . . . un-*soigné*, I suppose, dear."

In the final event I wore my old gardening clothes, washed my hair, and bought a lot of knitted ties from the Stonehenge

Woollen Industries shop. And got the part. Julie was glorious. A gift. We were joined immediately. She lived in a noisy flat in Earl's Court and slept on a lilo mattress. One morning (we were working in Paddington Station) she confessed that, during the night, it had sprung a leak and she was sleeping on the floor with a tribe of stray cats which she had rescued. She might therefore be rather tired. She had seen a proper bed, very expensive, she explained, but it was a big brass one with bobbles and bars in a junk shop in the King's Road, and as soon as she could, she'd save enough to buy it. Meanwhile she had asked someone to go and get her some puncture patches from a garage near the station. While she went off to have a pee in the Ladies, Forwood wrote out a modest cheque for the bedstead, and I did one for the mattress with a little left over for the blankets, always supposing that she needed them. Which seemed more than possible. We put them in her handgrip and she was surprised to find them rummaging through later for an apple.

"What's this then?"

"For the bed and the mattress."

She smiled happily and bit her apple. "Ta," she said. She was absolutely adorable, and taught me more about ad-libbing than anyone else in the business; she could ad-lib and overlap endlessly, so I had to learn; self-protection. It was a very happy film although, predictably, we ran out of money halfway through and no one really believed in it except for the people who were actually involved in it. Joseph Janni, our producer, came sadly into my room one evening at the end of work. Face putty, his eyes hooped with fatigue. "Disaster," he murmured sitting dejectedly on the arm of a chair. "I've mortgaged everything; car, flat, stocks and shares, everything except Stella, my wife. Can you help us? Will you accept a cut in salary and defer your deferments?" The reluctant backers sat glumly through the daily rushes; no big American name, an unknown girl and an, almost, unknown director. They also thought the story was, in the good old Wardour Street word, downbeat. Anything that didn't have a happy ending had to be downbeat.

"She's got a face like the back of a bus," said one of them unhappily at a screening of the first week's work. "She looks just like a feller! Look at that jaw . . . she could play bloody football." He swivelled round in his seat, and appealed miserably to Forwood, "Don't you agree? She's dead ugly."

Judy Garland with her children Lorna Luft, Liza Minnelli, and Joey Luft in their New York apartment, 1962.

Roddy McDowall

Welcoming Judy to a party at the Ad Lib Club, London, 1964.

A break during "Hot Enough for June", Padua, 1963.

The Elephant Gate. Red Fort, Delhi, 1957.

The last film in the Rank Programme: "The Singer Not the Song", 1960.

With Joseph Losey on location for "The Servant" in "The Queens Elm", Fulham, 1962.

". . . a shabby outfit for a mean and shabby man." Self as Barrett, with Wendy Craig and James Fox in "The Servant".

Nore, Hascombe, Surrey: from the chestnut walk. Spring 1964.

Nore: the drawing room.

With Julie Christie at the Royal Command Performance, 1966. We had both just won the British Academy Awards, for "Darling".

Trevor Humphries

Ingrid Bergman and Gareth Forwood at Nore, 1965.

"I think she's the nearest thing I've seen to Brigitte Bardot," said Forwood.

The anxious monkey face before us was blank. "You think she's sexy!"

"Very. She'll be a big, big star."

The monkey face looked in bewilderment at its partner who removed his cigar and blew a smoke ring into the dead air of the projection theatre.

"You heard what the gentleman said." He dispersed the ring with a polite cough. "I must be losing my wits. Sexy? It's all going mad."

But the news had spread that something remarkable was happening on "Darling". David Lean, at that time casting his epic of Pasternak's "Dr Zhivago" asked to see film on both Julie and myself. Losey allowed me to send a reel of "King and Country" and Julie got Schlesinger to send a bit of her best work. We waited, naturally curious, to hear the results of our exam. Julie heard that she was hired, on the lawns of Skindles in Maidenhead where we were doing some location work. She was sitting in a tweed suit and pearls, for her role, and reading Karl Marx in paperback. She came from the telephone quietly and serene.

"What happened?"

She opened Karl Marx and smoothed the pages. "I've got Lara. Rather good. But they want me to get out of this little picture . . . said it wasn't important and that I should get to Madrid as soon as possible and start working on the part; they say," and she closed her book and slammed it on to the grass, "I could get an Oscar for it; that I should leave John and all this . . ."

"And so . . ."

"And so what?" Her eyes were filled with tears of outrage. "I told them to stuff Lara or wait." She pushed a hairpin which had slipped loose back into her bun. "They'll bloody have to wait. Leave this? Leave John, all this? What kind of a business is this?"

"Not lovely."

"Did you hear anything?" She was cautious, gentle, knowing anyway.

"No. Nothing."

In the event she won the Oscar. For "Darling", the little film, and rocketed to stardom in Hollywood. All she ever got out of "Zhivago", as far as I know, was a theme song.

Losey and I worked together again on two more films in

succession, "Modesty Blaise" which was nearly a compromise between commercialism and intellect and which, to my mind, but not to his, never quite succeeded, and finally in 1966 the most exhausting, exciting and valuable work we ever did together, Pinter's "Accident". A perfectly hand-crafted piece of work from the first shot to the last and quite the most exacting work I had ever had to do on a screen. Once again the part had not been intended for me, but for another actor, and once again by some strange fluke I got the chance; and took it.

The work in those years with Losey gave me the self-respect in my work which I had never dared even hope for and strengthened my somewhat shaky belief that I must never again compromise no matter what the cost. But although my belief had been strengthened all right, it did not mean, sadly, that other forces far beyond one's control, would not cause it to bend; it is unrealistic to try and make films for a minority audience in a business which is geared above all things towards a mass audience. After we had finished "Accident", the most difficult and perhaps the most successful of our endeavours together, Losey and I found, regretfully, that the *boucle était bouclée*: we had used ourselves up; there was nothing more for us to say together; weary, drained almost, and to some extent disillusioned, we realised that we must separate for a time and go our own ways; even the Press was finally beginning to hint that our work together was becoming incestuous. We both of us, in our very different ways, knew also, for all our high intentions, that we should eventually be forced to have to bend a little in order to survive, but in the bending, I think we believed that we should be able to bring the same integrity to the commercial-compromises, should they arise, which we had brought to our own high endeavours in the past. I think that we did, as it happened; but the emotional cost was high.

On the last morning of shooting on "Accident", Arnold brought me my usual egg-and-bacon sandwich for breakfast. He tidied round the room a bit, laid out *The Times* and *The Guardian* and poured me a mug of coffee from his always-steaming coffee pot.

"Sad day today," he said.

"Yes; sad day."

"But I've just had some interesting news."

"Oh."

"You know Zelda? Zelda Barron?"

"Of course."

"She's doing Production Secretary on the new Jack Clayton film."

"So, good for her."

"Good for us too."

"What do you mean, Arnold, I'm tired."

"She read the script last night, says it's a real beauty. 'Our Mother's House'."

"And?"

"And there's a smashing part for you in it."

"Does Jack Clayton know, by any chance?"

"No. Hasn't a clue. Hasn't cast it. We thought you'd be perfect."

"You and Zelda?"

"Sure, she's going to suggest you at lunch time when she sees Jack. He's lovely."

"Maybe, but he might have his own ideas, Arnold, he'd have asked me if he'd wanted me."

"Hasn't thought of you! That's the point. It's our idea."

"Arnold! For the love of God. You can't go begging parts for me!"

"We've both got to live, Governor, and I've got a kid to think of."

"Yes, but you can't do this; it might be terribly embarrassing. He may hate the idea, he's probably got someone in mind you two don't know anything about."

"Hasn't got anyone in mind. Told Zelda. Dead worried. Super part too. Just what you want after all these neurotic blokes. Cockney dad with eight kids. Right up your street. All on location in a house in Croydon; you'll love it."

He was absolutely right; I did. Clayton was highly amused by this unethical approach, but we talked it over and he seemed to think that Arnold and Zelda might be right.

"Not a very attractive role . . . shifty, seedy, and you have to face a whole gang of kids all on your own, there is no one else in the film, and they are pretty tough, but if you'd like to have a try?"

On my first morning in the gloomy house in Croydon I was in a bit of a funk. Eight pairs of eyes, ranging from five to fourteen, gazed at me solemnly. Not a smile, no welcoming grin even. In the little caravan in the scrubby front garden which I had been given to change in there was a jam jar stuffed with privet and some wilting Michaelmas daisies. Under it a note. "Let's hope you are as good as you're cracked up to be. You'd better be. Sincerely; The Children."

I loved every second of the film which was one of the happiest I have ever made. The children were fantastic, good actors, kind, funny, devoted and professional. Clayton was a demanding, challenging, exciting director. We were all locked into a make-believe world which I found hard to break away from even at the week-end.

Perhaps we all got too lost in our Croydon existence, too isolated, too immune. For although we had all passionately believed and loved what we had set out to make together, no one else did. And the film was a failure. A distinguished failure to be sure, but failure none the less, it doesn't much matter about the adjective used. At the Venice Festival our hopes, reasonably high, were very soon damned by faint praise and light applause. Walking back from the cinema to the hotel the air was sweet, the night soft, the moon riding over a flat, silver Adriatic. And I hoped never to see Venice again. Clayton and I could not ease each other's distress very much. It is hard indeed to laugh off the severing of a limb, and so acute was our sadness that that is what it felt like to us. Even on the third or fourth glass of champagne we still tasted ashes, surrounded as we were by the noisy, happy audience who had attended our funeral and now seemed intent on turning it into an Irish wake.

Full of brave self-pity it is hardly surprising that I paid scant attention to the people all around me laughing and talking; instead I immersed myself in a deep and useless conversation with Clayton trying to work out, far too late, just where we had all gone wrong; so immersed was I that I quite failed to notice my future standing at the bar watching me. Luchino Visconti.

★   ★   ★

The chestnut candles, I saw, were almost ready to flower, the leaves below like small spread hands. A ring dove cooed above our heads.

"It hasn't come to that, surely?" I said.

248

"It surely has, it would appear." Forwood pushed open the gate and we walked up to the house slowly.

"Television commercials? Finally . . ." I was stiff with alarm.

"There is nothing else, is there?"

"Well, there are some scripts in the office . . ."

"You refused them all."

"They are all dreadful, that's why."

"Well, no one has exactly been banging on the door for some time, have they?"

"So why should I go and do a telly commercial . . . there's no panic."

"No money is a sort of panic, I should have thought."

"Well I'm buggered if I'm going to go running up and down the Spanish Steps in a pair of sun-glasses just because no one has asked me to do a film for a year."

"You'll be buggered if you don't."

"But why? You said the other day that the account was very healthy. You said so clearly."

"It is. But ninety per cent of what you have goes for tax."

"And what's left after that?"

"You'll have eight thousand pounds left."

"I see."

"Look; I absolutely respect your No Compromise rule, believe me. But you can't afford it any longer, that's the fact of the matter."

"What shall I do . . . ? I'm lost."

"Go to Rome, do the telly thing, it's a lot of money, and they have agreed never to show it in England, and have a look round. You've been asked to work there often enough; no one wants you here, it seems, there are hardly any Studios left anyway, the Unions have seen to that. Start again; somewhere else."

I looked hopelessly round the gardens, the wind shaking the apple trees, the Downs hard against the early April sky.

"I can't chuck this all up, the family, England. I can't, it's been too long."

Forwood stooped down and pulled a long straggly plantain from the path. "You're right. Far too long. Something's got to give."

12

THE Hassler hadn't changed in eight years, I can't imagine why I thought that it would; all good hotels, like the Connaught or the Lancaster or the Hassler never change. Everyone gets a little older over the years, they re-lay the carpets from time to time, re-paint a room, but otherwise everything is much as it was. Which is why one returns. Via Sistina still ran away to the left of my window, the Trinita dei Monti rose, crumbling, to the right, a little fig plant growing from a crack in the belfry now almost a sapling, and below flowed the Spanish Steps up and down which I was shortly to run, showing my elegance in sun-glasses, and my lack of pride in everything else I was doing. The only immediate change that I could see now was that instead of a rustling Christmas tree with a glittering star on top, giant azaleas in Tuscan pots tumbled down the wide steps, a splendid cascade of magenta, pink, and white. It was May; no longer cold December although my mood, for want of a better word, was still much as it had been then, strengthened, but still one of bewildered perplexity.

The last time I had stood here I had coveted the dream of making a change in my cinematic existence and was desperate that the changing patterns swirling all around me like marsh gas will o' the wisps would lead me into a smothering bog; I had longed for self-respect in my work. Well; in the eight-years' interval I had fortunately achieved this, but how odd it was that it should lead me back to Rome, where, as someone once pointed out, all roads end (rather than lead), in the cinema of the day, and where I was about to become more commercial than ever before. Advertising sun-glasses for an American company. There was an irony somewhere. But if my dreams had to end where they had begun there seemed no pleasanter place for the quiet finale than this city jumbled below in umber, terracotta, saffron and blazing white; St Peter's still hung serenely in the sky, the jelly mould almond green against the hard, clear blue. Familiar, reassuring; a great deal better than Earl's Court. The Eternal City; only proving my own transience.

I ran up and down the steps twenty or thirty times, inanely smiling, blacked-out by the sun-glasses which successfully concealed my face, mute, since I spoke no word, sweltering in a flannel suit and new shoes which slipped on the polished stone. It didn't take very long, and was less shameful than I had imagined, and when I was back in the cool of the suite, and had changed into a shirt and slacks, Forwood came in and announced that while I had been labouring so too had he; or meddling might be a better phrase, for it had only meant a few well-placed telephone calls about the city to say, casually, that I was there. Not what I was doing, but just that I was, well, about, if anyone cared.

Since the work Losey and I had done together a number of people in the Italian cinema did care, and I had only refused all the offers which temptingly came because I was loth to leave England, frightened to work in a foreign country and, truthfully, distrustful. Also, an important fact, the scripts, or the dialogue to be exact, of practically every subject offered was an appalling mixture of Hollywood and literal translation. Hollywood because all the scripts were translated by Roman refugee Americans, and literal translation because some bewildered secretary had sat at a desk with a dictionary and laboriously worked it all out. Since the Italians use a great many words to say anything at all, or nothing, the scripts were thicker than *Whitaker's Almanack*, and as dense as *Bradshaw*. So I had declined.

"There is a new revision of that 'Macbeth' thing which you got from Visconti," said Forwood, being English in the Roman heat with a pot of tea. "I said that you might have time to read it again, if they wished, before you left. I did not commit you," he added quickly, seeing my alarm.

"The first script was pretty dreadful. The part was so wet. I'm really not very interested."

He slopped the detestable tea-bags into an ash tray. "Well, just read it . . . maybe they've made some changes; no skin off your nose if you still say 'no'. Where do you want to eat tonight? Passeto?"

It was a much better version as it happened. I almost rather liked it. The part was still wet; Macbeth is, I have always thought, unless in a Master's hands. However, this version was clearly based on the Krupp family, and the parallel was intriguing. So, it had to be faced, was Visconti, even though, at this moment, he was slightly in the shadows softly cast by Fellini's rising moon. I agreed that we should meet and discuss the project before again rejecting it out of hand. It would have been a high-handed thing to do; and I had absolutely no intention of making another commercial, for no matter what, ever.

I offered to go and see Signor Visconti at his office whenever he so wished. I should have known better, of course; Signor Visconti did not possess an office nor would he, it appeared, have been seen dead in one; the message would, however, be relayed to him, could I repeat my name once again?

Just as I was about to leave for Passeto, hand on the light switch, a telephone call to say that Signor Visconti was dining in my part of the city and would find it possible to come to my hotel; would I please expect him within twenty minutes? And he drank, they assured me confidentially, Johnny Walker Black Label and soda water. No ice.

He was punctual, taller than I had imagined, immaculately groomed for his later appointment, steel hair, dark, steady eyes, weary but alert, beautiful hands which he waved towards his companion, a slight man in grey flannel, *his* hands primly folded before him, like a cardinal in mufti.

"Signor Notarianni; he will translate."

He wandered slowly to the windows and looked out. "Molto bene . . . c'est charmant . . . calm . . . eh, Notarianni? Molto bello . . ." He took his whisky and we sat in a sort of semicircle. He raised his glass. "Cin Cin." We drank in a restrained silence.

"You like the new scenario, eh?"

"It is much better than before."

His falcon's eyes were immediately hooded, he leant back in his chair.

"Once it was enough if I asked an actor to work with me; enough, you know? To be with Visconti. But now . . . ," he shrugged resignedly, "now they all demand a script to read." He picked up the blue-covered copy and weighed it in his hand. "They do not like the part, they do not like the words, they do not like not anything. They do not know." He clattered it on to the table as if he had found it sullied in a lavatory. "You imagine I will make this . . . merde? Vous comprenez le mot merde, j'imagine?"

"Oui."

"Pas très jolie. Not polite. Pas du tout polite. But it is so. I do not shoot that. Never. Is for the actors to refuse, for the American agents to understand, for the financiers to read and give us money." He sighed and stared at me solemnly. "But you think is better this new merde, eh?"

"Much."

"You think the role of Friedrich is good."

"No, truthfully no. He is so . . . wet, still."

The eyebrows raised fractionally. He turned to the Cardinal. "Non capisco . . ."

"Morbido," murmured the Cardinal, his eyes on the floral carpet.

"Ah so!" Visconti took a long drink from his glass, and placed it on the table by the blue folder. "Macbeth, you know this man? He is . . . morbido also? Macbeth is weak, a weak man, is Lady Macbeth who is the strong one. Is true, is not true?"

"True."

"Ecco! So?" His eyebrows questioned more than his word.

"I have to play so many weak men."

"Maybe you play them well? 'Accident' is weak, the man Stephen, and the Pappa with all the children; Clayton's so beautiful film."

" 'Our Mother's House'?"

"Certo! The Pappa is weak, but is different weakness. You have a big range; 'Il Servio' is weak, I am right?"

"Weak-strong . . . yes."

"Non capisco."

"Si," said the Cardinal quickly.

Visconti opened his arms wide to the whole of Rome. "So? Is a problem to be a weak man? I must have a *strong* actor to play a weak man, not a weak actor. I have Lady Macbeth for you . . . molto forte, stupenda . . ."

"Who?"

"Thulin. Ingrid Thulin. You know her work?"

"Yes."

"You like this work?"

"Yes, very much. Is it sure, Thulin?"

He looked at the Cardinal questioningly. The Cardinal nodded his head slowly. "Since this morning we have Thulin," he said.

Visconti raised his glass to his lips. "Ah! Bene . . . bene. Signatura?"

"Si, si," assented the Cardinal comfortably. "Signatura."

"I asked this Vanessa Redgrave to be my Lady Macbeth . . . but she too did not like the scenario." He shrugged again, spread his hands as if to count his nails. "Finally, it is good, I think. Too tall for you. Friedrich would be weak *and* short. Not good."

"No," I agreed, "not good. When do you start to shoot?"

"We will shoot all in English. Very terrible for me, I cannot understand, but we must be international." His voice heavy with sarcasm. "And we will work all in Germany . . . very terrible for me, I am Italian you know, in Essen, in Unterach, in all the places where it happened. It will be molto pericoloso."

"Yes, Signor, but when?"

"When I have found my Friedrich finally. Then."

"I will be him."

I heard Forwood clear his throat softly.

Visconti made a little nod in my direction. "Molto bene," he said.

★ ★ ★

Later in Passeto Forwood smiled across the table and laid his fork on his plate.

"You didn't waste much time."

"No . . . it was instant. The moment he came into that room I knew. I don't know quite what I knew. But I did. He had such power about him. Like an Assyrian bull, a Tartar Prince, something tremendous."

"He is a Prince."

"I know that; but it was a feeling of such determination, such assurance, I know he knows what he is doing. It's very . . ." I pushed the salt cellar about the table hunting for the word which I could not find . . . "very un-domestic, very un-Gerrard's Cross. Do you know what I mean?"

"I do. I don't know if anyone else would."

"Royal. I suppose." The salt cellar tumbled and hit my glass. "A sort of Emperor really."

"I understand actors very well," he had said on his third Black Label and soda. "Actors are surface. I prefer to use people in my work. People who become the personage on the screen. Most actors are surface creatures. Self-absorbed. Is not for me. In opera yes; that is different. You saw Callas in my 'Traviata', certo? Ah no? So . . . generally actors are like horses; you know? I was a trainer; you must be very, very careful with them . . . if they are to win for you. When they leave the travelling box some will come down very confidently, head high, eyes wide, very sure . . . others step very timid down, they test the ground, scent the air, ears flat, unsure, nervous, very tense . . . you must take the greatest care of him. He must be controlled, loved, treated very, very gently for he will win the race . . . usually he will win; but you must be aware all the time; a director is like a trainer, ecco . . . actor is like a horse." He had smiled for the first time suddenly. "You do not mind to be a horse?"

"Not if it means that you expect me to 'become' instead of to act only?"

"I expect you to become Friedrich . . . not put him on like a coat . . . it is too easy . . . not real . . . I think that you become in all the work I see of you . . . which one is the one you think is best? We play a little game now? Which part you feel you had become?"

"Stephen in 'Accident'."

"Exact. Certo. Parfait. Why?"

"Because he was absolutely nothing to do with the man I am. I will speak slowly."

"Please."

"When we finished, after three months' work, I was dead. Really dead. We stopped shooting by the river at Oxford one afternoon. At three o'clock I was still him, still Stephen; at three-thirty it was over and he had gone. My body and my mind were a vacuum; he had left. I could not return to myself. I drove to my home and I wept like a small boy for the man I had lost. I put all the clothes he wore in a suitcase and locked them away; it took me many weeks to get back to my body. I'm sorry, I bore you."

He shook his fine great head vigorously, "Not bore. Not bore. It is correct. Is what I want. So." He rose and looked at his Cardinal, who had looked at his watch unreproachfully. "So. We go now . . ." He put out his hand. "You remember one thing very important. I make the cinema like I make my operas. It is big, how I work, bigger than life . . . it is very hard but it is my way. This film . . ." he waved his hand disdainfully towards the blue-covered script, "this merde is 'Götterdämmerung', that is opera, no? Grand opera, like Germany in 1932. You will go to Essen, you will see the Krupp house, what folie! Quelle horreur! You will see the house in which you lived. You will become. You will be poor, morbido, Friedrich. It will be amusing, no? Ciao, Bogarde." He had smiled quietly and I saw him to the elevator and in a trance had gone to dinner.

Plans were rapidly altered, and I stayed on in Rome longer than

I had intended. Fittings, make-up tests, the deal itself; all this took time. It was May and the film was to commence in early July. Just time enough for me to go back to England and make the arrangements to be away from home until October at least; I would miss the summer, but a summer in Rome would not be untenable, especially since I would be working at something I really wished to do; dragging my heels around Sussex, weeding the shallots, removing tendrils from the sweet peas, bedding out geraniums, picking mint and playing cheerful host on Sundays had started to lose its pleasure. (Ingrid Bergman, staying at Nore while she was playing in "A Month in the Country" at Guildford, was constantly amused by my evening walk down to the vegetable gardens to pick the mint for supper. As she set off for her theatre, so I set off for my mint bed. It became, for both of us, a symbol of unemployment . . . a far more agreeable phrase than just out of work and one which we have used together ever since.)

There were many other more exciting and stimulating things to do—like going to the Krupp villa in Essen, as appalling as he had suggested, and meeting Joseph Strick, a devoutly esoteric director, who arrived the day before I was due to leave Rome with a first script of Lawrence Durrell's "Alexandria Quartet" which he persuaded me to do with him, playing the role of Pursewarden. It would start, he said, in November in Tunis; then studio work in Paris, and Anouk Aimée had already agreed to be his Justine.

After so much indifference in England this attention went, slightly, to my head. I had not had a single offer from a British Studio, apart from the job I did with Jack Clayton which Arnold and Zelda had so cunningly contrived for me, since "Accident" with Losey in 1966. It would appear that I had overstayed my welcome there to some degree, and nineteen years was a long time in which to have stayed anywhere. Too long. I had been exceedingly fortunate; I had had my training and had chosen my path. I was unable to go backwards now; the doors had all shut behind me, but the corridor went on and other doors were flying open in the welcome which was being extended to me now from Abroad. The temptation was much too strong to resist; the alternatives were unattractive, and the British film industry was showing such distressing signs of malaise that it could only be a matter of time before a final diagnosis would prove the malady to be terminal and the only thing that I could possibly be asked to do was to attend at its funeral; a prospect which filled me with the keenest sadness after such a long, fortunate, battling innings.

I had worked as hard as I knew how to help the industry. I had not exactly bled it white, and with Losey, Dearden, Clayton and earlier with Asquith, we had tried to give the audiences a better meal, so to speak. The fact that our audiences now were feeding at the breast of television and could not accept our richer diet was our bad luck. But at least we had tried; nothing wrong with trying until you fail. I was nearly fifty; I had overstayed my time; the only future I could see for me now was Abroad.

* * *

"Do you see what I mean?" I must have sounded desperate because Forwood stopped eating and looked up, he cupped his ear with one hand.

"Speak up. When in Rome . . ."

"Do you see what I mean? About leaving . . ."

"Yes. Yes, I do. But just because you have got two films to do in Foreign Parts doesn't seem to constitute a good reason for tearing up your roots and emigrating . . ."

"I think it does, it's not just two films in Foreign Parts either. There's another to follow if I like with Fliano. Resnais has asked me to work for him; Jean Renoir and Truffaut; all abroad. Now Visconti and Strick. It is going to my head; I want to work. I want to work with these directors. Do you realise that the last thing I was asked to do in England was a half-hour narration for the Forestry Commission?"

Forwood poured another glass of Valpolicella. "Point taken," he said.

A day or two later we drove home through a deceptively calm France; for just below the surface of this smiling May lay the possibility of a civil war. The Students were marching, barricades going up, shops closing, and the streets of almost every major city seemed strangely deserted and dead. A long, hot Sunday. In Paris there was a silence which was almost tangible. Little traffic, few people, the sound of pigeons' wings and hurrying feet along almost empty boulevards. A breath held; Alain Resnais sitting at a small table at the Café du Rond Point, almost entirely alone, waiting for me. We had made the arrangement to meet some days before to discuss the possibility of a film which he wanted to make, and which we had been trying to get financed by an American company for months, "The Adventures of Harry Dickson". Now the finance had come through finally; but Alain, staring at his coffee, felt that the steam, as he put it, had gone out of his ambition. He had had to wait too long, make too many idiotic compromises for our future bosses, so that, now the money was available, he felt that he could no longer face the challenge.

"I will not compromise to the extent which they demand. No. I cannot do it now . . . it is finished; you understand?" I did, of course, but was sad. It would have followed "Justine" and was a part which I longed to play above all others especially since Resnais, as he said, had written it for me.

"I have here a letter for Vanessa Redgrave, she has been so kind and patient to wait, will you give it to her in London, we have no post now with the events of these weeks. I think she will understand too. Explain to her for me."

I took the letter, declined his offer to cross the river and come, as he said, "to see history being made: the Students are fighting for their existence two kilometres from here." I left him standing on the pavement, tall, slightly stooped, a shabby raincoat, his red scarf, an airline holdall slung over his shoulder, the legend peeling: BOAC. He waved slightly as the car moved out into the thin traffic. He looked infinitely sad; infinitely worried. I put the letter for Vanessa Redgrave in my passport and we headed for Calais. And managed to catch the last ferry across the Channel before the strikes finally closed France.

Driving up through Ashford Forwood said that perhaps, with things as they were now in France, I had better think again about moving there to live. We agreed that since I would be working almost immediately, and for a lengthy time, in Italy, it would be wiser to rent a house outside Rome, and see how it went. But first of all, and irrevocably, I would go ahead and put the English house on the market while I was away. I'd tell no one, apart from my parents, and perhaps the staff, Antonia and Eduardo who had taken over from the much-loved Hans and Agnes, and who, for their own futures must be admitted into the plans, for they would, I hoped, come with me when I left for Italy. I had about five weeks to go before Visconti would need me; there would be a great deal to do.

*   *   *

There is an army saying that the camp tailor knows more about troop movements than the Chiefs of Staff; and sooner. The same thing applies to theatrical costumiers. From them, after standing mutely for five days, amidst a welter of half-finished suits and coats, being pinned and chalked and offered endless cups of lethal espresso's in Tirelli's in Rome, I was informed that Visconti, whom I had not met since the one evening long ago, it seemed, at the Hassler when I agreed to this enterprise, now wished my physical body presented to him, for one single shot, by ten o'clock tomorrow morning. Since it was already three-thirty in the afternoon I was in some degree of panic.

"But where are they?"

"Salzburg. Very pretty."

"How do I get there?"

"We have the plane tickets; Düsseldorf and you change for Munich then a car . . ."

"But I was told not for three weeks."

"Changed his mind; tomorrow ten o'clock."

"I have nothing to wear; no costume is ready." I threw a despairing hand about the cluttered, stuffy room, hung about with half-finished hacking jackets, coats and evening clothes.

"Ah si, si . . . all you will need is raincoat. And here he is; is only a big shot. Just your head. All is ready. Tirelli is always ready. Never late."

But I sure as hell was going to be late for my first day's work with Visconti. Something I felt absolutely sure he would not tolerate. How could I get myself on and off planes to bloody Salzburg; I had never moved a step unaccompanied either by Theo Cowan or Forwood ever since I had waltzed into this monstrous business. I was not about to do it now.

We drove. Packing two suitcases in the space of fifteen minutes, we left the Hassler holding all the rest of the stuff, and headed for Salzburg. It was a fiendish drive through the night with a four-hour stop-over in Trento, and a dawn start the next day. One hour late, that is to say at eleven o'clock in the morning, we drew up, dusty, exhausted, anxious and hot, at the door of the elegant hotel which was Visconti's headquarters. The manager was extremely polite; certainly this was the right place, and Signor Visconti was staying there; I could not possibly be late, he added in a hushed voice, since Signor Visconti was still asleep and would not be awake until at least four in the afternoon. He had attended the first night of Von Karajan's "Don Giovanni" the night before, and had also worked very hard at the film. There was no cause for me to be distressed by my lateness, since no one would work today because it was a rest day. He suggested that I might like to see my room, regretfully in the annex, because the place was completely full on account of the Festival, and that my chauffeur was accommodated in a small room in a pension up the hill.

White with exhaustion and anger I went to see my annex room. A small place under the eaves, overlooking the garage-wash area. The manager shrugged his shoulders sadly and said he regretted the situation, but for one night only . . . One night! At this rate how many nights would there be? Who was in charge, what had gone wrong, why had I been dragged through the night for absolutely no good reason? I was seething with anger, and shaking with fear. My first work in a strange country . . . not a good indication of things to come.

The day passed slowly. Salzburg is just another city when all is said and done, and apart from an exhibition of Egon Schiele there was nothing much to see. Or that I, in my present mood, cared to see. By the time I had returned to the hotel Visconti had, like Box or Cox, left for some unknown destination. He would not be returning for dinner. There was no note, no explanation, no form of contact. I might just as well have still been in Rome; probably he thought that I was. We walked, Forwood and I, forlornly up the hill behind the too-elegant hotel, found a small bar with high wooden settles, a juke-box and a pretty waitress in a swirling dirndl who brought beer, wine, and piled plates of wurst and röesti. Life seemed a little more tolerable. Until the next day when the same procedure took place. Signor Visconti was asleep, and would be until four in the afternoon; he could not be disturbed.

"This is very curious behaviour," I said. "Perhaps he doesn't know I am here?"

"He must do . . . he must have seen the car outside . . . the management have told him . . . he's just being an Emperor; is that what you called him?"

"Well, if he makes no sign this evening by six, or whenever he gets up, I'm off; we leave for Rome and pack the whole business in. I don't mind forgetfulness so much but I won't tolerate sheer bloody rudeness."

At precisely six that evening I went down to the bar; no sign of life, but a scattering of laughter from the garden beyond. I stepped out on to a gravel path and walked, rather self-consciously, towards a collection of elegant cages clustered around the trunk of a giant lime. There were golden pheasant, quail, a toucan; casually I looked through the wires across the lawns towards the terrace. Sitting around a large table in the evening sun, Visconti and his court; the Cardinal from the evening at the Hassler, five or six others listening to him, agreeing, clapping politely at some gentle joke, laughing, sipping cool drinks from long glasses, relaxed, casual, quite unaware that I was hovering furiously behind two blue macaws in the aviary.

"I'll give it another five minutes," I murmured to one, who clambered inquiringly down the wire to the piece of twig I offered. "Five minutes, and if nothing happens straight back to Rome and England."

But there was a slight pause suddenly in the laughter at court. Someone looked across to the aviary, a bending of heads, and just as I was about to leave and cross the lawn towards the annex the Cardinal came loping worriedly across, hand outstretched, the other buttoning nervously his immaculate jacket.

"Ah! Buona sera . . ." Saved by the bell.

They made room at the table, and drinks were ordered, but no explanation was offered beyond the fact that they had done some good work already, and that tomorrow I would do one single shot and then be free.

"Is very simple," said Visconti. "Just a close-up. You see your brother-in-law in bed with a boy, you are shocked, you shoot him, poum! poum! then you close the door. Is all. Then to Rome again; very simple, eh? A good beginning for you."

I was still angry and I confess bewildered, but remained exceedingly British and cool, and when he invited us to join them all at dinner in Salzburg I declined, politely, and said that I preferred to eat up the hill. He looked curious. "Up the hill? There is up the hill here, restaurant?"

"No, a little trattoria; very small, very ordinary, quite simple." We said goodnight and walked thoughtfully back to the annex.

There was a wedding party in the little bar up the hill, the bride red-faced and shy in white, swigging down pints of beer, the bridegroom tightly stuffed into a blue suit, a massive crimson carnation matching his complexion. Children ran about the room in wrinkled socks, laughing and rolling beer mats, bouncing balloons; someone sang a rousing song to an accordion, the waitress hurried through the throng balancing steins of beer and plates of sausage. It was warm, relaxed, noisy and cheerful; through the smoke and clattering children I suddenly saw one of the faces from Visconti's table, as he saw me. He came directly to the table, elegant in grey silk, politely he stood to attention.

"Herr Bogarde, Herr Visconti sends me to ask if there is room at your table perhaps?"

"Of course . . . plenty . . ."

"He will be here directly." The elegant young man clicked his heels and left. Two minutes later (he had clearly been outside in the car), Visconti entered with the court. Dressed in dinner jackets and with extreme elegance and care they made an impressive picture. The waitress hustled extra chairs about the table, threw plates down and hurried off to the kitchens. A child nearby burst a red balloon. Visconti removed his jacket and sat down beside me in his braces. He was grinning happily.

"I like," he said, indicating the wedding and the blasting accordion. "You like too?"

I nodded. He patted my shoulder comfortably and, taking up my glass, finished my wine.

*   *   *

Unterach was dressed all over in scarlet, black and white. Banners and swastikas fluttered all about the cuckoo-clock village on the placid lake, the streets were thronged with laughing, jolly, blond young men, clumping over the cobbles in their jackboots, brown shirts and breeches; belts and holsters sparkling in the sun. Girls in dirndls and modest blouses, hung on their arms, singing and smiling at the memory of a time they never knew, and the elders happily held their babies up to clutch the sailing banners and have their photographs taken by fat lederhosened fathers. A spirit of festivity was everywhere, and the villagers were enjoying it all; they were making a lot of money out of the Italian film company, and reliving a past of which they now remembered they were very proud. No one was in the least distressed, except for one unhappy tourist driving through in his Ford Taunus on the way to somewhere else, who, trapped in recreated history, had a minor heart attack and was carted waxen-faced to the nearest clinic; this evinced much laughter since he was Jewish, but he shortly recovered and, I was informed with much laughter by a jolly lady in the pharmacy, fled back to Zurich. I detested the smiling little village.

I did my first shot for Visconti at the end of the morning. They were in a hurry to get out of the small hotel in which they had been working for some weeks . . . and I was hustled, in my raincoat, to the door of the bedroom in which they were shooting.

"All you must do," said Visconti quietly, "is open the door; you see the wicked Konstantin in the bed with a boy. Orribile! Orribile! You fire. Paum! Paum! Paum!, make a little look, retreat, close the door. Is very easy . . . capisci?"

On his cry of "Actione!" I threw open the door, stared at Konstantin and his lover, suggested by a large apple crate with an X chalked on it . . . did my shooting and the look, and left. There was a silence. The door opened. Visconti stood there, cigarette in hand, one finger rubbing his chin. "You do again, this time you are smiling? Capisci?"

I repeated the process. Smiling . . . I did it Nervously, Ruthlessly, Sardonically, Coldly, and eventually with tears streaming down my face with Regret and Grief. Or whatever he had demanded in his low voice. I opened the door and shot Konstantin and his chalk-mark lover, six very different times, all within twelve minutes. The tears had taken a few moments to prepare. Visconti printed all six and strode off to his lunch at the hotel in the square. He said nothing. OK. So now I was through and could return to Rome. Albino Coca, his right-hand man, and chief assistant, caught me up crossing the cobbled streets, threading our way between the laughing Nazi children. He put his arm round my shoulder like an old friend.

"Six prints. Is amazing for Visconti . . . usually only one or two perhaps . . . but six, and all different, he prints all! Amazing. He liked what you do. I know, I work always with him. He is very surprised, I can tell. Very good." He squeezed my arm tightly, smiling.

"He didn't look very pleased; is that normal?"

"Ah si, si . . . he says nothing. Not ever; but I can tell."

"Well, bully for you."

"Scusi?"

"I suppose it's his way; what do I call him on the set? Visconti? Sir? Signor?"

Albino thought for a moment. "You must call him Visconti, for sure; not Sir, is very military, I think, eh? Fascisti?"

"I always call my directors Sir. It is simpler and quicker."

"Not Visconti . . . but never, never, never call him Luchino. That is very private name. Personal. No one calls him that on the film, ever. Remember."

The hotel was full, the restaurant, on a terrace over the lake like a ballroom. I found a small table with dirty plates and an empty wine glass. Suddenly, as I was about to sit, the Cardinal appeared at my side, smiling deferentially, hands clasped: "Please! To come . . ." I followed him through the tables to where Visconti sat in splendour round a white cloth sipping his wine and eating from a plate of beetroot salad. He motioned me to sit beside him, smiled at Forwood and indicated another place. He beamed genially about him.

"Some wine? The house wine is delicate . . . not too heavy. You like trout, Forellen blau? Some Kartoffel Salat? Molto bene."

I shook my head. "No, Visconti, no . . . some wine . . . no food yet."

He raised his hand in mock surprise, laying it gently on my own. "My God! So formal! Visconti! La la la . . . Luchino! Everyone calls me that! Capisci?"

*   *   *

I didn't return to Rome. Preferring to stay and watch him working, to see how he did it, and what he demanded. It was all very quiet, hardly a word was ever spoken. He never moved from his chair; instructions were given in a soft voice to Albino and relayed to the players or to the large crowd. It was an absorbing experience, and I stayed at his side, daily, sitting in a canvas chair, for the next three weeks. We hardly spoke, there was never any need to, he knew what I was doing and instinctively knew why; he was serene and happy, and together we developed what can only be described as, for want of a better phrase, a form of mental shorthand or even telepathy. I was the pupil. He became my Plato or my Socrates . . . although he would have scorned me had I told him.

However; all was not well elsewhere. By the end of the three weeks working on the Night of the Long Knives and sundry other pieces, we had spent all the money available. The German Finance had been suddenly withdrawn without warning because they considered that we were making an anti-German film. The locals grew tired of our presence, had fearsome battles with the Italian crew, whom they considered to have let them down as allies in the war, and put up the prices for everything from a glass of Coca Cola to a reel of thread. The battles were physical. The laughing Brown Shirts beat the living daylights out of the tight-shirted, and too-tight-trousered Italians, trapping them at nights, after dark, in small bars or walking through the bannered streets. At Visconti's suggestion the Italians bought up all the cheap tourist rings in the local jewellers shops, crammed them on to every available finger of each hand and thus armed with knuckle-dusters gave as good as they had got; and more.

We left the ugly little smiling village and headed to the next set-piece in Düsseldorf. Here we were locked in our hotels, the equipment and the film impounded, until the bills had been settled, and all cables to Rome were unanswered. The film was on and off again constantly. We sat about in dejected heaps with our luggage packed and the feeling that we were a broke variety troupe whose agents had abandoned them. The Cardinal flew about trying to find money, and Visconti, after rising late, lunched daily in regal splendour since he was paying out of his own pocket, as indeed, was I. Eventually some money came, we did the work needed and thankfully headed back to Italy.

*　　*　　*

The main set at the studio in Cinecitta was the ground and second floor of the Krupps' villa at Essen, the Villa Hügel. Complete. All of it. In all the years that I had worked in the cinema I had never seen a set like it. The great main hall, rooms leading off, Music Room, Drawing Room, Library, a great gallery with an immense staircase, and off that too, more and more rooms, all furnished, crammed with flowers, real fireplaces in which blazed real logs, and antique furniture of great worth and beauty. Tapestries, as well as faux Titians and Rubens, covered every spare inch of space, and every detail, from pencils and magnifying glasses in the vast library, to family photographs in silver frames and a half-finished piece of needlework lying, as if hurriedly put aside, in a huge armchair in the small Study, were in place. The flowers, fresh twice a day because the heat of the lamps caused them to wilt, were dozens and dozens of white lilies and deep crimson roses. "Gladioli are bourgeois flowers . . . for yachts in St Tropez . . . remove them. And no mixed flowers, it is vulgar to mix flowers, and the Krupps would know that; they were tinkers originally, but they had great pretentions towards 'comme il faut'. We do not make mistakes.'

Standing in awe in the midst of my villa, I realised immediately why we had gone broke. It must have cost thousands and thousands. It had. And more was to come. The entire place was carpeted, wall to wall, up and down stairs, in dark brown. Visconti, on the first morning of his inspection, with not one single cent left in the bank and some of the film still impounded at the airport in Düsseldorf for non-payment of bills, tapped his foot gently on the acres of carpet, shook his head gently, and said, "No". In appalled horror his designers and assistants and production staff, trailing behind him as if he was indeed an Emperor, implored him to explain. It was very simple. There was a *muffled* sound through the villa . . . no sound of feet clacking on polished wood, no sense of urgency would be heard, hurrying feet, running feet, frightened feet, stealthy feet. It was ruin to the atmosphere, it must be relaid, immediately with wood: parquet flooring, polished, shining, cold. The floor must play the music of fear.

It did. It took six men five days to rip up and relay, in oak and beech wood blocks, the two floors and staircase of the house. And Visconti was right. Now the house rang with a clear, cold steel sound. Of course. It caused a tremendous scandal in Rome; and everyone prophesied ruin for the film. They were nearly right. With the cost of the floors and the cost of the flowers and costumes alone, Losey and I could have made "King and Country" twice. But this was Visconti. The attention which he paid to the smallest detail was incredible. Always I had been brought up in the cinema to believe that they would never see it. They being the much maligned audience. This was the direct opposite of Visconti's theory which was that they would all see it, feel it, smell it; and they were not to be cheated. Fires were fires, and burned from real logs. The meals we ate at the dinner scene, which went on for three solid weeks in sweltering heat in the studios which were not air-conditioned, were cooked and brought in by Alfredo's in Rome. Wood was wood, never plaster, and wood was wood indeed. Silk was also silk. I had learned texture from Losey; but this was really texture, and if Visconti's excesses sometimes seemed self-indulgent he never, at any time, excused them. Save by example. The old man I must kill with my small revolver lay propped up in his vast walnut bed. The room softly lit, the sheets and pillows, vast and of the finest silk, he lay white and ashen, his veins green as malachite, raised across hands and arms, like tributaries of the Amazon. A dinosaur for dying. Visconti took up a pint plastic bottle of real blood (bought from a local Accident Clinic) and with careful aim sprayed the venerable corpse, his silken sheets, his pillows, his nightgown of finest lawn, the bed even, walls and carpets. It was a cavern of blood.

"Visconti! It is too much surely? Excessive?"

He looked at me from beneath his craggy brows, balefully, as if I had questioned his pedigree. With a swift movement he threw the plastic squeezy-bottle into my astonished grasp.

"You are English, Bogarde? You must know your heritage . . . Shakespeare? You know your text to 'Macbeth' . . . you remember, 'who would have thought the old man to have had so much blood in him?', is a line from 'Macbeth'? I am correct? Not excessive, Elizabethan perhaps. I tell you, I make opera in the cinema. Macbeth is opera, this death is opera. Ecco, capisci, Bogarde?"

But on occasion this desire for texture took up a great deal of time; and that, coupled with the on and off situation, grabbing money in small parcels whenever possible to pay for the excesses like the dozens of roses and lilies, the exact beautiful Art Deco jars to hold them, and his alarming rages if they were not immediately available, put the shooting time of the film in a frightful mess. My looming commitment to Mr Strick in Tunis bothered no one but myself; Visconti was, I feel sure, convinced that when the moment came for me to pack up on his opera and fly to "Justine" I would refuse, and stay on in Rome ignoring my future assignment. It was a repeat of "The Lonely Stage" situation, and I grew increasingly nervous as each day's delay continued either in a search of ready cash or else of a particular object with which to decorate a scene. I would arrive at Cinecitta every morning at seven-thirty in the hopes that work would proceed. Very often it did not. Sometimes there was no Visconti to be seen, and no one dared to telephone him to ask why. So I was often handed the instrument, after someone in the office had bravely dialled the number of his country house at Castelgondolfo, and asked to find out why.

"No one has paid me one single lira for two weeks. I do not work. Where are you?"

"At the Studio."

"Come to the house, is better here by the pool, Rampling is here too, she has not been paid. We do not work today."

I would then relay the news to the worried crew members and go to Castelgondolfo where Charlotte Rampling and one or two others of the cast not immediately working nor yet paid would be sitting in rather hopeless heaps round the pool. Visconti would be happily working away at something in his study. Charlotte, whose big break this was—Visconti had chosen her for his film because "she has the beautiful eyes of tragedy . . . she can be one day a big, big star . . . it is her decision, not mine: mine to have her, but hers to take the chance",—was naturally depressed. No work, no money, and what, we all wondered, would happen if the film was, like so many before it, quite suddenly abandoned? It was a possibility which seemed to go with the kind of pictures I had elected to make. A haunting.

"Luchino, you know I have to leave for Tunis in a few days?"

"Tunis! What for Tunis?"

"For another film. 'Justine'."

"Non possibile. We do not finish this yet! How to Tunis and this not finished?"

"I'll have to leave you and come back after I finish 'Justine'."

"When you finish, you think?"

"After Christmas."

"Ayee! Is now October! What do I do, Bogarde . . . you leave? We have one big, big scena, in the steel works, is essential, is not possible to go."

But go I had to. He was very philosophical in the end. He would have to shoot what he could of the film which remained without me, and then settle down until I could be released from Mr Strick. So be it. He would wait.

"But we must have a little party before you go. You must show your respects to the troupe, is very important. Some beer, some sandwiches, I will arrange. Very simple."

The night of the farewell party, my beer and sandwich "thank you" to the troupe, I arrived at the studio canteen at the appointed hour to find it dark, chairs stacked, a cool wind whipping through the pines in the shaggy gardens. A night watchman said that the party was being held on the set of the villa. Visconti had staged my party for me. Lights blazed from every corner of the immense set, fires crackled, a bar ran the length of one room, and the entire cast and crew was present, dressed in their best frocks and suits, all laughing and applauding as I walked, bewildered, to the high-backed chair in the centre of the great hall where Visconti sat smiling brightly and offered me a brimming glass of champagne.

"Is such a 'orribile place, the studio canteen, no? And we have this, all this, free; and the party is so big, everyone has come to honour you." He meant himself, but no matter. I accepted the wine and the compliment intended. "It is Krug, non-vintage," he said, looking at my worried face. "Beer is not right for this kind of parting."

It was a night of great happiness and also great sadness. I hated the idea of leaving them all tomorrow; we had fought such a tremendous battle together, from Unterach onwards, that I wanted to be there to the end. However, that was not possible; I would have to put "Götterdämmerung", for myself at least, into cold storage. At eleven-thirty, an enormous cake arrived in the shape of the dreadful, ornate villa, and amidst cries of delight and much applause I was presented with a cigarette case inscribed by every member of the unit. The gesture brought me to the edge of tears, it was so entirely unexpected, and Visconti, in his great chair, nodded smiling and demanded a little speech which I made, appallingly, in fractured Italian, with a very full heart.

It had been a splendid party, we all agreed. All that remained for me to do was to pick up the bill. Which rocked me gently when it arrived the next morning at the Hassler just before I left for Tunis. It had all been most tactfully done, Visconti had smiled only, waved a vague hand and called, "Ciao, Bogarde" as we parted, and I was left to walk alone through the night, under the sighing parasol pines to my car. He knew how to handle his horses.

*   *   *

Arnold was at the airport at Tunis to meet me. The sun sparkled on the blinding white city, on the dusty roads, on the walls of livid bougainvillaea. Rome was only forty-five minutes away by air, but already lost to me.

We settled into the car for the journey to the hotel on the beach where I would stay during the location. Arnold was full of news, but first of all, after a separation of some months, wanted mine.

"How's the family, Dad? Your Mum?"

"Oh fine . . . how's June? And your boy?"

"Great . . . he's almost talking. Visconti all right?"

"The greatest ever. I miss him."

Arnold stared out of the window at some passing camels. "You will, gov, you will. It is all a bit of a cock up here."

"Oh God! Not another?"

"This is the revised script." He handed me a fat package. "And there is one other thing which will make you happy, I hate to tell you, but we have to go to Hollywood for the studio work. Not Paris."

"What!"

"Changed their minds. L.A. now."

"I can't go to Hollywood! I haven't finished the Visconti thing . . . there is a week's work left to do."

"You'll have to fly back from lovely L.A., that's all."

In the dusty road a small boy thrashed a plodding donkey.

"What about Mr Strick, is he all right?"

Arnold lit a cigarette and blew smoke steadily ahead of him. "He's a nice man. A bit lost: they've only been working a week. It's early days. You know; it's a funny thing, do you know the aggregate age of the camera crew is three hundred?"

"The aggregate what?"

"The age. Is about three hundred and I'm not kidding. Everyone is into sixty knocking seventy . . . maybe more even. Goldie, now he's really nice, told me he already bought a double-plot at Forest Lawn. Cost him a bomb. It's on a hillside, see? No seepage. You pay more to stay dry. The Sound Mixer can't get around too well so they push him and his equipment about on a cart." He spun the spent match through the open window. "Trouble is they made the thing too wide for the doors, so he has to stay outside the Sets mostly and can't get to see the action. It's all a bit weird. Most of them did their first Movies with Constance Talmadge and the Gish Sisters. You're in for a few surprises, Gov."

"I have already had a few."

He laughed nervously: "Oh well . . . that's Show Business."

Hollywood has always been praised for its extraordinary efficiency. A German inheritance? It does not work, alas, outside the city itself. We were a lost rabble. Nothing was just exactly what it should be. Except for Mr Strick who was calm, apparently genial, and enthusiastic even though little of Mr Durrell remained in the revised-from-Hollywood script. Anouk Aimée was wan and sad for most of the time, since she had suddenly realised, too late, that her decision to accept "Justine" had most probably been, for one reason or another, a serious error of judgement on her part, and was now feeling abandoned and lonely; she had brought her two cats with her from Paris to keep her company and fed them on fillet steak which angered the waiters in the hotel who had to make do with chick-peas. Everyone got some form of Tunis stomach; the company flew in Jumbo loads of American Press weekly, whom we had to entertain and deal with socially in the "fabled city of Tunis" while they watched, with some degree of boredness, and eye irritation from the constantly blowing dust, the shooting of this "great saga of literature"; and I shortly discovered that none of my costumes fitted nor were right for the seedy character of Pursewarden with which I was trying, against all these odds, to come to terms. I was swamped by the gravest misgivings.

After four incredible, unorganised, miserable weeks we were flown off to lovely Los Angeles just in time for Christmas, and a total overhaul. That is to say, Mr Strick was replaced by George Cukor, the four weeks' work in Tunis was all scrapped, and everything started from scratch again. Cukor, once again stepping into the breach, employed three Literature students from nearby U.C.L.A. to sift through all four books which comprised Mr Durrell's masterpiece, and had restored, to what characters remained, some of the original dialogue, so that at least one felt one was speaking the writer's written word; it gave a little courage in a sagging epic. Cukor, as ever filled with boundless enthusiasm, struggled and fought and began wresting shape into the soggy mass. But the Studio, now alerted to the early disaster in Tunis too late, sliced the budget and applied the brakes; we were also constantly trapped by the idiotic rules of Old Hollywood. Forbidden, because of the Decency Laws or something, to use real children in the Children's Brothel, we were forced to employ elderly dwarfs instead, swathed in veils or strategically placed back to camera. Most of the sets looked like the Coffee Shop in the Tunis Hilton; everything was clean and neat; and even wretched Michael York was forced to wear a flesh-coloured pair of briefs for his seduction scene on a beach, and striped flannel pyjamas when he was in bed. Hollywood's decadent, fabled Alexandria had all the mystery, allure and sin of Derry and Toms' roof garden.

None of this was Mr Cukor's fault, perhaps the most cultured and erudite of all Hollywood directors. It was the Studio system to which he was, of necessity, bound. He had generously taken over an established production and just had to make do with what he found, and although he found some pretty rum things he made do marvellously, although he constantly longed to return to Durrell's books and remove the whole benighted effort out to Alexandria itself and shoot it all there. However, this was not to be; we struggled on under his blazing enthusiasm, his infectious love of the cinema, his boundless energy and quite extraordinary capacity for teaching. He wanted one to learn, and by Heaven, one learned. He swept us all along on a glorious wave of mounting excitement and determination, it was really very much like working with Visconti. The same dogged battles for perfection as far as it could possibly be achieved. And sometimes he was fighting against immense odds, and the perfection which he sought became ever harder to accomplish. There were some incredibly awful bits of original casting which he was powerless to change, and half his vibrant energies were spent in bullying, cajoling, pleading and encouraging performances of one kind and another out of these wooden, self-indulgent method actors. However, in spite of these harrowing vicissitudes, he fought bravely on, with the enthusiastic assistance of the splendid Philippe Noiret and Anna Karina, and we took every opportunity which he offered, and he was prodigal, to profit from his experience and knowledge.

"How nice it would be," he once said ruefully, "if some time, somewhere, you and I could do a whole picture together right from the beginning!" It was a compliment to cherish, but, alas! we were never able to manage it. And so we worked on into a wet, fog-shrouded, December.

But Christmas was coming, and after it I would be that much nearer to my return to Italy. Visconti sent constant sad little notes asking me when I thought I could come, and reminding me sternly that he had an Opera, a real one, to stage in Milan and that nothing should come in the way of it . . . please would I ask Hollywood and Mr Cukor, whom he much admired, to hurry a little?

No one wanted to hurry away more than I did. It was a forlorn Christmas when it finally came, spent in pouring rain; the plastic Christmas trees dripped and sagged along every street, absurd and vulgar among the palms, and "Jingle Bells" blared from speakers at every corner. Down on Wilshire Boulevard there was a small cage of reindeer, rhinestone in their antlers, coats dyed pink and hoofs gilded. They stood huddled in the rain in mute subjection while the pink puddled round their shabby golden hoofs, and the rhinestones scaled off like shining scabs.

"Happy Yuletide," cried my chauffeur as he dropped me at the hotel on Christmas Eve. "I don't wish you a Happy Christmas on account of this is a Jewish Town and they don't care for the connotation; so it's Yuletide; saves a lot of feelings; we don't have Christmas here."

In the bungalow, set amidst sodden palms and the squelching lawns of the hotel garden, a log fire crackled in the sitting room, a handful of cards cluttered the mantelshelf. Robins, a Mickey Mouse with plastic eyes, Tower Bridge in a blizzard. Arnold came in with presents and we had a beef stew for supper, cooked in the kitchenette, with a couple of bottles of Nappa Valley Beaujolais and watched the first men round the moon trying, agonizingly, to fire their motors and break away from its orbit. Which they did eventually; as they came round from the far side of the moon a low, and relieved, voice was heard to say, "Let it be known that Santa Claus does exist!" which put all the idiocy and vulgarity of Hollywood firmly into perspective.

It was still raining the next morning when we drove down to Noël and Sarah Harrison's house to deliver presents to their horde of children. They lived in a kind of mini ranch house up a dank, shadowy canyon, feet deep in thick brown mud, with two horses steaming miserably behind a split-rail fence, and flickering fairy lights looped mournfully round the dripping porch. Sarah was lying full length on a settee, covered in a rug, wearing green velvet and a long fox stole. She also had Hong Kong 'flu and a very high temperature; the children ripped packages apart and hit each other, and Noël, dressed for Katmandu and clinking and clonking with chains and lumps of Tibetan jade, opened gallon jars of Californian wine which he poured into hand-blown glass goblets capable of holding, at least, three goldfish apiece. Firelight gleamed on the knotty-pine walls, the beaming children's faces and the exhausted, fevered one, of their pretty mother who coughed and streamed apologetically into a steadily mounting pile of paper handkerchiefs and her black fox stole. But the Christmas Spirit, helped enormously by the gallon jars, prevailed and reached a splendid peak with the arrival of Lionel Bart dressed in early Carnaby Street and cowboy boots with a car load of Pretty People all bearing gifts and contagious good humour. We left, in the gathering afternoon, to the beat of "Lucy in the Sky with Diamonds" at full blast; the horses, up to their withers in mud, hung despondent heads over the split-rail fence in the still-teaming rain.

There was a party that evening at George Cukor's elegant house high up a hillside road. It was set in a walled garden, lofty columns, ivy, white marble figures shadowy in the heavy mist, ilex and magnolia. Inside, polished wood and shining silver, a great bowl of punch, the scent of pot-pourri and beeswax, flowers in profusion, books, paintings, elderly smiling maids in black, neat white aprons crackling, deep old chairs and gentle, amusing conversation. Proudly he showed us all a gift he had received, a kind of bird made out of pine-cones and nuts, which we all dutifully admired, since the donor was present, wondering privately what on earth he would do with it in a house so clearly unsuited to its rustic quaintness. One of his dogs, however, settled its future neatly, by eating it entirely, half an hour later, thus saving Mr Cukor a good deal of anxiety.

Driving back through the wet night I was happy that I had spent such a day with good friends in their own homes, it had given me a feeling of security and strength which I had needed, for much earlier, before setting off for the Harrisons, I had learned that I no longer had a home. The house in England had been sold. I had telephoned my father in traditional Sussex quite early that morning.

"Merry Christmas! I suppose you are only just starting over there aren't you? We're nearly over it here. Mother's just putting a little capon in the oven for supper."

"Just starting here. It's raining and cold."

"Never! But good about the moon-business, wasn't it? Extra-ordinary!"

"Yes, marvellous. All well with you? Any news from the house?"

"We're quite fit, thanks. Antonia and Eduardo are very well, and all the dogs and things . . . no messages this week . . . Judy

Garland called a couple of times, she said she couldn't reach you in Rome and didn't know where you were . . . by the way there is one thing; you remember the people I told you about who liked the house last week? Well, they want it. No conditions; accept the price and want possession as soon as possible. Mid-February too early for you?"

"I don't know. I still have to finish here, then go back to Italy to finish that. It might fit. Is it definite do you think?"

"Absolutely. I think they've signed their contracts and so on. They know they'll have to wait a little for you to pack up. Otherwise . . ."

"Well, look; I'll call you from Rome as soon as I get there in a week or two, but say mid-February should be all right definitely. Mother well?"

"Fine. A bit of a cold, just sniffles really, it's the weather here. So I'm to say mid-February for certain, right?"

"Yes. I'll need a week to pack the place up, you see."

How odd, I had thought, to pack up England. In a week.

★   ★   ★

"Funny feeling; not having a home any more." I was looking for spoons and knives. Forwood was boiling eggs in the kitchenette for Christmas Dinner.

"It's what you wanted."

"Yes, I know . . . but now . . . feels odd. Possession mid-February. Rather soon."

I started to lay the table with the hotel cutlery; Arnold was coming in to eat with us; they don't have egg cups in America so we were using tea cups; it all seemed a bit upside down, like the rest of the hideous place. The salt was damp, the bread wrapped, the white-plastic-frosted tree with all its scarlet ribbons stood dejectedly in the corner where the delivery-boy had left it two days before. It bore a label which said, in florist's writing, "Hi there! Happy Yuletide. Have Yourself Fun!" We didn't know who had sent it; probably no one.

"Do you think we could make February . . . all the packing; removal vans?"

"Don't know. You want two eggs or one?"

"One. I'll have a bit of cheese."

"You'll have to get your arse up from here pretty quickly," he said.

★   ★   ★

Fifteen mornings later we landed, ashen with jet lag, stale air, the in-flight movie and hours of taped Victor Sylvester, at Rome. The Cardinal was there to greet me, freezing in the bitter wind, huddled in a fur coat, neat little gloved hands clasped in eternal prayer.

"Visconti is in Spoleto; is quite near the place we shoot the Steel Works, but not today, not tomorrow, maybe three days' time."

"But I have raced across the world to get here for tomorrow!"

He spread the doe-skinned hands apologetically. "He changes his mind again . . . you have a good rest . . . two, three days we will be making the scene."

Later in the day, furious and fatigued, we drove through the snowy hills of Italy to Spoleto; the hotel was warm, modern, small and ugly. Albino smiling happily in the bar.

"So good to see you! Notarianni has told you we don't work tomorrow? Maybe two, three days . . ."

"But why? I left California yesterday I think . . . to be here in time . . . what has happened? Money?"

Albino was gentle. "No, no, not money, now we have all we need; they like the film. Eccellente! Bravo, the Warner Brothers say, bravo! Now we relax a little; we wait for one of the other actors to come from Milano. He is very tired, all week he is in a play . . . and the other actor, he must come from Berlin . . . he is also in a play . . . very fatigued. We work in a day or two, you rest, you will see, all is well."

"Where is Visconti now?"

Albino looked miserably at the terrazzo floor. Then he looked up, put his hand on my arm, to break the news gently. "In there; but please be very quiet, he is working very hard, not to disturb, anyone . . . please . . . do not trouble him?"

In there was a small, dark room. In there he sat. Alone amidst a sea of small metal chairs, in the dark, watching television. I crept in and settled beside him in a chair. It creaked. He looked up, anger reflected in the flickering blue light from the set. He suddenly saw me, anger flicked to a small smile. He put a finger to his lips.

"Ciao, Bogarde. You stay with me? Certo . . . not to speak . . ."
He was whispering, his voice hoarse with the effort. "Not to
speak. Is the Eurovision Song Contest . . . very exciting. United
Kingdom is bad, France is bad, now is Denmark; poor. Maybe
Italy will win? Capisci?"

13

THE removal vans trundled slowly down the long drive in a flurry of sleet and snow-showers, leaving the house empty, bare and strangely silent after the long racketing week of packing and crating-up of one's life.

Elizabeth had come to stay for the final week to comfort; and to assist Antonia with a woman's hand, to fold blankets, sort sheets and pillowcases, and also to make endless cups of tea, on the hour, hourly, for all the removal men who accepted them with gratitude when they were not busy swigging the last of the vodka, sherry and whisky from the decanters which huddled forlornly on a tin tray in the stripped Drawing Room.

And now she too had left, taking with her an odd assortment of house plants, one howling Siamese cat, a cage of tropical finches fluttering, and Candy, the ageing English mastiff who knew (only too well by her hooped eyes and drooping tail) that something cataclysmic was afoot, and that she too would be shortly starting a new life elsewhere, and how would she manage?

We were left, my parents, Antonia and Eduardo, Forwood, George and the ever-loyal Arnold, sitting in exhausted heaps on the window-sills of the empty Staff Sitting Room, drinking beer out of Italian-Spode breakast cups, waiting for the arrival of the new owners so that I could hand over the keys, a formality I could well have done without.

The house was cold, dead, a shell now that its life was packed and trailing off to a warehouse near Victoria to await a new beginning. Somewhere a tap dripped; agreed fixtures and fittings left, a drum of Harpic and a brush in the downstairs cloakroom, telephone directories neatly stacked, a list of local traders pinned to a cupboard in the kitchen, a box of keys labelled "Greenhouses", "Garage", "Linen Cupboards", a long-forgotten cigarette burn on the wooden shelf in the Boot Room.

The gardens were bleak; fine snow drifting, bare branches riding harshly against a grey sky; urns, statues, tubs all long since removed by George; goldfish motionless in the fish-pool under thin ice.

"You're not saying goodbye?" Arnold in a duffle coat beside me, anxious, pale, tired.

"Christ, no. Did that ages ago. Just checking, that's all."

George came down the path pulling on gloves. "Well; I'll be getting back now; before it gets too thick, it tends to drift up on the hill, don't want to get stuck with all that fragility in my van."

I walked up with him, helped him slam the doors on terracotta, marble, lead, and a sundry collection of garden implements. We shook hands warmly, he started up his engine and with a quick wave turned out into the lane and went off after the rest of the house. I watched him go; wondering when next I'd see the Drummer Boy, the saucer urn from Crystal Palace, the camellia pots . . . and where? He pulled in sharply, after two hundred yards, to let a metallic-blue Rolls inch past gently towards the house. The new owners.

"Here they come," said my father. "Well, I think Mother and I will just get off now, leave you to it. She's been saying goodbye to Antonia for ten minutes, both in floods of tears. Women, really; must say I don't like this moment myself."

"It's not as bad as all that, Pa, you know . . . I mean it's not as if it was my ancestral home, I haven't lived here for generations upon generations, it's not my heritage I'm leaving as some people have to, my roots never got that far down, you know, in the end. I don't quite know what I should have done if that had been the case . . . I'd rather not think, I suppose. And remember I'm leaving of my own free will. Before anyone lowers the portcullis. It's not too late to start again. Just."

He rubbed his nose with a gloved finger thoughtfully. "Suppose you're right. Well, good luck anyway, we'll come out and see you as soon as you say; when you're settled. April? May perhaps, when it's still coolish . . . Mother doesn't like the heat, you know. Not Rome heat anyway. Mother! Come along, dear, we'll be in the way if we don't get along now."

They drove away just as the Rolls stopped, pale blue, shimmering in the steel light. Doors slammed; the woman was wearing snow boots and a leopard coat, thin blond hair, clutching a lavender poodle in a jewelled collar.

"Hope we didn't interrupt anything?" She let the poodle down gently on to the gravel path where it squealed and shivered and cocked its leg nervously against the front door. "Look at him!

Marking his territory already." The woman laughed merrily and put out a diamond hand.

*   *   *

Forwood and I, with Antonia and Eduardo in the Rolls, Arnold hard behind in the Simca with all our luggage, left the house and drove up the hill, through the darkening afternoon, past the barns surrounded by softly bleating sheep huddled under the big oaks against the swirling flakes, which lay upon their fleece like powdered glass, and turned left out on to the main road. The journey had begun. We none of us looked back.

*   *   *

It was almost like a sailing; the room was crammed with flowers and the heavy scent of white hyacinths from Losey, daffodils from Irene, roses and roses, a wanton thrusting of early yellow tulips from someone else . . . notes, messages, cards and letters stacked, bottles chilling in beading silver bearing labels; "Bon Voyage".

"All we need," said Forwood tiredly, "are the streamers . . ."

In a collision of suitcases in my room I wondered exhaustedly which and what to unpack. A month here at the Connaught, to rest, one thought hopefully, from the long year of packing and unpacking before the final effort and final severance. First things first; I lugged a handgrip into the bathroom and set out shampoo, razor, toothbrush, lotions; from the window I could just see, under the tall lamppost, that the snow was settling in Carlos Place.

From the azaleas in early May on the Spanish Steps, the industrial sun of Essen and Düsseldorf, painted reindeers in California, bougainvillaea blazing in Sidi Bou Said, the blinding heat of Visconti's Steel Mills in Terni, the soft bleating of the sheep recently as we passed them on the hill . . . it had been a long time, a long way, many voyages; but perhaps the longest and most daunting was ahead. I would use this month to relax and prepare, just sleep perhaps.

But that was not possible. Every day was filled with luncheons, suppers, dinners, drinks and various entertainments. The generosity and love of one's friends was overwhelming. Everyone wanted to have a farewell party; and everyone did. The engagement book was steadily filled for days, even weeks, in advance.

Ten days after arriving in London I was desperately planning to leave it; a surfeit of affection, wine, food and too many late nights. One morning I looked through the crammed book and made a sudden and firm decision; this would be the last day of all. After the planned luncheon I would pack up and just clear off and head for Italy.

It was an amusing, decorative final luncheon. Kathleen Tynan, Caroline Somerset, Patrick Lichfield, Angelica Huston, a representative gathering of loving, if all-unsuspecting, friends, and when they had finally left, promising to meet again within a few days, I telephoned Arnold and alerted him to be ready with the Simca to drive down to Dover that evening, and called my father.

"We're leaving, tonight, try and get an early boat tomorrow morning."

"A bit sudden, isn't it? Thought you had another couple of weeks?"

"On my knees; if I don't go now I'll never go. It means I can't get down to see you and Mother; do you mind?"

"Goodness, no! Don't you worry about us; we'll see you very soon anyway wherever you land up, I mean unless it's somewhere like Turkey." His laughter cheerfully unbelieving.

"No. Rome . . . it'll be Rome I think for a while, to try it for size."

"Well, have a word with Mother, and don't worry about us."

"You are sure you wouldn't come with me? Follow in a month or so?"

A little pause.

"No, my dear; as I said, we're both a bit too old now; might have said yes ten years ago . . . but we'd be pretty lost, you know; all our friends are here, the ones who remain . . . I'd miss the Rose and Crown in Fletching and my Worthington . . ."

"I'm sure you could get Worthington in Rome."

"No, off you go; good luck, and God bless you. Get some in for me though; I'll need a little strength after the journey."

"Get some what?"

"Worthington, of course . . . you are dense!"

*   *   *

281

We were the first two cars in the queue at the Customs shed next morning for the first boat across. The night before at dinner in the local hotel we had made the final plans for our journey. Arnold would leave us at Arras and go by way of Macon, we to Paris; and the next night, all things, and the slightly aged Simca, being equal, we would meet up again at the Hotel de l'Europe in Avignon, then to Genoa and on to Rome; it all seemed perfectly straightforward. The Customs official, a tall gaunt man, his arms wrapped around him for warmth in the bitter wind, leant down and said good morning.

"Wonder if you'd mind stepping out, sir; bit chilly, but I'd like to have a little chat, if you don't mind."

I stood beside him in the dirty shed, gulls wheeling and crying, wind whipping a flag taut, scraps of torn paper eddying in a corner.

"All yours, is it, Sir?"

"Yes . . . both cars."

"Quite a lot of luggage, eh?"

"Yes; a lot."

"How much money are you carrying, sir?"

"Three hundred and fifty pounds."

"That would be all, would it?"

"That's all."

"And the other gentlemen?"

"We have three hundred and fifty between us all."

He wandered to the back of the Simca and peered in.

"Record player, I see. Spare tyres?"

"For the Rolls. Expensive in Italy."

"Going on a little holiday?"

"No."

"Ah . . . what are you going for then, sir, with all this luggage?

"Ever."

He stood and looked at me impassively, his coat tails whipping around his legs, arms still wrapped.

"I see. Thank you, sir." The barrier went up and we started the cars.

In the shuddering British Rail cabin, grey as the morning, one tartan rug on the bunks, I replaced the papers and passports in the briefcase, gave Arnold his, and rang the Stewards' bell for something hot to drink.

"Aren't you coming up top?" Arnold looked worried, huddled in his sheepskin.

"What for? It's bitter."

"To see them go . . ."

"The white cliffs?"

He shrugged, and sat on the bunk.

"You go up if you want to, Noldie. I've done it so often before."

So often before. With Lally and Elizabeth for holidays from as early as I could remember, sitting on deck eating lemons against seasickness, on Lally's stern advice, repeating the phrases she thought we might need on the other side—"Bonjour", "Merci", "Le Doublevey Sey, s'il vous plait"—watching the gulls swoop and glide behind us on the wake, smoke stream away from the black and red funnel, the water all about us like foaming ginger beer. We hadn't ever looked behind then; no last looks, no silly waving, "Full Steam Ahead!" Lally used to cry happily. Ahead to Abroad, to adventure, a return rather than a parting. And that's how I would think of it today in the sullen light; not a severance, a beginning.

*   *   *

The London flight was on time when we got to the check-in at Fiumicino; Arnold was pretty silent all the way down in the car. No one felt much like speaking.

"I wish you'd let me stay a bit longer; just to see you settled in somewhere." He stared miserably out of the window.

"No, don't even think of it, we'll manage . . . got three houses to see today."

"Just don't like leaving like this. It doesn't feel right."

He checked in his baggage, a small handgrip. I handed him the presents which he'd bought for June and his child. A bottle of Chianti, a long sausage in a net bag, a wind-up police car with flashing lights.

"I'm going to miss you, Gov. Miss you bad."

"I am too. It's the only thing I really feel guilty about; leaving you, Noldie."

He rallied swiftly. "Aw Hell! We had a good innings though, didn't we? Fifteen years . . . a long time . . . couldn't ask for much more, could we?"

We walked together towards Immigration, no sense in hanging about.

"Maybe when we're all settled you could come out for a holiday . . . bring June and Aidan? In the summer—have a real relax . . ."

"Sure. I'll miss all those early morning calls though; the bacon sandwiches. Always had the coffee ready, didn't I? In my little percolator."

"You'll be doing it for someone else soon, you see."

We stopped at the barrier, he rummaged for his passport and boarding card.

"No. Not me . . . I don't want to stand-in for anyone else now. Try and get my ticket on the Floor somewhere. Assistant . . ."

"Give June my love."

"I will; and take care, right?"

"Sure."

"It was a really *great* time," he said and turned away abruptly.

★ ★ ★

Rome seemed, then, to be full of ladies who ran Estate Agencies, or at least worked in them, and I got to know a varied selection of both the ladies and the properties which they had on offer to rent. All pretty awful.

An elderly Russian Princess, dressed as if for a tough shoot in the Highlands, and with an inaccurate, not to say completely erroneous knowledge of my station in life, implored me round a number of decaying palazzos in the hills and ornate villas on the Appia Antica, promising that the central heating would be mended, the pools made watertight, the furniture returned, and that the views, on clear days were incredible . . . all the way to Frascati or even further. That these sad villas lay in vast, unkempt gardens amidst mouldering columns and crumbling putti, that they were cold, damp and neglected and often furnished as if by a mad Maharaja left naked with a cheque book in Drages or Maples, never caused her a moment's care or worry. Everything, she insisted, could be done by tomorrow—and quite clearly, from the neglect and disarray of most of them, never was. Although I continued to insist that my funds were very modest, and that I only wanted a very small house with a swimming pool if possible, not as a luxury but as a dire necessity in summer in

Rome, and that it should be as easily run and compact as possible, I still had to make fruitless journeys into the smart areas of the city, or up into the hills, where wreathed in mists and scrofulous with damp, yet another rusting crested gate was thrown open and warrens of rooms and corridors explored.

Signorina Dora was a little easier to convince, and far less grand; her agency was small and seemed to cater for a more modest client. The flats she offered were often small, foul, in dark streets, or high blocks, and had all been used for one kind of a business or another. Usually one kind. She didn't do houses very often. She was a wan girl, bleached blonde hair with an angry black parting, plastic alligator boots and a fur coat which moulted in the rain. She chewed thoughtfully at her pencil and made copious notes, a telephone glued into the crick of her neck, Italian streaming from her lips like bullets from a Tommy gun. Eventually she hung up, ran her hand wearily through the harsh blonde hair and pushed an address towards me.

"It is north of the city, not chic, very not chic. Via Flaminia; not a good address. The big cemetery is there, Prima Porta. Molto doloroso, eh, va bene. It has what you want, is empty, is cheap, has telephone, pool . . . and you must pay the gardener."

Villa Fratelli was twelve kilometres out of Rome on a small hill stuck all over with parasol pines, mimosa, magnolia. Below it lay a clutter of squatters' houses, apparently built overnight, from blocks of porous tufa. Bilious yellow, tin roofs, an open sewer running through the dirt streets, dumped cars, a football pitch, television aerials, enormous refrigerators incongruously standing in the muddy yards linked to the main electricity cable by meters of tangled wire. There was one Bar with green walls, striplights and a pin-table; a butcher, a baker, and a shop which sold Kodak film and wedding enlargements or confirmation photographs in vivid colour. Otherwise there was nothing much there apart from a few scrawny chickens, starving dogs, and an old man who rode about in an invalid car with a musical box, a monkey and no legs.

The villa, when you finally reached it through the unmade roads and dank tufa houses, was not so bad. Surrounded by a walled garden, with stout wooden gates, it was a modern reproduction of a casa colonica . . . and commanded the most marvellous views; from the upper windows. It was cool, light and not depressing. A good swimming pool in the garden, reasonable kitchen, sparse furniture, most of it awful, but it was cheap and it was in the country; if you ignored the sprawl of suburban Rome below the hill. There was even an empty chicken run, and a small vineyard. I made arrangements to re-visit and finalise it the following day and hurried back to Rome to warn the Princess.

"Where is this villa?" she said darkly, the commission slipping through her anxious fingers. "Near Prima Porta! Dio! Not possible . . . you can not live near Prima Porta! only dead people are there . . . no one goes to that part of the city except on the day of the dead. It is appalling, dangerous, and not chic . . . I have all arrangements made for you to see Palazzo Gondoli . . . is divine, is the house of our Ambassador to Uruguay . . . is ravishing. 2,000 dollars a month. You come now. Immediately."

"But I have seen the Palazzo, Princess, it is too big, too grand and too expensive for me . . ."

"We can make an arrangement, maybe they take 1,800 . . ."

"But it overlooks the city dump yard."

"No. No. Is not true!"

"I've seen the trucks, big trucks dumping the rubbish. The fires . . . you can see it from the gardens clearly."

"Ha!" she cried cheerfully. "Only when you stand up!"

Villa Fratelli belonged, as might seem reasonable, to Signora Fratelli, a newly widowed lady, of considerable charm, reduced circumstances, and lost hopes. She was about thirty, pretty, vivacious when she was not melancholy, which was all the time now, and smart in a last-year's-model kind of way. Something had distressed her greatly in the past, and she was not about to relinquish her grief easily. Her husband, she told me the first day we met, had been a very handsome man, very brave and dashing; if not particularly bright about finance, he was extremely good about guns and hunting which had led to his tragic death, by falling from a low flying aircraft, a Piper Cub she thought, attempting to shoot his first zebra in Kenya. He had unhappily lost balance and had fallen into the galloping herd below. Without having fired a shot. She herself was told the dreadful news while sitting on a Nile steamer floating gently towards Luxor and unsuspected widowhood. It had destroyed her. The house which they had built together was now too full of memories, so she had ripped out the furnishings, save for a few odds and ends, and put it on the market. The last, and indeed they had been the first, tenants, were an American family, very friendly, with many children. They were employed at NATO and he had been posted away suddenly; so the house was free. Would I care to rent it, or buy it? It didn't matter much one way or another.

I rented it for a year, and paid the slightly astonished Signorina Dora her first deposit. Capucine and Julie Christie, both of whom happened to be working in Rome just then, lost no time in having a look at it and both pronounced it acceptable if bleak.

"You need masses of flowers and cushions everywhere!" they said, and later sent both to prove it.

Two days later Signora Fratelli came up and did the inventory, which took very little time, since there was really very little left to check. Some ash-trays from local Roman restaurants, beds with straw mattresses, some chairs, a large refectory table too heavy to cart away, and a dining-room suite of spartan simplicity and ugliness. There were no sheets, naturally, and no electric light bulbs. Little things had to be found; like knives and forks, and something to cook in.

"Ah! Si . . . I forget. I will find at the casa de Mamma where now I live alone . . . you understand."

She showed me how to work the central heating, where the water main was turned off or on, how to empty and fill the pool, and that the gardener's name was Peppino and that he had been in the service of her mother's family for fifty years. He was now, she thought, about eighty and useless. "The gardens," she indicated them with a sad shrug, "we had so many plans to make it pretty . . . but God was unkind," implying that what was left was for me to get right.

It was a wilderness of red earth, clumps of frosted oleanders, long-dead geraniums, and a scrappy piece of grass outside the drawing room which might, once, have been a lawn. The tall pines dropped their needles endlessly, the magnolias shed enormous rusty leaves, the raspberry canes were a thicket. Through an overgrown hedge lay Peppino's province, the vegetable garden where he grew tomatoes, onions, asparagus and ragged rows of beans in a vague haphazard way. Down at the bottom, the empty chicken run. All about the mimosa, pines, twisted olives, and at their feet, a cobalt carpet of violets scenting the March air. There was plenty of time; as soon as the house was livable I'd start on the garden with Peppino, useless or not.

Signora Fratelli drove off in her small red car, a list of promises in her hand which I hoped she would remember, but already expected her not to; I was, after all, quite used to Italy.

Eventually, with a certain amount of pressure from Signorina Dora, bits and pieces of missing inventory returned to the villa, and by the time that Eduardo and Antonia arrived to join me from Valencia, where they had been waiting, the place was almost a going concern. At least one could eat, sleep and cook in it, and they were delighted by the views all around, by the simplicity of the house, and by the fact that they could go to Mass anywhere they liked within minutes of the slummy village below.

Peppino proved to be willing, kind, and eager to help. Ignored for years by the Fratellis, hardly spoken to by the American family from NATO, he clumped after me through his domain, chattering in incomprehensible Italian, apparently explaining what he could do with a few packets of seed, some encouragement, and a new spade and fork. His smelly little shed, in which he spent his siesta, beside the chicken run, was the centre of his life and his domain. A sagging bed, a wooden chair and table, Gina Lollobrigida on one wall and a Milan football team on the other, the beams wreathed with drying chillis, pomodori and onions. We shared a glass of repellent house wine and I promised him the tools he needed, and Antonia willingly agreed to cook him a meal daily in return for baskets of fresh fruits and vegetables, providing that he stopped hurling bricks at the cringing little dog, rib cage showing, foreleg smashed and bloody, with bone sticking out, riddled with worms and heaving with ticks, which haunted us day and night. He explained that it had been the property of the Americans who had bought it the year before as a puppy for Christmas for the children; and that when they left, apparently in a great hurry, they abandoned it, with two cats, now gaunt and starving, to fend for themselves, leaving him a small amount of money to buy them food. Since he reckoned that he needed the food far more than the beasts, he had spent it (compassion for animals is not in the Pope's recipe for Holy Salvation); and most of the day chucking stones and bricks at the bewildered animals which refused to leave. I determined to find a vet to come out and painlessly destroy the three of them. They would obviously be a problem when Candy eventually arrived from England. In the event the vet wormed and mended everybody, which cost a fortune I had not budgeted for (I was on a tight rein here), and the house now had three more occupants who took over the place as a right. Under Antonia's loving eye and gentle care, they prospered well. The dog was called Labbo, the cats Prune and Putana. Villa Fratelli was complete.

Elizabeth was our first staying guest in the ugly Blue Guest Bedroom.

"I admit the wallpaper is a bit dizzy-making, my dear, but still . . ."

Blue roses and sweet peas writhed across walls, ceiling, curtains, bedspread and the one upholstered chair which Prune had claimed as his; the floor was of blue shining tiles.

"It's a bit like sleeping in a knitting-bag or something."

"Signora Fratelli calls it her bower."

"Her what?"

"Bower . . . I think it was their room."

"How peculiar. Hope he doesn't come back haunting people in his safari hat, I'd really have a frightful turn if he did; perhaps I should have brought old Candy after all . . . oh dear."

It had been the original intention that she would accompany Candy from England; but she had come alone, finally deciding that a mastiff was, at nine, too old to make the trip in a small cage, and that it would be far better off in the cooler climate of Sussex with her own family. She arrived instead with a pile of much needed bed linen, custard powder, Bisto, and three pudding bowls which Antonia said she could not possibly manage without; and was much impressed with the villa and the gardens, which were already starting to show promise, since Peppino and I spent hours attacking weeds and thick red clay, pruning, planting and mowing, making large compost heaps and dribbling beans and peas into long carefully-measured trenches. As the spring wore on more and more people started to arrive, Rome was a very busy place, and all roads seemed to cross there, even if they did not always end there, as I had been told. Eventually Villa Fratelli became just like Bendrose, Beel and Nore, with much the same cast, all coming out for holidays or long week-ends. Xan and Daphne, Moura, Irene, Gareth, the Lerners, Bumble and so on. The Blue Room was hardly ever without occupants. With the pool at the edge of the terrace, the Frascati wine in barrels, the soft spring sun of Italy, and three excellent meals from Antonia it was a happy temptation; instead of feeling a lost, wistful immigrant I was once again in the bosom of my friends, or they were in mine, whichever way you put it, and all that seemed to have happened was that the set and background had changed, but little else.

One of the things which I surprised myself discovering was the sheer delight of marketing. Something I had not been able to do for over twenty years. In England it had been impossible to walk about in shops or streets alone; I was always accompanied by Forwood or Theo Cowan to ward off the inevitable scatter of curious people who would constantly follow me about from place to place making life sadly uncomfortable. Eventually I resigned the business of shopping at all, hating the stir it always caused which irritated both me and the shopkeepers. People were never rude intentionally, merely unthinking, and it was just better to keep out of the way. I never carried money in my pockets, Forwood paid for everything, and for many years I never even signed a cheque; this was done at a much higher level by a group of black-pin-striped gentlemen who were my accountants and lawyers and so on. Life was totally unreal in this direction, even in the village where I lived, unless I was very careful and went about looking like a tramp. Now to be able to wander among the towering piles of fruits, fish and flowers in the market at Ponte Milvio every morning at eight o'clock, alone and unheeded, was a delight that I had almost completely forgotten. Daily I would return to Antonia's kitchen with baskets of fresh green beans, artichokes, new potatoes the size of bantams' eggs, loaves of still-warm bread, kilos of gleaming coral-pink prawns, bunches of amber grapes, arms full of carnations and heavy-scented stocks. No one asked for autographs, pulled my clothes or asked for signed photographs for relations. If I was recognised it was always politely, with a smile, a salute, or sometimes even an offered flower. And if, after the exertions of bargaining with Elsa at the fish-stall, I went into a bar for a coffee, no one asked me to come outside and put up my fists to impress the woman they were with, which had been a frequent hazard before in pubs from Chiddingfold to Bristol. I naturally found it all very refreshing and even exhilarating to feel so free. I inevitably came to grief in the supermarkets, which for the first time in my life I now entered bravely with my trolley and clattered up and down the aisles plundering like Attila the Hun arriving back at the villa with a varied assortment of goods ranging from tinned beans, toilet rolls and pot-scrubbers to a five-foot cactus in a plastic pot. Having money in my pocket was a serious problem for the accountant, Forwood, who, after a few hysterical weeks of my assaults on Super-Romano or Standa, managed to bring my polka down to a slow foxtrot, if not a complete halt. The first showing, in private, of "Götterdämmerung" now retitled "La Caduta degli Dei", managed to do that quite well.

I was deeply impressed with the tremendous scale and theatricality of the film, of the breadth of Visconti's vision and work and of all the performances save for my own. Clearly I had done what I could with the role of "Friedrich", but what I had done was not, perhaps, quite enough. He still remained wet; this was not, I hasten to add, entirely my fault. Visconti admitted that he was eventually the villain of the piece, because he had decided to favour the second plot-line rather than the first; and had hacked most of the big set-piece scenes between Ingrid Thulin and myself out of the picture in favour of those of the incestuous son and his mother—which was the line he wished to pursue in his story. The fact that so much that had been strong was now eliminated, and that what was left was mostly played on the back of my head, rather diminished the effects which I had tried, successfully, I thought at the time, to achieve. Milestone had said years ago that you could make a good script bad but that you could never make a bad one good. It applied also to the parts. Now I learned the hard way.

"You are sad, Bogarde. Va bene . . . but I change my mind, is my privilege, no? I make this not just the story of the Macbeths, it is the story also of the corrupted youth . . . so . . . we have to cut. Already the film is four hours; too long! And you will agree," he smiled when he said it, "that you give the best back-to-camera performance that has ever been seen!"

"But the big scene in my study, the one with Ingrid in the salon, the one after I have done the first murder . . . all gone, Luchino?"

"All gone . . . were perfect, molto bello, molto, molto; but they distracted the story from the boy. He must be the pivot, not Friedrich, they had to go."

He looked sad enough for me to doubt his sureness; I tried once again.

"And the big scene, walking through the house all alone. The big terror scene?"

"Ah!" said Visconti, holding up a warning hand. "In that you were not good. Orrible. Troppo Mozart and not enough Wagner . . . capisci?"

But at least I was proud of the film and prouder still that, however wet, I was in it. It had not been a wrong decision; just a lesson in tactics and acting.

At dinner that night, in his house on Via Salaria, among white-gloved footmen, sparkling crystal, and excited and congratulating company, he became Emperor Supreme knowing that the smell of the film was good, and that the great efforts he had made had not, apparently, been in vain; leaning across the gleaming cloth, he placed his hand gently on my arm, "Salute!" he said warmly. "The Friedrich you have given me is the Friedrich I wanted; not so happy for you . . . but happy for me. And one day, you will see, I will give you a present. I will not forget; it will be a present, not a reward. Remember." He raised his glass and took a sip of his wine. "I drink to that, Bogarde."

In the early part of June my parents arrived, and settled into the Blue Room, my father ravished by the brilliant light all about him, armed with sketch books and boxes of paints; my mother bewildered by the smells of pine and roses, the dizzying sun, the squalor of the squatters' village below the hill, and the splendours of the city itself, spent a great part of the day, however, in the kitchen, discovering, with Antonia, the mysteries of pasta, which the latter had learned to make herself.

"Aren't women funny?" said my father, squinting over his easel at the hills. "Came all this way to see Rome and she spends all her time in the kitchen and says she hates cooking. Funny lot. Odd."

"As long as she's happy."

"What else could she be? This lovely place. I suppose this is all quite usual for you, isn't it? Breakfast on the terrace, the light through the pines, those cricket things singing away."

"No. Not usual. But cherished. I'm not even getting used to it yet."

"How many suitcases did you bring?" He raised gentle white eyebrows, mildly, and went back to his hills.

"Ah. You remembered! More than two, I'm afraid, and the Rolls, and a record player and books, and all of this is a bit more than a flat. But it is a start in the right direction; I wouldn't go back now, I can manage this much quite easily . . . somewhere warm, simple, easy to run."

He unscrewed a tube of paint carefully. "I think it was a good move."

"You don't mind that I left?"

"Left? Goodness no . . . an Englishman's right still. As long as it makes you happy. I feel it wasn't just work, was it? A bit political?"

"A bit; yes."

"If they lose the next election?"

"They'll get back. I just hope they manage it better than we all did."

He mixed some colour on his china palette. "We didn't do so badly . . ."

"We think that. But the kind of life we thought we were fighting for in our wars was all the past really. The things we knew were worth keeping have all become class symbols now. They'll never come back. *We* finished in '39; I know that."

He mixed a little yellow busily. "I suppose so. You'll be honourable, won't you? Wherever you finally settle. Become a resident, you know. You won't just flit about . . . evade things?"

"No. Never."

"Because I wouldn't like that."

"I promise you."

He turned away suddenly and cleared his throat; his face furrowed in concentration. "I can't ever get the right green for olives. How did Cézanne do it? And Bonnard? It's not green it's blue, not blue it's silver, not silver it's, I don't know, I can't get it. Mother says all my olive trees look like broccoli. It *is* a worry."

"I'm thinking that if I start pulling out of the acting now, it would be a good idea. I never really wanted this to happen as it did. It was too much and too soon and too fast. I hate the struggling for power, the pushing and shoving, the battles to try and do anything decent . . . it's too much of a fight now; I'm not a starry-eyed idiot any longer. I don't think I ever was. Lost the glitter a long time ago."

"What would you do . . . write or something? Painting again?"

"No, write. I want to start my book . . . I've done the first three chapters already up here. About Elizabeth and me and the Cottage."

"I've been looking out stuff for you as I promised. School reports, letters, that sort of thing. They might be helpful one day . . . What about money, can you manage?"

"If I was very, very frugal and lived carefully."

He laughed at the word frugal and flicked me a shrewd look.

"No Antonia, no Eduardo, no Rolls of course; a small house like this, small amount of land. I'd manage I think."

He brushed a ladybird off his paper, and applied a little brush of green. "It's *just* green, isn't it? What do you think? Green, not *olive* green."

"But not here in Italy. I think I'd go over to France. Wiser in the long run."

"Italy's always been a bit of a mess," he laughed shortly. "Charming people but all a bit volatile, not awfully stable really." He started carefully blocking in a tree.

Forwood came across the terrace with bottles and glasses, my father looked up in relief. "A little refreshment? Splendid . . . I'm having a dreadful time with my olives again."

Forwood set everything down on the table. "Margaret is about to be instructed into the mysteries of a real Bolognese sauce. She didn't know there were chicken livers in it, or that you pound pine nuts for a *pesto*."

My father snorted. "She'll have a hell of a job getting pine nuts in Haywards Heath, I can tell you. You've heard Dirk's plans for becoming an old man, I suppose?"

"Yes; I rather think he means it this time. He could manage; carefully. Maybe do one film now and again, just to keep the bank happy. We'll see."

In the evening, after dinner, we sat out under the trees among the fireflies, the frogs chanting down in the field below the house, a warm wind rustling through the pines scattering needles into the pool.

"What about film work though?" said my father. "Wasn't there something with Jean Renoir? Now *his* father could mix the green I want. Used it in all his paintings, that olive green I can't get, Margaret, you know? Renoir found it."

"And Renoir lost it," I said. "I mean the film, well he didn't lose it, but after the troubles in France last year everything got rather set aside. But there is a lot of work here; mostly commercial stuff, historical, police, adventure stuff, nothing I want to do. I'm not going back to that ever again. Not those films."

"Oh dear!" said my mother. "What a pity." She lit a cigarette, a sudden spear of vermillion light among the fireflies. "I think you are very snobbish about those kind of films as you call them. I don't know where you get it from; not *me*. If I had had half the chances you have had . . ." She dropped her lighter into her handbag and snapped it shut. "I'd have adored to have done the things you have; I just didn't have the chance." She leant back in her cane chair and it creaked a little. My father took up his brandy and patted her knee kindly.

"Now, Margaret, we don't want to go through all that again, dear, you had a very good career as a wife and a mother. Did it quite brilliantly. Very good mother, dear."

She smoothed down her skirt and sighed. "Yes I know, Ulric, don't patronise. But it wasn't the career I had intended. Never mind, I won't bore you all with me again . . . I have my memories, you know. But we did have such lovely times on those films. All the places you took us to. Padua, I'll never forget, darling Padua; and that funny place, what was it called, where people sat in hot mud all day and you made a frightful fuss because the food was so bad in the hotel that belonged to the man who built Big Ben?"

"Abano Terme. Yes, the trips were fun, but the films really weren't; for me."

"Margaret dear, the man didn't own the hotel, he only lived there years ago when it was his private house. You've got it muddled."

"I'm not muddled! It's the same thing, isn't it? I don't know why you have to make everything so complicated, you two . . . it's no fun really; it's negative thinking."

Forwood laughed in the soft blue light. "Trouble with your son is that whenever he's not working he becomes negative. He's very positive when he is working though."

My mother reached for her glass and took a thoughtful sip. "Well, I think he's been damned lucky, if you ask me," she said. "And that's positive."

★ ★ ★

They were both right. I remembered the conversation a few weeks later going down in the evening to feed Peppino's fifteen white pullets which now occupied the hen-run. Not working made one introspective, slightly neurotic, and certainly negative. The temptation to accept, just one, of the fat scripts which now cluttered the small room I used as an office, was very great. They were all commercial so there would be no battles to

295

get them off the ground . . . but the very thought of playing yet another light weight, another bantering hero, another elegant Englishman, filled me with dread. I had made a definite decision which had very possibly cost me dear; I must stick to it, pick the mint and feed Peppino's chickens, do the daily marketing, amuse the team who came to stay, chill the wine, and try, in between the chores, to get on with my writing; I was finding it pleasanter to look backwards rather than look forwards. A danger signal which I chose to ignore.

The fifteen pullets came cluttering round me as I went into the run, craning necks, leaping, flapping scrawny un-fledged wings. I scattered the corn and kitchen bits in a wide arc and saw Peppino running towards me through the pines, holding his battered hat with one hand, the other waving a piece of paper.

"Telegrammo! Telegrammo!" he cried and thrust it folded through the wire. He didn't stop, and with profuse, if unintelligible, excuses turned round and ran back down the hill towards his train to Viterbo, still holding his hat.

I sat on the upturned bucket, kicked a chicken bone among the cannibal hens, and opened it. "Thinking of you. Stop. Desperately sorry about Judy. Stop. Know how much you loved her. Stop. Hope she has found her rainbow now." The signature was one I vaguely knew. Past tense. Past tense. The pullets blurred before me. The triteness hurt as deeply as my own knowledge of failure. I had broken the promise I had made her and turned my back. I hadn't walked away facing her smiling as she feared, I had done a far worse thing, I had left her and closed the door behind me. Rejection. What crueller weapon could I have found to use. And why? The demands had been too many and too strong for me to support; she had gone her own way, as she always said that she would, and I had determined to go mine. As she spiralled slowly downwards into her particular black well of despair and fear, I had ignored the outstretched hands imploring help. How can one halt a blazing meteor in its fall? It was no consolation; I walked up to the villa filled with shame, but also filled with a fury at the waste, the sheer bloody waste, of a husked-out, rejected, once glorious life destroyed by the cinema.

At least fury was positive, so positive indeed that when Visconti telephoned an hour later he knew that I was angry.

"You don't want to speak to me?" His voice was mild.

"No, I love to speak to you."

"You sound molto furioso. You are ill?"

"No. Forgive me; a telegram with bad news, personal. Nothing . . ."

"Ah! I have bad news too. From the Warner Brothers in America. They like very much our film but they wish to make more cuts in it than I agreed. They will butcher me, my work, everything for the dollar. I hate this business: it is always the money. Will the film be understood in Wisconsin? If you do not make money you are rejected like robaccia, capisci?"

"Yes, very well."

"Can you make me an English lunch perhaps? This week? I will bring my very nice cousin, Ida Cavalli. You will like her and she will like some Pudding Inglese. Is possible? I want to speak with you also . . ."

Antonia's reputation for making an English trifle was almost the main reason that Visconti ever braved the dangers of the journey from Via Salaria to the Via Flaminia. He ate it in great quantities making Antonia's cheeks flush with sheer delight. But he hated the journey always. "Ecco! You must drive through Inferno to find Paradiso, only an Englishman would have found this house. It is a miracle!"

They arrived for lunch a few days later, as if they had crossed China in a cart. Dusty, unbelieving, exhausted. We had a splendid lunch and spoke mostly about the wickedness of Warner Brothers and the cuts they wished to make in the film. Contessa Cavalli was a plump, cheerful, chain-smoking woman of about the same age as Visconti. She coughed constantly, wheezed like a bellows and spoke perfect Nanny-English. "I have emphysema, it is fatal," she said with great good nature, "but they tell me it will take a long time, and so why do I worry? And therefore I don't. We can't have Mr Glum about the house, can we? We must all die one day." She rummaged in her bag for her cigarettes and handed Visconti a small, wrapped packet, which she found there apparently by mistake.

"This is yours?" she asked him. He took it in one hand and weighed it carefully.

"No. Is for Bogarde here." He placed it by my hand on the table. "A present; not for anything, but for the Pudding Inglese, certo . . . for that."

I took it, wrapped in ribbon, a gold and black paper. "You should give this to Antonia perhaps, she makes the trifle."

He laughed and pulled the almost empty glass dish towards him: "I take a little more, Ida? You will have a half with me?" But she refused, laughing at his gluttony, and as he started to eat I held in my hands a paperback copy of *Death in Venice*.

"You know it?" He was smiling over his spoon.

"Yes, ages ago."

"We make a film together, you and me. You like?"

"Yes. When?"

"Spring, I think, March maybe; maybe early summer. Venice is difficult later with tourists. I must have the light of the sirocco."

"It is sure? Certain?"

He laughed and placed his spoon neatly in his bowl. "No, not certain. For *me* is certain, but there are many problems. There is money, it will be expensive; it is difficult, only one man, one beautiful child; is not Box Office, you see? I must speak with the Warner Brothers, maybe if I say yes to some more cuts they will say yes to this. But you will be von Aschenbach?"

"Yes. No conditions. Am I too young?"

"Why? He says no age, after fifty only. You know it is about Mahler, Gustav Mahler? Thomas Mann told me he met him in a train coming from Venice; this poor man in the corner of the compartment, with make-up, weeping . . . because he had fallen in love with beauty. He had found perfect beauty in Venice and must leave it in order to die. If you ever look upon perfect beauty, then you must die, you know that? Goethe. There is nothing else left for you to do in life. Eh! We will shoot from the book as Mann has written it, no script. You will trust me this time?"

"I trust you."

"I watched you the first day in 'La Caduta degli Dei', remember? You made six shots for me all different, the first day? No dialogue, just the mind. I saw. And I knew that I had found my actor. Voilà! I promised you a present, I drank to it, and now you accept it. Molto bene, but you must do nothing else whatever until we do it. Promise? No Fliano, no Resnais, you wait for me only? Capisci?"

"Positive. I'll wait for you as long as you ask."

He nodded approvingly and pushed his bowl away from him. "You must start right away to learn. You must hear all the music of Mahler, everything. Play it and play it. We make a study of solitude, of loneliness, if you hear the music you will understand, and you must read, and read, and read the book.

Nothing else. You must live the book. I will tell you nothing finally. You will know. Because Mann and Mahler will have told you; listen to what they say and you will be prepared for me. When the time comes."

Which was anybody's guess. It might be never at all. There was every possibility of that. But I was now working. I had nearly ten months, if there was a possibility of starting in March, to prepare. The negativity which had so irritated my poor mother was now replaced by an active positivity which would have exhausted her. I thought how strange it was that everything was slipping into shape gently after all. If Forwood hadn't forced me to run up and down the Spanish Steps in a pair of somebody's eyeshades; if Arnold and Zelda hadn't suggested me to Jack Clayton and Visconti had not been present that night in Venice; if I hadn't spoken to a blue macaw in a cage in Salzburg— but there were too many ifs in life. Like the doors, one must not question them; accept them and never regret them. And there was a very long way to go before anything could be certain. But I must reject that thought too and do as I was told to do; prepare myself so that if the time came I should be ready.

Closing the gate on the mint fields for the time being I took up the corn bucket and the kitchen stuff and wandered up in the evening sun to the hen-run. Sitting on the upturned bucket among the scrabbling pullets where I had heard of her death made me feel nearer; she had taught me more about loneliness than anyone else I had ever known.

* * *

I didn't see Visconti again for a long time. Nor did I expect to. He went off to his castle in Ischia to prepare. I spent the rest of the summer driving about looking at houses for sale with the fading idea of living in Italy permanently, fading because the prospects were always poor rather than good, and the astounding amount of bribery and corruption which seemed to be a regular part of the life disconcerted me deeply. It appeared that you could do almost anything if you knew who to speak to and absolutely nothing if you did not.

Every transaction, from registering one's car, leasing a villa, applying for a *carte de séjour*, receiving a parking ticket or obtaining a table in a restaurant was accompanied always by a flurry of paper money, or surrogate contracts. Nothing was above board, nothing ever seemed to be exactly what it was. This, coupled with the agonizing poverty crushed against quite nauseating and overt richness, made me miserably apprehensive and aware that this, apparently, smiling, sunny, extrovert country was marking time before catastrophe. I had gone through one cruel and bloody war of Liberation in Java as a soldier: I had no wish, if it could be avoided, to repeat the experience in Italy as a middle-aged civilian. Once was quite enough.

I made up my mind that as soon as the premiere of "La Caduta degli Dei" was over, in October, I would leave for France and see what possibilities lay there.

It was a very grand premiere indeed. The Barberini Cinema had been closed and redecorated especially for the event. Visconti and I took our places in the front row of the balcony in a theatre smothered with a million pink and white carnations and an audience composed of all Rome society and the entire Government, in lounge suits in deference to Visconti's apparent political sympathies. He claimed to me to be Communist but I found it hard to accept the fact among the palaces, Picassos, footmen and cooks and the splendour and abundance of his living style. So I placed him vaguely Left, which irritated him constantly and made him promise that one day he would explain it all to me. For the moment none of that mattered. The film was received as a masterpiece, and at the finale, as the lights came up in the vast auditorium, Fellini leapt from his seat in the stalls and facing us, he saluted Visconti with a great cry of "Il maestro! Il maestro!" which brought the entire audience to its feet cheering and applauding and Visconti to his, modestly bowing in his dark grey suit and neat blue tie. He smiled but never moved a muscle, suffused with quiet triumph. Rome had restored its Emperor.

14

I SUPPOSE it is fair to say that I fell hopelessly in love with Simone Signoret the very first time I clapped eyes on her in a modest Ealing film called "Against the Wind" some time during the period that I lived in Chester Row and was attempting my own passage into the cinema. I placed her then on the very peak of the profession, and as far as I am concerned she has never budged from it and I still love her dearly. For many years we were often not more than paces apart; my table at the Colombe d'Or in St Paul de Vence was just across from hers summer after summer, year after year, whenever we managed to get there. But we never spoke, nor did we ever recognise each other by nod or smile. There was no reason indeed why she ever should, but every reason that I might. However, apart from an occasional slow, considering, look out of those extraordinary eyes, the years passed in total silence; and I was left to worship from a discreet distance over the *gigot* or *loup de mer grillé*.

One day in the early sixties, with a hangover of the most punishing dimensions, I lay flat on my back in the sun beside the swimming pool, too weak to move, too ill to sit up, just wishing to be left alone and for the world to stop swinging about my aching head. A shadow fell across my face. And stayed there. Reluctantly I opened my eyes to the blazing light and saw, immediately above me, a pair of ravishing brown legs and two motionless fists. In the right a large Bloody Mary, in the left a packet of Marlboroughs clutched, an enormous gold bracelet glinting in the sun. I recognised the accessories and attempted to sit, but the voice bade me stay where I was.

"Don't move," it commanded. "I may not stay long."

At seven in the evening, as the staff were setting up the tables on the terrace for dinner, we finished luncheon together; it had to be a long luncheon to bridge the many years which we had spent sitting apart, she at her table under the big fig tree, me at mine a little along the wall under the oranges. We had, and still do have, a great deal to talk about.

The one thing I finally became absolutely positive about, living in Italy, was exactly where I wished to live in France. I

301

stuck the point of a compass into the village of St Paul de Vence and measured a half arc in pencil towards the south in a radius of about twenty kilometres. I had got to know and love this area, and a great deal beyond and above it, intimately, through Michael Powell with whom I had, in the early fifties, made a film based on the extraordinary exploits of Patrick Leigh-Fermor during the war in Crete. Mickey knew every hamlet, track, crag and olive grove. Together we had explored them and I had quickly grown to share his passion for the calm and peace which lay not so far beyond the cruelly ravaged coast. In this gentle, undulating, wooded land as yet almost untouched by the rotting fingers of the prospective property tycoons, I determined to seek and acquire my house. St Paul, once so sweet and calm and lost, except to a fortunate few, when I first came to it at the end of the forties, was now, in 1969, slowly but inexorably turning itself into a kitschy ruin of faux art galleries, Provençal boutiques, Vietnamese restaurants, and tarty little shops selling postcards, hideous porcelain, olive-wood salad bowls and key-rings.

Only the Colombe d'Or managed to stand aloof from this onslaught of quaintness, remaining a small, bright island around which all the flotsam and jetsam of package tours and coach trips ebbed and surged hourly, red-skinned, hot, smelling of sun-tan oil and *pommes frites*. Yvonne and Francis Roux who own it, were patient and polite and listened to my plans with no shred of astonishment, merely shaking their heads thoughtfully, if sadly, insisting that what I wanted (a small, tumbled down old mas or shepherd's house in a few isolated acres for very little money) simply no longer existed in the area of the village. Everything had been bought and converted, the land was almost the highest priced in all Europe per square metre, and I would have to search well down into my compass-inscribed perimeter to avoid tremendous prices, swimming pools, macadamed drives, wrought iron, or Manniken-Pis and storks in every garden; the dreadful attributes of Paris-rustic, well-heeled New Jersey, Frankfurt, or Bexley Heath.

Since M. Roux had been born in the village and knew his way about things extremely well, I saw absolutely no reason to doubt their word. But Simone was ever brave, ever courageous, and at this present time a little bored with picking mint. She said that she would come with me on the journeys I would take, and offered herself as guide and translator, since my French was almost limited to the phrases which Lally had taught us years ago and those, I felt, were hardly enough to deal with plumbing, contracts, rights of way, electricity and septic tanks. This was indeed generous of her, and we all set out confidently on a course of house-hunting.

Simone's presence, alas, was a mixed blessing. Although she dealt fearlessly, vocally, and expediently with rights of way, septic tanks and land boundaries with the agents, the householders fell back in awe and delight at her presence and brought out the bottles of Marc, or Cognac and endless cups of coffee. The social delights tended to obscure, rather, my desperate search in the limited time I had for my next, and I hoped, final abode in the soft hills of Provence. We visited many possibilities that November, none of them remotely acceptable.

Eventually, with time rapidly running out, I took another look at my map with a weary eye and discovered, almost by chance, that the pencil line of my perimeter neatly bisected a small village on its southernmost tip in which lived a much admired actress Yvonne Mitchell. Indeed she had been the recipient of the very first fan letter I had ever written in my life. She had lived there for over six years. How on earth could I have forgotten? Surely she must know the region pretty well and perhaps even know of something for sale, or someone who could advise me? Of one thing I was perfectly certain: Yvonne would know exactly what I was after. And she did. Indeed she did; and knew of a house, quite remote, near a village which had almost entirely been by-passed. It had, she thought, quite a bit of land, would need restoration, but not, she said firmly, at the price which I envisaged. For that, all I could hope for would be a studio flat with a small balcony in one of the new blocks which were spreading like white fungus along the coast from Juan-les-Pins to Antibes. However, she agreed to call the owners, whom she knew slightly, and see if they would consider selling. They were anxious to move into Nice because the land was becoming too much for them and their children were now growing up and should be nearer schools and so on; although the place was not actually on the market she had a feeling that a fair price might tempt them. The next evening she telephoned to say that they would consider selling, and the price they were asking. Which was rather more than half my savings; she assured me that it was reasonable, that the family had owned the house for more than four hundred years, that they were very distinguished and honourable, and that if I really did wish to settle in that part of France it was the ideal place for me.

It was. It stood three sides full to the winds; the north sheltered by a high hill and a wood of ancient oaks; the east had the sea far below as a distant border, shimmering white in the November sun; to the west rose the seven hundred metre hump of the Bois de la Marbrière which would help to deflect the mistral which roared down from the Rhone Valley from time to time; and to the south the terraced land fell steeply to the plain and the wooded hills which rose eventually towards the craggy line of the Estoril range. Twelve acres of long abandoned vine and jasmine fields surrounded it, and four hundred venerable olive trees sheltered it from view, an uncompromising, stone-built, pink-tiled, shepherd's house, approached by a long rutted track. Above the front door leading directly into the stone-sink and tiled-floored kitchen was a stone with the date deeply incised upon it. 1641. I knew that I had arrived.

The next day I went again, taking Simone (there were no householders to be bewitched; they had very discreetly vanished), and we were shown round the house by a plump girl listlessly sweeping out a shed. There was much to be done. But there were a lot of possibilities. Simone approved of the rough-cast walls, the tiled floors, the great oak beams, and a large photograph of Che Guevara pinned to the wall in the only, rather small, sitting room upstairs. Below were just stables and the kitchen with its immense open fireplace. She pronounced herself satisfied, said the place was "une vraie maison", and that, knowing my obsession for privacy and solitude, she didn't think I need look further. I knew that I didn't, and by the following January the house and its land were mine to do as I pleased. I made arrangements to move in immediately after "Death in Venice" was finished, some time in mid-summer, and for various alterations to be made in that time. I knew that living there would be a great challenge both financially and physically, but beyond that I had no doubts whatsoever. Yvonne Mitchell had secured me my foreseeable future.

*　　*　　*

It really would be refreshing to report that preparations for

"Death in Venice" went ahead smoothly, calmly and confidently. The reverse, alas, is true; it was all perfectly normal. We had to fight, cajole, push and batter to get Mr Mann's classical work even near a screen. Money, naturally, was the first problem; this was finally more or less overcome (we thought) by a grant, modest enough, from the Italian State. But we needed a great deal more.

"La Caduta degli Dei" (now re-titled "The Damned" for English-speaking countries) was a tremendous success in America with eulogistic Press reports and highly encouraging attendances in the cinemas. We were the hit of the season and Visconti put it down to the fact that New York was a predominantly Jewish city (as were many of its critics) and the film was splendidly anti-German. Whatever the true facts we were successful, the only thing you need to be in America, and they offered to back his next venture. On certain conditions. First I must be replaced by one or other of two British players who, at that time, brought in a great deal more money to the box office than I did. Or ever would. This Visconti refused outright, insisting, to their bewilderment, that I was exactly like a pheasant hanging by its neck in the game larder, ready and perfect for the pot. They eventually agreed but promptly halved the budget which they had originally offered. Visconti still refused to yield me up, and settled for half-money.

Secondly, they insisted, or tried to insist, that Tadzio, the boy, should be played by a girl. This, they declared, would be far more acceptable to American audiences; if the story was left exactly as Thomas Mann had written it, it could only possibly mean one thing in that shining new country: "a dirty old man chasing a kid's ass." Visconti heard them out in a stunned silence. "But if I change Tadzio to a little girl, and we call her Tadzia, you seriously believe that American audiences would be prepared to accept that?"

"We certainly do."

"You do not think that in America they mind child-molestation?"

There was, he told me, a nervous pause and then the spokesman bravely shook his head and said that they didn't see it like that.

"Mister Visconti, we do not envisage that kind of problem. We are not as degenerate here as you are in Europe," he said comfortably. Vietnam was still to come.

"This is a search after purity and beauty," said Visconti. "Surely people will recognise that? They have been reading the book for many years. Even in America."

The battle went on for almost a week; and finally, reluctantly, suspiciously, they capitulated on both points; and Visconti flew back from New York victorious, battered. There was not enough money to make the film exactly as he had planned unless everyone concerned with the project would accept severe cuts in their salaries. He himself said that he would accept no fee whatsoever. And did not. Setting an example which was impossible to ignore. I accepted the salary offered by an extremely embarrassed producer (Visconti quite properly always avoided personal confrontations over money) of 40,000 dollars for five months' work (plus a large percentage of which, to this very day, I have never seen a cent). Silvana Mangano, who played the lady of the pearls, Tadzio's mother, waived her salary altogether, working only for her hotel expenses, and the rest of the troupe from the great Pasquale de Santis to the set decorators accepted equivalent reductions. It was more important to us all that the film was made; and buoyed by our co-operation Visconti set out, in an immense fur hat and a pair of seal-skin boots, to search for his Tadzio in the northern capitals.

He found him right away, on the first day of his search, in Stockholm. A slim, pale, blond boy of thirteen, Björn Andresen, who had been brought to the auditions by an ambitious grandmother and who was, in spite of a strong predilection for black Bubble Gum and The Beatles, the ideal choice. Anyone else was unthinkable; although Visconti, always a man of honour, carried out the rest of the tour from Copenhagen to Helsinki and only signed Andresen at the very last moment so as not to disappoint the many eager parents and children who flocked to his presence in the hopes of landing the part. Björn was not immediately impressed by the idea himself, but once it was promised that he would receive at least enough money from the modest salary that was offered him to be able to purchase an electric guitar and a motor bike he accepted, and the perfect Tadzio was ours.

We were on our way. Except for one very minor-major matter which seemed to cause Visconti not the least shred of concern. The rights to the subject. He was so sure that he would be able to secure them with no trouble at all, since he knew the Mann family well and was convinced that no one else would even want to attempt such a difficult proposition, that he simply never bothered to find out if they were free or not. Robin Fox telephoned from London four weeks before we were due to start work and very politely suggested that, if Visconti really did want to go ahead, mightn't it be a good idea to check the rights? He had heard from a fellow agent in New York that they did in fact belong to someone else, who planned not only to play von Aschenbach, but to write the script himself, direct it and produce it. A one man band. He had owned them for some long time and was not about to give an inch.

Consternation filled the quiet, elegant rooms of via Salaria when Forwood and I, after an urgent request for an appointment, arrived one evening with the news and came face to face with an ashen Visconti. The first time, and indeed the last, until his illness some years later, that I was ever to see him shattered into helplessness. At first he absolutely refused to believe that our news was correct or that Robin Fox knew what he was talking about and it was only by forcing him, almost physically, to lift his receiver and call the agent in New York that we succeeded in making him realise that the appalling rumours, as he had insisted on calling them, were in fact true. He hadn't even known how to dial New York, and when this was done for him, and when he had spoken at some length, the silence which followed his replacing of the receiver was frighteningly eloquent.

For a few moments he stared helplessly before him, one hand toying with a small ball of lapis lazuli, the other nervously flicking a Cartier lighter.

"It is true. True what they tell you. This dreadful thing. Orribile! He bought the rights long ago . . . but he does not set the film up . . . now he waits patiently like a tiger in the grass. What to do? Quel catastrophe! I am helpless; what can I do . . . eyee!"

It was distressing to see him sitting slumped in his great velvet chair among the Picassos, Klimts, Schieles and glittering bric-a-brac, his greatest plans in ruins about him like an exploded house of cards. Despondently we drove back to the villa on the hill near the cemetery with leaden hearts. "Death in Venice" was was clearly lost.

But Visconti rallied swiftly after our departure and three days later we were summoned back to via Salaria and a triumphant, if disgusted, victor explained in confidence that, after a long and bitter altercation on the telephone to America, followed by numerous vitriolic cables, in which he had threatened the unfortunate owner with every possible kind of indignity and a "great mischief in all the newspapers of the world which I will make personally," he managed to buy him out. For a vast sum. The rights were now ours. But at such a cost; the already slender budget had further been depleted. Visconti's over-confidence had cost us all dear. There was even less to work with now four weeks before starting, and strict and even savage economies had to be made. I for one lost my entire wardrobe which had been meticulously planned down to the last button and hook eye, and made do with a couple of old second-hand suits, a too small evening jacket, and hats and shoes which Piero Tosi, the designer of the film and probably the most brilliant of them all, had somehow found for me from stock in the enormous wardrobe at Tirelli; but the crowd, so important to the film, and all carefully hand-picked by Visconti himself, had to be halved and on it went, one slashing cut after another to try and balance up the shaking budget. But we were all cheerful in spite of this, and felt confident that once we really started, help, if we needed it, would come from somewhere. Although not one of us dared to consider where that somewhere could possibly be.

I, after all, was well used to working under duress and actually found that it increased the intensity of concentration. I spent the next three weeks reading and re-reading the book, and going through the unmitigated hell of having a nose built to resemble Mahler's own. This entailed hours of lying prone while plaster of Paris was poured over my face, two straws shoved up my nostrils so that I could breathe, and then anxious days of fitting the plastic model made to fit over my own nose. Once all that was done we had to start the packing up of Villa Fratelli—taking the cats to the photographer in the village who promised them a home, sorting out the possessions which we had all of us accumulated in the year, and trying to placate Peppino who wept silent tears in his little shed with Gina Lollobrigida, his hat twisted in his fist, his face buried in the crook of his arm, even the sight of two months' salary failing to get him to raise his head. Signora Fratelli mistrustfully checked her very inadequate inventory, told us to leave the keys under a flower pot in the garden, and accordingly one dark, bitter March morning, exactly one year to the day that I had arrived there, we all drove away in convoy again, much as we had left the house in England, but this time for Venice; and with the addition of an extra passenger, since Labbo, the abandoned dog, had now become so much a part of life that to leave him would have been unthinkable.

Equally unthinkable to cart him round the hotels of Venice for five or six months, and to this end Visconti, who was deeply attached to the beast whom he called Poverino, sought and found a small house with an acre of garden which he persuaded his friends the Volpis to allow me to rent, assuring them that though I was, unfortunately, a cinema actor, he could guarantee that I would not wreck it, turn it into a bawdy house, or receive any members of the Press there. This having been solemnly agreed to, and accepted, we all moved into Ca' Leone, a ravishing eighteenth-century house which, although cold, damp and often flooded, stood in an acre of flowering gardens on the lagoon immediately joining the gardens of the Redentore. We were all ravished by its calm and tranquillity, by the many arched colonnades, secret little piazzas, vines and trees, white walls, and elegant simple furnishings. The only one who actively disliked the whole project, acreage and trees included, was the dog. Ca' Leone was to become my evening sanctuary from the exhausting problems which beset "Death in Venice" daily.

The first, I suppose, was the matter of Mahler's nose. It fitted perfectly and looked exactly as it should. After three hours of make-up on the very first morning of work, dressed in the old second-hand suit we had found, and from which I had hastily removed a tailor's label bearing the date of its making, April 1914, lest Visconti reject it out of hand as being four years ahead of the story, my button boots and the uncompromising felt hat, I looked, in the mirror at least, very like Mahler himself. Visconti was in raptures.

"Ah!" he cried, clasping his beautiful hands. "Ah! My Mahler! My Mahler!"

The only problem was that I was quite unable to move my head or face. Embalmed as I was in three hours' work of plastic, wax and glue, the very slightest movement caused the nose to crack immediately round the edges, from which oozed an extremely unbecoming fluid. The perspiration, which had gathered between my own unhappy member and its plastic and rubber addition, trickled implacably from the fissures which appeared every time I moved a muscle even to speak, and slid inexorably down my chin, beading there like crystal warts.

The groans of anguish which emanated both from Visconti and the unhappy Mauro, my make-up man, were as nothing to my own distress. It was impossible to use the nose; without it, I knew, I would have no character. I would be reduced just to my old familiar face, of which I was exceedingly weary, peering out from a baggy, brown suit. Although Visconti stubbornly insisted that we go ahead in the Mahler mould, I equally insisted that the only way I could go through the film under those conditions was in a wheel chair bolted by the neck to the head-rest. It would, I felt, be at least a still performance. Eventually it was decided that Silvana Mangano's make-up man, a retired gentleman of great experience who had agreed to leave his peaceful retreat in Tuscany to work again for his adored Mangano, should be the one to give the casting vote as to whether the nose could or could not be made workable. He pronounced it, after a good ten minutes close and agonising inspection, as impossible and sadly left the room.

There was a dreadful silence. So still was the small room in the Hotel des Bains where I was dressing that I could hear the gulls crying across the gardens, and the sea flap-lapping softly against the distant sands. Visconti sighed, lit a new cigarette and stared out of the windows; Mauro turned to the wall and leant against it, his tears quietly falling; Forwood looked stoically over my shoulder into the mirror, and I wrenched the sticky mess from my face and dropped it into the waste-paper basket. Visconti quite suddenly slammed the window and looked at his watch.

"In one half an hour you must come downstairs to the big Saloon, we will have a glass of champagne there for the good luck. The Press are waiting, many friends are there to wish us success. At 2 o'clock we will make the first shot of the picture; it is necessary for the insurance people. Ciao."

He and Mauro left the room and closed the door. I stared at my crumpled reflection. I looked exactly like a depraved choir-boy with bags under his eyes and a badly running nose. Mann and Mahler had never been so far away.

"What shall I do?" I was relieved at least to hear that my voice had broken.

"Difficult. You'll have to start from scratch again."

"I have half an hour, I gather."

"Well, you'll have to hurry up, won't you? Start thinking him."

"But I just look like myself. They will all expect Mahler, that's what they've been told."

Forwood was fingering through a small box of moustaches which Mauro had left behind in his grief. He handed me one at random. I stuck it on; it was bushy, greyish, Kipling. In another box of buttons, safety pins, hair grips, and some scattered glass beads he disentangled a pair of rather bent pince-nez with a thin gold chain dangling. I placed the hat back on my head, wrapped a long beige woollen scarf about my neck, took up a walking stick from a bundle of others which lay in a pile, and borrowing a walk from my paternal grandfather, heavily back on the heels, no knee caps, I started to walk slowly round and round the room emptying myself of myself, thinking pain and loneliness, bewilderment and age, fear and the terror of dying in solitude. Willing von Aschenbach himself to come towards me and slip into the vacuum which I was creating for his reception.

And he came, not all at once, but in little whispers . . . bringing with him the weight of his years, the irritability of his loneliness, the tiredness of his sick body, and stiffly he went out into the long, long corridor which lead to the great staircase, walking heavily, thumping firmly with the stick for confidence, frighteningly aware of the rising sounds of voices and laughter from below, some idea of tears behind the glittering, pinching pince-nez. At the top of the staircase he stopped suddenly, one shaking hand holding the cool mahogany rail, trying to square the sagging shoulders which emphasised his agonising shyness; below, the hall seemed jammed with people he didn't know and had never seen before. Arrogance slid in like a vapour; carefully, firmly, no longer shaking now, he started to descend towards them, head held as high as it would go, legs as firm as they would allow, hand lightly touching the rail for moral support. There was a sudden hush in the crowded room. Faces swiftly turned upwards towards him, pink discs frozen. He continued slowly down, allowing himself the barest smile of German superiority. From a long way away he suddenly heard Visconti's voice break the almost unbearable stillness. "Bravo! Bravo!" it cried. "Look, look, all of you! Look! Here is my Thomas Mann!"

★   ★   ★

I led a curiously isolated and protected existence for the next five months. I seldom, if ever, joined in with the troupe, or the other players, or met Visconti, or anyone else for that matter, socially; my life was in a state of limbo. Daily I sat alone on the Lido beach in my little cabana aloof and distant, silent and yearning as von Aschenbach himself. Indeed I had absolutely no doubt that I was him, and the exterior shell of my normal body was only the vessel which contained his spirit. My main objective at this time, which was understood and respected by everyone around me, was to remain in total, exhausting, concentration at all times and under all circumstances in order to contain this spirit which was so completely alien to myself. It was a fragile thing; I was constantly terrified that he would at one moment or another slip away from me. But he stayed. Eventually, even in the peace of Ca' Leone, alone in my garden massed now with nodding spikes of white hollyhocks, or walking through the silent piazzas of the city after I had changed into jeans and a tee-shirt, I still retained his walk and mannerisms which might have surprised anyone who didn't know that I walked as a man possessed without consciousness of the present world.

My relationship with Visconti was extraordinary. We were fused together in a world of total silence. We seldom spoke, and never ever about the film. We sat a little apart from each other, admitting each other's need for privacy, but never much more than a metre away. Incredibly we had no need of speech together. We worked as one person. I knew, instinctively, when he was ready, he knew when I was. We worked very much on sign language; a raising of eyebrows from him signified that all was set when I was. Should I shake my head, then he would sit again, and light another cigarette until such time as I felt myself in condition, and then I would touch his arm and walk towards the lights. We hardly ever shot two takes of anything—occasionally he would murmur, "Encora" and we would do it again—but that was all that was ever said and it happened very few times.

Our behaviour startled the occasional stranger to the set. An American female photographer, forced upon us by our American bosses, haunted us for a few days, and was dispirited and furious at the same time, at our total lack of co-operation, which must, I suppose, have seemed rude to her. One day, in a bitterly sarcastic whisper I heard her remark that she had just heard us say "good morning" to each other . . . right beside her.

"They've stopped feuding!" she said triumphantly.

Feuding! I told Visconti with a wry smile, and he patted my hand comfortably: "Non capisce matrimonio, hey?" And it was a marriage indeed. We had never, at any time, discussed how I should attempt to play von Aschenbach; there were no discussions at all about motivation or interpretation. He chose the three suits I should wear, the two hats, the three ties, all my luggage and the shabby overcoat and scarf—and he had chosen me. Apart from that not a word was spoken. Once, just before our departure from Rome, I requested him to give me just half an hour to discuss the role. He grudgingly agreed and, telling me to help myself to wine on the table beside him, asked me how many times I had read the book. When I told him at least thirty, he advised another thirty and that was that; nothing more was ever said.

I think that the only direct instruction he ever gave me was one morning when he requested that I should stand upright in my little motor-boat at the exact moment that I felt the mid-day sun strike my face as we slipped under the great arc of the Rialto bridge. I did not know why I had to make this specific movement at such a precise time until I saw the final film with him some months later, and it was only then, too, that I realised he had been choreographing the entire film, shot by shot, blending all my movements to the music of the man he had wanted to embody the soul of Gustav von Aschenbach. Gustav Mahler.

*　　*　　*

The partial withdrawal from ordinary life was not, when all is said and done, as depressing as it might seem. Although I moved about in a sort of trance for most of the time I did manage to attempt some kind of normality on Sundays, the one day we had free, and Ca' Leone with Antonia and Eduardo at the helm welcomed carefully chosen, and sympathetic, guests—Kathleen Tynan, Rex Harrison, Alan Lerner, David Bailey, Alain Resnais and his wife Florence, Penelope Tree and Patrick Lichfield with all his cameras, and others who were understanding of what has been called my obsessional privacy and who allowed me to wander off back to the attendant shade of von Aschenbach whenever the need arose, without question.

Nor was I absolutely unaware of things which went on around my solitary figure sitting in the cabana on the beach. I noticed, casually, one day, that some of the troupe, carpenters, the script girl, an assistant property man for example, were walking about wearing neat little squares of white paint, no bigger than a postage stamp. I didn't pay very much attention, but after three or four days, and an ever-increasing amount of little white squares appearing on people's arms or legs or, once, on a forehead, I asked Mauro what was happening. His very evasiveness gave me a worrying clue. They were testing some kind of make-up. The more I took notice the more I saw that the patches were being worn on the most sensitive areas of the skin. It was a worrying clue because of all the things which I had to face in the film the thing which frightened me most was the actual, final, death scene, which I knew I would find difficult, and which I also knew Visconti was keeping to the very end of the work in Venice. Clearly that moment was upon us. They were testing special make-up because the one I would have to use must be a total death mask: it was to crack apart slowly, symbolising decay, age, ruin and the ultimate disintegration of a man's soul. But I kept silent, as was my habit, and merely watched with mounting terror the daily proliferation of little white patches among the troupe. Whatever they were using (or Mauro was trying to invent) was going to be both unpleasant, and possibly from the amount of care being taken, dangerous. The bolt hit me one morning, heavy and hot with the sirocco; the sea grey and flat, the wind spinning burning grains of sand across the beach, the heat almost insufferable. Visconti's perfect weather for his grand finale. I was told that today, towards four in the afternoon when the light would be exactly right, I should have to play the final death scene. In the make-up room Visconti was quiet, firm, and very gentle.

"Today is the perfect light, you see . . . the real sirocco . . . it will help you . . . the heat; you are sick now, and old; remember what Mann has said, you will have lips as ripe as strawberries . . . the dye from your hair will run . . . when you smile to Tadzio, your Summoner, your poor face will crack, and then you will die . . . I tell you all this because when you have the make-up on your face you will not be able to speak, it will be dead as a mask . . . we only do one take for that reason . . . it is hard like a plaster."

"But what is it?"

"The make-up? Very good. We have tested very much. All will be well, you will see."

314

He left me to Mauro who held in his hand a fat silver tube of a white substance which, when he applied it, immediately burned like fire and started to stiffen. It was too late to protest; for two hours I sat immobile while the stuff was plastered and smoothed to my wretched face. Before he had gone too far I was able, just, to implore him not to use it round my eyes, for from the intensity of the burning I was sure that it would blind me; he nodded sagely, and continued his work implacably. When it was finished I looked like a Japanese puppet. I was carried into a car and driven down to the beach lest the least movement should cause the by now iron-hard mask to crack or chip before the cameras turned. Two strong men carried my inert body across the burning, copper sand to the deck-chair placed ready for my demise. I had thought, foolishly, that the beach would be deserted and that tact would have been used to remove any idle bystanders from my eye-line. Not so. Twenty feet away from my electric chair, for that is how it felt to me, ranged a line of eager spectators all seated comfortably under umbrellas, all with Instamatics, Nikons, Leicas and even, I noticed miserably, one pair of binoculars. In the very centre of this array sat Visconti himself, the host to his invited guests from Milan, Rome and Florence, who, led by Alida Toscanini, had been offered the great privilege of witnessing the final shot of his film. They all looked very jolly and relaxed, sipping cool drinks. If comparisons with the Coliseum flashed into my mind they could be forgiven. Someone removed my hat and fixed, with dexterity, a small plastic sac of black dye . . . this was to break with the heat generated under my hat, when the moment came, and would run down my painted face. I noticed hopelessly that someone had placed three long pieces of bamboo cane in the sand before me. One quite near, one further away, the third five metres out into the leadened sea. Albino, leaning close to my ear, whispered that the first cane marked the position of the fight between Tadzio and Jaschiu; the second would represent Tadzio after he had broken away; and the third his ultimate position in the sea beckoning to me, and pointing out an immensity of rich expectations.

Since I could not speak, let alone breathe (it is exhausting to breathe only through one's nose for any length of time) for fear of cracking the scalding mask, I was able simply to reply by hand movements and when Albino asked me in a deferential whisper, a priest giving the last rites, if I was ready, I drew the figure 5 with one finger on my knee. This he interpreted as five minutes, correctly, so that I could prepare. The silence was intense. The visitors were stiff now with apprehension. I could hear the hot wind flipping the little frills of the sheltering umbrellas; somewhere miles away a child laughed. I looked at the three markers, felt the heat rising within my body, my heart racing, the blood surging, and raised my hand for the cameras. We had three to cover this supreme moment and I never even heard Visconti's accustomed cry of "Actione!"

Back in the make-up room Mauro was beside himself with joy, slapping his thighs, hitting the walls with the flat of his hand, brushing tears of happiness and triumph from his glowing eyes. Everything, as far as he was concerned, had worked. The hair dye had run perfectly, the face had cracked, the strawberry red lipstick had smeared, my tears had coursed through the wreckage; it had been splendid. Apparently the dying bit had been all right too.

We worked for an hour with soap and water, a palette knife, cold cream, petrol, and a pair of blunt scissors to remove the white make-up. My face, when parts of it emerged, was crimson and blistered, burned like a severe scalding.

"Tomorrow will be better; you see. We put some pommade on; you will sleep, all finished by tomorrow morning. Is sure." Mauro was highly encouraging.

"What was it?"

He picked up one of the many squashed tubes which littered the table before me. "Is the idea of me, Mauro! Is English preparation, very safe, is English, made in England, must be safe for you."

I took the flattened tube from his hand. He had carefully scraped off most of the label. All that remained were the words "—ghly Inflammable. Keep away from eyes and skin". It was a preparation used for removing oil stains from fabric.

★　★　★

We finished shooting on August 1st in a plum orchard high up a mountain outside Bolzano, precisely at lunch time. There was no celebration; after five months of work, six days a week and mostly between the hours of two am and seven am, in order to catch the dawn light, a substitute for the overcast light of the sirocco, and also to avoid the traffic and tourists of day-time

With George Cukor, working on "Justine", Hollywood, 1969. On the back he has written: "As you can see, I am doing my best (controlled) to teach you the very rudiments of acting. You can also see that you are sulking and resisting . . ."

Arriving at the Barberini Cinema, Rome, with Luchino Visconti for the premiere of "The Damned", 1969.

Jack Clayton on "Our Mother's House", 1967. One of the happiest films I have ever made.

MGM Films

With "Gussie" Henry. The youngest of my "family" in "Our Mother's House". Croydon, 1967.

Eve Arnold

Self as Friedrich Bruckmann in Luchino Visconti's "The Damned". Rome, 1968.

"...never much more than a metre apart..." Visconti, self and Forwood. Grand Hotel des Bains, Venice Lido, 1970.

"...we shall shoot the book as Mann has written it..." Venice, 1970.

With Silvana Mangano as the Lady of the Pearls.

". . . you will have lips as ripe as strawberries. . . ." The "Death" make-up for the final scene.

Von Aschenbach.

Films and Filming

With Piero Tosi.

Venice, we were all far too exhausted even to think of celebrating anything except the fact that we had actually, amazingly, finished the project. Visconti and I shook hands in silence; I had my hair cut, changed into jeans and a shirt and went to take my leave of him in the local village Pensione, where, in spite of everything, he was starting his lunch.

"You eat nothing, Bogarde?"

"No, thank you. I'm all packed now. Cars ready."

"You drive to Provence now? Is long, no?"

"Twelve hours about . . . we'll stop in Cremona . . ."

"And you have Poverino, certo . . ."

"Sure. He's very happy. Hated Venice."

"You take him from his country, poor Poverino . . ."

"He'll like France. There are twelve acres."

Deliberately he cut himself a thin slice of sausage and removed the skin. "So now you both become Frenchmen. One English, one Italian. Avventuroso!" He pulled out a chair beside him and patted the rush seat. "Sit down, one little moment. Good. Now."

He closed his eyes for a moment. "I am thinking to make the Proust, *La Recherche*. You know this?"

"Yes. A long time ago."

"But you like?"

"Of course."

"I am thinking in my head of Olivier for Charlus, good eh? You must think of Swann perhaps, yes?"

"But not for a long time surely?"

"Ah no, maybe two years. Who can tell, there is much work to do first."

"Because I want to stop acting now for a few years."

His eyebrows rose in chevrons of polite surprise.

"To stop? How so?"

"Had enough. I'm nearly fifty. I've done fifty-five films. Basta."

"But you came to Europe to work, you told me."

"I know. But during this film I came to a decision. I don't know if I am good in it, or if it is good, how can I? But I do know that whatever happens it marked the peak for me in work. The summit. Where do you go from the summit but down?"

He laughed suddenly and punched my arm. "I am on a summit too, Bogarde. I go on to another one; I do not descend! To do Proust maybe . . . or *The Magic Mountain*, you would like this? Another Mann, I go on, I have many summits to reach and I am sixty; we have much we can do together, more to say, eh?"

"Yes; but today I know I finished one part of my life, in a few moments I will start off to begin a new part in a new country. It is not easy. I want time to settle, to think, to rest. Maybe two or three years. I am now out of the competition, I don't want to fight any more. Resnais has brought me a beautiful script, the Marquis de Sade in the Bastille. Poetry, beauty, but he will never get the finance, it will be the old battles all over again; one man in a cell! Who will care? If it was one man in a cell with two naked women and whips then they will care. But the fight we have had with the Americans to make our film has made me revolted. No more. I stop. It was the finish for me. I know what their Press will do to us; you remember the man from Chicago?"

He brushed the wooden table thoughtfully, cupping a pile of crumbs into his hand and spilling them into his plate.

"Ah, the Press," he snapped his fingers, "you live by the Press, you will die by the Press. They say I am losing touch . . . that I shoot only the surface of the emotions, that I am degenerate, that I am operatic! They say so stupid things. They have only theory not practice, they cannot construct only criticise, and if they find something they do not comprehend they get angry and destroy like children! Pouf! You must think nothing of them. They do not *risk*, nothing ever. How can they know, eh? Callas risks. Stravinsky, Seurat, Diaghilev all risked; even *we* risk. All true creators must. Think only of the people for whom we work. The audiences. They understand, they know, they encourage. You see."

"Well, for the moment I have had enough; today I finish. I'm not 'retiring' exactly, but I will no longer seek employment from now on."

"You are just tired old horse, eh? No more race."

"Exactly. No more racing. I don't want to try to win anything any more."

"So you go out to grass; excellent. But you will come to me if I call you, for a little lump of sugar?"

"Of course I will, in time . . ."

"Ah yes, in time. There is much to think about. Maybe, you know, we even do the life of Puccini. Opera! Really Opera. The Press will comprehend that at least. You think of Puccini too in your shepherd's house. We have many possibilities together, I think. But we have not finished yet with Mr Mann, you know, there is still work to do. Looping for the sound, I think. Not much, some."

"Of course. When will you know? How soon will you see all the work, the first assembly of 'Death in Venice'?"

He broke a piece of bread and kneaded it thoughtfully. He never, ever, saw the daily work on the film, relying only on the great de Santis, his cameraman, who did, for assurance that everything was as it should be; with five months work to look at I was sure it would be an age before he could give me a verdict on our joint effort which had started in such turmoil and which had ended so peacefully just now under the plum trees. He took a sip of his wine, wiped his lips carefully and smiled suddenly at me.

"Ah! You do not know; but I have already seen nearly all, nearly all, just not the last three or four days is all. You did not know, hey?"

"No. And . . . I mean . . . is it all right, Luchino?"

He folded his hands carefully before him on the wooden table. "You look for compliments, that is it?"

"No, Christ no . . ."

"Your work transcends anything that I even remotely dreamed of." He suddenly took my head and kissed me roughly on both cheeks. "Go away!" he commanded and turned back to his lunch.

★   ★   ★

It was a long, and silent, journey down the valley to Brescia and Cremona in the blistering afternoon sun. The dog slept trustingly in the small space available to him left by a junk-shop of coats, books, typewriters, plastic bags and an ornate silver-plated salver, a gift from the troupe on parting. Forwood doubtless had his own problems; the furniture vans from England would arrive within thirty-six hours, Antonia and Eduardo would be arriving shortly at Nice airport after their brief holiday in Spain to join us, for six months only, in order to settle us into the new house. He was also probably mourning the loss, months before when we left Villa Fratelli, of the Rolls which had been shipped back to England and sold, since the tax on such a car in France would have been prohibitive; and, anyway, who could use a Rolls up and down a goat-track? The big cut-down had started. And although it was far away from the two-suitcase small-flat syndrome, it was a determined start on a different way of life, and one to which, under the waves of fatigue, I was eagerly looking forward. Fatigue had smothered reaction so far. I was not yet in the desperate state which the ending of "Accident" had induced; no tears on this journey for the departed von Aschenbach, for he had not lingered long. His hair had tumbled greyly about my heels under Mauro's ruthless scissors, his buttoned boots I had seen being tied together, labelled and thrown into a vast wicker hamper by Maria in the wardrobe room; she had bundled up his white suit and battered panama hat, tied them roughly with string, and sent them to follow, reserving only, at the last moment, with gentle Italian insight, the pair of steel-rimmed spectacles which, wordlessly, she had slipped into the pocket of my jeans jacket. When the last dyed lock of hair had fallen, when Maria slammed shut the lid of the hamper and wrestled with the padlock, I knew, for certain that he had gone. It was not so much a hamper which had closed but another door. And how nearly I had turned my back on that door in the gardens by the aviary of blue macaws so long ago in Salzburg. Notarianni loping anxiously across the evening lawns buttoning up his jacket: "Buona sera . . ." Just in time.

I knew, clearly, that "Death in Venice" was, for me at any rate, the culmination of years of work and training, of learning from and striving under such teachers as Dearden, Leacock, Ralph Thomas, Asquith, Cukor, Milestone, Losey, Clayton and Schlesinger, a not inconsiderable fraternity, which had prepared me for the hardest job I had ever had to do. Apparently I had satisfied Visconti and since he appeared to me to be the Emperor of my profession I was content.

I had not seen even a millimetre of the work we had done together; I must rely on his word. Perhaps eventually we should be savaged by the Press, for we had attempted to film an unfilmable, it was said, minor masterpiece, and that was always a dangerous, precocious, thing to do. The slightest degree of failure would mean disaster. But my instinct told me that whatever happened to it finally, it could have a deep and lasting effect upon the audiences who might come to see it . . . at least in Europe. In America one could not be sure; generally their culture is so very different from ours, the barrier of the common-tongue so firmly in place, the nuance, diplomatically, intellectually and above all conversationally, so despairingly extinct, the dislike and fear of degenerate Europe so strongly imbedded, that there we might easily be destroyed.

I had remembered the man from a big Chicago newspaper eventually managing to corner Visconti in a stinking alley while we were setting up a shot. Hot, sweating, furious at having been avoided, he attacked like an Evangelist, his pencil and pad shaking with righteous anger. "Look, I came all this way . . . I even passed up the really *big* picture they're doing in Padua with Loren and Mastroianni just to try and give you a *break* . . . and what is this? You say you don't care about publicity! You refuse to see me . . . I came from Chicago . . . we can do you a lot of good in our columns . . . you be careful . . . this is a very, very dangerous subject you are making, I understand . . . just who the hell are you making it for, Mister Visconti?" He sat back in his canvas chair fanning himself with his note pad, a hot toad.

Visconti raised his eyes slowly, looked at me with a little smile, deliberately patted my hand, "For Bogarde and myself," he said pleasantly.

Chicago left shortly after, and wrote nothing. I had laughed aloud at the splendid conceit. But now it was all over, and I, sitting speeding towards my brave new life, was too tired, drained and, it had to be admitted, apprehensive for the future which lay ahead. However, of one thing I was now very certain; I would never go back into competition again. The doors along the corridor could all remain closed as far as I was concerned, I would not push one, nor venture again towards them, however tempting they might seem. I would wait until they were opened for me; until someone came out and literally dragged me protestingly in. I was no longer curious, anxious to prove, seeking; I had, it seemed to me, reached a point beyond which I now no longer wished to explore. What I had been taught, what I had done eventually with that teaching, what I had worked for had, as far anyway as I was concerned, at last been achieved; I did not think that I could better myself. I would happily go out to grass now, as Visconti had said. But if one day he, or Resnais or some other magic piper as yet unknown to me called, I should, most likely, follow. For me now the game, for such is what it had all been really, was almost over. But not quite.

Forty years ago, in her little parlour in Twickenham while Elizabeth and I had placed the cups and saucers after supper tidily back on the dresser, Lally would take down the box of games from the mantelshelf. "One last game of snakes and ladders before we go up the wooden hill to Bedfordshire!" she would say. The board would be laid out on the bamboo table before the glowing range, the counters and dice scattered, and in the honey-glow of the hanging lamp we would be off. Up the ladders and down the dreadful snakes we would go, tongues hanging out with the intense concentration of willing the dice to tumble with the numbers which we needed; and then one of us would hit the base of the tallest ladder and whizz right up to the top of the board a few squares only away from the one marked WIN. And this was the most dangerous part. For lying-in-wait was the tip of the tail of the longest snake who would lead you terrifyingly all the way down to START again. A three and a one, or a double two, and you were lost.

It seemed to me that afternoon on the road to Cremona, Genoa, the frontier and France that this was just exactly where I had now got to in this dangerous game of ups and downs and that the next throw of the dice would be decisive. It was a game of chance, not skill, and although I might close my eyes, cross my fingers or murmur a couple of Hail Mary's, only fate could possibly decide on which square I should land eventually . . . the one with the snake's tail or the other marked WIN. I tried to comfort myself with the thought that it was no good worrying, there was nothing much I could do about it anyway; Judy's song from long ago came back to me:

> *But it's all in the game,*
> *and the way you play it,*
> *and you've gotta play the game*
> *. . . . you know . . .*

APPENDIXES

Man in the Bush

*I saw him move
his head
behind that green
bush.
I must wait until
he moves again.
The mist is rising,
soon the sun will
come, the cautious sun,
and probe with tentative
fingers into this sombre
undergrowth.
My gun is heavy to
hold,
and my arm is aching.
Man in the Bush,
does your arm ache
as you watch me?
These nettles here are
bejewelled with the
night dew,
And here brambles,
all strung with
liquid diamonds,
clutch at every move
I make.
I saw him move
again
behind the green
Elder Bush, green
with new born shoots.
The mist is risen now
and turned to rain,
soft rain.
My gun and hands
are one.
Are yours too, Man in*

*the Bush?
Why won't he move?
This tree is my
protection,
pressed against
the roots I lie
and wait.
A pigeon
cried.
I think it was
a pigeon.
He moved again.
And now, with
stealthy hands,
he parts the greening
branches of the Elder.
I must not move.
Slowly his head,
in steel encasement
rises, gleaming with
the rain.
His face, pale and
haggard,
peers at me;
but I am not
seen;
this pine is my
protection.
Move my gun
slowly
O! so slowly
to the aim.
Stretching himself
yet crouching
he peers unseeing.
Watch his face,
white and muddied,*

expressionless.
To the aim.
A crack!
Startled, a pigeon
blusters through the bushes.
A wisp of smoke
eddies in the damp
air.
He has rolled,
a sand bundle
amongst the Elder
branches, a huddled
lump,
with legs and arms
awry,
and the rain
glinting on his
helmet.
This is the first man

I have killed,
And blood, not
dew, bejewels
now the nettles,
rubies strung
on all the trembling
leaves.
And now, with
cautious fingers, the
sun peers amongst
the pillars of the
wood and sparkles
on the barrel of my
gun.
Sad Elder!
And sad the rubied nettle!
A thrush has sung.
It is the Morning.

D.B.

'The Times Literary Supplement', 1941

Steel Cathedrals

It seems to me, I spend my life in stations.
Going, coming, standing, waiting.
Paddington, Darlington, Shrewsbury, York.
I know them all most bitterly.
Dawn stations, with a steel light, and waxen figures.
Dust, stone, and clanking sounds, hiss of weary steam.
Night stations, shaded light, fading pools of colour.
Shadows and the shuffling of a million feet.
Khaki, blue, and bulky kitbags, rifles gleaming dull.
Metal sound of army boots, and smokers coughs.
Titter of harlots in their silver foxes.
Cases, casks, and coffins, clanging of the trolleys.
Tea urns tarnished, and the greasy white of cups.
Dry buns, Woodbines, Picture Post and Penguins;
and the blaze of magazines.
Grinding sound of trains, and rattle of the platform gates.
Running feet and sudden shouts, clink of glasses from the buffet.
Smell of drains, tar, fish and chips and sweaty scent, honk of taxis;
and gleam of cigarettes,
Iron pillars, cupolas of glass, girders messed by pigeons;
the lazy singing of a drunk.
Sailors going to Chatham, soldiers going to Crewe.
Aching bulk of kit and packs, tin hats swinging.
The station clock with staggering hands and callous face,
says twenty-five to nine.
A cigarette, a cup of tea, a bun,
and my train goes at ten.

D.B.
Poetry Review, 1943

Final Scene from: "I Could Go On Singing"

Casualty Dept. St George's Hospital.
Small room off Consulting room.
Jenny in chair. One bandaged foot resting on stool.

JENNY. Don't ever go to an exhibition of "Abstract Art for the Millions."
DAVID. No. I won't.
JENNY. And if you *do* go, don't drink the Martinis.
DAVID. No.
JENNY. Because they're half gasoline.
DAVID. And you've had enough.
JENNY. I've had enough to float Fire Island, does it show?
DAVID. Someone told me.
JENNY. Well, that's pretty sneaky. Oh! there is a young Lord I must warn you about.
DAVID. Oh?
JENNY. Mmmm . . . Lord George Hell, whatever his name was. He asked me if he could take me home, and I said thank you and we got into a cab, and the next thing I knew, it was all fall down and I wound up with this. (Indicates bandaged ankle.) He knew where he lived all right, but I was out; I was out cold. I was out. Nobody asked me where I lived.
DAVID. How did you get here?
JENNY. Cab-driver named Gerald. Gerald brought me here. And they fixed my foot, and they gave me . . . coffee. Somebody asked for an autograph for their cousin Marilyn. (Covering face with hands.) Oh! I feel AWFUL David.
(David pours coffee.)
DAVID. Drink some of this, come on.
JENNY. (Waving it away.) No! No more coffee. I couldn't drink anymore coffee; you'd have to feed me through a vein. I'm full . . . I'm full to the brim with the whole Goddamned world.
DAVID. Be good. Drink this. Come on.
JENNY. Have you come to take me home?
DAVID. No, I've come to take you to the Theatre.
JENNY. Oh no you haven't! I'm not going back there. I'm not going back there ever, ever again.
DAVID. They're waiting.
JENNY. (Furiously.) I don't care if they are *fasting*! You just give them their money back and tell them to come back next Fall.
DAVID. Jenny, it's a Sell-Out.

JENNY. I'm *always* a Sell-Out!

DAVID. You promised. They're waiting. George and Ida . . .

JENNY. (Interrupting.) George and Ida and two-hundred thousand. I KNOW that! I KNOW! Well just let them wait . . . to hell with them all . . .

DAVID. Come on now . . .

JENNY. I can't be spread so thin. I'm just one person. I don't want to be rolled out like pastry so everyone can have a nice big bite of me! I'm *me*. I belong to *myself*. I can do whatever I damn well please with myself and nobody's going to ask any questions!

DAVID. Now you know that's not true, don't you?

JENNY. Well I'm not going to do it any more, and that's final. It's not worth all the deaths that I have to die.

DAVID. (Kneeling beside her.) You have a show to do tonight. You have to do it, and I'm going to see that you do.

JENNY. Do you think you can MAKE me sing? Do you think you can? Do you think George can make me sing? Or Ida? You can GET me there, sure, but can *you* make me sing?

DAVID. No . . . no . . .

JENNY. (Voice rising.) I sing for myself! I sing when I want to. Just for me. I sing for my OWN pleasure, whenever I want. Do you understand that?

DAVID. (Taking her hands.) Yes, I do understand that; just hang on to that, will you? Hang on to that.

JENNY. I've hung on to every bit of rubbish there is to hang on to in this life. And I've thrown all the good bits away. Now can you tell me why I do that?

DAVID No, no I can't tell you that. But I can tell you this. You're going to be late.

JENNY. I don't care!

DAVID. Darling. (Arms round her.) I don't give a damn who you let down. But you're not going to let You down.

(A long pause. When she speaks her voice is very low.)

JENNY. You haven't called me that . . . for years . . .

DAVID. I haven't been able to call you that for years. (She quickly averts her head.) Now come here, look at me . . . please . . . look at me. Are you listening?

JENNY. (Nods. Eyes brimming.) Mmmmm . . .

DAVID. There's something else I haven't been able to say to you in years . . .

JENNY. (Her hand swiftly covers his lips.) David, don't. Don't say it. Because if you said it now, and didn't mean it . . . (Weeping.) I think I'd die . . . I think I'd die.

DAVID.   I'll mean it. I love you.
JENNY.   (Sobbing.) Oh David! David!
            (They hold each other close.)
DAVID.   Help me! Help me!
JENNY.   Help you?
DAVID.   Help us. Help us!
JENNY.   David, he didn't want to go away with me. He didn't want
            to. He made all kinds of excuses; he didn't want to stay with
            me.
DAVID.   Darling, darling . . . I know, I know. Help me, please help
            me . . .
JENNY.   I want . . . I want to help you, but I don't know how.
DAVID.   Come with me now, come Jenny . . . please?
JENNY.   David? You wouldn't cheat me would you?
            You wouldn't pretend to me?
DAVID.   Darling, I wouldn't cheat you . . .
JENNY.   You wouldn't say those things to me . . . ?
DAVID.   I wouldn't say I loved you if I didn't.
JENNY.   Tell me again David. Please tell me again . . . please?
DAVID.   I'll tell you as often as you want me to. I've always loved you.
            (A long pause. She wipes her face wearily.)
JENNY.   That's where it ends, isn't it?
DAVID.   That's where it ends. We were the right people, who met at
            the wrong moment. With all the right ideals. But we were
            both too strong to give up everything for each other.
JENNY.   We just didn't fit?
DAVID.   We fitted. The rest didn't though.
JENNY.   It doesn't make much sense . . .
DAVID.   The loving does.
JENNY.   Yes. The loving does. The loving always does.
DAVID.   Are you all right now?
JENNY.   (Small smile.) Mmmmm. All right.
            (She tries to rise from the chair.)
JENNY.   I think that your going to have to help me. With my foot . . .
DAVID.   (Helping her.) Can you manage?
JENNY.   Uhuh. (They face each other.) You know, there's an old
            saying that when you go on stage, you don't feel any pain at
            all. When the lights hit you, you don't feel anything. It's a
            stinking lie. Will you stay with me?
DAVID.   I'll stay.
JENNY.   How long?
DAVID.   Until you can stand on your feet . . . again.
            (They stand in silence together. CUT.)

FILMOGRAPHY

The dates given are the approximate date of release

Dancing With Crime	1947	The Doctor's Dilemma	1958
Esther Waters	and 1948	Libel	1959
Quartet	1948	Song Without End	
Once A Jolly Swagman		The Angel Wore Red	
Dear Mr Prohack	1949	The Singer Not The	
Boys In Brown		Song	1960
The Blue Lamp		Victim	1961
So Long At The Fair		H.M.S. Defiant	1962
The Woman In Question	1950	The Password Is Courage	
Blackmailed		The Mind Benders	
Hunted	1951	I Could Go On Singing	
Penny Princess		The Servant	
The Gentle Gunman		Doctor In Distress	1963
Desperate Moment	1952	Hot Enough For June	1964
Appointment In London	1953	King And Country	
They Who Dare		High Bright Sun	
Doctor In The House		Darling	
Simba	1954	Modesty Blaise	1965
The Sea Shall Not Have		Accident	1966
Them		Our Mother's House	1967
Doctor At Sea	1955	Sebastian	1968
Cast A Dark Shadow		The Fixer	
The Spanish Gardener	1956	Oh! What a Lovely War	
Ill Met By Moonlight	1956	The Damned (La Caduta	
Doctor At Large	and	degli Dei)	1969
Campbell's Kingdom	1957	Justine	
A Tale Of Two Cities		Death In Venice	1970
The Wind Cannot Read	1958		

Films made AFTER 1970

Le Serpent (The Serpent)	1972	Providence	1976
Il Portiere di Notte (The		A Bridge Too Far	1977
Night Porter)	1973	Despair	1978
Permission To Kill	1975		

British Film Academy Award, 1963, for "The Servant".
British Film Academy Award, 1965, for "Darling".

Main Theatre Appearances

	Director
Power Without Glory.	
Fortune Theatre, 1947.	Chloe Gibson
With Beatrice Varley and Kenneth More.	
Point of Departure. Duke of York's, 1950.	Peter Ashmore
With Mai Zetterling.	
The Shaughraun.	
Bedford, Camden Town, 1952.	Judith Furse
With William Shine.	
The Vortex. Lyric, Hammersmith, 1953.	Michael MacOwan
With Isobel Jeans.	
Summertime. Apollo, 1955–56.	Peter Hall
With Geraldine McEwan.	
Jezebel. Oxford Playhouse.	Frank Hauser
With Hermione Baddeley.	

Films for Television

Little Moon Of Alban. Hallmark, U.S.A.	1965
With Julie Harris.	
Blithe Spirit. Hallmark, U.S.A.	1966
With Rosemary Harris and Ruth Gordon.	
The Epic That Never Was. Documentary. BBC	1963
Upon This Rock. Documentary. U.S.A.	1969
With Dame Edith Evans, Sir Ralph Richardson and Orson Welles.	

INDEX

Abeles, Arthur, 239

"Accident", 235, 246, 255, 256, 320

Actors' Reunion Theatre, 76, 77

"Adventures of Harry Dickson, The", 258

Aeolian Hall, 83, 95, 192

"Against the Wind", 301

Aimée, Anouk, 256, 271

Alexandra Palace, 82, 83

"Alexandria Quartet, The", 256

Alfredo's Restaurant, Rome, 266

"All Quiet on the Western Front", 136, 138-9

Aller, Victor, 176, 177, 179, 181, 182

Amersham, Buckinghamshire, 9, 141

Andresen, Björn, 306

Angel, Daniel, 223, 242

"Angel Wore Red, The", 223, 242

Anouilh, Jean, 168

A.P.I.S. (Air Photographic Interpretation Section), 59, 60

"Appointment in London", 135

Arnhem, Holland, 47, 48, 62-3

Aschenbach, Gustav von (character in "Death in Venice"), 298, 311, 313, 320

Asquith, The Hon. Anthony ("Puffin"), 170, 171, 172, 193, 257, 320

Attenborough, Richard and Sheila (Sim), 122, 236

Baildon, Nan, 110-16, 118, 120, 125, 130-1

Bailey, David, 313

Bandoeng, Java, 38

Bardot, Brigitte, 245

Barn Theatre, Shere, Surrey, 73

Barnes, Clive, 166

Barron, Zelda, 247, 256, 299

Bassett, Ernie, 25-7, 29, 30

Batavia, Java, 63

Beatles, The, 306

Bedford Theatre, Camden Town, 4

Beel House, Amersham, Bucks, 147-148, 151, 152, 153, 156, 165-6, 170, 184, 186, 195, 196, 199, 289

Belsen, Germany, 56, 63

Bendrose House, Amersham, Bucks, 130, 134, 140-1, 144-5, 147, 148, 152, 156, 234, 237, 238, 289

Bergman, Ingrid, 256

Berlin, 48, 55

Betti, Ugo, 168

Bickford, Charles, 215

Blackburn, Lancashire, 47, 59

"Blue Lamp, The", 128, 129

Boatwright, Alice Lee ("Boaty"), 237

Bogaerde, van den, Elisabeth (Mrs George Goodings) (sister), 29, 30, 50, 52-3, 57, 64, 98-9, 117, 191-2, 205-6, 208, 209, 226-9, 236, 238, 242, 274, 278, 283, 289, 293, 321

Bogaerde, van den, Gareth (brother), 29, 51, 52, 53, 54, 58, 64, 118, 238

Bogaerde, van den, Margaret (mother), 29, 51, 53, 54, 55, 57, 64, 68, 69, 98, 117, 187, 191, 274, 279, 281, 292, 294-5

Bogaerde, van den, Ulric (father), 29, 51, 54, 57, 98, 117, 187-9, 190, 191, 199-200, 279, 281, 292-4, 295

Bois de la Marbrière, 304

Bolzano, Italy, 316

Bombay, 48, 63

Bond, 118, 142

Boussicault, Dion, 168

Box, Betty, 139, 140, 152, 153, 169

Box, E., 109

Bristol Hotel, Vienna, 182, 238

Brook, Peter, 151

Brooks, Elsie, 31, 50, 51

Budberg, Baroness (Moura), 289

"Caduta degli Dei, La" ("The Damned", Italian title), 291, 298, 300, 305
Café Royal, London, 240
Calcutta, 48, 63, 113, 115
Ca'Leone, Giudecca, Venice, 309, 312, 313
Callas, Maria, 254, 318
Canterbury, 217
Capucine (Stage-name of Germaine Lefebvre), 177, 181, 182, 187, 194, 201, 287
Carnegie Hall, New York, 206
Castelgandolfo, Italy, 267, 268
Catchpole, 142
Catterick Camp, Yorkshire, 6, 9, 31, 48, 58, 80, 240
Cavalli, Contessa (Ida), 297
Chanctonbury Ring, Sussex, 226
Chelsea Polytechnic School of Art, 51
Chester Row, 44, 105, 109, 130, 166
Chevalier, Maurice, 157
Christie, Julie, 243, 244-5, 287
Christopher, Jordan and Sybil, 237
Cinecitta Studios, Rome, 265, 267
Clayton, Jack, 247, 248, 256, 257, 299, 320
Clayton-Hutton, Michael, 97, 98, 99
Clift, Montgomery, 186
Coca, Albino, 263-4, 276, 315
Colombe d'Or, St Paul de Vence, 301, 302
Columbia Picture Corporation, 174, 176, 178, 194
Connaught Hotel, London, 177, 231, 237, 240, 250, 280
Cooper, Gladys, 164, 185, 186
Country Life, 110, 209
Cowan, Theo, 240, 241, 259, 290
Coward, Noël, 102, 104-5, 117, 145, 155, 168, 207-8, 235, 238
Craig, Wendy, 231, 232
Cronin, A. J., 153
"Cruel Sea, The", 134
Cukor, George, 182-3, 186, 188, 193, 195, 210, 215, 271, 272, 274, 320
Cuvillies Theatre, Munich, 181, 183
Cyprus, 136

Dalrymple, Ian, 104, 105, 124, 133
"Damned, The" (see "Caduta degli Dei" & "Götterdämmerung"), 305
Darjeeling, 115
"Darling", 245
Daubeny, Peter, 75, 81-2, 103, 117
Davis, Allan, 77-8
Davis, John, 153, 157, 166, 167, 169, 170, 172, 194, 204, 205
Dawson, Beatrice ("Bumble"), 233, 237, 289
Dearden, Basil, 128-9, 134, 135, 154, 155, 166, 193, 195, 199-200, 201, 210, 220, 221, 224, 231, 241, 257, 320
Dearden, Melissa (Stribling), 199, 241
"Death in Venice", 298, 304, 305, 307, 319, 320
Dehn, Paul, 166
"Delbo, The Case of Helvig", 82, 83
Dietrich, Marlene, 157
"Diversion", 21
"Doctor at Sea", 154
"Doctor in the House", 139
"Doctor Zhivago", 245
"Doctor's Dilemma, The", 172
Dodds, Olive, 117-18, 121, 122, 133, 134, 140, 145, 152, 153, 171, 224
Donne, John, 35
Dora, Signorina, 285, 287, 288
Dorchester Hotel, London, 152, 166
Driel, Holland, 62
Duke of York's Theatre, London, 77
Durrell, Lawrence, 256, 271, 272
Düsseldorf, Germany, 265, 266, 280

Ealing Studios, 127-8, 167
Eddy, Nelson, 214
Eduardo and Antonia (Boluda Ariguel), 258, 274, 278, 280, 288, 289, 290, 292, 294, 297, 313, 319
"Epitaph for George Dillon", 204
Essen, Germany, 280
"Esther Waters", 104, 106, 123, 124, 125, 133, 140
Eton College, 241
Eurovision Song Contest, 277
Evening News, The, 84
Everest, Mount, 115

Farrar, David, 104
Farrell, Charles, 214, 222
Feldman, Charles, 176, 178, 179, 187
Fellini, Federico, 251, 300
Fielding, Daphne and Xan, 237, 289
Fliano, Enno, 257, 298
Forestry Commission, The, 257
Fortune Theatre, London, 103
Forwood, Anthony (E. L. L.), 74–6,
    77, 79, 80–1, 101, 103, 117, 118,
    119, 122, 123, 130, 139, 144, 145,
    157, 160, 168, 175, 176, 180, 181,
    182, 184, 188–9, 201, 205, 209, 210,
    230, 245, 249, 251, 254, 257, 259,
    260, 275, 278, 280, 290, 294, 295,
    299, 307, 310–11, 319
Forwood, Ernest Harrison, 142
Forwood (Family), 140, 148
Forwood, Gareth, 158, 187, 237, 289
Fox, James, 230, 231, 237
Fox, Robin, 204–5, 229, 231, 307
Fratelli, Signora, 286, 287, 289
Fratelli Villa, 285, 289, 319

Garbo, Greta, 160
Gardner, Ava, 145, 186
Garland, Judy, 28, 65, 161, 162, 163,
    169, 196–9, 206–7, 210–22, 224,
    274, 296, 321
Gaynor, Janet, 214, 222
"Gentle Gunman, The", 133
Gibbons, Carol, 81
Gibson, Chloe, 85–6, 93–7, 117
"Gigi", 157
Glasgow, 10, 40
Goetz, Edie, 194
Goetz, William, 176, 178, 194
Goodings, George, 53, 117, 191, 205,
    208, 209, 226, 227, 228, 229
Goodings, Mark, 208, 227, 228
Goodings, Sarah, 208
Gooley, Paddy, 2–4, 5, 8, 10, 11, 13,
    15, 17, 18, 19, 24–5, 30, 34, 48,
    162, 169
"Götterdämmerung"   ("The
    Damned"), 255, 269, 291
Gough, Annie (Anne Leon), 145,
    151, 184, 237
Gough, Michael, 145, 151, 237

Grade, Leslie, 231
Granger, Stewart, 82, 99
Graphic, The Daily, 135
Greaves, Flt. Lt. Christopher, 62
Green, Janet, 202
Green's Hotel, Calcutta, 48
Gritti Palace Hotel, Venice, 238
Grunwald, Anatole de, 171
Guardian, The, 246
Guest, Val, 134
Guinness, Sir Alec, 172, 209
Gumm, Frances Ethel (Judy Garland),
    214

Hamilton, Patrick, 19
Harri, 58, 65, 70–1, 136, 158, 160,
    164, 165
Harrison, Noël and Sarah, 237, 273
Harrison, Rex, 150, 151, 156, 163,
    184, 185, 313
Hassler Hotel, Rome, 238, 250, 259
Hassocks, Sussex, 51, 72
Havilland, Olivia de, 173
Haywards Heath, Sussex, 36, 52
Hepburn, Audrey, 157
Herkashin, Captain, "Sonny", 89–90,
    92
Hillside Cottage, Clayton, Sussex, 64
Hilton Hotel, Tunis, 271
Hinxman, Margaret, ix, 166
Hollywood, 173, 183, 185–6, 270
Hope, Vida, 6, 8, 20, 32–3, 58, 119,
    240
Horn, Mary, 102
Hotel des Bains, The Lido, Venice, 310
Hotel de l'Europe, Avignon, 282
Howard, Irene, 145, 210, 237, 289
Hubialla, Doctor, 88
Huston, Angelica, 281

"I Could Go On Singing", 222, 327

Janni, Joe, 242, 244
Joachim, Frederick, 79–80, 81, 82,
    83, 84, 86, 87, 105, 106, 107, 117,
    166, 204
Johns, Glynis, 74, 122, 123, 145, 187,
    237
Johnson, Nunnally, 186
"Journey's End", 38

337

"Judgement Day", 20, 21
"Justine", 258, 267, 268, 271

Kanchenjunga, Mount, 115
Karina, Anna, 272
Kee, Robert, 243
Kelly, Gene, 145
Kendall, Kay ("Kate"), 145–9, 156–7, 158, 159, 160, 163, 164–5, 183, 184, 185, 187, 196
Kendall, Kim, 158
Kettners Restaurant, London, 101, 105
Kilmuir, Sylvia, (Countess of) 161
"King and Country", 242, 245, 266
Kleve (Cleves), 63
Kramer, Stanley, 207
Krupp Family, 251, 266
Krupp Family House (Villa Hügel, Nr Essen), 255, 256, 265

"Lally" (Nurse to Bogaerde children), 38, 39, 52, 54, 156, 189, 192, 282, 321
Lancaster, Burt, 207
Lancaster Hotel, Paris, 250
Laughton, Charles, 100, 222
"Lawrence of Arabia", 170, 171
Leacock, Philip, 135, 154, 166, 224, 320
Lean, David, 122, 245
Leigh-Fermor, Patrick, 302
Leighton, Margaret, 145, 158, 237
Leon, Anne (see Gough, Annie)
Leon, Beatrice de, 72, 80
Lerner, Alan Jay, 150–1, 157, 158, 289, 313
Lerner, Nancy (Olsen), 150, 151
Lichfield, Patrick (Fifth Earl of), 281, 313
Lilliput Magazine, 110
Liszt, Franz (Film based on the life of, entitled "Song Without End"), 175, 176, 177, 181–3, 186, 193, 194, 199
Lollobrigida, Gina, 288, 308
"Lonely Stage, The" (original title for "I Could Go On Singing"), 211, 267
"Look Back in Anger", 170

Loren, Sophia, 321
Los Angeles (L.A.), 178, 183
Los Angeles Times, 183
Losey, Joseph, 154, 166, 193, 223, 227, 229, 230, 231–2, 233, 234, 240, 241–2, 245–6, 251, 257, 266, 320
Luft, Joey, 212, 218
Luft, Lorna, 212, 218
Luft, Sidney, 196, 206
Lynn, Vera (Mrs Lewis), 64, 65, 67, 68, 69
Lynne, Ralph, 77
Lyons Corner House, Coventry St, London, 6, 32, 240

McCarthy, Senator Joseph, 223, 224
MacDonald, Jeanette, 214
McIndoe, Sir Archibald, 146
Magic Mountain, The, 317
Mahler, Gustav, 298–9, 308, 309–10, 311, 313
Malraux, Florence, 239, 313
"Man in the Bush", 30
Mangano, Silvana, 306, 310
Mann, Thomas, 298–9, 305, 311
Maria (Wardrobe supervisor, "Death in Venice"), 320
Markham, David, 81
Marshall, Herbert, 100
Mary, H.M. The Queen Mother, 104
Mason, James, 82, 104
Mastroianni, Marcello, 321
Matlock Bath (Spa), Derbyshire, 47, 59
Matthews, Jessie, 143
Maugham, Robin, 225
Mauretania, R.M.S., 157
Mauro (Make-up supervisor, "Death in Venice"), 310, 311, 314, 315, 316
Mayer, Louis B., 216
Medmenham, Buckinghamshire, 61
Melford, Jill, 237
Men Only, 22, 23
Metro-Goldwyn-Mayer, (M.G.M.), 172
Miles, Sarah, 230–1, 237
Milestone, Kendall, 149, 150, 151, 291, 320
Milestone, Lewis, 136–9, 149, 151

Millar, Gertie, 43
"Mind Benders, The", 210, 221, 231
Minnelli, Liza, 212, 218
Mitchell, Yvonne, 303, 304
"Modesty Blaise", 246
Monarch of Bermuda, R.M.S., 36
Moore, Henry, 51
More, Billie (Mrs Kenneth More), 185
More, Kenneth, 96, 97, 98, 140, 185
Motion Picture Herald, 167
"My Fair Lady", 151, 156

Nares, Owen, 113
Neame, Ronald, 220
Nesbitt, Cathleen, 158
New Lindsey Theatre, London, 96, 97, 98, 128
New York, 158
Newnes Handy Touring Atlas of the British Isles, 58, 62, 63
Nichols, Dandy, 96
Niven, Forrest (Grandfather), 81
Noiret, Philippe, 272
Nore, Hascombe, Surrey, 210, 237, 289
Notarianni, Pietro ("The Cardinal"), 252-3, 255, 261, 265, 276, 320
Novello, Ivor, 19

Oak Room, The Plaza Hotel, New York, 163
"Oklahoma", Drury Lane Theatre, 103, 117
Oliver, Maurice (*see* Fox, James), 229, 230
Olivier, Sir Laurence, 169, 317
Osborne, John, 170, 204
"Our Mother's House", 253
Oxford Book of Modern Verse, 8, 24
Oxley, David, 237

"Palace, The" (Family nickname for Drummer's Yard, Beaconsfield), 206, 210
Palace Theatre, New York, 161
"Palmers Green", 4-5, 11, 12, 13, 14, 15, 17, 30, 169
Parry, Natasha, 74, 151
Parry, Nina, 74

Passetto Restaurant, Rome, 252, 254
Pasternak, Boris, 245
"Peace in Our Time", 104
Peppino the Gardener, 287, 288, 289, 296
Perry, Lusia (later Mrs Gordon Parry), 73-4, 75, 119, 151
Philpot, 143, 234
Picturegoer, 135
Piffard, Frederick, 86
"Pigskin Parade", 161
Pinewood Studios, 121
Pinter, Harold, 225, 227, 235
Plaza Hotel, New York, 238
Pöllitsch, Florian, 148, 184
Pook, Maureen (later Maureen Prior), 85, 86, 94, 96, 102
Powell, Dilys, 166
Powell, Michael, 302
"Power Without Glory", 97, 117
Price, Dennis, 82
Proust, Marcel, 317

"Q" Theatre, Kew Bridge, 4, 9, 73, 128
Queen Elizabeth, R.M.S., 238
Queen's Royal Regiment, 41

Radio Batavia, 70
Rampling, Charlotte, 268
Ramsbottom, Lancashire, 41, 42
Rank Organisation, J. Arthur, 82, 100, 105, 124, 127, 133, 134-5, 139, 146, 153, 157, 190, 194, 204, 205, 208, 224, 240, 241
Rattigan, Terence, 170, 172
Recherche du Temps Perdu, A La, 317
Red Dean, The (The Rev Hewlett Johnson), 217
Redgrave, Vanessa, 253, 257
Renoir, Jean, 257, 294
Resnais, Alain, 257-8, 298, 313, 318
Rice, Elmer, 20
Richardson, Sir Ralph, 113, 225
Richmond, Yorkshire, 5
Rome, 187, 250, 255-6, 259, 260, 266, 281, 285, 286, 287, 289, 292, 300
"Rope", 19, 21, 80, 240
"Ross", 172

Roux, Francis and Yvonne, 302
Royal Corps of Signals, 9–10, 38
Rubin, Dolly, 194–5, 204
Rubinstein, Artur, 161
Russell Taylor, John, 239
Rutherford, Margaret, 172

Sacher Hotel, Vienna, 182
Sade, Marquis de, 318
St John, Earl, 82, 121–2, 135, 140,
    141, 153, 167, 170, 171–2, 173,
    204, 205
St Paul de Vence, 301
St Suplice, Normandy, 61
Salaria, via, Rome, 292, 307
Salzburg, 259, 260, 261
Sandhurst, 41
Santis, Pasquale de, 306
Sardi's Restaurant, New York, 194
Saturday Night and Sunday Morning, 170
Savoy Hotel, London, 72, 73; Grill,
    105
Schiele, Egon, 260
Schlesinger, John, 242–3, 245, 320
Schönbrunn Palace, Vienna, 181
Schulkes, Aidan, 284
Schulkes, Arnold, 239, 240, 246, 256,
    269, 273, 278, 279, 280, 281, 282,
    283–4, 299
Schulkes, June, 270, 284
"Servant, The", 225, 229, 231, 235,
    236, 238, 239, 241
Shulman, Milton, 168
Sidi Bou Said, Tunisia, 280
Signoret, Simone, 301, 303, 304
Sikkim, 115
Simmons, Jean, 145
Singapore, 14, 20, 36
"Sleeping Tiger", 224
Smith, Alexis, 224
Soltau, Germany, 56, 63
Somerset, Lady Caroline, 281
Sourabaya, Java, 52
"Spanish Gardener, The", 153
Spoleto, Italy, 276
Standing, John, 237
"Star is Born, A", 210, 215
Strick, Joseph, 256, 257, 267, 268,
    270, 271

Sunday Express, 185
Sutherland, Graham, 51
Syms, Sylvia, 201

Tagore, Rabrindranath, 48, 110, 112,
    113
"Tale of Two Cities, A", 169
Tamiroff, Akim, 149
Tamiroff, Tamara, 149, 150, 151, 157
Taylor, Elizabeth, 145
Tearle, Godfrey, 113
Telegraph, The, 135
Terni, Italy, 280
"They Who Dare", 136
Thomas, Ralph, 140 152, 153, 169,
    320
Thompson, Bob, 154, 166
Thompson, Kay, 198
Thulin, Ingrid, 253, 291
Tilly, 7, 11, 17, 20, 23, 34, 169
Times, The, 7, 22, 23, 30, 110, 239, 246
Tindzhe Dzong, Sikkim, 115
Tirelli, Umberto, 259
Toscanini, Alida, 315
Tosi, Piero, 308
Tree, Penelope, 313
Trento, Italy, 259
Troodos Mountains, Cyprus, 137
Truffaut, Francois, 257
Tunis, 268, 269, 271
Tynan, Kathleen, 281, 313

U.C.L.A. (University of California,
    Los Angeles), 271
Unterach, Upper Austria, 262
Ustinov, Peter, 73

Van Thal, Dennis, 97, 204–5, 209
Varley, Beatrice, 96, 99, 102
Venice, 248; Film Festival, 298, 309
"Victim", 201, 243
Vidor, Charles, 176–8, 179, 182
Vienna, 181
Visconti, Luchino, 248, 251, 252–5,
    257, 259, 260, 261, 262, 263–4, 265,
    266–9, 270, 272, 276–7, 280, 291–2,
    296, 297–9, 300, 305, 306, 307–8,
    309, 310, 311, 312, 313, 314, 316,
    317–19, 320, 321

Volpi, Count, 309
"Vortex, The", 155

Wallis, Minna, 165
"Wally, Mr and Mrs" (Mr & Mrs W. Theobald), 142, 145
Walters, Mrs, 143
Warner Brothers, 239, 276, 297
Warner Cinema, London, 32, 240
Waugh, Evelyn, 35
Wilde, Cornel, 178

Wilding, Michael, 100, 145
Woolley, Geoffrey, 171
Wyndham's Theatre, London, 21

York, Michael, 271
Young, Kay, 144, 145

Zaharias, Babe, 212
"Zhivago, Doctor", 245
Zwickl, Hans and Agnes, 148, 172, 184, 208, 258

44 Chester Row 1947.